LIKE A BOSS

The Process and Privilege
of Supervising People

K. L. Morgan

Melbourne

First published 2022

Copyright © K. L. Morgan 2022

ISBN: 978-0-6481050-4-6

Published by K. L. Morgan
11 Mannix Sq
Wantirna Vic
Australia 3152

E-mail – kenmo2006@gmail.com

Web – www.likeabossbook.com.au

Unless otherwise noted, Bible quotations are taken from THE HOLY BIBLE, NEW INTERNATIONAL VERSION®, NIV® Copyright © 1973, 1978, 1984, 2011 by Biblica, Inc.™ Used by permission. All rights reserved worldwide.

Some quotations are paraphrased.

Cover Design – Leanne Beattie

To Mark
This book began with your leadership,
all those years ago...

Ken Morgan has built a career around the management and leadership of people, both as a Human Resources professional and as a trainer and coach.

A graduate of Tabor College, Victoria University and The Family Systems Institute, he makes his home in Melbourne.

Read this first

Getting what you need from this book

It may sound weird for an author to say this, but I'm not expecting you to read the whole book – not all at once, anyway. What I really hope is that reading some of this book will help you become a more effective supervisor. I'm inviting you to read what you need to make progress.

Becoming an effective supervisor is a journey on which you'll hopefully remain for most of your life. It's my desire that this book will be one of your companions for the journey, and will introduce you to other, wiser companions as well.

Novels are great to sit and read cover to cover over a couple of days, immersing yourself in the world created by the author, the characters and the unfolding plot. This is not a novel. The world of this book is the context where you work as a supervisor, the protagonist is you and your workers – paid or volunteer – are the main cast. The plot unfolds as you apply (or don't) what you're about to learn as you read.

We humans have a very limited capacity to integrate new learning. Sure, we can absorb a bunch of information and regurgitate it onto an exam paper, but actually embracing new ideas and putting them into practice requires personal change, and there are powerful instincts and habits that will thwart your efforts.

I encourage you to read a manageable chunk, then think about how it impacts your current ideas and presuppositions. Thanks to some sage advice from my editor, I've included a quick summary at the end of each chapter. You can use these as a prompt to come up with a plan to make a change or two in how you go about being a supervisor and then put your plan into practice. Come back to the book when you're ready.

Where to begin

I invite you to take a look at the index and find what makes you most curious, or what seems to most directly address your learning need – and begin reading there. That said, I want to stress that some solid theory lies behind the design of the book. It's structured according to the four main questions of human learning, in the order that the human mind generally asks them: *Why? What? How?* and *What if?* If you have the patience, there's good reason to begin at the beginning.

You'll get to know me a little as you read so I might as well be up front and confess that I'm one of those impatient learners who is always thinking (and sometimes saying), "Can we just get on with it?" I tend to learn by doing, and I've lost count of the number of times I've sat in a lecture or workshop feeling deeply frustrated with the presenter's need to get through their entire theory in finely granulated detail before getting to implementation.

If like me, you're a 'cut to the chase' kind of person, you may want to skip straight to Section 3, which deals directly with the mechanics of being an effective supervisor. It's all about the practice of supervision. Read enough to get clear on what you could do more, less, or differently, and then have a go at putting it into practice. Let your experience throw up some questions. And you may come back to other chapters in search of the answers.

You may be one of those people who needs to be satisfied that something is important and valuable before investing your time and effort into learning about it or developing skills to become competent in its implementation. 'Why is this important?' is an important question – a question of philosophy – and the first major section is written just for you.

I have a couple of dear friends and colleagues for whom the finely grained detail is prerequisite for them to begin any kind of implementation. They want the topic defined, analysed, explained and systematised before they're willing to give it their trust. And fair enough too. If that' your approach to learning, you may want to begin with Section 2 and dive into the theory of supervision before you think about philosophy and practice.

I have other friends who begin with an idea and in no time at all they're bursting with possibilities. They see connections with other ideas and contexts, wonder about ways to test and implement; and implications for microbiology, macroeconomics and everything in between. Sometimes they get misdiagnosed with Attention Deficit Disorder. If you're one of those visionary types, you could do what many authors believe is unforgivable and start at the end (well, at the last section, anyway). You might be inspired enough to come back to the other sections.

If you've read this far, you're probably going to read it all from start to finish.

Really getting the most out of this book

If you're committed to maximising your effectiveness as a supervisor, there are a couple of techniques I can recommend to turbocharge your learning.

Firstly, pull together some like-minded people and form a reading group (this will of course increase my sales but that's not why I'm recommending it). If you read a chapter or two at a time, meeting with your colleagues in-between to discuss your learning and to share your efforts to apply your learning, you'll gain more out of the book, guaranteed. You'll have some peer accountability to motivate you to implement your learning, and you're more likely to finish the book!

Secondly, get yourself a coach. Having a person sufficiently committed to your growth to give you an hour of their undivided attention on a regular basis and to hold you accountable for your commitments is the best way I know to ensure you will grow and mature as a leader. If you need help finding a coach, drop by the website at www.likeabossbook.com.au, contact us and we'll see what we can set up.

Be warned, coaching is expensive. A competent coach will charge you about the same fee per session as a psychologist, although they will probably see you less often. If you're not pulling down a six-figure salary you may struggle to afford coaching. Your employer may not be willing to stump up the cash, either. Yet coaching is one of the most powerful means of accelerating your growth and improving your performance.

Elite athletes get to where they do because they get a coach when they show potential, long before they've become wildly successful. Coaching is an investment in your own development. Think carefully before you say, "I can't afford it." It's more likely, you can't afford not to.

Here ends the user-guide. Let's get started...

Contents

Introduction – Don't skip this

Can we really make a better world?

A story is told of a man walking along a beach littered with starfish, washed up on the sand. Ahead of him he saw the figure of a little boy, engaged in a process of repeatedly bending down, picking up objects from the beach and throwing them into the water. As he came closer he realised the child was throwing starfish. He engaged the boy in conversation.

"What are you doing?" The man inquired.

"Saving the starfish!" replied the child as he flung another into the waves.

"But there are thousands of starfish washed up on this beach! How can you, by yourself, hope to make any difference?" The boy paused, looked at the starfish in his hand, looked up at the man, and hurled the starfish as far from the shore as he could.

"I made a difference to that one!"

Why would I write this book (and why should you read it)?

"It takes all kinds to make up a world," my dad would often say, "But not all of them make it better."

This book reflects my effort to be one of the ones who makes the world better. Like the kid rescuing starfish, the difference may be indiscernible to global humanity, but I hope I make a significant difference for the people I supervise. I hope this book makes a difference for you, and for the people who think of you as their boss.

What you and I do both for money and for the sake of our communities is important. Whether they're trying to make a profit or purely pursuing a purpose, organisations have the potential to be of enormous benefit to people, especially the people who work within them.

Talk to someone who claims they have a great job, and one of the key factors will be, "I have a great boss." Talk to someone who hates their job and they're more likely to be much less complimentary toward their supervisor. Whether you're the CEO of a multinational corporation with a turnover equivalent to a small country, or the leader of a scout group with two volunteer assistants and a dozen kids, your contribution makes a difference in the lives of the people you supervise.

From teenagers in our first volunteer role or our first after-school job, right through our adult career and on to the volunteer work we might do in our retirement, we spend a very significant part of our lifetime working for people. If the experience of working for people is enriching and satisfying, it goes a long way toward a rich and satisfying life. Being a great boss plays a significant part in giving people a great life.

The best supervisors for whom I've worked have brought enormous benefit to me and to my development as a leader (read on and you'll get to meet some of them). That's the kind of impact I want to have as a supervisor, and I'm assuming that's the impact you want as well. If you think the world might be a better place if people's experience of work and volunteering is both enriching and facilitates their development, we're going to get on very well as we journey together.

Filmmaker and educator Marlon Hall describes himself as "a curator of human potential."[1] I believe it's an excellent way to understand the role of supervision. You and I might only impact a handful of people, but like a dying starfish tossed back into life-giving water, it makes a pretty significant difference to them.

Bottom-line impact

The Gallup organisation's research into employee engagement compared business units scoring in the top quartile for engagement to business units in the bottom quartile. The results for the top quartile include 41% lower absenteeism, 17% higher productivity, 24% less turnover in high-turnover sectors and a whopping 59% less turnover in low turnover sectors. Quality

---

[1] Quoted by Victoria Atkinson White in Alban Weekly *"How do you curate human potential?"* https://faithandleadership.com/victoria-atkinson-white-how-do-you-curate-human-potential?utm_campaign=faithleadership&utm_medium=content&utm_source=albanweekly

defects were 40% lower, safety incidents were 70% lower and profitability was 21% higher. It's not hard to see how engagement can improve profitability.

Simply put, engagement is about the answers to four questions.

What do I get? People want a clear understanding of what to expect of their boss, what the boss expects of them and having the right resources to do their work well.

What do I give? People thrive when they have opportunity to contribute what they do best, receive recognition and encouragement, and experience care from their boss or someone close to them at work.

Do I belong? People want to feel like they have a say, that the purpose or mission of the company makes them feel that their work is important, that other members of the organisation are committed to doing quality work, and that they have a close friend in the workplace.

Can I grow? People want opportunities to learn and grow, and to have conversations with others about their progress.

The supervisor's contribution to gaining positive answers to the four engagement questions cannot be overstated. While a range of workplace factors influence employee engagement, Gallup estimates the supervisor's contribution at about 70% of the whole.[2] A good boss gains more profitable work from their workers at less overall cost than a bad boss.

Al Winseman's work translating Gallup's engagement measure into the Christian church context showed even more positive results with essentially the same four questions. Engaged participants volunteered more time, gave more money, and were vastly more likely to invite their friends and family to join.[3] Clearly, engagement works just as powerfully in the community-based volunteer organisation as it does in the paid workplace – possibly more so.

---

[2] The four engagement questions and the research results are summarised from Clifton, J. and Harter J. *It's the Manager* (Gallup New York 2019).
[3] Winseman, A. L. *Growing and Engaged Church* (Gallup, New York 2018).

While I haven't written this book as a response to Gallup's research, we will address nearly all the aspects Gallup measures in their engagement surveys (just in case you're curious, I'm not touching the 'best friend at work' thing…).

The grim reality

I have worked in fields related to Human Resources Management for more than 20 years: I've worked in multinationals, family businesses and not-for-profit organisations. I've coached hundreds of leaders who have supervision responsibilities and whose work is in turn overseen by others. I've coached people overseeing staff payrolls in the millions of dollars, and I've coached people just taking on their first volunteer report. I've come to the conclusion that, generally speaking, most supervision is done poorly. It seems that the majority of people are pretty much flying blind when it comes to supervising those who report to them. And it's as true of seasoned and senior leaders as it is for beginners.

I doubt that there's any need to regale you with stories from the frontlines about lousy bosses or inept leaders. Everyone I know who's spent more than a year or two in the workforce can tell stories starring people who've royally botched the task of supervision. Everyone has a bad boss story. Even as you're reading this, I just know that you're recalling your own experiences of a bad boss. And if you're over 30, I bet you have more than one.

The tragedy of many of these stories is that they often feature people who are trying to be good supervisors and who believe they are doing well. When it comes to supervision, it seems like we're experiencing some kind of collective managerial blind spot.

As a coach, I've lost count of the number of conversations I've had with people who are struggling with the basics of managing their employees and volunteers. People are trying hard to do something they've never really been trained to do.

What supervision is…

When I googled 'Supervision for Dummies' I was surprised that there is yet to be a book published with that title. Supervision is one of the basic skill sets that hundreds of millions of people are expected to exercise in the leadership and management of people in all kinds of organisations – from families, community groups and small businesses right up to huge corporations and governments.

If gazillions of people have been doing this for thousands of years, it would be safe to assume that there has arisen some kind of consensus as to the theory and basic process of supervision. It just can't be that hard, surely?

Well, if you have a spare weekend, you and google could turn up a whole host of different ideas and theories about supervision. There's a broad range of views and presuppositions as to what supervision actually is. So let's get clear on this first.

There are a few different applications of the term 'supervision', and this book is about only one of them. If you're a psychologist, social worker or priest, you'll probably have a professional supervisor – a person with whom you reflect on your practice, think about the application of theory and ensure you're staying within the bounds of your professional role. Professional supervision ultimately focuses on the client (i.e. the person the supervisee is serving). This book is *not* about that kind of supervision.

Related to the above is the supervision of trainees and interns, where a supervisor facilitates an action-reflection process. This book may inform that process somewhat, but it's not directed at that kind of relationship either.

This book is about achieving outcomes through the action of an employee or volunteer under your direction. It's about the relationship where you have some degree of responsibility for the conduct and performance of another person. That might be very close supervision where you observe their work multiple times per day, or it may be very distant supervision where they report to you every month or so and you may not see them between times. It may be overseeing a simple and infrequent role as part of a community group, or it may be a complex and intensive relationship as part of a high-stakes undertaking with do-or-die ramifications.

Put another way, this book is about you fulfilling your responsibility by appropriately exercising legitimate authority over the activity of another person at a defined time and in a specific setting. Some of you may rankle at the use of the term 'authority.' It's one that has copped a lot of bad press because authority is so easily and frequently abused. We'll spend some time thinking about the relationship of authority and responsibility a little later.

As a supervisor, your responsibility and authority come from somewhere. In most cases we'll consider in this book, supervisory responsibility is given to an individual by an organisation (not necessarily a 'company'). An organisation is any group of individuals who cooperate for mutual benefit or a common cause. A family is an organisation. So is a sporting club, a small business, a community legal centre, a local residents' collective, a body corporate, a church. Companies and corporations are also organisations.

Human organisations generally operate by the same process and principles because they're made up of the same elements – people. Despite the diverse purposes of various organisations (from delivering a return to shareholders, to saving endangered species, to winning at badminton) the interactions and chain reactions are eerily similar. So I won't be making too many distinctions between organisations that aim to turn a profit and those that don't.

You're a supervisor because your organisation has made you responsible for the actions of one or more employees or volunteers. Throughout this book I'll refer to 'the organisation', or 'your organisation' and when I do, I mean the organisation that gives you your supervisory responsibility.

A word of warning – and encouragement

As you've picked up this book, you've felt the weight of 400-odd pages – i.e. there's a lot in here. Sooner or later as you read, you're likely to experience a sense of overwhelm, or at least mutter to yourself, "This guy is asking too much." If you're like most of the bosses I coach, you're busy, stretched, scrambling to do a great job at work while mindful of your responsibilities at home and everywhere else.

Supervision is not all that complex in and of itself. You are however, dealing with complex beings – people – and over the following pages I'll take some time to explain the 'Why?' as well as the 'What?' and 'How?' Putting it all together to be the kind of boss you would really like to be will take effort and discipline – so I'm probably asking already busy and stretched people to do more. Initially.

The encouragement is that improving your practice as a supervisor will in time lead to you doing less: less of the stuff like performance management and conflict resolution and constantly recruiting to deal with staff turnover.

You'll do more of the things I find enjoyable: coaching, developing people, finding ways to improve organisational processes and improving people's experience of being a part of your organisation.

Like any other effort to improve ourselves and our performance, working to be a better boss will probably mean you're up for a bit of short-term pain. And in the longer term, you're signing up for some much greater gain.

A word on culture

I'm writing from a western-world perspective – which tends to be more direct and linear than other perspectives. And I'm an Australian, which means I'm probably more direct than more 'civilised' westerners. We Aussies are fairly unvarnished.

Australians are also very egalitarian – we address our Prime Minister by his first name. So supervisory relationships tend to be more peer-to-peer and based around functions. In other cultures hierarchy is more evident and there may be issues of honour and shame. Positional power and influential power may be more pronounced. Communication may be less linear and less direct. If your situation is not characterised by western culture, or if you're in a multi-cultured situation, you may need to do some translating.

The principles will hold, but the approach may need some finessing.

Section 1
A boss worth working for

This first major section is about understanding your approach or posture to supervision. I suspect most supervisors haven't thought sufficiently about their role. Many seem to just blunder along with a collection of unexamined and inconsistent assumptions dancing about in their heads.

While I've encouraged readers to begin where their curiosity takes them, sooner or later a person committed to being a good supervisor will need to develop a solid and explicit philosophy to ground their approach to the task.

You won't become a boss worth working for by accumulating a grab-bag of tools and tricks and techniques, any more than you can become a competent surgeon by standing next to a tray of surgical instruments. Being a great boss is fundamentally about clarity and about character.

In this section we're going to spend time developing clarity about our responsibilities as supervisors: to ourselves, to our organisation and to those who work for us.

There's not much I can do directly to develop your character, but I can set out the convictions and attitudes of character that will make you a boss people will want to work for.

Chapter 1
Enjoy responsibly

Supervision is about responsibility.
To the organisation, no matter how small, the supervisor is responsible for the prudent deployment of resources to the organisation's benefit and the advancement of its purpose.
To the person supervised, the supervisor is responsible for ensuring that the person's participation in the organisation is to their benefit.

This sounds like a lot of responsibility – why would anyone want to shoulder that load?

As you read the statement above, you might wonder why I've stated that supervisory responsibility goes in two directions – firstly toward the organisation that gives you the responsibility to supervise, and secondly toward the person that you are responsible for supervising.

While responsibility to the organisation seems obvious, we're going to look at it in detail. As a supervisor you are entrusted with some of the organisation's resources and opportunity in the hope that you will steward them to the good of the organisation and the furtherance of its cause. We'll unpack the various dimensions of these in chapter two.

Less obvious is your responsibility to steward the human resources under your care. This goes far beyond merely eliciting their energy and directing it toward the organisation's goals. The people serving under your care are profoundly important and valuable by the simple fact of their humanity. These people are putting their energy in for a reason, and your supervision can contribute to their satisfaction or their resentment, their growth or their being diminished, their joy or their regret. In supervising other humans, you're touching on the sacred. We'll explore that further in chapter three.

You might also be wondering how the principle of benefit to the person being supervised might apply in situations where one person may have authority to direct another person into harm's way. I guess that's where the concept of supervision ends and the idea of 'command' begins. In a law-enforcement or military context, a person 'in command' may have a supervisory posture most of the time, but once they're charged with ordering a lower ranking person into an action that may result in their harm or demise, the principles of supervision give way to the more strident principles of command. This book is not about command.

Responsibility begins with you

I'm assuming you're reading this because you already have people reporting to you, be they executives with broad responsibilities and six-figure salaries, or volunteers with narrow responsibilities and no recompense other than the satisfaction of being helpful.

Writing to his protégé, Timothy, somewhere around AD 63, the Apostle Paul states, *"Here is a trustworthy saying: Whoever aspires to be an overseer desires a noble task."*[4] Now the term 'overseer' (literally, one who sees from above) is synonymous with 'supervisor' (literally, one who looks over). Supervision is a noble aspiration.

This leads me to ask you (or for you to ask yourself), "Why are you doing this? To what are you aspiring as someone in a position to direct others? What's in this for you?"

Your answers are likely to be complex – perhaps a mix of motives and aspirations. Perhaps it's the cold reality that no one else was willing to shoulder the load, perhaps the hope of making a difference or the desire for influence. Maybe it's just about the career, and having staff comes with the territory. You may be a natural leader and it's come to you easily, or you may be a reluctant leader and it's not something you've really wanted.

Why would I ask these questions? Because it's likely that the answers are already apparent to your people. Perhaps not explicitly, and perhaps filtered through their own assumptions and backstories – but whatever is driving you to be a supervisor will have a profound influence on how you approach the responsibility.

---

[4] 1 Timothy 3:1 – *Holy Bible: New International Version* (International Bible Society, Zondervan, Grand Rapids 2011).

I'm not assuming your motives are dishonourable. Paul says supervision is a *noble* aspiration and I'm going to assume that all of us are trying to do good and to be responsible – more or less.

Paul goes on from his statement to list a bunch of prerequisites for being an overseer. He includes in his list a couple of competencies: able to teach and able to manage. The majority of the list however, is about character: sober, temperate, self-controlled, generous, hospitable, gentle.

In summary, overseeing people is a noble aspiration and so should be reserved for those of noble character. For us, exercising supervision nearly 2000 years later, the challenge is to live up to what's been entrusted to us.

Now you may not relate to a first century religious teacher. You may protest that your business operates in a dog-eat-dog industry requiring tough-mindedness and a certain ruthlessness. At the risk of jumping from one extreme to another, here's some thinking from Chinese military philosopher Sun Tzu from his third century BCE classic *The Art of War*.

"There are five dangerous faults which may affect a general:

1. Recklessness, which leads to destruction
2. Cowardice, which leads to capture
3. A hasty temper, which can be proved by insults
4. A delicacy of honour which is sensitive to shame
5. Over-solicitude for his men, which exposes him to worry and trouble"[5]

Examine the two references carefully and they're not that different. Supervision is a leadership function and effective leadership takes character.

The first person to supervise is yourself

We like to use the phrase 'leading your life'. It implies the exercise of taking some initiative, some agency and some responsibility for the results our lives produce. If we're each responsible for leading ourselves, it begs the question, 'What kind of boss are you to yourself?'

---

[5] Sun Tzu *The Art of War* Translated by Lionel Giles (Harper Collins, London, 2018), 35.

It may even lead to questions like, 'How well do you work for you?' If you stop and contemplate these questions for a while, the answers may have far-reaching implications.

Now you may find yourself protesting, 'I bought this book to improve my supervision, and now this mad Aussie is taking me down some self-examination rabbit hole.' Well yes, I am – for the reason of improving your supervision. Let me explain.

Your staff will either observe or make assumptions about how well you work for you. If they perceive that you don't do a good job of leading yourself, they'll likely find it hard to respond well to your efforts to direct them. Think about your own experiences of working for a boss you've struggled to respect. It's likely to elicit memories tinged with all kinds of unpleasant emotions – not exactly motivating.

So, let's look at some dimensions of being a supervisor worthy of respect, a leader worth following.

Self-management
First off, if you want the people who work for you to get things done, you need to be a person who gets things done. This is a question of both organising and motivating yourself.

If you're game, you might want to ask yourself some questions like:

- How effective am I in completing the tasks associated with my job?
- Do I forget or neglect things?
- Do if follow through on my commitments?
- Am I on top of my work and up to date, or always running behind?'
- Can I look at my personal output at the end of the day and say, 'I put in a good effort and made a useful contribution today?'

If you feel good about your answers, read on. If you feel a little uncomfortable, you might want to take some steps to improve your boss-worker relationship with yourself. Take a look at *Getting Things Done*[6] by David Allen, *Do It Tomorrow*[7] by Mark Forster and *Work Smarter: Live Better*[8] by Cyril Peupion.

I can't over-emphasise the importance of being able to manage yourself well. Let's be candid – if someone can't manage themselves well, they'll probably struggle to change themselves, so it's unlikely that they'll implement what they learn from reading a book (even a really helpful book like this one!). It may be that this paragraph is evoking some uncomfortable feelings for you. If so, it's important that you pay attention to them. If you feel like you're struggling to manage yourself, that previous efforts at leading yourself to change have failed and you're feeling a little powerless, please don't just plough on reading. Please, take some steps right away to get yourself a coach. I'll talk more about coaching later, but for now, it's important that you get some degree of mastery of your own life, and a coach will help you do it.

Getting a grip

When was the last time you told yourself or someone else to 'Get a grip'? It's a more contemporary version of the older expression 'to take hold of yourself'. It carries the idea of not letting yourself get 'out of hand'.

Keeping yourself 'in hand' or 'under control' is not a popular idea nowadays. Fearing that their kids will end up repressed, resentful and riddled with Freudian complexes, parents nowadays are counselled to encourage their children to express their feelings for fear of repressing their emotions. While that may seem very therapeutic, sooner or later we must develop some maturity. Maturity, as defined by family systems writers like Jenny Brown,[9] is about having your feelings but not allowing your feelings to have you. It's about being able to experience your feelings without losing your thinking, being able to reflect on your feelings and make thoughtful choices about how you respond.

---

[6] Allen, D. ***Getting Things Done: The Art of Stress-free Productivity*** (Penguin, New York 2001).
[7] Forster, M. ***Do it Tomorrow: and Other Secrets of Time Management*** (Hodder & Stoughton, London 2006).
[8] Peupion, Cyril ***Work Smarter: Live Better*** (Peupion, Melbourne 2011).
[9] Brown, J. ***Growing Yourself Up: How to Bring Your Best to All of Life's Relationships*** (Exisle, Wollombi 2012).

Maturity means acting responsibly even if you're feeling the intensity of anger or fear (up to a point). And it's also about making responsible choices when you feel compulsion, desire, aversion or distaste. That may mean saying 'no' to dessert or an online purchase, or 'yes' to the unpleasant task or the unpleasant conversation that is part of your job.

It's also about being able to tolerate the unpleasant emotions that arise out of taking responsibility. When we take hold of ourselves, get clear on our responsibilities and do what we know we should, we can expect to experience some very unpleasant emotions.

Taking up our supervisory responsibilities will sooner or later lead us to having difficult conversations with our people. Whether it's telling someone that they've not met performance expectations, or that their behaviour is not acceptable, or that their idea has been rejected, we can expect them to experience some unpleasant feelings in response. Whether they get angry or sad, their unpleasant feelings, or even our anticipation of their unpleasant feelings can trigger a corresponding emotional reaction in us.

Those of us that prefer the world of facts and tasks may find all this emotional stuff a little tiresome, so let me be blunt. Doing your job as a supervisor will at times mean experiencing discomfort, and that is usually triggered by the necessity of having conversations that make others feel uncomfortable. Prerequisite to being an effective supervisor is the ability to tolerate discomfort – in yourself and in other people.

Of course, not letting yourself get out of hand also means managing your own upset. While some bosses use a fierce temper to control their employees through fear, there's a good deal of research to demonstrate that fearfulness actually inhibits good thinking and promotes reactive 'fight or flight' responses. Your people may perpetually look busy if they know you've got a short fuse, but they won't be bringing their best thinking to their work.

It almost goes without saying that most people find it hard to trust and respect a supervisor who loses their temper. My guess is that you'll possibly be forgiven for one meltdown, and maybe two if there are strongly extenuating circumstances. Much more than that and people will become nervous around you and withhold information to avoid upsetting you. If your people get into this posture toward you, your chances of effective supervision begin to shrink – rapidly.

If the previous paragraph made you squirm, you owe it to yourself and your organisation to take some steps to change. A great place to begin is *The Anger Fallacy* by Steve Laurent and Ross Menzies.[10]

Self-leadership

Being a good boss to yourself goes beyond self-management and self-control. Beyond finishing your to-do list, following through on the difficult things and keeping calm all the while, self-leadership is about taking yourself somewhere. This usually takes the form of orienting your effort toward future goals.

Let me give you some examples. My current goals include restoring a fifty-year-old car, writing this book, and running ten kilometres in under fifty minutes. None of these are quick or easy. The car I hope to have mostly completed by the end of the year (so I might be driving it before you're reading this!). The ten-kilometre run has been a saga of injury and recovery for several years. I hoped this book would be a two-year proposition, and it's going to be closer to four.

Each of these roles plays into the kind of person I want to be: a craftsman, an author, and fit enough to be in good health well into my eighties. These are goals I lead myself to pursue. They're the tangible pursuits that, taken together, help me to become the kind of man I want to be.

Now you might read the previous two paragraphs and think, 'This guy's going soft on himself.' You're entitled to your opinion. Or you might think, 'That's okay for you, but I struggle just to get through the day, let alone hold aspirations to be a craftsman or an athlete.' And that might be all you can do. Stay with me for a minute.

Working toward longer-term goals is a key means by which people grow. Setting challenges and then aligning energy and resources toward them is a primary mechanism by which people develop strength and increase their

---

[10] Laurent, S. and Menzies, R. G. *The Anger Fallacy: Uncovering the Irrationality of the Angry Mindset* (Australian Academic Press, Samford Valley 2013).

capacity. As a supervisor, part of stewarding the people entrusted to your care is to help them grow and develop (we'll talk more about this in Section 4). There's a better chance that they will grow and develop if you can provide them an example.

You may not feel able to pursue a bunch of goals simultaneously. But if simply meeting the demands of the day leaves you with a completely empty tank and no resources left to dedicate to your own development, you may want to stop and ask yourself, 'Is this worth it?' You may be in a situation where you really don't have any viable options to change (e.g. holding down a demanding job and at the same time parenting little kids), or perhaps you could decide on just one goal – even if it's quite modest – and commit yourself to pursuing it.

Self-limiting

Self-limiting can sometimes be confused with 'self-defeating'. I'm not talking about maintaining scripts and presuppositions in your head that impede your growth and progress. I'm talking about leading yourself by setting boundaries for yourself.

I once read an account of an incredibly successful businessman who'd built a stellar career and made a huge fortune. And on his fiftieth birthday he found himself alone in a hotel room contemplating suicide, because he had no real friends and had become estranged from his wife and children.

How did that happen? Much like the guy in Harry Chapin's 1974 song "Cat's in the Cradle", there were 'planes to catch and bills to pay', and small decision by small decision, the businessman's career spilled over the limits of sustainability and eventually displaced just about every other priority in his life. His career became just as powerful and destructive an addiction as would drive someone to drug and alcohol rehab.

Getting a grip on yourself includes keeping the various aspects of your life within limits of balance and sustainability. You might think working seventy hours a week is an example to those you supervise, inspiring them to greater commitment and aspiration. Chances are, they'll see you as a workaholic and wonder what it's costing you in other areas of your life. There's a solid body of research showing that work efficiency peaks at less than forty hours per week, and productivity plummets after about fifty-five hours a week. [11]

Setting limits on yourself also includes how much you take advantage of your entitlements. Over recent years in Australia, we've had a string of high-profile politicians and trade union leaders forced to resign because they've claimed entitlements that, while technically within the bounds of the law, failed the common-sense 'pub test' – i.e. what the consensus opinion would be if the facts were laid out to the patrons at the local bar.

Showing discipline, restraint, modesty, even frugality when spending the organisation's money on yourself will do much for your credibility. Being seen as having your 'snout in the trough' will rob you of the moral authority necessary to call your people to account.

Servant leadership

While the idea of servant leadership can be traced variously to Taoist philosophies from the fourth century BCE, Jesus of Nazareth of the first century, and Indian thinkers of the sixth century, it came to prominence in the Western world from 1970 through the writing and work of Robert K. Greenleaf[12].

As a philosophy, servant leadership stands in opposition to the narcissism and entitlement that seems to underlie so much of the cult-of-success speakers and writers doing the rounds nowadays.

It gets down to this – if the organisation has entrusted people to your supervision, are you willing to set aside your own comforts, your prestige and even your reputation in order to serve the organisation by serving their best interests? Right now you might be thinking, "He's joking right? No one ever does that for their subordinates!" Well yes, some people do. Let me tell you a story.

Early in my management career I was placed in charge of workplace health and safety plus a Total Quality Management project at one of the sites

---

[11] E.g. John Pencavel *The Productivity of Working Hours* (Institute for the Study of Labor sIZA DP No. 8129 April 2014).
[12] https://www.greenleaf.org.

11

operated by Pacific Dunlop. At the time, it was Australia's largest and most diverse manufacturing company. The company had over-indulged on acquisitions like a kid in a chocolate shop and it was financially cantilevered over the abyss. There was pressure to increase profitability – and fast.

In the plant where I worked, we were under pressure from a newcomer to the market, with better and cheaper product, eating our market share. We were not meeting our EBIT (Earnings Before Interest and Tax) targets. EBIT was important at PacDun. It was repeated like a mantra. Head office was the temple of EBIT. I worked for a guy named Mark, who will pop up from time to time throughout the next few chapters.

To keep their jobs, the divisional managers submitted to group management a budget that was – let's just say – a little on the optimistic side. Budget variance reports required 'scaling' to be meaningful. Group management was kept from knowing the truth of our iffy profitability through fairly creative financial management and reporting strategies.

This was just before the electronic mail era and we communicated by the now antiquated means of the 'memo'. One such memo from me to my colleagues in the operations team made passing reference to "...the fantasy sometimes referred to as the budget." The memo was never meant to get to the 'suits' in the divisional finance department, but somehow a copy found its way onto the Financial Controller's desk.

The FC was a brilliant but difficult kind of man, one who would happily ignore safety rules, social conventions and the principles of accounting transparency. As you may guess, he also had scant regard for industrial relations regulations and he issued instructions down the chain of command for Mark to show me the door forthwith.

I wasn't privy to the conversation between Mark and the FC, other than to be informed that Mark had put his own job on the line to bypass a couple of levels of bureaucracy and have the fierce conversation directly with the FC, all in order to protect me. Mark had a fat mortgage and three kids in high school. Australia was mired in an economic recession (one which, Federal Treasurer Paul Keating assured us that we 'had to have'). Mark had an awful lot to lose, and he risked it for a junior and no doubt expendable member of his production team – me.

That's what I mean by servant leadership. And you can bet that from then on Mark had my absolute and unwavering allegiance.

Summary

- Supervision is a noble task that requires noble character. That means
    - managing yourself – getting your own stuff done
    - controlling yourself – not letting your feelings get out of hand
    - leading yourself – pursuing life goals
    - limiting yourself – keeping balance and proportion.
- People follow servant-leaders: Bosses who put their worker's well-being ahead of their own comfort and convenience.

Discussion

- In which aspect of your life and leadership do you feel most challenged by this chapter?
- What's the one thing you could do more, less or differently to respond to this challenge?

Action

- What tangible action will you commit to taking in the next three days?

Chapter 2
Responsible to…

*"People will confer authority or volunteer to follow you
because they are looking to you to provide a service."*
Ronald Heifetz[13]

Way back in my early twenties (yeah, I know, last century) I was part of a production crew working for a small chemical company. We made all kinds of specialist cleaning agents: evil-smelling potions to clean printing presses and jet aircraft, to strip graffiti from walls and road-grime from trucks.

My supervisor asked around the crew if we knew anyone who needed a bit of casual work, since one of our team had just moved on to a sweeter smelling, better paid and more secure job that was less irritating to the mucous membranes. I had a friend who had just been put off by his employer, so I recommended him. He started a few days later, and I was assigned to set him to work filling twenty litre drums with a blend of solvents.

The average crew member doing this kind of work would fill and label a couple of hundred drums in less than half a day. My friend, at the end of the first day, had managed not much more than 30. The next morning I let him know that he needed to speed up. At the end of the second day he still hadn't finished the batch he'd started the day before.

My boss pulled me aside. "Your mate's not up to the task. You're gonna need to tell him not to come tomorrow. You recommended him, so you get to give him the bad news." It was possibly the hardest conversation of my life up to that point. My friend cried. I felt awful.

Let's talk about responsibility.

The idea of responsibility is to some extent expressed by the prepositions around it. As a supervisor, I'm responsible *to* my organisation. And as a

---

[13] Heifetz, R. Grashow, A. and Linsky, M. *The Practice of Adaptive Leadership: Tools and Tactics for Changing Your Organisation and the World* (Harvard Business Press, Boston 2009), 24.

supervisor, I'm responsible *for* my staff. There's a reciprocal flow to it. We'll take a look at responsibility *to* in this chapter, and responsibility *for* as a distinct idea in the following one.

Delegated responsibility

As a supervisor in an organisation, you're generally responsible to some kind of hierarchical up-line. A team leader is responsible to a service manager who is responsible to an operations manager who is responsible to a general manager who is responsible to a CEO. The CEO is responsible to the chair of the board who represents the rest of the board of directors. The chair is responsible to the board who are responsible to the shareholders. It's a bit like the song about the old woman who swallowed a fly. The number of layers is largely determined by the size of the organisation.

In the not-for-profit space it works largely the same way, except there will be members instead of shareholders. Notice that the owners (shareholders or members) delegate to people (a board) a certain set of responsibilities who in turn delegate some of their collective responsibilities to an individual.

The important idea to grasp is that responsibility is nearly always delegated to you. You have a part to play in a bigger system that is pursuing a broader purpose than your division, department or team. Your role exists to contribute to that bigger purpose, and your remuneration and/or other forms of recognition is (or should be) the return you receive for your part in achieving that purpose.

Organisation over individuals

All that is to say, your first responsibility is to the organisation that entrusts your role to you. This becomes crucial when, as a supervisor, you feel the inner conflict of your sense of responsibility to your organisation and your sense of responsibility for your workers pulling in opposite directions.

If you're a business owner, you may not relate to the delegation flowing down to you. You may, however, recognise the delegated responsibility inherent in your overdraft or business loans. Further, you'll probably feel the weight of responsibility for providing work that provides a livelihood for those who work for you. If you think about being responsible to the community of people associated with your business that depend on the good conduct of your business for their welfare, the structure may be different but the sense of responsibility is similar.

In his book *The Advantage* Patrick Lencioni sets out the problems that arise when a supervisor's sense of responsibility *for* their people takes precedence over their responsibility *to* the organisation.[14] None of us want to foster interdepartmental rivalry, competition, secrecy, mistrust and blame-shifting, yet when looking after our people's interests comes at the expense of the purpose of the organisation, we're failing in our responsibility to those who have given us our role.

What's at stake

Now I realise that this kind of thinking will have some of you choking on your Weet-Bix. The line of thinking in reaction to this goes straight to a question of values. "People are more important than corporations." Agreed. "Corporations exist to serve people, not the other way around." Yep, agree with that too. So how can I possibly say, with any credibility, that the supervisor's first responsibility is to the organisation that they serve, rather than the people they supervise? How does that square with the servant leadership ideals outlined a few pages ago?

More specifically, should I have fired my friend? Great questions.

Here are the hard facts I had to face. The inherent work-for-pay bargain entered into between the company and my friend was for the company to buy his labour in order that they might gain a return on the buildings, plant, raw materials and intellectual property in which they had invested. My boss made the call on behalf of the company that my friend's labour was not worth what the company was paying: they were not getting the expected return. Further, the slow work was holding up hundreds of thousands of dollars' worth of plant, which could not be used to make more product until the product already made was packed out. So the bargain was terminated.

For my part, I had recommended my friend when I had no accurate assessment of his work capacity. I'd taken a risk that had proven to be unwise,

---

[14] Lencioni, P. *The Advantage: Why Organizational Health Trumps Everything Else in Business* (Jossey Bass, San Francisco 2012).

and the price for my risk-taking was the experience of some unpleasant emotions.

The company had not entered into an agreement to provide a supported role for a struggling worker who had a naturally slow pace, and my supervisor would have been failing his duties if he had allowed the unsatisfactory bargain to continue. Allowing an employee to continue to perform at less than the expected standard may have put the profitability of the company at risk. If the owners were not getting their expected return on their investment, they might look at outsourcing or offshoring, putting all our jobs at risk.

While it was uncomfortable for me and a bitter pill for my friend, it would have been inherently unethical to put other people's interests at risk (when they were fulfilling their responsibilities of work and management) simply to avoid causing unhappiness to one person. My boss knew his responsibilities well enough to know he could not let the underperformance continue.

The happy ending is that my friend found a job that was much better suited to his skill set and pace soon afterward.

Here's another illustration from the late twentieth century. When I was working in HR, a worker in the manufacturing area of the company I served dropped by my office for a chat. She was concerned about the conduct of the shop steward (the labour union representative on the factory floor), who had made a habit of passing unkind and unnecessary comments about the worker.

This was before 'workplace bullying' was a common term, but, if proven, it was clearly in breach of our anti-harassment policy. I asked if anyone had witnessed the behaviour and was given a couple of names. When I interviewed the witnesses, they reported that the shop steward was engaging in much more widespread harassment, including threats of violence. I took statements and interviewed more witnesses. Over the ensuing week I built a thick dossier of wide-ranging misconduct.

When I presented a summary of the evidence to the shop steward and her supporter, she flatly denied every allegation and offered no possible alternative explanation for the complaints. Given the seriousness of the claims and the high likelihood of the shop steward retaliating against the complainants (I figured she could guess who they were), I fired her. Summarily, on-the-spot-take-your-stuff-and-leave-the-premises. I told the shop steward her right to dispute the decision and even gave her all the information she needed to issue proceedings. Then I marched her out.

There's an unwritten law in industrial relations that says, 'you can't sack a shop steward.' I had guessed that in this case the shop steward had been banking on this and imagined she could act with impunity. I fully expected the union organiser to show up the same day and call a strike. I would have a lot of explaining to do, and there was a chance I would have been forced by my management into a humiliating back-down. Still, I believed that it was my responsibility and in the best interests of the company to do what I had done.

An hour or so after I had ensured the former shop steward had left the premises, the receptionist buzzed me. "The union organiser is on the phone." I took a deep breath and picked up the phone.

"I hear you just sacked our shop steward."

"That's right."

"I'm guessing you had your reasons."

"Yeah, plenty. There was a long list of stuff including harassment and intimidation."

"You followed procedure?"

"To the letter."

(Not long prior to this, the union had contested a disciplinary action I had taken when a worker had made threats against her supervisor. A registrar of the Industrial Relations Commission had gone through our policy and procedure and found it solid. Reviewing how we applied the policy and procedure in this particular case, the registrar recommended to the complainant that they not take their case to a hearing. The organiser knew the strength of our processes and the rigour with which we followed them).

"Well, let's see if she wants to take this to the commission."

"That's her prerogative."

And with that we exchanged the perfunctory pleasantries and the call ended. I never heard a word from the shop steward. The union took no further action.

The next day I took a walk around the manufacturing area just to check the mood. A number of workers – died-in-the-wool union members – approached me to offer their thanks and appreciation for ending the fear and intimidation that had become part of their everyday work experience.

The company and its workers were all better off for the sacking of a single worker. Truth be told, the union was better off too. A rogue shop steward was doing nothing to help their cause.

Before I go on, let me take a minute to clear up some possible misconceptions. Firstly, I'm not for union-bashing. My father served on the executive of a trade union. His father had been the secretary of a trade union; his father had been a leader in the movement for workers' rights in the UK. He moved to Australia because he had been blackballed by the building companies in England. I am proud of my heritage. I have been a member of a trade union and represented my fellow workers in enterprise bargaining negotiations. I believe unions have a legitimate place in the industrial relations landscape.

Second, I'm not advocating a Donald-Trump-on-reality-TV style of management that yells, "You're fired!" at the first sign of a mistake. I'm a big believer in procedural and substantive fairness. I would rather help someone learn and grow and become a great contributor than to fire them.

All that said, when a supervisor allows an individual to continue to perform poorly, or to breach the policy and procedure put in place for the good governance and management of the company, they risk undermining the welfare of the rest of the people who make up the organisation. Servant leadership means serving all your constituents.

In his life-altering book *Deep Change*, Robert Quinn boldly asserts, "If you're not risking your job, you're not doing your job."[15] There comes a time when your convictions will lead you to act contrary to your political instincts (i.e. those times when you know you're acting in the company's best interests *and* it could get you fired). Sometimes fulfilling your responsibilities is not in your own immediate best interests. Welcome to leadership.

---

[15] Quinn, R. **Deep Change: Discovering the Leader Within** (Jossey Bass, San Francisco 1996), 156.

Let's sum up the discussion over the past few pages. I've argued that the supervisor's first responsibility is to the organisation that charges them with the role of supervisor. The organisation entrusts the supervisor with responsibility for using resources (in our discussion on supervision, the primary resource is money to purchase people's labour and expertise) to further the purpose of the organisation. To act contrary to this, or to prioritise other things that may impede the company's purpose, is a breach of that trust.

Before we leave this part of the discussion, there is one question to clear up: 'What happens when pursuing the purposes of the company leads us to act contrary to our personal values?'

Occasionally supervisors will be called upon to act in a manner that might be for the apparent benefit of the organisation, but which compromises their own sense of what is right and fair. Over recent years in Australia there has been a string of high-profile hospitality and retail organisations that have been found to be breaching minimum wages standards. The term 'wage theft' has arisen to describe the systemic underpayment of workers – usually those already on minimum rates.

So what should a supervisor do if they find themselves party to something like wage theft? Isn't their first allegiance to the organisation? Well 'yes', in a way, and 'no' in another.

In the wake of the appalling revelations emerging out of the string of recent royal commissions in this country, issues around integrity in governance have come to the fore. Public confidence in large institutions is at a low ebb. There has been a push for governance processes to be more transparent, for whistle-blowers to be afforded more protection, for values to be given more consideration and be a more prominent point of reference for decision-making. In updating their governance principles, the Corporate Governance Council of the Australian Stock Exchange contemplated incorporating the idea of social licence.

The Ethics Centre, a Sydney-based non-profit organisation dedicated to ethics in every sphere of life, defines social licence to operate as "the informal acceptance granted to an individual or organisation by a local community".[16]

---

[16] https://ethics.org.au/ethics-explainer-social-license-to-operate/.

Increasingly, an organisation's sustainability and success in the longer term is dependent on its social licence. When the community perceives that an organisation is acting unfairly or unjustly, the organisation's sales and share price can be adversely impacted.

What's this got to do with your role as a supervisor? Plenty. If you go along with an organisation's unethical behaviour, you're collaborating in the erosion of the company's social licence and putting the company at risk – just as you would be if you were to look the other way when substandard products and services are offered to customers. Viewed from this angle, your responsibility to the company is to call out unethical practices like wage theft.

Sometimes the stakes are higher. Sometimes it's hard to see how the organisation could possibly benefit from your drawing attention to unethical behaviour. As the 2013 Royal Commission into Institutional Responses to Child Sexual Abuse discovered, some organisations are inclined to actively cover up unethical behaviour, pressuring their members to maintain secrecy in the vain hope that it will all blow over and be lost in the mists of time.

I would venture that in such cases, the organisation has lost the right to your allegiance. It becomes a question of your own integrity. Acting ethically in this situation may put your reputation, your livelihood and your entire career at risk. The question then becomes one about the price of your integrity. You may choose to quietly resign; you may choose to become a whistle-blower. There are no simple answers.

Summary

- Your first responsibility is to the organisation you serve.
    - The organisation gives you your authority to act.
    - Executing your responsibility to the organisation generally. benefits the workers who do their jobs faithfully and comply with standards.
    - Act according to conviction, not expediency, even if it means calling out bad practice.

Discussion

- In which aspect of your supervision do you find it hardest to meet your responsibilities to your organisation?

Action

- Is there a specific course of action you need to take to step up to your responsibilities?

Chapter 3
Responsible for…

Stewardship

Consider the recent case of a globally recognised non-government organisation (NGO) involved in relief and development, where its senior management in one country was found to be engaging in sexual exploitation of local women. In response, an estimated seven thousand donors pulled their giving and governments withdrew funding, causing a financial black hole to the tune of £16 million. Celebrity ambassadors terminated their associations, and several host countries ended up banning the NGO.

The funding deficit led to life-giving programs being cut and aid workers losing their jobs. Those already desperately poor were so much the poorer as a result.

As it turns out, there were signs of things going awry in the host country a full year before the scandal erupted. These complaints were sought to be 'managed' rather than properly addressed. The behaviour of a very few employees caused enormous and long-lasting damage to this NGO, and at critical junctures, people in senior supervisory roles failed to discharge their responsibilities.

It might be much smaller in scale and severity, but when one of your staff is discourteous or dismissive to a customer or stakeholder, or they fail to fulfil their responsibilities to serve a client or address a public concern, they are to some extent eroding your organisation's brand. And if you as their supervisor tolerate their failure, you're contributing to the erosion of the brand entrusted to your stewardship. I've already touched on the idea of stewardship, although not using that term. As a supervisor, you are entrusted with some fairly valuable assets. If you're supervising paid staff, obviously there's the money the organisation is spending on you and your staff. The implicit expectation is that you will exercise responsible stewardship of that investment.

In one of the stories I told earlier, I described how a slow worker tied up a whole lot of machinery. The capital resources your staff use – buildings, machinery, computers, furniture etc. – all cost money, and money costs money. If you're in the not-for-profit sector, money can be even more expensive, since it often takes a higher investment in goodwill, trust and partnership to raise money. The implicit expectation of responsible stewardship extends to the stuff you and your staff use. You have an obligation to show some return for it, be that in terms of money earned or a mission accomplished.

Some resources are harder to quantify on a balance sheet, such as reputation or 'brand'. These are most directly brought into play when your staff are facing the customers, clients, or members of the public that interact with your organisation. In every interaction (or non-interaction in the case of unanswered calls and emails) you and your outward facing staff are stewards of the organisation's brand.

If you're in the not-for-profit space, you might be tempted to think that the whole branding idea is a concept from the corporate world that doesn't apply to you. Yet as the story at the top of the chapter illustrates, branding is in many ways an even more sensitive issue for not-for-profit organisations.

Before you get too discouraged, let me pull a few threads together. Remember the words of the Apostle Paul I quoted earlier: *"Whoever aspires to be an overseer desires a noble task."* Supervision is a noble task, because it enables large groups of people to leverage their collective energies and skills for enormous good. Without humans in organisations directed by careful supervision, we would have no civilisation beyond a simple village and no technological advancement beyond basic metallurgy (we'll develop this idea a little further in chapter six).

If you're a supervisor, yours is a noble task. And it carries some far-reaching responsibilities.

And that's before we even begin to consider the sacred.

Stewardship of the sacred

Buddhism and Hinduism imply a certain sacredness to all forms of life, with humanity occupying a place close to the divine. Similarly, the three great monotheistic religions of the world maintain that human life is sacred because humans are created in the image of the divine. Just as one offends a monarch should they deface a coin bearing the monarch's image, so it is an offence against the creator to 'deface' the divine image borne by the human.

Even if you're not religious, it's unlikely that you would deny the ideas enshrined in documents such as the United Nations' Universal Declaration of Human Rights. While many would like to see some of the rights in the UN-UDHR conferred to other life forms, the broadly accepted rights therein apply uniquely to humanity. It's hard to imagine conferring rights to privacy, nationality, marriage, and ownership of property upon any creature that has no sense of these concepts, or guaranteeing freedom of thought, conscience and religion to a creature without the massive cerebral cortex that makes such faculties possible. In the minds of most people, humans occupy their own category.

Humans confer rights on other, unrelated humans. Humans have concepts of justice and fairness. Humans act to protect unrelated humans and even other life-forms from harm. The Holocaust is so named because it was inherently *inhuman.* We react with outrage when strangers' rights are violated and we call it 'man's inhumanity to man.' For reasons that evolutionary biology has struggled to explain, the very idea of being human carries the notion of being valuable – even priceless – and dare I say it, sacred.

All this means that supervisors are not just deploying a labour market commodity, purchased for the purpose of exploitation to maximum profit. As supervisors we are stewards of the sacred to the extent that we're directing the efforts and attention of unique and priceless beings we call humans: while at the same time ensuring that we discharge our responsibilities to our organisation.

Remember, *'whoever aspires to be an overseer desires a noble task'* – it's a noble task, not an easy one. As a boss, sooner or later the burden of discharging your responsibilities is going to cost you sleep. Getting our responsibilities and our ethics straight is especially difficult when, for reasons that are beyond their control, our workers are unable to fulfil the responsibilities we've entrusted to them. It may be that they have a family crisis, an illness, a legal problem. I wouldn't be writing this and you wouldn't be reading it if this were obvious and straightforward.

God's gift to...

We've all met the muscular, self-obsessed alpha-male, and possibly muttered, "He thinks he's God's gift to women," being reasonably confident that the women in question have other ideas (usually involving exaggerated gestures of fingers down throats). That's not the kind of gift I'm thinking about.

You'll remember right at the opening of this section, in speaking about responsibility, I included the quote 'To the person supervised, the supervisor is responsible for ensuring that the person's participation in the organisation is to their benefit.'

Can a boss be a kind of gift to their staff, helping to shape their work as an enjoyable, fulfilling, maybe even joy-producing experience? I reckon they can. Let me tell you a story.

Back when I was studying my undergrad, newly married and just beginning the odyssey of foster parenting, I needed a part-time job that would fit around my study and parenting. A relative of a relative offered me a job driving the rescue ambulance for the Royal Society for the Protection of Animals (RSPCA), which had its main operations centre a couple of suburbs away from where I lived. They already had a regular weekday driver; my job would be to take over on the weekends. The industrial relations environment of the day meant both Saturday and Sunday attracted generous penalty rates. I would make three and a half days pay in just two. It sounded great.

As it turns out, animal rescue is expensive and risky, so if there was any way the RSPCA rescue centre staff could encourage a member of the public to capture and transport the sick or injured animal they were reporting, they would. While most days I would have a couple of calls to attend to, I spent a good deal of time working as a kind of roustabout back at the centre.

Clad in waterproof pants and gumboots (galoshes or wellingtons for those not familiar with Aussie parlance) I would spend hours cleaning out the large network of dog pens, often up to my ankles or even elbows in dog excreta, trying to avoid being bitten by nervous, nasty little terriers, or trying to avoid being covered by the poopy pawprints of boisterous retrievers that were pleased to have any kind of company. And all the time immersed in the din of a hundred dogs barking incessantly. If I wasn't there, I was taking care of similar duties among the (quieter) feline inmates.

While the pay was good for a virtually unskilled job, the work was – on the face of it – pretty unpleasant. Yet, I count it as one of most enjoyable jobs I've had, and I looked forward to the weekends.

The key to enjoying my work at the RSPCA was the culture among the rescue centre staff, especially those working 'outside' in the maze of enclosures and compounds. The keeper of that culture was Deb. Slightly built and sandy haired, looking the business in regulation bib-and-brace overalls and checked flannelette shirt, Deb was positive, patient, funny, compassionate and a wealth of knowledge about animal husbandry.

The team were a quirky bunch ranging from passionate animal-rights advocates to volunteers with intellectual disabilities, to people serving out their court-ordered community service hours (plus the weekend ambulance driver who was overconfident and didn't know as much as he thought he did).

All of us were offered the same breezy humour, patience and grace. All were recognised and thanked (except perhaps for the very laziest of those on court-orders). Despite the often unpleasant and sometimes confronting nature of the work, it felt pretty good to be a part of Deb's crew.

Deb was a gift – a gift to me, to the volunteers, and to the constant flow of people who streamed through each weekend, tearfully (and occasionally heartlessly) surrendering the pets they could not keep, anxiously hoping we might have their lost Fido or Tiddles down in quarantine, or excitedly perusing the sales pens for a new best buddy.

Deb was my firsthand experience of the RSPCA, as she was for the rest of the team and thousands of members of the public. Because that experience was overwhelmingly positive, we had a positive attitude to our work, and so we worked hard. Deb was a gift to us and to the organisation.

Learning to trust

The cemetery is full of indispensable people. Although we all know that no one is indispensable, it's common for organisations to have a person within who's deemed to be so. On the other hand, the ill-advised corporate restructure often surfaces the person whose contribution *was* close to indispensable – right after they collect their severance package and walk out the door, leaving us to realise that they've taken with them a whole lot of tacit knowledge that we desperately need. It's notoriously difficult to estimate the value of a person's contribution to the organisation. We're constantly over or underestimating how 'dispensable' a person might be. Usually it's after people leave that we wonder what the dickens they ever did, or recognise with profound regret that they knew and did an awful lot more than we imagined.

Systems that standardise and document processes go some way to helping us more realistically estimate people's contribution to the organisation. Clear and unambiguous performance metrics (we'll talk more about that in the next section) also take out some of the guesswork. But it's hard to get a clear line of sight to everything a staff member or volunteer does. Sooner or later we'll either stop caring about their work (this happens more often than you might imagine), micromanage them, or come to trust them.

That brings me to the crucial point I want to make in this little section. ***Trust is critical to the supervisory relationship***. People tend to trust those who trust them, so who goes first? As a supervisor, there's a sense of leadership in establishing a trusting relationship. I'm not saying you should cut every new employee a set of keys to the safe. I am saying you'll need to take the risk trusting people with as much as you reckon they can handle, and be prepared to take responsibility for dealing with the aftermath if your trust proves a little optimistic.

For the purposes of this discussion, 'trust' could be simply defined as believing in the reliability, truthfulness, or ability of your worker. More specifically, it's believing that your employee or volunteer will discharge the responsibilities with which they're entrusted – that they'll perform to your expectations.

How can we be certain people will perform to expectation? Well, actually, we can't – not with absolute certainty. Over time we can develop confidence in a person's character, commitment and abilities based on their track record. But early in the relationship, we supervisors will need to make an educated estimate of what responsibility we entrust to people and learn to live with the risk.

Trusting someone sends them a message. If I handed you the keys to my fifty-eight year-old classic car – a car that I laboured for thousands of hours to restore – I would be telling you I think you're a good driver (the old thing is a handful to drive) and I would be telling you that you're important enough to me that I'm prepared for your sake to experience the angst I will undoubtedly feel if someone else were to drive it. I'd be saying, "I believe in you, I want you to experience what I experience when I drive the car." I'm implying you mean something to me, that you're valuable to me.

Think over your own experience. What was it like when someone entrusted you with something important? How did you feel? What was the implied message behind the person trusting you?

For most people, being trusted feels good. When we're trusted, we instinctively want to live up to people's faith in us. We want to prove to them (and perhaps to ourselves) that their positive assessment of our ability and character is well-founded. Trust tends to motivate, to bring out people's best – sometimes they'll surprise even themselves as to what they can achieve.

For the supervisor, there is something of a risk-reward ratio at play.

If you can get the 'stretch-to-achieve' factor about right, people feel empowered, motivated and they'll likely perform close to the top of their capacity. They'll likely enjoy their work more and be more engaged, using their creative abilities to think about ways of contributing further or solving problems or improving practices in the workplace.

It may even be that their job becomes a pleasure. Imagine being the kind of boss who facilitates their staff deriving genuine enjoyment and fulfilment from their work.

However, entrust someone with more than they're willing or capable of doing, and they may feel like a failure. They may be overcome by feelings of hopelessness and lose motivation. They may push too hard and become fatigued. They may feel abused and resent you. When their shortfall comes to light, as a supervisor you'll likely have some explaining and some repairing to do.

Conversely, trust a person with too little and they may feel belittled, micromanaged, disparaged and bored. They may feel unappreciated and resent you (sooner or later someone is going to resent you – you can pretty much count on it).

You're not going to accurately gauge a person's trust 'sweet spot' with perfunctory supervision conversations that are just about tasks, or if the supervision conversations are infrequent or fleeting. Being able to gauge the trust equation for each individual comes from getting to know them, learning about their strengths and challenges, and giving feedback that invites a conversation. It takes investment of time and emotional energy on your part. To bring out the best in your people, it will take giving of yourself.

Now let's take it back to the organisational side for a moment. Unless you're paying piece-work rates or your team are all subcontractors, you're paying the same whether you get mediocrity or brilliance. By appropriately trusting people (while still holding them accountable) you may just create an opportunity for them to shine. The organisation benefits through better return on their money paid in wages and the worker wins though greater enjoyment of their work, greater satisfaction and the opportunity to learn new skills. We can't give everyone blue-sky opportunities all the time, but we can be thoughtful about what we might encourage people to attempt.

Treat everyone like volunteers

Nowhere is this more important than in the volunteer space. Although the organisation does not stand to get a better return on the money paid in remuneration, everything else holds true.

A good chunk of my time nowadays goes toward coaching church ministers. Some of these ministers have staff, some don't. All of them, directly or indirectly, oversee a large crew of volunteers. One of the major issues that ministry coaches talk about is that of 'growth barriers' – or the tendency of churches to grow to certain size limits and then stagnate (the reasons are more about anthropology and organisational theory than theology, so even if you're not religious, stay with me).

A critical factor in breaking through these barriers is the role of the leading minister. In small churches (less than about 50 people) the minister tends to have no other staff and operates like the owner of a small business – they're everything from CEO to janitor, receptionist to marketing manager, head of HR and agony aunt. They are the only one getting paid and they tend to hold the conviction – either explicitly or just by instinct – that it would be unfair to ask someone else to do something they could do themselves. And that, more than just about anything else is what keeps small churches (and businesses) small.

A similar dynamic goes on in smaller not-for-profits. A board of directors – usually unpaid but emotionally invested up to their armpits – works 'tirelessly' to keep the show on the road, while other members, program participants, community partners all watch and sometimes cheer them on (I put 'tirelessly' in inverted commas because, ironically, most people so described are on the verge of exhaustion).

This came into razor-sharp focus when I recently began working with the board of a small not-for-profit. I'd been a participant in their programs for years and partnered with their staff on some collaborations. I'd come to regard these people as friends.

Something I heard the CEO say gave me an inkling that all was not well at the top of the organisation. I contacted her later and asked if she could use a little consulting assistance – pro bono (like I said, they're my friends).

In my first meeting with the board, I went through the basic reality checks that any consultant would. It turned out that the organisation's forward-orders (in their case, enrolments) were very, very thin and cash was very, very tight. It was clear that the organisation needed to do some quick revenue generation to get some working capital. The obvious solution was a series of one-day events around single topics that would pull a paying crowd beyond the usual suspects (generating quick cash) and give opportunity to promote their longer-term programs (marketing to build up enrolments).

I looked around the room at the directors. All the colour had drained from their faces. The very idea of pulling off more than they were already doing seemed like asking them to swim the English Channel. The unspoken assumption among the board was that they held the only resources available to the organisation.

I looked at them quizzically. "Didn't you guys just graduate a bunch of people?" I'd seen some of these new grads lead side-seminars at the organisation's annual conference. It was worth the price of admission to hear them speaking on their areas of speciality.

In the next ten minutes we listed four people to approach to host and present workshops under the organisation's brand – for free (i.e. the organisation would retain all the gate money after costs). Of the four, three agreed to host workshops – putting in all the preparation and all of the logistical work for the benefit of the organisation, simply because they believed in the cause, had benefited from the organisation's work and wanted to give something back.

I had simply challenged the board to think beyond themselves and their resources and recognise that there was a body of untapped goodwill that could be an enormous resource to the organisation, if only the leaders had mind to look for it. To quote St James, "Ye have not because ye ask not" (James 4:2 KJV).

Sometimes we ask not because we say 'no' on behalf of the people we might otherwise invite to step up. A mantra I recite to leaders constrained by their own capacities goes like this: "Try to get to the point where you only do what only you can do." And by that I mean delegate or cease to do everything possible without breaching your own employment contract or going broke. Another way of putting it: "Don't do what you could delegate to other staff or hand over to appropriately trained volunteers."

Whether it's a not-for-profit, a business or a local bowls club, if the leader spends all their time just taking care of business as usual, the future will look a lot like the present, except everything and everyone will be older, and the world around will have moved on. Getting other people doing more stuff they can do gives you more time and energy to the stuff only you can do.

I bet you can guess the predictable response from leaders when I challenge them to work toward a situation where they only do what only they can do. 'But I don't have anyone I can delegate to...'

Let's use a few worked examples. In a small business context, let's say the owner insists on (inefficiently) doing their own IT, their own web design and their own invoicing – tasks they could hand off to a part-timer or a subcontractor while they do what only they can do, like the face-to-face meetings with potential customers that will build the business. The growth engine of the business is stymied and the business never develops. The small business owner remains a sole trader who puts in 80-hours a week.

To take a not-for-profit example, imagine a sporting club where the president does everything from clean the clubrooms to cutting oranges. They may feel like they're super-dedicated, but they're actually impeding the involvement and investment of others. Imagine if they partnered with a local disability job placement agency and got some volunteers cleaning the clubrooms. If the volunteers were shown some kindness and some appreciation, the agency's clients and their families will become more interested, possibly more involved and progressively more committed to the club. They might even want to relieve the president of their orange-cutting and uniform-washing duties. Meanwhile the disability service's clients gain valuable work experience and that veritable golden ticket, a verifiable work reference.

Return on trust investment

Let's say a church minister reports to me that they spend four hours a week building a PowerPoint deck for their Sunday service (yep, in case you haven't been in a while, most churches have ditched the hymn books and gone multi-media). I reply, "Wow, that's half a workday – it's like, ten per cent of your work time. Can't you flip that to a volunteer?"

"Nope."

"Why not?"

"We don't have anyone in the church who can use PowerPoint."

At this point I really want to say, "Really, have you asked everyone?" but I usually bite my tongue.

The minister will usually go on to explain that it's too much trouble to try to train someone because they won't do it right and it will take just as long to work with someone so they may as well do it themselves. The subtext being, they're not willing to take the risk to put in the investment to develop someone else's abilities. The implication: they're not willing to take on the role of a competent and responsible supervisor. The result being, theirs is a church that will likely stay small.

If they had a change of heart and *invested* those four hours a week into a newly retired person or newly arrived immigrant volunteer with some basic computer literacy, over time the volunteer would need less and less time in supervision, and the minister would have more time to do other things. Meanwhile the volunteer's commitment to the church would have increased. People commit to what they're involved in – not the other way around. If you want more commitment, ask for more involvement.

Whether you're paying staff or leading volunteers, offering people the opportunity to take on new responsibilities (providing you're not being manipulative or abusing their goodwill) often leads to the supervisor having more of their time and effort to give to the things that will drive forward progress, while releasing untapped potential in staff and volunteers. It usually takes a willingness to trust and a shift in the supervisor's mindset.

What lies within

A conversation about trust and inviting people to take on more responsibility naturally leads to some thinking around the kind of raw potential that might be lying latent within the people we lead in the workplace and the community group.

In general people are a little reticent to offer their resources and abilities. Perhaps it's the fear of a knock back, perhaps it's not wanting to appear pushy – I'm not sure anyone's put any research effort into the question. Sometimes I'm not sure why I'm reluctant to put myself out there.

At times the skill and knowledge that our staff and volunteers carry is hiding in plain view. People in our organisations have understanding and know-how that we may never discover. More often than not it's carried by older people, and sometimes those older people will take a bit of coaxing to bring their skills and knowledge to bear.

A good chunk of my HR career was served in the agricultural sector. Specifically, I worked for a sprawling, vertically integrated agribusiness that in one way or another handled about twenty percent of Australia's apple, pear and stone fruit crop. Head office was located in the middle of an eighty-acre orchard that included the original tract farmed by the founder just after World War II.

Kevin had been an employee of the company for as long as anyone could remember. He'd worked shoulder to shoulder out in the paddocks with the founder in the early days.

During my time with the company, Kevin was close to retirement and could be found in a triangular-shaped workshop wedged between a dam wall and one of dozens of huge cool rooms located on site. Kevin was in charge of maintenance for all agricultural machinery across the dozen-or-so farms that made up the orcharding side of the business.

No one would ever accuse Kevin of being easy-going. He seemed to resent the fact that his influence was on the wane – the farther-flung farms were getting local mechanics to repair their machinery. Worse still, the founder – his mate of long-standing – was now enjoying retirement while Kevin languished in the workshop, up to his elbows in grease.

I especially came in for some fire from the old guy. When I started with the company, my first priority was to improve occupational health and safety management practices across the group. At the time, farms were the most dangerous worksites in the country, and the people most likely to be killed on a farm were older men who'd worked on farms all their lives – just like Kevin. The directors feared that someone would take a shortcut, end up as an on-farm fatality statistic and they would find themselves explaining it all to a County Court judge.

With the authority of the directors behind me, I implemented regular inspections of all the machinery, and pushed the orchard managers to get things repaired quickly. I even threatened to 'tag out' (i.e. ban from use pending repair) machines that were deemed unsafe. Clearly Kevin and I were on a collision course.

I must admit, I saw Kevin as a bit a relic. I had a begrudging admiration for his encyclopaedic knowledge of anything powered by a diesel engine, and his ability to wring service out of ancient machines that were long past their planned obsolescence. But in my mind, he was the kind of stubborn 'I'll do it my way' kind of guy who would likely land us in court. I guess in my mind I wrote him off.

It so happened that one day I needed to chat with the orchard manager at the home site, and I found out from the farm hands that he was up at 'Number Three', which was about a half-mile walk from my office back at the main complex. I found the orchard manager standing on the headland watching an eighty horsepower Case tractor with a disc plough shaping up long mounds of soil in preparation for fumigation prior to planting. I squinted toward the tractor labouring about 200 yards from us. At the controls of the Case was Kevin.

"So why's Kevin discing up the block?" I enquired of the orchard manager.

He looked back at me with a kind of expression that conveyed "only an idiot would ask a question like that." "Kevin's a genius with a disc plough," he explained. "There's no one in the whole group who's even close to his level of skill. It will take me years to learn to do what he can do."

By this time the Case had reached the headland. Kevin had alighted and was walking toward us. Ignoring me, he addressed the orchard manager as a sensei would a student. He explained how and why he'd done things as he had, described what would be needed in the next pass down the row and how to set the attitude of the plough to achieve the required result.

The orchard manager listened in respectful silence, then approached the tractor and set off down the row, endeavouring to do as he had been instructed. I watched in silence as Kevin gave a muttered-under-the-breath commentary. I listened just to see what I could learn.

When the orchard manager returned from his pass, Kevin gave him a fairly blunt critique and further instructions. He nodded appreciatively, set his jaw and turned the tractor toward the next row. In the meantime, I had forgotten what I had wanted to discuss with the orchard manager, and quietly departed for the sanctuary of my office.

Clearly there was a lot more to Kevin than I estimated, and he deserved more respect than I had afforded him.

Kevin was a walking, grumbling, treasure trove of what we call 'tacit' knowledge. The kind of know-how that's not in the procedures manual and that can't be learned in a university course or from reading a book. Fortunately for the orchard manager, he had some insight into Kevin's value and sought to draw upon it. From then on, I made an effort to do so as well.

Chances are, there's a Kevin or two in your organisation, and they're quietly sitting on expertise that you could use. You may have written them off because they're a bit difficult or seem unwilling to change.

Herein lies the conundrum for the leader. We could have people among our staff and volunteers, our membership, graduates, client base or among our broader network with all kinds of knowledge and skills that would be useful to our organisations. What's more, they may be willing to offer that knowledge and skill for free.

But we'll never know if we don't get to know people, if we're not open about our needs, and if we're unwilling to loosen up our own grip on the tasks and responsibilities that give us a sense of belonging and identity in our jobs.

Sometimes it's not even about a person's pre-existing knowledge and skills – it's about what they might be able to do with some on-the-job learning and perhaps some formal training. We'll talk more about this in the final section of the book.

Summary

- You're not just responsible to the organisation you serve, you carry responsibility for stewarding its assets:
    - Tangible assets like equipment
    - Less tangible assets like brand reputation
    - Sacred assets – the people who work for you
- You can be a gift to your organisation and your workers by:
    - Trusting people enough for them to flourish
    - Developing their skills and delegating responsibility
    - Seeking out the capacities that lie within your workers

Discussion
- Where do you find it hardest to entrust responsibility to people?

Action
- What will you do to enhance your stewardship of the people under your direction?

Chapter 4
The responsibility shift

Your workers *are* your job

Most people get their first shot at supervision in the workplace by being promoted from a non-supervisory role. It doesn't seem like that big a change. In my early twenties I was a chemical process operator and after a while I was put in charge of three other process operators. I didn't think much of it. As long as they knew what to do and how to do it (and I assumed they did), I just needed to keep an eye on them and answer their questions. In the meantime, I could get on with my own job of churning out batches of paint or fixing broken machinery. In my mind, the tasks I did personally were my real job and my crew were somewhat of an interruption.

Taking the role of supervision seriously reveals just how wrong the assumptions of my younger self were. As soon as we have supervisory responsibilities, our workers become our real job. Sure, we have other things we need to do (as I write this, I still maintain close to a full-time list of clients even though I lead a team of four), but other than ensuring we ourselves are in a fit space, our staff take priority over our own busy-work.

The financial consideration is obvious. If my staff are not delivering good value for the organisation's money, and the reason is because I'm not providing them with appropriate supervision, I'm wasting the organisation's money. If a member of my team is being unproductive because they're waiting for me to make a decision or provide a resource or give directions, I'm failing them and the organisation. If one of my employees is beavering away at whatever they think is most important when it does not line up with company strategy or priorities (this happens a lot more than you might imagine), I'm misusing a resource by not redirecting them to core priorities.

If my staff have staff, the problems multiply further. As a coach and consultant, I am fairly regularly confronted with leaders who are yet to make the shift – sometimes these leaders are in CEO or equivalent roles, with payrolls running into the millions and several layers of staff under their direction. The cost of mismanaged and misdirected resources is staggering.

Further, when our workers are confident that we're interested in them and their work, and when they have ready access to us as their boss, they will generally reward our investment with higher quality work. Conversely, even the most dedicated and intrinsically motivated employee will find it hard to stay focused when they suspect their boss just isn't that interested.

Since we employ people and recruit volunteers to contribute effort to advance the cause of the organisation, the inherent logic is that workers and their interests are not the primary purpose of the company, but rather a means to an end. We may not verbalise or even think this explicitly, but it's implied in the basic mechanics of the work-for-pay bargain that is the foundation of the employment relationship.

There's a growing movement in the corporate world that would challenge this tacit assumption. It's typified in the dedication of Jim Clifton and Jim Harter's book, *It's The Manager:*

To those who believe maximising human potential
is now the primary purpose of all organisations.[17]

Now you might think the two Jims are taking the idea of the altruistic organisation a little too far. Perhaps, but it nonetheless brings into focus the importance of the supervisor taking seriously their responsibility for the stewardship of the human resources placed under their care. Focusing on the organisation's priorities to the extent that we fail to see the people who fulfil those priorities can bring us unstuck. Let's look at a couple of ways this can happen.

When the 'people' responsibilities are neglected...

Most of what I've written so far has assumed that the relationship between the organisation and the employee or volunteer will be mutually beneficial. The relationship will enable the organisation's cause to be advanced while the worker, paid or unpaid will flourish. For many employment and volunteer relationships, such benefit to both parties is well within the realms of possibility. I've experienced a number of settings where my work has been a

---

[17] Clifton, J. and Harter, J. *It's the Manager* (Gallup New York 2019).

win-win for the organisation and for me personally. I hope you can recall similar stories from your own experience.

However, sometimes it's just not going to work out that way. Some workplaces seem set up to exploit people, and some people seem to make a career of making their workplace pay for their maladaptive behaviours. Let me illustrate.

Organisations that burn people

In Australia we have a prevailing narrative that we impress upon our hapless children. It goes something like this: Work hard to get a good study score at the end of high school (in Australia we call this an Australian Tertiary Admission Rank or ATAR). A good ATAR means getting into a good university course. For example, you'll need an ATAR of 99 (i.e. in the top one percent) to have a shot at the best law school in Australia. The same goes for medicine. If you get into a good uni course, so the story goes, you'll have a decent shot at getting a good job. Get a good job and you'll have a shot at saving to buy a house, and once you've achieved that, you can have kids. Then you'll be happy. Great story: finish with a crane shot pulling back to a wide angle, some stirring music, gradually fade to black and roll credits.

A young woman I know well was naïve enough to buy the narrative, and studiously set about meeting all the required milestones. She studied hard in year 12, finished dux of her school, got an ATAR a little north of 98 – tick! She enrolled in the second-best law school in the state (remember the best one needed a 99), studied hard for five years completing a double degree, graduated well above the average (remember, that's the average of a bunch of kids that all scored in the top two percent of the country at the end of high school). To improve her chances, she did a couple of clerkships with respected law firms and some voluntary work at a community legal service – check! She was accepted into a graduate program with a well-known firm – done! That house and the kids are now only a matter of time...

Except this is where it all begins to go off track. In this respected law form our heroine was beavering away assisting a bunch of admitted lawyers who are all carrying the kind of caseloads you would expect in a modern law firm. Lawyers don't do 9-5. The young woman found that overloaded lawyers are not on top of the details of their cases and, being rather conscientious, she set about getting case files in order, getting salient facts established, and following up details so that, when the case went to conciliation or court, the lawyers operating the files were well-advised and properly briefed. Her supervisors noted her diligence.

Then one of the lawyers quit because the workload was too much, life was out of balance and out of control, their relationships were suffering as was their health. The departing lawyer was operating fifteen or so case files, and many of them were significantly behind in their progress (i.e. their court dates were approaching and there was a lot of work to get the evidence collected and the arguments set out).

The partner leading that area of the firm had a brilliant solution. "How about we give half of the files from the lawyer who just quit to that bright young grad who's doing so well? Oh, and she can also maintain her current workload (with which she's barely keeping up) as well. Sure, she's not even an admitted (i.e. licenced) lawyer yet, but we can work around that. When our heroine reluctantly agreed on the condition that she was given a legal secretary to assist, the partner was delighted – and refused to give her the legal secretary. And of course, there was no rise in pay.

Pretty soon our eager young grad was drowning in the workload, developing some worrying health symptoms and asking her husband to take more and more responsibility at home as she worked longer hours. The happily-ever-after narrative began to unravel, and the real story became clear. This is what law firms do. They pay grads barely above the minimum wage, and then flog them mercilessly, all the time holding out the carrot of admission to the court, followed by advancement, and if they really sell their soul to the firm, partnership. Surely a young woman's health and marriage is a fair price to pay. Not this young woman. She quit – leaving the firm down another key staff member, and potentially a diligent lawyer who would have made them a good chunk of money.

This kind of abuse is not confined to the legal profession. It's perhaps worse in medicine, where young medical interns work double normal working hours under unimaginable pressure. Nurses report that the intern error rate is nothing short of scary. Young female doctors commit suicide at 2.27 times the rate of the general population, and one in five medical students report experiencing suicidal ideation. [18]

Remember these are the two professions that attract those diligent, hardworking young people with the rarefied ATAR scores.

Some organisations are just as hard on their volunteers. I know I just got through waxing lyrical about the hidden potential among those in our orbit to be invited to be a resource to our organisations. But remember, I talked about the relationship being mutually beneficial. Some leaders and indeed some organisations develop a track-record for burning people. The anecdotal evidence from the field suggests a volunteer who is committed to the cause but pushed to make an unreasonable contribution will last about eighteen months – it seems that's about how long it generally takes for the impulse for self-preservation to become more pressing than the desire to serve the cause.

If your community group, sporting club or church seems to turn people over after eighteen months or so, you might want to do some exit interviews.

What's all this got to do with supervision? You may not be in charge of interns in a hospital or a partner in a legal firm. If you are, you might feel powerless since 'it's not me it's the system.' Now let's dare to tell ourselves the truth. People who are part of a system that causes harm to its workers, and benefit from that system by remuneration and career status, are complicit in the abuse. It's your call.

People who burn organisations

There's a particular subspecies of employee that, despite appearing to make a valuable contribution to the organisation, actually functions more like a malignancy. Malignant cells function differently to healthy cells in three particular ways. Firstly, malignant cells are unregulated. The normal processes for cellular regulation – metabolic rate, division, and termination when DNA is degraded – don't operate in a malignancy. They grow and consume resources, often at an alarmingly rapid rate. Even when they mutate they just keep going and growing. Second, malignant cells are

---

[18] Swannell, C. *Reducing Risk of Suicide in Medical Profession* Medical Journal of Australia – https://www.mja.com.au/journal/2018/reducing-risk-suicide-medical-profession.

undifferentiated. A healthy cell in a brain or a heart or in the bloodstream has a unique set of properties and functions that interact with the rest of the organism to maintain the function of the system. Malignancies just invade the space and interrupt the functioning of the cells around them. Thirdly, malignancies do not serve the life force of the organism's survival and reproduction. Instead, the malignancy serves only its own ends, even if it means eventually killing the organism in which it is growing.[19]

Some organisations find themselves home to a person who operates like a malignant cell – they're a person who seems to operate as if the normal rules don't apply. I worked with one branch of a dispersed organisation where a mid-level employee was a personal friend of the leader of the whole enterprise. This employee profoundly disagreed with and personally disliked the person in charge of the branch and would actively sabotage their leadership. When challenged, they made oblique references to their connections further up the food chain. The branch leader felt hamstrung.

Then there's the person who seems to have the organisation over a barrel. It might be that they, and only they, can maintain the software that the organisation relies upon, or they have unique and well protected relationships with key clients – whatever the basis of their special status, it seems to be a hall pass for all kinds of behaviour that would get anyone else fired.

One manager I came across (we worked in the same organisation, but this manager and I were in different management lines) simply did as they pleased, ignoring whatever policy, procedure or process they deemed to be inconvenient to them. However, their 'protected species' status lay in their ability to manipulate the appearance of the organisation's finances to give the illusion of profitability. If the managing director crossed this guy, the whole charade would have unravelled and heads would have rolled. So the unregulated manager remained at large in the organisation.

I've seen sporting clubs look the other way when a particularly gifted, 'indispensable' player broke the booze rules, failed to turn up at training or

---

[19] Adapted from Friedman, E.H. *A Failure of Nerve: Leadership in the Age of the Quick Fix* (Seabury, New York, 1999).

otherwise thumbed their nose at the standards expected of all the other players on the list.

In his classic story, *The Five Dysfunctions of a Team*, Patrick Lencioni has the main character relate her experience of being a rookie leader who fell into the trap of protecting and even promoting a 'malignant' employee because they outperformed the rest of the analysts in her crew. When the crunch came, it was the rookie manager who got fired, not the malignant employee.[20] Lencioni is a master at teaching through stories. One you've finished this book, read some of his.

In addition to Lencioni, there is no shortage of literature lamenting the cost of the toxic employee. Harvard Business School went so far as to put a dollar value on savings associated with quickly firing a toxic hire.[21] Curiously, the paper also found that toxic employees tend to demonstrate above-average productivity.

All this is to say, as a supervisor, your integrity is on the line. If you allow a different set of rules for people who can cause you short-term grief, you're engaged in what Susan Scott terms an 'integrity outage.'[22] The research and the anecdotal evidence both point to this being an increasingly costly approach. Your staff will lose their respect and eventually resent you. Productivity will go south, turnover will go north. Don't be that boss.

In short...

Let's review the journey so far. We've talked a lot about responsibility: both in terms of responsibility to the organisation that entrusts you with a supervisory role, and responsibility for the resources under your direction, particularly human resources. We spent a bit of time discussing stewardship and dipped into the idea that there is a sacredness to humans that calls for them to be treated with a certain care and respect.

---

[20] Lencioni, P. *The Five Dysfunctions of a Team: A Leadership Fable* (Jossey Bass San Francisco 2002).
[21] Houseman, M. and Minor, D. *Toxic Workers* Working Paper 16-057 Harvard Business Review http://www.hbs.edu/faculty/Publication%20Files/16-057_d45c0b4f-fa19-49de-8f1b-4b12fe054fea.pdf.
[22] Scott, S. *Fierce Conversations: Achieving Success in Work and In Life One Conversation at a Time* (Berkley, New York 2002).

We thought about developing people through your supervisory role, whether through your organisation's formal policies, or whether it's just taking advantage of the development opportunities that supervision presents. I talked about being a kind of gift to your staff, helping to shape their work as an enjoyable, fulfilling experience.

In this chapter we've looked at the shift in priority that supervisory responsibility demands. As a boss, your people *are* your job and it makes good leadership and economic sense to prioritise them over your own busy work. To illustrate we considered two extremes: companies that burn people, and people who burn companies.

I know it's tricky to keep it all in your head when you sit down with your staff member or key volunteer for a formal supervision conversation (yes, you should do this, and we'll look at the how and why in the next section). But the most important concept I'm hoping you'll take into your supervision conversations is that you're dealing with a human being who has a backstory and a family, perhaps some aspirations, hopes and aversions. They have some skills and capacities that they may or may not be using in their role, they have potential to develop new skills and perhaps take on greater responsibilities. If you can bring your best to the supervision task, they, you, and the whole organisation will likely benefit.

Summary

- As a supervisor, your job is to ensure your workers have clear focus and the resources required to do theirs.
    - This takes priority over your personal to-do list.
    - They're more likely to be interested in their work if they're confident you're interested in them.
- It is a failure of supervisory responsibility when:
    - the organisation's priorities lead to workers being exploited. This was illustrated by common practice in law and medicine.
    - a 'malignant' employee is allowed to continue in their ways because they're a protected species.

Discussion

- When do you find it hardest to put your supervisory responsibilities ahead of your personal priorities?

Action

- Are there some areas where you're allowing workers to be overburdened or to get away with undesirable behaviours?

Chapter 5
With responsibility comes authority

Back in the 1970s, a lot of people had a crack at communal living – the Jewish kibbutz movement came to wider attention, neo-monastic movements sprang up, and communities like the House of the Gentle Bunyip (true story) popped up in the inner suburbs of Melbourne.

A colleague of mine and a bunch of her friends were living in one such community, growing their own vegetables and trying to embody their religious values in a shared life. So far so good. Because they valued equality and sharing of power, they reached a consensus that every decision should be reached by consensus. And so came the conversation about relocating the shed. These people were all university-educated adults (i.e. smart people). Some were academics (i.e. *officially* smart people). Yet the debate over the location of the shed raged for six months, and in the end a compromise consensus was reached to move the shed approximately two metres. Nobody 'lost' – and nobody 'won'. If the purpose of the community cooperating was mutual benefit, it's hard to see who was better off for all the energy expended.

Consensus seems attractive because it appears to banish those evil twins, 'authority' and 'hierarchy'. It achieves this by giving everyone equal authority and equal responsibility – along with infinitely variable degrees of frustration as our story illustrates. Consensus gives the same authority to the least mature, least functional and least responsible participants as it does to the most.

While consensus and other flat-as-a-pancake structures have the apparent appeal of being abuse-proof, they're actually just as vulnerable – it's just that the abuse takes different forms. A consensus decision can be held to ransom by the least mature member of the group holding out, either from fear or bloody-mindedness. Further, consensus and other democratic processes can be manipulated through subtle and less-than-subtle manoeuvring outside of the main forum of conversation.

Every process for collective effort – from consensus at one end to dictatorship at the other – suffers from the same root problem. We humans have a selfish streak. Whether you want to think it as the result of competitive evolution or a fall from grace, humans throughout history have a propensity to use power to their own advantage and at the expense of others. So when the organisation affords an individual power, the possibility for abuse of that power is never far away.

'Authority' and 'hierarchy' have come in for some bad press because they tend to be associated with large corporations and bureaucracies. I'm not here to defend large institutions as noble and beneficent. In my home country of Australia, we've had a succession of royal commissions which have laid bare wholesale abuse on the part of churches, banks, and aged care facilities. Big institutions have provided a context where corrupt individuals have ruined people's lives. Without the power and protection afforded by the sheer size, influence and resources of large institutions, such abuses would not have been possible to sustain.

History is littered with sad and even appalling stories of large organisations doing very harmful stuff, sometimes in the name of God. But here's the rider: it's also rich in stories of large organisations doing remarkable, magnificent, redemptive stuff. Amazingly, sometimes the very same organisation will feature in both kinds of stories.

Further, history generally does not record the harmful things that have gone on in smaller, independent, less-organised groups because these groups themselves largely go unrecorded in history, and the scandals are too isolated to make the headlines. But most of us have heard enough sad anecdotes to know that what happens on a big scale in big organisations can happen on a smaller scale in smaller organisations, even families.

The size of the institution is not the issue. Let's do a bit of organisational theory here; and the importance will become apparent.

Organisations, by definition, form and function around cooperation for mutual benefit. Let's take the organisation most familiar to all of us, the family. Until fairly recently my nuclear family comprised four adults, each with varying degrees of responsibility and authority (the kids have since flown the coop). Sometimes I would have the pleasure of eating a dinner cooked by my daughter. I benefit from her work. To gain that benefit, I have to give up some power – I don't get my first choice for dinner. She's a vegetarian, and when she cooks for us, we're all vegetarians.

For an organisation to work, the various players give up some things in order to receive others. Cooperation requires letting go of some power in order to gain a benefit.

Ain't a dirty word

Hierarchy arises when some people have responsibility for an aspect of the functioning or wellbeing of others. Another way of looking at it is that some of the power handed over for benefit accumulates with certain individuals. While it's generally viewed pretty negatively – it is both efficient and inevitable.

Sociologists studying leadership have discovered that hierarchy seems to emerge spontaneously. In one set of group experiments, a bunch of strangers were thrown together and given a problem to solve. In next to no time people adopted functional positions of leaders and followers. And the groups that settled into some kind of structural functionality the quickest tended to solve the problem more quickly and efficiently, because they could more quickly put their best efforts toward the challenge at hand and expend less resource on the fairness of the process.

Hierarchy in various forms is evident in the histories of nations, institutions and the world's great religions. In the history of the children of Israel, as recorded in the biblical book of Judges, the twelve tribes that made up the nation had no central means of government. "In those days Israel had no king; everyone did as they saw fit."[23] The book records an apparent rollercoaster of social breakdown and malaise, followed by deliverance under a skilled leader, followed by another social breakdown, and subsequent deliverance under another leader. Their fortunes improved under the federated leadership of King David and his successor, Solomon.

Without leadership, people tend to do as they please and things inevitably turn to custard. Just and stable societies flourish under the rule of law, which is in turn administered by institutions. These institutions are generally large

---

[23] Judges 17:6 – *Holy Bible: New International Version* (International Bible Society, Zondervan, Grand Rapids 2011).

enough to require structures of delegated authority, necessitating both leadership and hierarchy.

When we throw out hierarchy and structure because we see these concepts as vehicles for abuse, we throw the baby out with the bathwater. In order for a group to cooperate and gain mutual benefit with any degree of efficiency, it's necessary for people to take up specific responsibilities. In order to fulfil those responsibilities, people must be afforded the power to decide and act. And that power may include the power to direct the actions of others or to allocate resources.

The bigger the group, the more potential for collective good and the greater the power that may necessarily accrue to a small group of leaders. For hierarchy and leadership to be beneficial and not abusive, the aspiration of those with power must be for the benefit of others. We'll come back to hierarchy when we talk about structure in Section 4.

If you follow the chain of reasoning over the past few paragraphs, the clear implication is that civilisation depends upon people being ethical and effective supervisors. Being a good boss really is that important.

Sources of authority

As a supervisor, your primary source of authority comes from your position in the hierarchy. Draw out the organisation chart and it should be clear about who has authority over whom. My boss has authority over me, and I have authority over my team. This is not a value judgement, but simply a statement of fact. The smooth fulfilment of responsibility and the maintenance of accountability depends on clear reporting relationships.

But hierarchy is not the only source of authority in an organisation. Some authority comes from expertise. Imagine working in an architectural firm, and a world-renowned architect visits as the guest of the CEO. Professor Fahrenheit (he has a lot of degrees) chooses to wander about the design studio, stops by your workstation and looks at the job you have modelled in 3D on your screen. "You'll want to change that cladding combination." He advises. "That style direction has been around for three years and the more progressive studios have already moved on. That look will date the building terribly."

What will you do? He's not even on the organisation chart, he has no power to make you change your design. But you would have to be pretty sure of yourself to ignore his counsel.

Cast you mind back to the earlier story of Mark, who as my boss, stuck his neck out to save my bacon after I shot around an ill-advised memo. From then on, I knew without a doubt that Mark had my back. It led to a subtle shift in my mindset. Sure, my contract and my payslip indicated that I worked for Pacific Dunlop. But at the gut level I worked for Mark. In fact, even after I started a new job, I still spent a few evenings back at PacDun completing a project that had been held up. After all he had risked for me, it felt like the least I could do.

Authority is afforded by position in a hierarchy, but it also comes through expertise and reputation along with character and relational commitment. If you can build a sense of commitment in your staff and volunteers that's based on respect for your character and appreciation of your commitment to them, you'll seldom need to rely on your position in the organisation chart as your source of authority.

Your workers will probably *obey* you just because of your position. They will *follow* you because of your expertise and character.

Here's Sun Tzu again.

"Regard your soldiers as your children, and they will follow you into the deepest valleys; look upon them as your own beloved sons, and they will stand with you even unto death... If however you are indulgent, but unable to make your authority felt; kind-hearted, but unable to enforce your commands; and incapable, moreover of quelling disorder: then your soldiers must be likened to spoilt children; they are useless for any practical purpose."[24]

In a nutshell...

In this chapter we've looked at the necessity and inevitability of bosses carrying aggregated responsibility and wielding delegated authority through supervision. This basic mechanism of hierarchy is essential to the functioning of a modern civilisation, both in terms of the institutions that govern and

---

[24] Sun Tzu *The Art of War* (Translated by Lionel Giles. Harper Collins, London 2018), 48.

serve society, and the corporations that deliver the complex goods and services we now enjoy and depend upon.

Yet the decency and sustainability of society depends on its leaders exercising authority with noble motives and high standards of ethics.

I referred to Australia's major financial institutions, insurance companies, aged care facilities, churches, schools and other organisations being scrutinised by a series of royal commissions ordered by the Australian Government. Time and again leaders who carry responsibility and wield authority in these organisations have shown less than noble motives and disappointing ethical standards. Their failures have caused irreparable harm to thousands of people.

You may be thinking, "But I'm just a team leader," or "But I lead such a small company." That may mean the scale of your influence is limited. But to the extent that your responsibility gives you authority to shape people's jobs, it gives you power to impact people's enjoyment of life now and their career prospects into the future.

A supervisor's motives and ethics shape the fundamental nature of the employment or volunteer relationship. In the next chapter we'll look at a case study, some research and some practical wisdom as to how the shape of the employment relationship plays out to the benefit or detriment of the organisation.

Summary

- While the concepts of authority and hierarchy tend to have negative associations, they're essential and inevitable aspects of a large and diversified civilisation.
- Being a good boss is primarily about responsibly exercising the authority afforded to you by your place in the hierarchy.
- Good character and commitment to your workers will enable you to rely less on hierarchical authority.

Discussion

- When do you find it hardest to appropriately exercise authority?
- Do you rely on your position as your sole source of authority, or do your expertise and character also give weight to your influence?

Application

- Do you need to actively change your thinking about authority in order to change the way you exercise authority?

... ...

Chapter 6
The working relationship

When I was entering the workforce, manufacturing was a significant proportion of the Australian economy. Five different makes of car were manufactured in Australia. There was a large textile, clothing and footwear manufacturing industry. Whitegoods and TVs were made here. Australia was also an immigration economy. One manufacturing plant where I worked had a huge contingent of East Timorese workers, about half of whom spoke English. All of them worked hard, put up with the arduous, noisy conditions and cranked out tons of product. It was commonplace to hear stories of migrants from Europe arriving on Friday and starting work at Ford or Toyota the following Monday.

Unskilled but willing labour was a commodity, and so were unskilled employment opportunities. As a high school student, I could usually find a job in a factory or warehouse during my summer holidays.

That economy has all but disappeared in Australia. There are virtually no jobs standing at a machine punching out widgets. Nowadays even entry-level jobs usually require English and computer literacy, and decent interpersonal skills. Australian employment is largely in services that require a much higher suite of general and job-specific skills. Employers are looking for vocational qualifications even for entry-level hospitality roles.

Employment nowadays has higher barriers to entry. Jobs require a much greater investment both on the part of the employee and the employer. Those unable or unwilling to participate because of the higher barriers either choose (generally employers) or are forced (always workers) to resort to insecure employment arrangements or the gig economy with all its tenuousness and opportunities for abuse.

Unfortunately, it seems that supervision practices left over from the commodity era or leaking in from the shadowy world of the gig economy are finding their way into the world of skilled employment, often with disastrous results for the employer.

A relationship, not a commodity

Let me paint you a picture, based on an actual case study. A young IT worker, armed with a vocational diploma, landed an entry-level help-desk job at one of the Australian sites of a global pharmaceutical company. The company manufactured and distributed products that are almost certainly in your medicine cabinet right now. The site where our IT guy was employed had about a hundred and fifty workers in various specialised roles, most of which required a desktop or laptop PC. The manufacturing area was home to a well-established production line that had been running the same IT, right down to the tractor-drive printers (remember those?), for more than 20 years.

The young, enthusiastic IT guy set about his work, which came to him in the form of job-tickets. Every day he picked up a ticket, went to the computer or server listed, talked to the operator or person somehow in charge, figured out the problem, resolved it using his specialised IT skills, smiled, headed back to his desk and repeated the process. It turned out he was good at this and had a good work ethic. Pretty soon he was clearing more tickets than anyone else, by a considerable margin.

Sometimes tricky issues landed with the IT department. One of those aforementioned tractor-drive printers gave up the ghost one day, grinding a multimillion-dollar production line to a halt. That model of printer, and the type of connections it used, went out of production literally last century, so simply buying a replacement was not an option. Because pharmaceutical production has incredibly stringent process-validation requirements, simply plugging in a newer computer that would drive a newer printer was not a desirable option as it would have required expensive and time-consuming re-validation.

The young IT guy jumped onto eBay, found a second-hand machine of the same model in some faraway place, bought it and got it express-freighted to the plant. In next to no time the process was up and running again. The boss of the IT department was impressed.

In a similar vein, complaints began to ramp up about slow internet speed. The more senior techs looked into it. The on-ramp to the telecommunications network had plenty of capacity, and all of the equipment downstream from there was working correctly. The data was flowing thick and fast. No one could see the problem – yet the complaints kept coming from the end-users.

Unbidden, and between clearing all those tickets, the young IT guy started to do a bit of his own research into the slow internet. He traced the huge dataflow to a single server that was trying to back-up to storage off-site. It would get so far, hit an error and recommence – over and over and over, constantly sending a huge volume of data and overloading the internet on-ramp.

Once isolated, the problem was an easy fix. You'd think the young IT guy would get a raise or a promotion. And he did. He was quickly put in charge of the help desk team. You would also think that he would deserve little niceties like payment for public holidays, some sick leave and annual leave as laid down in Australian employment law. You would think so, but he didn't get any of those.

You see, the IT guy was not an employee of the pharmaceutical company per se. He worked for a multinational IT company, to which the pharmaceutical giant contracted out their IT work. But he wasn't an employee of the IT multinational either. He worked for a labour-hire company that had contracted his work to the IT company that had contracted to the pharmaceutical company. And he actually wasn't an employee of the labour-hire company either. He worked, technically for himself, as an independent contractor, selling his services to the labour hire company who sold it on up the food chain.

Let me say this straight out. The arrangement described above is illegal. If it had come to the attention of the Australian Taxation Office (ATO) or the Australian Fair Work Commission, there would have been penalties handed down and a lot of entitlements back paid. The young IT guy knew this, but he needed the job, and he needed a positive reference to get his next job, so he didn't want to risk his future by making waves.

It's pretty obvious what the IT guy is losing out on here. But the cost to the pharmaceutical company, while harder to identify and more difficult to quantify, is nonetheless real. The risks, aside from a trip to the ATO or an industrial relations tribunal, are even greater.

The employment relationship is a mutual investment on the part of both the employer and the employee. When the employer decides to cut their costs and exposures by putting in a couple of degrees of separation between themselves and a worker who would otherwise be a direct employee, they decouple some other aspects that accountants can't put numbers around.

Mutual disinvestment

When the employer weasels out on their part of the mutual investment, it's naïve to assume that the employee won't follow suit. Sure, the young IT guy took some initiative and solved a couple of tricky problems – but not out of a sense of partnership with his employer-twice-removed. He was earning his stripes on his way to a better gig. If he could get a better job in the same context, well and good. If not, *hasta la vista*.

Further, the young IT guy was steadily building his own knowledge base about the quirks and peculiarities of the hardware and software infrastructure with which he worked. No matter how much general technical knowledge a person may have, it takes a while to pick up the particular undocumented knowledge of how the various parts work (or don't work) together in practice. The pharmaceutical company was putting several degrees of separation between itself and the people who held the knowledge needed to maintain the company's operations. As a contractor, the young IT guy could pull up stumps at a moment's notice and take with him all the tacit knowledge he'd accumulated. He's got no accrued leave entitlements to worry about, so there's nothing to gain by giving notice.

It's folly to employ smart people only to treat them as if they're stupid. People treated as commodities will only hang around for as long as it takes to get what they want and for a better offer to materialise. Perhaps it's just enough time in the role to make their resume look respectable, perhaps its building enough exposure to a methodology or software package to make themselves more marketable. Whatever it is, their resume is probably on someone else's desk already – or will be sometime soon.

The leader matters more than the job

Bill Adams tells about working on a grad program in a large corporation, where high potential university graduates were recruited into the 'talent pipeline' for developing a new generation of leaders for the corporation. The new grads were given exposure to a range of the corporation's various entities and departments. Once they had gained a feel for the corporation, they were settled into stable roles where they could take on responsibility and grow into their careers. Adams observed that there was significant competition for gigs in particular departments.

Adams found that it wasn't the nature of the work that was the basis of the competition, it was the calibre of the leader in the sought-after departments. He concludes, "They were voting with their feet and moving to work for great leaders."[25]

Treat your staff as a commodity to be consumed and they'll probably treat their job as an opportunity to be exploited, even if they're diligent and trustworthy while they're there. This kind of working arrangement belongs in an era long gone, and it was never much use back then either.

Conversely, treat your people as valued partners in whom you are interested and they will likely go above and beyond for you. Your organisation will likely be seen as an attractive option for high-calibre talent.

People with good work ethics, valued skills and up-to-date knowledge will eventually leave an organisation where they're being treated shabbily, leaving only those without better prospects. Over time, these kinds of people accumulate. The organisation ends up as a collection of clock-punchers.

Good organisations are less likely to tolerate people with poor work ethics and substandard skills. With robust processes and skilled supervisors, low-performing workers are managed up to improve their performance or managed out. Either way, good organisations tend to accumulate good people.

What kind of people are accumulating in your organisation – people who would rather work for you than anyone else, or people who couldn't get a job anywhere else with the same pay? How do you tell? Think about the last five people to depart your organisation: your organisation is probably collecting people who are the opposite kind to those who are leaving.

---

[25] Anderson, R. J. and Adams, W. A. *Mastering Leadership: An Integrated Framework for Breakthrough Performance and Extraordinary Business Results* (Wiley, Hoboken 2016), 3.

Challenge to some personal work

I opened this section drawing from some ancient writings that supervision is a noble task and from time-to-time returned to this idea, adding that it's not easy.

I've set out to show that effective supervision can be a very personal interaction. We've looked at being the kind of supervisor that people will respect, even the kind of leader that people will follow. I've touched on self-leadership, self-development, self-control, self-limiting, when you might think a book about supervision would be more about leading, developing controlling and limiting others.

I've spoken about the sacredness of the humans you supervise, the possibility of you being instrumental in their job being a joy. I've discussed trust, empowering and equipping others and the fundamental shift that's required when you start supervising.

All of this is underwritten by your responsibility *to* the organisation that made you a supervisor, and responsibility *for* the people you supervise.

Supervision is not a responsibility to entrust to the immature, to those lacking concern for others, or to people who are short on self-awareness. You might argue that no one is therefore ready to supervise, since all of us have some way to go in developing maturity, compassion and insight. To a certain extent, you'd be right. As bosses, all of us will fall short of the ideal here and there.

Because supervision is a person-to-person interaction, the kind of person you are – your character and maturity – has an enormous bearing on the quality and effectiveness of the relationship. At the heart of being a great boss is a commitment to growing into the kind of person required to supervise well.

In view of the six chapters that you've read to get to this point, I'm advocating that you begin by examining your own life. It's really tempting to grab a theory and immediately apply it to your team members, your boss, your partner, your kids and even your pets.

Beyond adding a new theory and some novel terms to your knowledge base and vocabulary, my challenge to you is to make a serious commitment to your own growth and development, to engage the journey that Robert Quinn calls

'Deep Change.'[26] You might even begin by reading Quinn. He'll argue that organisational change always begins with personal change. The theories to which I referred – and any other theory with which you might resonate – should be used firstly to help you better understand yourself, and then your staff. This will provide perspective, enabling you to make more thoughtful supervision decisions. It's not about psychoanalysing, diagnosing or fixing people.

Summary

- The employment relationship is more about the relationship than the contract.
- Seeing people as a commodity to be exploited is an unenlightened idea that dates from a long-gone era, although it remains the modus operandi of the gig economy.
- Using questionable contracting arrangements to avoid employment commitments robs a company of the commitment and loyalty of those it pays to work for them.
- Research suggests people will choose a great boss over other work preferences.
- Good bosses accumulate good people, and poor supervisors accumulate people who have no other options.

Discussion

- Does your organisation forge trusting relationships with its people, or is it more a case of each using the other to get what they want?

Application

- Do you need to do some work on your character and maturity to become the best boss you can be? What's the first step you could take on that journey?

---

[26] Quinn, R. *Deep Change: Discovering the Leader Within* (Jossey Bass, San Francisco 1996).

What we've covered

Section 1: A boss worth working for

- Your first responsibility is to be the boss of yourself
  - Manage yourself
  - Control yourself
  - Lead yourself
  - Limit yourself
- Your next responsibility is to your organisation
  - Your responsibility is delegated to you by your organisation
  - Prioritising individuals over the collective is (mostly) irresponsible
- You are responsible for the stewardship of humans
  - Humans are deeply valuable, perhaps even sacred
  - It all hinges on trust
  - Treat everyone like volunteers
- Your workers are your job
  - Not just an add-on
  - When supervision is neglected, organisations burn people and people burn organisations
- Exercising responsibility requires authority
  - Authority is necessary, but vulnerable to abuse
  - Authority comes from more than just your position
- Supervision is a working relationship
  - Don't treat workers like commodities
  - People work for people more than they work for companies
  - Work on yourself before you set to work on your organisation and your people

Section 2
The task of supervision

The first section was all about a philosophy of supervision. It set out to answer the question, 'Why is this important?' and went on to wrestle with some of the implications, which were fundamentally about what kind of person with what kind of attitude will people want to work for.

Now we come to the theory of supervision. This section sets out to answer the questions, 'What is supervision?' and 'What are the underlying principles at play?' That's going to lead us into some psychology and some management theories – but only enough to give you an understanding of where particular ideas come from, and perhaps what those ideas assume.

We'll begin with a brief look at some of the theories that emerged through the twentieth century. These provide a backdrop against which I'll set out the theory I'm espousing, beginning with a bare-bones framework and going on to build a narrative as to what's required to discharge our supervision responsibilities with excellence.

Chapter 7
The ghosts of theories past

In search of optimal performance: Theories X, Y and Z

Supervision has been around for at least as long as the idea of paid employment. I imagine that the question of getting the best return for the wages paid arose fairly quickly afterward.

Over the last century or so, various theorists developed approaches to getting the best out of people. Understanding these theories provides a lens through which to look at contemporary practice.

Theory X and Theory Y are terms coined by Douglas McGregor, management professor at the MIT Sloan School of Management in the 1950s. His 1960 landmark book *The Human Side of Enterprise*[27] has probably had more impact on your experience and practice of supervision than you realise.

Theory X

In short, Theory X works on the presupposition that workers are not particularly ambitious or motivated, and it's the manager's job to get them to do what's required, using punishments and rewards (in that order of preference). To be fair to McGregor, he was writing in a time when behaviourism was the psychological theory *du jour.* Pavlov's earlier observations of salivating dogs produced the stimulus-response theory of classical conditioning. B. F. Skinner developed the idea further into the theory of operant conditioning, where reward and punishment variously served to reinforce behaviours.[28] It's not that Skinner or Pavlov were wrong, it's more a case of humans being a little more complex and nuanced than perhaps their animal experiments suggest. A rat stuck in a box that delivers both food and electric shocks is probably not wondering if they're important to the lab technician who handles them, and neither are they likely to be contemplating

---

[27] McGregor, D. *The Human Side of Enterprise* (McGraw-Hill, New York, 1960).
[28] Ferster, C. B. & Skinner, B. F. *Schedules of Reinforcement*. (Appleton-Century-Crofts New York 1957).

meaning and a sense of existential fulfilment over their lifetime. We humans share a good deal of our neurobiology with other social mammals – and we have unique mental capacities unknown in any other species.

Also prevalent at the time was Frederick Taylor's scientific management theory. Early in the twentieth century, Taylor published *The Principles of Scientific Management*,[29] which set out the idea that work could be analysed and broken into discreet tasks. These tasks could then be optimised and standardised so that they could be performed with maximum efficiency. The scientific approach uses techniques like time and motion studies to ensure a task is performed in the shortest time while expending the least energy possible. Taylor got down to optimising the design of shovels so furnace stokers could work for longer periods. The judgment of the individual worker is removed and the worker operates according to standardised practice to achieve optimum productivity.

While this looks draconian now, at the birth of the mass-production line it provided a tangible means to drive down the cost of mass-produced goods. Taylor's thinking informed much of the operating practices in American automobile manufacturing in the first half of the twentieth century. In advocating standardisation, Taylor anticipated the mid-century dawn of quality assurance (QA).

Pull all of this together and you get Theory X. The worker is a resource from which the supervisor extracts labour. The volition and aspiration of the worker is discounted. The supervisor takes on a kind of stern parent role, pushing the worker into the position of an irresponsible child. It may seem outdated and unenlightened, but Theory X remains the principle by which most of the manufactured goods in the world are produced: from the clothes we wear to the technology we use. Many large-scale order fulfilment centres and the app-driven delivery services attached to them are pure Theory X. The only difference between them and the Taylorist factories of a century ago is that the supervisor is now an app driven by an algorithm. It's made rich some tech entrepreneurs and some investors, but I'm not sure how enriched the workers feel.

---

[29] Taylor, F. W. *Principles of Scientific Management* (Harper, New York 1919).

Now you may well have come across workers to whom Theory X seems perfectly suited: workers who lack drive and initiative. At times supervision is reduced to pure behaviourism. But it's only perfectly suited to some of the workforce some of the time.

Theory X-style supervision can get quick results and drives high productivity, which is why it's so prevalent in economies where workers have limited opportunities and few rights. In higher-wage, more liberal economies it tends to drive the workers who do have initiative and ambition out of the organisation, leaving a depleted talent pool from which to develop leaders. Some workers just don't want to leave their brain at the door and work like a robot.

McGregor wasn't holding up Theory X as an example to follow so much as a backdrop against which to contrast Theory Y.

Theory Y

Theory Y on the other hand is pretty much the polar opposite. Drawing on Abraham Maslow's Hierarchy of Needs,[30] Theory Y presumes workers are motivated and ambitious, seeking to work their way beyond mere survival and security (which according to Maslow lie in the lower, more basic categories of human need). Workers also look to their workplace for relationship, fulfilment and growth toward their potential (which in ascending order lie in the upper categories of Maslow's hierarchy).

Applying Theory Y leads to a more democratic workplace, where workers are empowered to make more decisions. Workers are presumed to have initiative and to take responsibility for their performance. It presumes that workers are, if managed well, creative and committed to doing things well. Theory Y supervision is therefore more collaborative, guiding and facilitating.

While there's a lot to like about Theory Y, it's as optimistic about humanity as Theory X is pessimistic, both in terms of their competence and in terms of their motivation. The presumption behind the theory is that given the right circumstances, people will know what to do. In reality, there are some challenges that cannot be solved by a team of stakeholders with good

---

[30] Maslow, A. H. *A Theory of Human Motivation.* Psychological Review, *50*(4), 1943 pp370-396.

intentions – even if they're well-trained. Some challenges require specific technical expertise or management acumen beyond a shop floor work team.

The presumption that everyone will choose correctly given the right circumstances, at best has tinges of Pollyanna and at worst is a post-structuralist denial of the evidence. Log onto any news site and you'll be bombarded with stories of how humans can seek their own gain at the expense of others, can be dishonest, cruel, irresponsible and stupid. And that's just the politics section.

When we can muster the courage to be honest with ourselves, most of us will admit there is a shadow side of ourselves that we'd prefer not to think about: a side of ourselves that doesn't do the right thing, and occasionally shows traces of all that we despise in the worst of humanity. Writing nearly 2000 years ago, the Apostle Paul said, "I do not understand what I do. For what I want to do, I do not do, but what I hate I do."[31] Yep, like he said.

People are a mix of motivations, instincts and reactivities. Sometimes we play nice in our little workplace sandpits, sometimes we won't share the toys, and we occasionally throw sand at others. A workable supervision theory needs to acknowledge a range of human possibilities, from the divine to the diabolical.

Theory Z

Japanese-American Dr. William Ouchi propounded Theory Z in the early 1980s, focusing on job security and employee wellbeing.[32] It's not really an alternative to Theory Y as much as a prescription for the kind of environment in which Theory Y can flourish. To understand Ouchi, you need to begin with W. Edwards Deming.

Deming advocated disciplines of statistical process control and methods of continuous process improvement. His work has been popularised as the 'Plan-Do-Check-Act' cycle. Although an American, Deming rose to prominence in post-war Japan, where the shattered Japanese manufacturing sector eagerly embraced Deming's thinking as a means of regaining strength and competitive advantage. Over the ensuing thirty years, Japan rose to become the world's

---

[31] The Apostle Paul, letter to the Romans 7:15 **Holy Bible: New International Version** International Bible Society (Zondervan, Grand Rapids 2011).
[32] Ouchi, W.G. **Theory Z** (Avon Books New York 1981).

manufacturing powerhouse. The Total Quality Management movement of the 1980s and early 1990s was founded on Deming's thinking and drew on examples of Japanese lean manufacturing like Toyota. His legacy can still be seen in process improvement disciplines like Six Sigma.

Ouchi's Theory Z looks at the kind of organisational culture that allows Deming's philosophy to bear fruit.

Like the rest of the alphabet of theories, Ouchi's Theory Z is based on some fairly big assumptions. Japanese manufacturing culture is in some ways an extension of Japanese culture itself, valuing predictability and order, discipline and rigour, hard work and harmony. It plays out in the way Japanese trains run to schedule and Japanese customs embody formality, simplicity and respect – think of two Japanese executives greeting one another compared to two Americans. Efforts to apply Theory Z outside Japan have shown mixed results –simply because it requires a significant shift in organisational culture to be sustained and effective. The underpinning values of Theory Z are embedded in culture, where they're presupposed rather than made explicit. It takes more than just a 3-day off-site workshop to embed them into an organisation.

Fads

At this point I'd like to introduce a couple of fellow Aussies called Frederick Hilmer and Lex Donaldson. Their helpful book *Management Redeemed* patiently unpacks the management fads of their day (it was written in 1996) to expose the simplistic naivety that believes a short and flashy intervention with a three-letter acronym can achieve lasting transformation.[33] Many of the fads to which they refer seem to be underpinned by a similar set of presuppositions to Theory Y/Z. Hilmer and Donaldson counter that management is complex, requiring discipline, knowledge and expertise. In short, management is difficult.

The problem with our alphabet of theories is that they tend to presume people are like this or like that. Fads tend to assume that the complexity can be

---

[33] Hilmer, F. G. and Donaldson, L. *Management Redeemed: Debunking the Fads That Undermine Corporate Performance* (Free Press, Sydney 1996).

reduced to a 'breakthrough' prescription. Hilmer and Donaldson counsel us, 'Not so fast.'

Some people do lack motivation for some or a lot of the time. Some people are reticent to take initiative. Some people actually perform better in an environment biased toward Theory X. But not many, and generally speaking, not all the time. Some companies and some occupations won't support the application of Theory Y. Some contexts have a rigid command and control culture because they're dealing with dangerous situations where ambiguity can be fatal. If you want to pursue Ouchi's Theory Z, you'll need the cooperation and commitment of the entire leadership structure of the organisation, and you'll need a long timeframe to adapt. Even if you're just experimenting with a pilot program, without the cooperation of the leadership, the project will inadvertently (or perhaps deliberately) be sabotaged.

A unique dance

Ronald Heifetz, Alexander Grashow and Marty Linsky, in their very helpful work *The Practice of Adaptive Leadership* distinguish such procedural tasks from those requiring adaptation, experimentation and judgement.[34] Problems that have a well-worn, predefined solution (like a flat tyre or an inflamed appendix) they describe as 'technical problems'. Those without a well-defined and well-known solution, that might require a degree of experimentation and may involve some new learning, they define as 'adaptive challenges'.

Achieving optimal performance involves too many variables to be treated as a technical problem, where application of technique and procedure will reliably produce a prescribed outcome. As we'll see in the coming chapters, supervision involves a degree of unpredictability. It requires careful judgement, juggling issues of capacity, context and a range of other variables that pop into the equation from time to time.

I use the term 'optimal performance' rather than 'peak performance' advisedly. We can all work beyond our sustainable capacity for a short time. A woman can labour and give birth, but I'm not sure she'd survive going through

---

[34] Heifetz, R., Grashow, A. and Linsky, M. *The practice of Adaptive Leadership: Tools and Tactics for Changing Your Organisation and the World* (Harvard Business Press, Boston 2009).

that kind of ordeal every week. I can run 100 metres at a faster pace than I can maintain over 10 kilometres. Our goal is to facilitate the highest level of performance that is sustainable, and even beneficial, for our workers.

For each worker, you'll probably begin with a reasonably generic approach, but as the supervisory relationship unfolds it will take on its own character – a kind of dance between you and your worker where you both respond and adapt. In time the relationship will find its own equilibrium.

As I write this chapter, I have three staff and each enjoys a unique relationship with their boss. For one, we've been together six years, we 'get' one another pretty well and the relationship is very trusting, with a high degree of transparency. Another has only been on board for three weeks and they're trying to make their way amongst the COVID-19 curveballs. We're still figuring each other out and what each of us means by what we say. There's some consistency between these two relationships in terms of the management practices I bring to framing our conversations, but the conversations themselves, both by video conference and by email, reflect the history, temperaments, skill set, personal capacity and developmental stage of *both* participants.

On top of that I have an array of coaching clients both in my regular job and in my private practice. These range from first-time leaders still finding their feet to seasoned professionals who are highly respected leaders in their sector. For some we're no more than five conversations into the relationship and for others we've been working together for over a decade.

While every one of those coaching relationships follows the same framework in terms of the agenda I send them and the notes I write, the content of each conversation is a unique adaptive response to all the variables that each of us brings to the table. Each one challenges me in a different way. Some press my buttons, others stimulate me to bring my very best thinking, leaving me exhausted and exhilarated.

Hopefully by now you're sold on the idea that for the supervisory relationship to be productive, there are a number of variables to take into account and a simple theory that reduces a nuanced task to a formula is simply not going to cut it.

I agree with Hilmer and Donaldson that management, particularly supervision, is difficult. Not difficult as in arduous, like climbing Mount Everest, but difficult in that it requires discipline, wisdom, and courage. Life offers up many difficult roles, like parenting children or caring for elderly parents. These require similar discipline, wisdom and courage. This is why I began with the kind of person who makes an effective boss, rather than handing you a bunch of tips and tricks.

Over the coming chapters we'll walk through some theory that will give you a way of understanding supervision. Theory won't make supervision easy per se, but it will help you make sense of your role and give you confidence to tackle the task of fulfilling your supervision responsibilities.

Summary

- Theories about managing people's work have been around a long time, but took particular shape in the twentieth century.
    - Theory X assumes a worker has little more to bring than their obedience, and so the manager must take all the responsibility for efficiency and performance.
    - Theory Y assumes the worker is engaged and motivated, and is able to solve problems and take responsibility for their productivity.
    - Theory Z is about the kind of culture and processes required to make Theory Y work.
- Fad theories look attractive and promise a lot, but ignore the complexity and challenge of management.
- Supervision is an adaptive challenge involving a number of variables, and requires a thoughtful, nuanced approach.

Discussion

- Where have you experienced supervision that seemed to be like Theory X? What was it like?
- Where have you experienced supervision that seemed to be like Theory Y? What was *that* like?
- Where would your default supervision style fall on a continuum between Theories X and Y?

Action

- Observe your supervision over a month or so. See if you can identify Theory X and Theory Y behaviours.

Chapter 8
Expectation and support

As a seventeen-year-old I got a summertime job in a fibreglass factory. The company made a diverse range of parts and components out of 'pultruded' fibreglass. One of my first tasks was to glue brass connectors onto the ends of feeder rods – which were fibreglass rods about a metre long, about 8mm in diameter and coated in black PVC. This was a multi-stage process, which meant using a stripping machine to remove about 30mm of PVC sheathing from the end of the fibreglass rod, making a series of small cuts in the exposed fibreglass with a hacksaw, and then gluing the brass connector onto the prepared end using epoxy resin. It's not that complex. Yet there was plenty of scope for me to mess it up.

The supervisor demonstrated the process once, then immediately left me to it. He neglected to tell me that sometimes the stripper doesn't remove all the PVC, which prevents the epoxy from adhering properly. If that happens, the brass connector will likely come off the feeder rod during use in the field. Oblivious to this important quality control information, I beavered away for the rest of the day, honestly believing I was doing a stellar job.

Several days later I was informed that my work was substandard and that an unacceptably high proportion of the feeder rods I had made had to be discarded. I thought I was working to the supervisor's expectations, but he had not been sufficiently clear about them. Further, his feedback about whether my work met his expectations had been too late to be helpful.

I've never really thought about it....

At its most elemental, supervision is simply a matter of making your expectations clear and providing timely feedback as to whether your expectations are met. Expectations and feedback are not in themselves difficult concepts, but it's not uncommon for supervisors to overlook them and assume people will just know.

You're probably thinking, 'Well Ken, that's a fine theory you've got there, but it's actually not that simple.' And I would agree with you. And even if it were that simple, it's not well understood.

While I was wondering whether I should write this book, I did a little informal market research – which is a more 'professional-sounding' way of saying I asked just about everyone I met about their understanding and experience of supervision. I was surprised that only one person came up with a simple concept or maxim that acted as their guiding principle for supervision. Their principle was, "Your job is to do whatever I say." I'm not sure that's going to cut it.

Everyone else (including some highly experienced senior managers) kind of stumbled around proposing some vague ideas, then paused and said something like, "You know, I've never really thought about it." Even if they have extensive experience, few supervisors have thought deeply about supervising people and even fewer have an articulated theory of supervision.

Some of those leaders were overseeing annual staff payrolls of several million dollars. Think about that for a minute. There are organisations out there entrusting millions of dollars in human resources to people who have not really thought about what it means to manage them.

As you're reading, you're probably asking yourself, 'What's my theory of supervision?' If you have one, you might want to bounce it off the one I proposed earlier in the chapter. If you don't have one (and it seems most people don't), you may want to take a minute to reflect on your experiences of being supervised. Here's a few key questions to ask yourself:

- What have my supervisors done to bring out my best?
- What was my supervisor's contribution during the times when I was performing well?
- What have my supervisors done that's strengthened my motivation and commitment? And what have they done to erode my motivation and commitment?

As you reflect on your answers to these questions, you may notice some particular ideas that seem important or recurring. These would likely become clues as to your own emerging philosophy of supervision.

We tend to create our approaches to tasks and responsibilities based on our experience. Sometimes we uncritically replicate what we've experienced because we presumed 'that's just the way it's done' – like eating dessert with an egg-shaped spoon and soup with a circular one. And sometimes our approaches are shaped by us seeking to avoid replicating our negative experiences.

No doubt you can see how my experience of inadequate supervision in the fibreglass factory has shaped my approach, and I'm hoping that, with a bit of thought, your experiences will shape yours too.

Meanwhile, at the Australian Institute of Sport

High expectations

The Australian Institute of Sport (AIS) is about performance. 'As Australia's strategic high performance sport agency, the AIS is responsible and accountable for leading the delivery of Australia's international sporting success.'[35] The AIS is dedicated to getting the absolute best performances from the highest potential athletes in the country. We can probably learn a lot about getting the best out of our people from the AIS.

Using my theory statement above as a lens to look through, you would have to describe the AIS as a high-expectation environment. If you're an athlete who's a part of an AIS program, there are a lot of people expecting an awful lot of you. They're expecting you to stick to a strict diet and strict training regimen; to go to bed at a certain time and get up at a certain time; to put in a 'try-so-hard-you-throw-up' effort in every training session. The expectations are set out with crystal clarity and any athlete who does not measure up is given unambiguous and immediate feedback. So far it fits my philosophy quite nicely.

High support

But here's the balancing factor to all that expectation – the AIS is also an incredibly supportive environment. Athletes have a variety of experts helping them with endurance, strength, technique and psychology. There are doctors, physiotherapists, masseurs, psychologists and nutritionists all committed to the athlete's wellbeing. Athletes have the best facilities and equipment available for their use.

---

[35] http://www.ausport.gov.au/ais/about.

High expectations combined with high support is the recipe for high performance. It's not a guarantee (the AIS has plenty of dropouts), it's simply the approach most likely to produce the desired outcome.

My staff will assure you that the team I currently lead is not the equivalent of the AIS. I don't expect that kind of performance and I can't afford to provide that kind of support. But I do have expectations that stretch my staff a little: asking them to aim a little higher than their default settings, and challenging them to keep learning and growing, deepening their knowledge base and developing their in-field practice.

At the same time, I try to offer better than routine support in the form of coaching, training and as much pastoral care as I can reasonably muster.

I'm not hoping for elite-level performance, but I am expecting my staff to operate close to the top of their game. My job is to create the balance of expectation and support that will enable them to do that sustainably and beneficially.

Balancing expectation and support

Over the years of thinking about and teaching supervision, I've come up with a little chart to explain the expectation/support relationship.

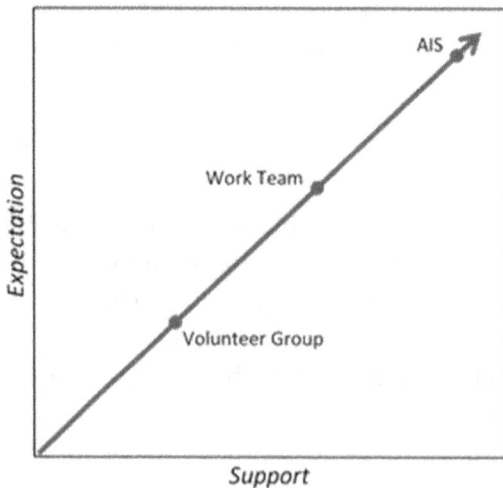

The arrow represents the balance of support and demand. Each type of organisation or sub-group within an organisation will need to find its place on the continuum. It would be ridiculous for the local scout group to put the kind of expectations on its volunteers that the AIS puts on its athletes, and the scout group simply could not provide the corresponding degree of support.

What is the reasonable and necessary level of support and demand for your organisation? Aim too low and your people will not perform to the level required to meet the objectives of the organisation. Aim too high and you'll begin to see symptoms like turnover and difficulty filling positions.

The second key idea is illustrated by the added arrows in the chart below. Too much expectation without the corresponding support leads to people becoming disillusioned and leaving. Too little expectation while lavishing people with support can make them kind of whingy and entitled. Balancing expectation and support is critical.

As you look at the two imbalanced possibilities – too much expectation with

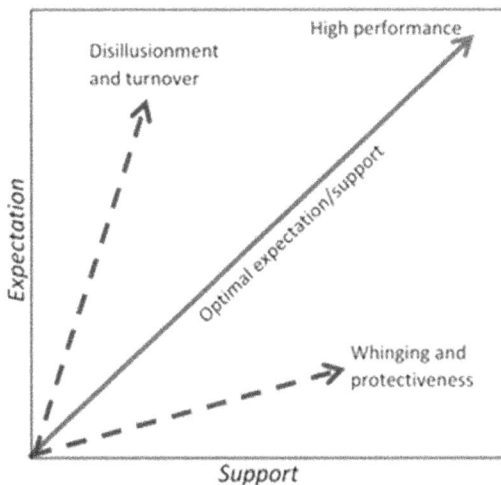

too little support, or too much support with too little expectation, you may be surprised at the 'results' I've described in the chart. Yet as I've reflected on the dozens of organisations I've served, this has been my fairly consistent observation.

People will tolerate high expectations and low support for a surprisingly long period – in some cases for years (although this is usually a sign of their personal dysfunction, but more on that later). In general, the 'elastic limit' of people in high expectation – low support environments averages around eighteen months. If you're seeing people dropping out or moving on after a year or two, this might be telling you something.

It's a little counter-intuitive to think that a high support – low expectation environment will produce a whingy, self-protective team. In Australia in the 1970s and early 1980s, most of the bitter and protracted industrial relations disputes did not involve the most disadvantaged or lowest paid workers – but rather workers who already had it better than just about everyone else. (Now don't get me wrong: I recognise the contribution of courageous collective action on the part of workers in shaping Australia as the land of the 'fair go'. As work becomes more precarious and employers are emboldened to operate outside the law, it's my belief that trade unionism is ripe for a second wind in Western democracies.)

In volunteer organisations, those who have been pandered to will usually be those quickest to complain. And those who have been given the most support will be reticent to allow others into their circle of influence.

If you have a team or group that bickers, whinges, stonewalls or makes threats, it's possibly because they've developed a sense of entitlement fostered by too much support and low expectations.

The purpose of the organisation will always be expressed more in what it expects of its employees and volunteers than in the support if offers them. Erring on the side of too much support runs the risk of the organisation's greater purpose being lost. Peter Senge said, "In the absence of a great dream, pettiness prevails."[36]

If you try to redress the high support – low expectation imbalance, be prepared for some turbulence. The bickering and whinging will get worse and will often descend into undermining and sabotage.[37] No one said this was going to be easy.

A conversation about high expectation without appropriate support invites a conversation about burnout, which we'll deal with in a later chapter.

---

[36] Senge, P. M. *The Fifth Discipline: The Art and Practice of the Learning Organization*, rev. edn (Currency, New York, 2006), 195.
[37] Friedman, Edwin H. *A Failure of Nerve: Leadership in the Age of the Quick Fix* (Seabury, New York 1999).

Summary

- In its simplest form, supervision is a matter of making your expectations clear and providing clear, timely feedback as to whether your expectations have been met.
- In order for supervision to be effective and sustainable, expectation must be balanced with a corresponding level of support.
- When expectation and support are out of balance, predictable indicators will be observable in your organisation.

Discussion

- How would you rate yourself on being clear about your expectations and providing feedback?
- Do you observe any of the signs of expectation and support being out of balance?

Action

- What's one thing you could do this month to be clearer about expectation and performance with your workers?
- Do you need to tackle any issues around the expectation/support balance being askew?

Chapter 9
Defining your expectations

Getting your expectations right

Despite searching on eBay and Alibaba, I can't seem to find anyone selling an instrument that will provide an objective measure on the balance of expectation and support. I suspect that's because the balance is not objective, nor necessarily uniform across individuals, or even consistent for a single individual over time. So what is reasonable to expect?

Getting clear

I guess it's time to admit the uncomfortable truth. Most supervisors aren't clear on what they expect. I'm sometimes unclear on what I expect. It requires thought and effort to become really clear in my own mind as to what I think is a good return for my investment in my worker. Sometimes I'm just a bit too tired, or distracted, or mentally overloaded to put in the hard work of thinking through exactly what I want to see.

Logically, if I'm not clear in my own mind as to what I expect, the chances of my staff knowing what I expect is close enough to zero. They'll beaver away at their best guess and hope I think that's okay. As a supervisor I need to hold up my half of the supervision relationship, and that means getting clear on my expectations of those who work for me.

Understand the job

If you have multiple employees doing similar work, over time you'll be able to gauge an average expectation. The forces for homeostasis that bind work teams together will generally serve to keep the output across the team within a fairly consistent band.

If you have two workers in an outbound call centre each making 120 calls a day, you can expect a third worker in an identical role to do about the same. If the psychologists in your practice each handle about 20 clients a week, you can reasonably expect that of any of the psychologists, all things being equal. The problem being all things are seldom equal.

As soon as you get beyond tasks that have a pre-determined labour input (like assembling an iPhone), the output you can reasonably expect from a worker becomes harder to define. If you have a Human Resources department in your organisation, you could ask them to do some job analysis which would give you a more accurate picture (although, getting your average HR person to perform that analysis outside of a recruiting, budgeting or restructuring exercise might be a tough ask).

I've had pretty good success simply talking the job over with the worker. If the worker has a position description (PD) that's great place to start. If they don't (and I'm going to argue later that they really should), perhaps the task of creating a PD gives you opportunity to collaborate with your worker to get a good idea of what you can reasonably expect. We'll look at developing a PD in a minute.

You can begin by listing out the tasks that make up the job. Once you have a list of tasks, you can begin to measure how much time each task would reasonably take. This can be done by estimate, or more accurately by getting the worker to log their time usage on tasks over a number of measurement periods. If the worker's job is similar each day, you might get them to log their activity over a few days. If the worker's job has more of a weekly rhythm, it might mean logging a couple of weeks of activity. Some jobs – like accounting – have a monthly rhythm.

Even management jobs that seem to be very different day-to-day and week-to-week will usually have some kind of recurring pattern. My job is very fluid, but I know that over a month I'll coach about 30 clients, run an average of two workshops, supervise three staff, facilitate three communities of practice, write two reports and write a column.

The variable nature of management and the ebb and flow of initiative and response means such jobs are hard to analyse down to the minute. A rough rule of thumb is that about 60% of management is predictable, and the rest is responsive. So, if my predictable responsibilities like those listed above add up to about three days a week, it's fair to say mine is a full-time role.

Unless the person you're supervising does a job that is absolutely predictable with no variations, getting the expectation level right will require your careful observation and consideration of the information available to you as a supervisor. In other words, you'll need to pay attention to your people and exercise professional judgement. We'll think a little more about this when we look at how to gather that information.

Tuning your expectations

However you decide to figure out a fair level of expectation, your estimate will eventually come up against the realities of your worker's efforts to meet those expectations.

Stop and think for a minute. What might be the signs that your expectations are out of whack? Let's look at some ways to identify the problems early, before things become difficult to rectify, or lead to some of the problems we considered in the previous chapter.

Early indicators of overly high expectations include:

- People working longer hours than is reasonable
- The human niceties like being polite and considerate begin to slide
- People being grumpy or petty conflicts arising
- Absenteeism
- Errors and things being forgotten
- Deadlines and targets frequently being missed

You can probably add a bunch of other indicators based on your own experience. As you look at the list, you're probably thinking, "Well those things could be caused by a number of things other than high expectations or low support." And you're right. If you listed the indicators of support outweighing expectations (i.e. things being out of balance in the opposite direction), many of the same things would be included. The trick is to watch for signs that things could be out of balance either way, then move toward the issue to find out what's behind it.

The power of position descriptions

We've already made a couple of brief references to position descriptions (PDs), so now's the time to dive into the document a little more. A few years back I was lured into one of those reader-comment conversations that spring up around articles published in online newspapers. The author of the article was making the case for position descriptions being redundant because everything changes so fast that something as static as a position description is out of date before it's even put to use. A bunch of other people piled in, mostly in agreement, claiming that their PD bore no resemblance to their work and was not a point of reference for their day-to-day activity. I suspect the author and the majority of commenters were working either in start-ups (where things do seem too changeable and chaotic to bother drafting out a PD) or in poorly-run organisations.

I put forward the view that basic HR functions like recruitment, performance management, performance appraisal and determining remuneration levels all required the information contained in a PD. The commenters dismissed my comments as 'old economy'. You might think the same. Allow me to attempt to change your mind.

As someone trained in HR disciplines, but who doesn't always work in the HR department, I'm always amused at the huge variation in style, scope and content I've encountered in PDs over the past 30 or so years.

Working on a recruiting job a few years ago, I was handed a detailed PD that had been spat out of the client's triple-quality assured Human Resources Information System. It was truly impressive, with linkages to all sorts of other aspects of the HR system, and the service delivery standards to which the company was certified. There was really only one flaw in it. Nobody could tell me what it meant. It was constructed in that third-person, passive voiced, present-continuous tense kind of language that seems to be written by an actuary who is standing in for an art critic tasked with writing tasting notes for an obscure variety of wine. It may have been good for quality assurance certification, but it was useless as a guide to recruit and select a new general manager.

What makes for a useful PD? We'll begin with the most fundamental questions that PDs should answer, then look at some other details you might want to add.

Purpose
Firstly, and often overlooked, is the fundamental purpose of the role. If you can link the role's purpose with the organisation's purpose, all the better. Imagine a house building company called OZ-Home describes their purpose as: 'Make a reasonable profit by building homes that Australians love to live in'. The marketing manager's role purpose might be to 'foster the conviction in

the Australian public that life is best lived in an OZ-Home, and so motivate people to make OZ-Home their builder of choice'.

A not-for-profit where I served as chair of the board articulated its purpose as: 'Helping people achieve a safe, secure and stable home where they can build their future'. The corporate services manager's role could be to 'ensure the operational teams have the process and systems that enable them to give their very best to the people they serve'.

You'll notice these purpose statements are a little idealistic, but that's okay. The idea is to give a clear picture of the employee or volunteer's contribution, not just their tasks. It becomes a clear reference point to reinforce when the worker gets lost in the immediate demands and details of their role.

Imagine a volunteer at a soup kitchen, whose task it is to serve food to the people who stop by to eat there. If their PD (yes, PDs are very useful for volunteer roles) defines the role's purpose as 'ladling soup from the pot to the bowl', the volunteer might try to do this with all speed and efficiency, while appearing dismissive and disinterested in the people who file by, bowl in hand.

Yet if the role's purpose is to 'contribute to guests experiencing dignity and personal value by serving their meals', the tone becomes totally different. Sure, being quick and efficient is useful, but not at the cost of connecting with the guests as you would your friends.

So much of my coaching centres around leaders directing their efforts toward their key purpose in their organisation, when so many forces, including their own emotions, pull them in other directions. I have a cheeky line I like to use (always with a smile on my face): "Let's play a silly game – let's pretend that you're the CEO (when that *is* their role) and it's your job to..." It's usually met with a wry smile, a bit of an eye roll and, "Yeah, I know, I know..." A clearly defined purpose statement in a PD becomes the central navigation point for the role.

Take a minute now to see if you can articulate the purpose of your job in a sentence or two. If you have staff, you might want to see if you can do the same for each of them. Remember, not just the task, the essential contribution.

Reporting relationships

Next on the list of PD fundamentals is the reporting relationships. Most fundamentally, 'To whom does the role report?' If this question is answered in the plural, i.e. if the role is designed to report either to a number of people or to a board or committee, there's pretty good potential for the role to drive the incumbent crazy. A wise old consultant once said to me, "Anything with two heads is a monster." A role with more than one boss is asking for divided loyalties and conflicting expectations, not to mention the potential for the worker to play their respective bosses off against one another.

A person may provide services to a number of people (a shared executive assistant, for example), but their line of accountability should go to a single individual who carries responsibility for that employee's performance and conduct. That individual should conduct regular supervision and periodical appraisal conversations with the employee. A shared responsibility is a shirked responsibility. Workers with more than one boss invariably receive little or no supervision.

Responsibilities

The next key ingredient is to set out responsibilities. This might look like a list of tasks in some roles, but the list should go beyond what to do and address how it's done. So, in the PD for our call centre operator working through that on-hold queue, responsibilities listed might include:

- Receive inbound calls from computer-routed customer care system using greeting script
- Determine caller's need using provided categorisations
- Address caller's need using protocols set out in customer care system
- Re-direct caller to specialist if required
- Prompt caller to appropriate decision using closing script
- End call using closing script
- Complete product awareness and system update training modules within specified time frame

In some organisations, particularly those with a quality assurance system, the above information will be contained in a procedure or work instruction. The worker's PD in such a case may be rather generic. The key issue here is not the title or format of the document, but rather that the worker has a clear understanding of their supervisor's expectations for their specific job.

Results

'Results' or 'outcomes' is the final essential element of a PD. People have various terms and acronyms for this, whether it's Key Performance Indicator (KPI), Key Result Areas, Performance Standards or whatever else communicates 'this is what we want to have to show for our money'.

For our call centre operator, it might be as simple as taking a set number of calls per shift. That's pretty unambiguous. Most computerised customer service systems will track this kind of KPI automatically. A KPI for an accountant might read: 'Ensure accurate and complete financial and statutory accounts are prepared to Australian accounting standards by the 10th of each month'. When I was managing occupational health and safety, my key result areas included number of lost-time injuries, overall days lost to injury, and completion of site safety audits.

In some roles the expected results can be hard to quantify. You may even need to set up a specific system to gather information – remember those customer satisfaction surveys we talked about earlier?

Earlier I alluded to the huge variety of formats and categories represented in the PDs I've encountered. You've probably seen plenty in your time as well. Don't be intimidated by the fancy formatting, complex language or attempts to cover every conceivable detail. What we're after here is simply to make clear what you expect.

If your organisation doesn't have PDs as part of its HR processes, start by creating a document for each employee or volunteer. Then address these four prompts as clearly as you can:

- The purpose of their job is...
- They are accountable to... (write your own name here if they report to you)
- Their responsibilities are ...
- Their work is expected to achieve these results ...

It's not fancy and it's not comprehensive but it will get you started.

To make it easier, there's a simple PD template on the resources page at www.likeabossbook.com.au. It has a few other categories that we'll get to shortly.

If your organisation already uses PDs, you might want to go over the PDs for your staff and make sure they're abundantly clear on the four topics above. If you're allowed to amend them, do so as needed. If not, you might need to start a conversation with your HR or QA departments.

If you're stuck with an inadequate PD, you can always use notes from your supervision conversations to document the information. You just need to make sure your worker gets a copy and that you can lay your hands on the notes to remind and reinforce when need be.

If you're writing a PD for a worker who doesn't have one, be mindful that any significant changes to a worker's job needs to be implemented carefully and in consultation with the worker. Don't go making significant changes to what you expect and present it wholesale to your worker. Consult, negotiate, and seek advice if necessary.

Depending on your context, there are some other pieces of information that are helpful to include in a PD. Most obvious is the job title. Alongside this may be the job's award classification. In Australia, a large percentage of jobs are covered by the national industrial awards scheme. You may need to refer to an industrial award or an enterprise bargaining agreement if the job is covered by one of these. The Australian Fair Work Ombudsman can help you. Other countries have different industrial relations systems, so you may need to seek out some local advice, particularly if you're in a strongly unionised workplace.

If you're in a unionised environment, job classifications can be very important, as they specify which tasks can be performed by the various workers according to their classification. If you write up a PD that's at odds with the prevailing collective agreement that covers your workers, you risk sparking an industrial dispute. Get some advice and avoid facing a picket line.

Other information that might be set out in a PD includes the roles that report to this one, plus document control and currency information like the date of approval, name of approving person, version number, and date of next revision.

Some organisations include selection criteria in their PDs – i.e. the qualifications, skills and qualities required to do the job. This can be a helpful reference if you choose to include it. Other organisations put these in a separate document.

Responsibility and authority

We've spoken at length about balancing expectation and support. In supervision, the other balance to consider is the balance of responsibility and authority. We've already talked about the idea of authority attracting some negative connotations, in much the same way as words like power or hierarchy. Yet properly delegated authority is an essential part of even the most junior role. Authority is simply authorisation to act. If a worker has absolutely no authority at all, they are unable to undertake the work you expect of them.

Nonetheless, authority can get a bad reputation when people assume it, overstep it, or abuse it. As a boss it's imperative that you're clear with your workers as to the decisions they are authorised to make. It's also important to define the limits to your worker's authority. The more senior the role, the clearer we must be about the delegated authority that attaches to the role.

Some organisations include statements of authority in a PD – i.e. what decisions, including expenditure, can be made by a person in this role. For our discussion, hiring, firing and corrective action of workers are important considerations. Other organisations set this out in a delegations document. The key issue is making sure authority parameters are documented in some way and the worker is clear on their own level of authority. Equally important is the supervisor's responsibility to ensure the workers under their care are held accountable for the exercise of authority, and that instances of exceeding one's authority are appropriately confronted. This will reduce your chances of needing to have that awkward conversation with a junior manager who orders themselves a super-expensive laptop that's way outside their scope of requirements. It might also save your organisation from an unaccountable autocrat.

The balance

Most of the authority required by a worker to do their job is self-evident, especially in roles closer to the base of the organisation. Authority such as that required to make a sale and initiate a credit card transaction are basic to a retail assistant. But what's their authority on exchanges and refunds? Discounts? Are they authorised to call around to other stores to see if the item required is in stock at another outlet? Don't leave them to guess.

The more responsibility a role carries, the broader the scope of authority required to fulfil those responsibilities. It makes defining a worker's level of authority either tediously detailed or somewhat ambiguous. To avoid writing a book within a book, let's just look at some headings.

Financial authority is the most obvious. Can a worker authorise purchases – i.e. spend the company's money? What are the limits on the amount of money and the type of things that can be purchased? What must be reported specifically, and what needs separate authorisation before making the purchase?

Next comes HR authority. If a worker has staff, it's logical that they should have authority to supervise their staff and to give them day-to-day direction. I would argue they should have authority to initiate performance review and management, up to termination. For senior management it may be absolute hire and fire.

Then there's authority for the deployment of company resources: scheduling of activity, stopping or interrupting an activity, authorising the use or forbidding the use of equipment and materials. You could get lost in this if you try to cover every eventuality. Think over the basic decisions a worker will need to make to get their job done and state their authority in making them. If the authority is clearly implied in the responsibilities statements, you may not need to state it specifically under a separate section.

The general rule of thumb is that a worker should be granted sufficient authority required to fulfil their responsibilities and no more. Some managers prefer that their reports consult them before making a decision. While this allows control, it also makes for inefficiency and stifles initiative. The manager becomes a decision-making bottleneck. Far better to grant workers authority to make decisions right up to their level of competence and insight, then hold them accountable through appropriate supervision and reporting.

Careful thought is required here. Giving a person authority to make decisions for which they will not be held responsible is the making of a loose cannon. This is especially true if a person can spend money from a budget for which someone else is accountable, or make decisions about people and resources for which someone else will be held responsible. Family companies are notorious for this.

On the flip side, too little authority at best results in inefficiency as workers wait around for people higher up to make decisions. Even worse, they may simply be stymied in fulfilling their responsibilities, resulting in exasperation or even 'resigning in place'. If a worker has a colleague making decisions that interfere with their work, their frustration will likely translate into sufficient stress to trigger some of the anxiety patterns we looked at in the previous chapter and may even result in a workers compensation claim or a resignation.

From PD to clear understanding

Once the PD is settled, what then? For some supervisors, the assumption is that the PD can be stapled to the letter of offer, and on their first day on the job the new worker will read the document and simply obey.

We'll talk about processes for inductions and orientations in the next section. My concern here is helping your worker to translate the responsibilities they read in the PD into the actions they perform in undertaking their job.

If we go back to our call centre operator working next to a couple of others performing identical work, the performance expectations are pretty easy to define. If Operators A and B can get though 120 calls per shift, then it's reasonable to expect that operator C will clear 120 calls per shift too. Job done, right?

Not so fast. Let's think about quality standards safety expectations, and what I like to call 'playing nice'– codes of conduct and issues around treating all people decently. Every volunteer and employee needs to be clear on the organisation's expectations with regard to quality, safety and personal conduct. And they need to be absolutely clear that you, their supervisor, take those standards seriously enough to ensure all your staff uphold them.

I can hear some people protesting, "Isn't that the HR department's job?"

Well, yes. And no. Depending on your organisation, you may have an HR team that handles induction training, including all the policy stuff around safety and standards of behaviour. But it's up to you, their supervisor, to keep quality, safety and propriety clearly in your worker's field of view. If it's not abundantly clear in their minds that you expect them to uphold these standards, it's highly likely that they simply won't.

For that person answering inbound calls, the tasks are concretely defined and the outcomes easily quantifiable. As long as the quality and courtesy angles are covered, there's not much to misunderstand about 120 calls. If your worker's responsibilities are more complex and ambiguous than our friend the call centre operator, getting clear on your expectations is going to take some careful thought. A PD is always a great place to begin, but these are seldom sufficiently specific to provide an unambiguous standard of expectations week-to-week, month-to-month or year-to-year.

In the next section we'll spend some more time breaking these ideas down a little further. At this stage, the main thing is the need to be absolutely clear in your own mind about what it means to meet your expectations. A more immediate and concrete question is to ask yourself, 'What do I want to see done the next time I talk to this worker?' This will usually be a list of standards, targets and milestones. Standards might include things like, 'all customer inquiries answered within 24 hours'. Targets might be things like 'produce two hundred units per labour-hour' or 'complete all routine maintenance tasks according to schedule'. Milestones might include things like, 'complete project proposal by June 1st'.

For more complicated and more autonomous roles like a teacher or a sales rep, the translation from PD to performance will require a plan: 'Plan the work, then work the plan' goes the old adage. To execute the tasks required to meet your expectations, your worker needs a work plan.

The work plan

Quite simply, work planning involves identifying all the main tasks to be done, and then scheduling when they will be done. It's more than just maintaining a to-do-list.

As a younger manager I was a classic 'to-do lister'. I identified all the tasks to do – some urgent, some not, some current, some good ideas I thought I might consider working on at some undefined time in the future. All of these were mixed up together in a huge, three-page to-do list. Each morning I would review the list and identify seven or eight tasks I thought I should probably tackle that day. These I highlighted and I would set about chipping away at them, mindful that I had a range of appointments in my diary to keep as well.

I would rarely finish the highlighted list, would allow myself to get distracted, procrastinate and generally be inefficient, since I had no sense of whether I was on top of things or behind, beyond the fact that my boss wasn't threatening to fire me.

If you're reading this thinking, 'Yeah, that's me', I suggest you stop reading this book and order a copy of *Do It Tomorrow* by Mark Forster or *Getting Things Done* by David Allen.[38] You can't lead where you haven't gone yourself.

The other half of work planning is scheduling the tasks on the to-do list. I'm talking about going beyond choosing a few tasks for the to-do list each morning. Nowadays I generally schedule a month of tasks at a time. Some people schedule a week at a time. Forster suggests an interesting 'next day' planning regimen. Regardless of method, a worker who's not closely supervised would do well to have a system for planning what they'll do and when.

Professions such as nursing are highly responsive and require a new work plan each shift. Others follow a one or two-week cycle, while others have a monthly rhythm (like accounting). Professions like teaching combine a weekly or fortnightly rhythm with quarterly and annual rhythms. If a job has a recurring pattern or several layers of recurring patterns, it makes sense to set up a planning pattern to match.

These roles often do well with a model week (or fortnight, or month) where the recurring tasks are scheduled. Put simply, a model week looks a lot like one of those school study planners that all of us were encouraged to use (and none of us actually used) back in high school. It looks like a week-to-an-opening diary, with seven days represented in parallel columns divided up into half-hourly or hourly blocks. A model week allocates appropriate blocks of time to the recurring tasks.

I don't use a model week or month for my professional activity, which is too adaptive to follow a pattern. That means I have to plan every month of my professional life almost from scratch. However, I do use a model week for my

---

[38] Forster, M. *Do It Tomorrow: and Other Secrets of Time Management* (Hodder & Stoughton London 2006); Allen, D. *Getting Things Done: The Art of Stress-free Productivity* (Penguin, New York 2001).

personal development. My five different physical exercise activities are slotted in over the mornings of the week, along with my spiritual exercises. Reading and journaling are scheduled in respective evenings.

Given there will be emails and slack threads and interruptions and unforeseen emergencies, it's unlikely that any plan will be executed perfectly. This becomes even more unlikely if every minute is scheduled, or the estimated time for each task is based on the best case scenario. Generally speaking, if more than about 60% of work time is locked down with commitments, the work plan is vulnerable to being disrupted beyond recovery.

An increasing number of organisations are using workflow planning software like Monday.com. These packages integrate work planning with project planning, strategy and budgeting. The software provides supervisors with an immediate line of sight on their worker's plans, and progress in executing them. If you have the basic disciplines in place, the software will make it all work with less effort and with fewer tasks falling through the cracks. But the software is not a substitute for discipline, and without discipline things will drift.

There are some aspects of workflow planning software that have potential for some downside risks, but we'll talk those through in a later chapter.

What has this to do with supervision? Everything. As a supervisor, you have a responsibility to satisfy yourself that your worker has a high likelihood of meeting your expectations. The most reliable way of predicting that is to know that they have a list of tasks that, put together, will fulfil their responsibilities as set out in their PD (which is your expectation in document form). Then you need to be confident that they have a credible plan to complete those tasks.

How closely do you need to observe the creation and execution of this plan? That depends on a range of variables. The first one is the nature of the job. I tend to categorise jobs either as predominantly initiating or responding. An incoming call centre operator is a role that's largely responding. There may be a bit of reporting or follow-up or learning that needs to be planned, but largely the inbound call centre operator is taking the work on as it comes. A receptionist, a production line worker, an order-picker in a warehouse, and customer-facing retail are all jobs where the work is initiated by the context and the worker responds.

The more that a job constitutes responding, the less it's likely to require comprehensive planning, and the more likely it is to be supervised by direct observation. For predominantly responsive roles, a simple calendar with the few non-responsive tasks (like cleaning, balancing the till, training, etc.), listed out is probably enough.

This of course begs the question: should a supervisor have one-on-one supervision meetings with the people they directly supervise by presence and observation (like a floor manager supervising wait staff in a restaurant, or a foreman on a building site)? I believe they should. It's a chance to address small issues of performance and conduct, to resolve the worker's problems and answer their questions. If you're game, you might even ask for feedback. If you make a habit of these fairly quick conversations, your workers will become accustomed to talking one-on-one with you, they'll relax a little and be more likely to trust you. You'll have solid lines of communication already established in case you need to have a more difficult conversation.

In jobs where the worker is initiating the tasks, like a sales rep, a more detailed work plan is required. That doesn't mean you as the supervisor need to see a weekly plan every week and ensure that every minute is allocated to a relevant and productive task. It does mean you need confidence that the worker has an adequate system of planning their work to ensure they meet your expectations. That may mean paying close attention to their work plans early in the supervisory relationship, and then relaxing a little once you're confident that the worker has an adequate and reliable planning regimen.

The next dimension to consider is the level of the job. As the chair of a board of directors, I've supervised CEOs. I doubt the relationship would go well if I insisted on seeing how every half-hour block was allocated, and then demanded a report as to whether the time blocks were spent as allocated. By the same token, I would not expect a new outreach worker in their first role out of college to have a well thought through planning regimen.

With a CEO, I'm going to keep the supervision to broader-brush items on the PD and the strategic plan (more on that in Section 3) as well as issues requiring urgent attention and action (e.g. a change in legislation or an employee relations issue that could have broader implications for the organisation).

If the CEO is not executing as expected, or seems to be swamped or disorganised, I might drill into their planning regimen. I may even step them through my regimen as an example (I'm constantly amazed how unplanned and reactive many senior managers are). If it seems like I need to hold their hand to plan every month, I clearly have bigger issues to address – they're probably not up to the job.

With the new outreach worker in their first role, I'm likely to coach them through listing out the key tasks for their first week or two. I may even help them put that list together if they're really green. Then I'll ask them to schedule the tasks into a work plan and get back to me. I'll check that the plan is reasonable, then let them loose. In their next supervision meeting (probably a week later, and no more than two), I would ask them how they went, how much they got done and what was outstanding. As they grow in competence and I grow in confidence, I'll step back and supervise more by outcomes and less by activity.

For workers somewhere between these two extremes of seniority, supervisors should find a sensible middle ground, having regard to the worker's experience, the complexity of the job and the degree to which the worker completing tasks on time and in order impacts on the productivity of other workers.

A generalist manager supervising special workers

Some of you may supervise people who have specialised expertise that's beyond yours. Typically, a CEO will know more about the specifics of their industry sector than the chair to whom they report. A CEO will likely have a CFO who's more financially savvy then they are, and a CIO or CIT manager who's more tech literate. In the engineering and technology sectors there will always be people with particular expertise in a narrow field supervised by a manager with a more generalist skill set.

So how do you supervise technical specialists who know more than you do? Wanda Wallace and David Creelman put together four helpful points in their 2015 article on this thorny issue.[39] In summary, they advise:

1.   *Focus on relationships, not technicalities*

Put the same effort into getting to know your staff as you would a key client. Don't try to get up to speed on your worker's 20 years of hard-won learning.

2.   *Add value by enabling things to happen, not by doing the work*

Get solid information on what's going on and intervene when trouble threatens. Be the sponsor, not the professor.

3.   *Practice seeing the bigger picture, not mastering the details*

Seek to understand issues for their broad effect on the wider organisation rather than granulating issues down into their component parts – think integratively, not analytically. This is a big one. Typically, when things go gnarly for a technical expert, it's not their expertise that's the problem, but more generalist issues like people skills or the ability to manage themselves. You can be a resource here.

4.   *Rely on 'executive presence' to project confidence, not on having all the facts or answers*

Carry yourself more like the president of the company and less like the technical boffin from R&D. This is particularly hard if you recently were the technical boffin from R&D.

You will undoubtedly need to get into the details sometimes, but you simply can't be across all of it and maintain your broader focus as a supervisor. Learning enough to know if you're being baffled with bull can be tricky. Sometimes it's helpful to have another expert you can quiz or consult, especially when you're relying on your expert worker's opinion in making a

---

[39] Wallace, W. and Creelman, D. *Leading People When They Know More than You Do* Harvard Business Review June 18, 2015 – https://hbr.org/2015/06/leading-people-when-they-know-more-than-you-do.

high-impact decision, or when you suspect that your expert worker's opinion may be incomplete or incorrect.

Fitting the job to the worker

So far, we've considered the means of defining your expectations of a particular role, be it operating a call centre line or running a company. In theory, this should be enough: "Here's the job, let's figure out how you're going to do it this week or month given the situation as it is, now have at it. See you next week (or next month)." But between theory and lived experience lies a range of variables, and those involve the particularities of your worker and their lives.

I know it's obvious, but bosses seem to overlook the possibility that a worker's capacities will vary. There could be an almost endless list of variables (not excuses) outside the control of the organisation that will impact a worker's capacity to meet their supervisor's expectations.

Let's be clear, I'm not saying that any and every challenge faced by a worker gives them a free pass for sub-par performance. I am saying that you'll need to be thoughtful about what you expect and may need to modify your expectations, and perhaps even the PD, in response to the unique challenges and circumstances of your workers.

Most of what we've discussed about clarifying your expectations so far has been fairly procedural: analysing and defining the role, then figuring out how to fulfil the role in the present context of the organisation.

In chapter seven I introduced you to *The Practice of Adaptive Leadership* by Ronald Heifetz, Alexander Grashow and Marty Linsky. You'll remember they differentiate technical problems (problems with a well known proven solution) from adaptive challenges, where the course of action is a little experimental and the outcomes far from guaranteed.

The task of getting the job to fit the person is more of an adaptive challenge. It's going to require your careful observation and for you to exercise some judgement. Keep in mind your role and responsibilities to the organisation – the worker's contribution must be a fair exchange for the benefits they receive. If you set up what amounts to a bad deal for the organisation, you're not doing your job.

Keep in mind that you're also stewarding a human being. If you set up what amounts to a bad deal for the worker, you're probably acting unethically, and possibly illegally as well.

It may be that you decide that the difference between the worker's capabilities and capacity on the one hand, and the requirements of the roles on the other, are simply too different to reconcile. If that's the case, my counsel is firstly to talk the challenge over with your own boss. Sometimes an organisation will be willing to 'carry' an underperforming worker because they're facing extraordinary challenges in other spheres of their life, or because they're close to retirement, and it would seem cruel to performance-manage them out of the organisation.

Exceptional circumstances aside, if the gap between your worker's ability and the requirements of the job cannot be bridged by some tweaks that don't put either side to significant disadvantage, you'll need to move them out of their role. I encourage you to seek some help from your HR team, or from an employee relations advisor, especially if you opt to terminate the worker's employment rather than redeploy them in a more suitable role. Depending on the jurisdiction in which you work, there may be a variety of legal risks and requirements to manage. For example, Australia has much more stringent federal laws about unfair dismissal than the United States, which has a patchwork of state and even enterprise-based requirements, along with a more litigious culture.

To summarise the last few paragraphs, it may take some thoughtful tailoring to get the job to fit the person. We'll touch on getting the person to fit the job (recruitment, selection and development) a little later.

Summary

- The primary means of defining your expectation is the Position Description.
- A Work Plan is an important mechanism for translating the Position Description into actual performance.
- You'll need to tailor how much you are involved in planning and observe its execution based on the nature of the job and the worker's skill set.
- You may need to adjust your expectations and approach to fit the circumstances.

Reflection

- How clear are you on your expectations of your workers?
- How clear are your workers on your expectations?
- Do you have a solid basis for confidence that your workers can and will meet your expectations?

Action

- From what you've learned in this chapter, what changes do you need to make to be clearer about your expectations and more confident they will be met?

Chapter 10
Super-vision

Getting a line of sight

Beneath the question of reasonable expectation lies the challenge of getting enough information about your employees' or volunteers' work to know what you can expect. Once that's been settled (at least enough for you and your worker to have a clear and shared understanding of the job and what's expected), the challenge becomes getting a clear enough line of sight on the worker's output to know whether your expectations are being met. It may not be as easy as it first appears. Over the years I've observed supervisors utilise four generalised strategies.

Strategy 1: Ignore

It's probably no great surprise that a significant proportion of supervisors effectively abdicate their responsibilities. I've had staff transferred into my department who had never met with their immediate boss for routine supervision. They would only speak if there was an issue to be resolved and the conversation would be confined to that issue. On several occasions I've asked coaching clients how often they meet with their boss, and they've replied, "I don't." Apparently, the supervisor assumes that the PD is all the worker needs and they will do exactly what's required without further attention from the supervisor. I generally equate this approach to one of those little clockwork monkeys with a pair of cymbals in their hands. You wind them up and set them going. You only really pay attention when the spring unwinds and they stop – or they fall off the table.

Sometimes it's more subtle. Some bosses think of their roles solely as pastoral – they catch up with the workers for a bit of a chat, make sure they're happy enough, metaphorically pat them on the head and send them on their way. Others confuse positional supervision (which is what this book is about) with professional supervision (not what this book is about), where the 'client' brings an issue or challenge from their professional practice and the supervisor guides their reflection. While a boss might perform that function, it's not their primary purpose. Psychologists, social workers and ministers who seek professional supervision usually go outside their organisation to find it, and they pay.

Strategy 2: Perception

You would be amazed how many supervisors, and indeed entire organisations use unexamined perception as their major determinant of employee performance. My dad was a bricklayer, working on major commercial building sites, often in Melbourne's city centre. He tells the story of a labourer with whom he worked in the late 1950s, building what was at the time the city's tallest building. My dad's a bit of an efficiency buff, and he was particularly impressed with this man's work

It's a brickie's labourer's job to keep the brickies supplied with bricks, mortar, water and wall ties. They need to keep an eye on the clock and where the wall is up to in relation to the scaffolding. There's no point mixing another batch of mud and loading up the mortar boards right before knock-off time. The mud will not get used and will set on the boards overnight. There's no point stacking the scaffold with bricks if the brickies are already reaching above their heads and it's nearly time for another 'lift' of scaffolding.

The labourer in question was expert in timing his work to ensure the brickies had everything they needed but never too much more. When he was loading up the mortar boards, he'd sling a bucket of water from the barrow handle and top up the water dippers at the same time. He always made the most of every movement around the site. Consequently, while he kept the brickies constantly working, he never really looked busy. One day the foreman noticed the labourer standing idly rolling a smoke. Without a question, the foreman marched over and summarily fired him for slacking.

Dad confronted the foreman and pointed out that all the brickies on his team had enough bricks to last to the next lift and had plenty of mud on their boards. "That bloke is smart, not slack. You just sacked the best labourer on the site."

The boss's humility was as minimal as his management smarts, and he refused to reinstate the labourer. The next labourer ran around like a madman while the brickies waited for him to catch up.

Some law firms evaluate their junior staff by the time they arrive for work and when they leave, because it takes too much time for partners to pay attention to the actual quality of their performance.

Looking busy is not synonymous with effectiveness. Management by perception risks rewarding the wrong behaviours.

Strategy 3: KPIs

If there was ever a three-letter acronym guaranteed to induce anxiety and eye rolls it's 'KPI', the dreaded Key Performance Indicator. Used judiciously, KPIs can help organisations measure performance, target attention where it's needed and steadily improve efficiency. Used without careful thought, KPIs become just another criterion by which workers determine how little their bosses know about the organisation.

Yet KPIs are virtually ubiquitous. If you work in consulting or in the legal field, the almost universal KPI is 'billable hours'. Play your cards right and you can work a 50-hour week but bill even more.

In sales it might be as simple as gross dollar value in sales for the week, or something more sophisticated like 'cost per conversion'. In project management it could be 'on-time completion percentage'.

You know those little online surveys you get sent after talking to a customer service agent on the phone? That satisfaction score will be – or relate to – a personal or team KPI for the operator with whom you just conversed. Feel the power.

Yet the use of KPIs has a number of pitfalls. Firstly, they sometimes fail to be a key indicator of what's good for the business. Lots of organisations borrow KPIs from other organisations, without realising that they don't readily transfer. Let's say a furniture retailer tracks people through the doors of their shops against gross sales for the day and finds that the two figures directly correlate – the more people, the more sales, with roughly the same transaction value. They run a few experiments to see if the relationship holds and find it's pretty stable and predictable. So, they set 'people through the door' as their marketing team's KPI. I know it's a bit simplistic but go with me for a minute.

Now imagine a building supplies retailer decides that they'll adopt the same metric, and without any research opt to run a bunch of loss leader promotions to attract foot traffic, which trebles by diverting customers from big-box hardware stores. (A loss leader is a special price where the seller makes little or nothing on the sale of a particular product, with the aim of attracting customers who will also buy other products at a much higher margin). At the same time, their trade accounts sales drop because the tradies are forced to wait while the staff help DIYers. The DIYers only buy the loss leader product and perhaps a few bits and bobs. Tradies typically spend thousands on their trade accounts each month. Selling loss leaders plus losing some key trade accounts puts a huge dent in profit. Be careful what you measure.

Second, KPIs sometimes incentivise undesirable behaviours. The recent Australian Royal Commission into banking found that lending agents (banks call them 'originators') were rewarded by the total value of loans written. Now, anyone with a brain stem could predict that would incentivise bending the lending criteria a little. As it turns out, those criteria were bent like a pretzel and money was lent to people who had no real prospect of servicing the loan. Be careful what you reward.

An outbound call centre might set a KPI around closed sales, only to find operators being pushy and using inappropriate tactics. They might push up total sales, but in the longer term they risk trashing the company brand. An inbound centre might set a KPI around calls taken, only to find their operators rushing to end calls, leaving customers feeling dismissed and misunderstood.

In manufacturing, a great way to improve machine uptime is to simply avoid shutting down for maintenance. The machine availability KPI improves just until the lack of maintenance leads to breakdowns – then machine availability falls off a cliff.

Thirdly, KPIs can be sabotaged. A recent inquiry found that police in Victoria had faked thousands of random breath tests just to meet a KPI. People find ways to move the numbers, sometimes with outcomes that are the opposite of those intended.

Some individuals or teams will concentrate so much on their own numbers that they fail to adequately cooperate with workmates or other teams. They may even act in a way that harms another person's or team's KPIs for the sake of improving their own.

If you're going to use KPIs, be careful that they actually measure something that's related to success – you might want to do some research and test your hypothesis before implementing KPIs. Check that your KPI doesn't incentivise perverse outcomes (hopefully you'll have more insight than those banking execs). Also be careful to ensure that the KPI can't be manipulated or faked.

In general, using a dashboard or scorecard of KPIs, some individual and some collective, will help to prevent the pursuit of one KPI distorting things. In recent years software has been developed to track employee work time, especially work that primarily involves working at a computer. While this may seem to relive a supervisor's anxiety about a home-based worker slacking off, it risks transferring that anxiety to the worker, who begins to feel like they're under constant surveillance. Ongoing anxiety, even at low levels, interferes with a worker's concentration and clarity of thinking. Software to measure employee performance can be very useful if used thoughtfully and transparently. Software used to constantly monitor workers has Orwellian overtones and at best will gain a short-term spike in productivity. In the long term it will cause the most internally motivated and creative workers to move to a more trusting work environment.

We'll talk a little more about the rise of computer software to measure employee performance in chapter 27. The cautions above apply very particularly to the emerging trend of using data fed into an algorithm to measure performance.

Strategy 4: Measuring activity

This is a slightly more sophisticated version of the story of the brickie's labourer a few pages ago. It stems from looking at how much activity a person undertakes without asking a few key questions. 'Busy' and 'effective' are not synonymous concepts. Sometimes a person looks really busy when they're simply inefficient. Some people are incredibly busy doing stuff they should have delegated to others. I've watched people working their fingers to the bone doing tasks that are simply not their job – even to the point where some of what they do is actually nobody's job and it would make no difference to the organisation if the activity was abandoned. You would be amazed how many people write reports that no one reads or generate data that no one uses.

A few years ago I was doing some job analysis in an accounts department. I was interested that they had five accountants and two clerks. Accountants outnumbering clerks is either a sign of highly automated accounting processes, or that the CFO is not paying attention to the people who work for them. As I analysed one accountant's job, I discovered that they took data from a Quicken file and manually entered it into an Excel file, along with some other data from an MYOB file. Then they took the data from the Excel file and manually entered it into the mainframe GL system. I was incredulous. This had been going on for at least a couple of years. I took my findings to the senior leadership group and recommended a process review. After some process streamlining and automating some data transfer, they were down to two accountants and three clerks – less than half the original payroll value for the department. If the CFO had been appropriately supervising their staff, they would have realised the inefficiencies and saved hundreds of thousands of dollars. But the accountants were always busy, so the CFO assumed they were being productive.

An even more subtle version of this strategy is when a person looks at their job description and sees a range of tasks listed under the 'responsibilities' heading. They furiously set about doing their tasks with all the energy they can muster. Imagine a sales rep whose PD includes:

- Services existing accounts by maintaining regular contact
- Develops new customers by initiating contact
- Keeps customers informed of new and upgraded products
- Adjusts content of sales literature to ensure content is correct and contemporary

Now imagine that rep works for a retailer who sells replacement parts for cars. The rep's primary customers are small mechanic's workshops, where the boss is 'on the tools' and may have two or three other staff.

Being keen to show their commitment, the rep decides to contact every customer every week. The rep is careful to identify one new product and one special deal to advise as a reason for their call. For the next three months, they faithfully call every customer every week. On top of that, in their daily 'road work' they visit customers to offer them the latest promotional materials, work through prices and attempt to 'upsell' by pitching products they think the customer might like. Each visit takes about 30 minutes. They also work hard to drop in on mechanics who are not yet customers to give them a similar pitch. Because they're so committed to their job, the rep spends their evenings working on updating promotional material to ensure it is fresh and up to date.

If you were measuring that rep by activity, you'd have to say they're a high performing worker: diligent, with lots of initiative and a great work ethic. They're doing exactly what their PD requires. The only problem being, that rep would send sales southward at an eye-watering rate, because they waste so much of their customer's time.

Now I can hear some of you protesting, "But you just warned about managing by KPIs, now you're warning about managing by activity." Yep. Stay with me.

If we're going to manage by activity, we have to be sure that the said activity actually produces the desired result. (That's why you get those surveys after the phone call to which I referred earlier). If the rep's supervisor had put in sufficient effort to understand the rep's approach and the supervisor knew their industry well enough to know how much tradies dislike reps wasting their time, the supervisor would have counselled the rep to channel their energies differently.

A motor trade rep I know would visit a particular mechanic in a particular country town every time he was in that part of the state, which was about every two months. He would drop in, see how the guy was doing and ask him if he'd like to do a price comparison or product comparison. The mechanic would always politely refuse, saying he was happy buying from the rep's competitor. The rep would smile, say, "Thank you" and be on his way, having taken no more than a minute of the mechanic's time. So far we've got activity with no results. If you were the rep's boss, what would you say? Before you answer, let me finish the story.

After perhaps half a dozen such visits, the rep dropped in to find the mechanic at his wits end, stuck with a technical problem he could not resolve. The rep happened to have a virtually encyclopaedic knowledge of the particular system that had the mechanic stumped. Five minutes later the mechanic's problem was solved and the rep landed $50,000 worth of orders over the following year.

How do you determine the rep's performance? Simply measuring activity would not help – the rep's activity was unremarkable. Measure by results?

Again, until the rep had the opportunity to help the mechanic, his results with that guy had been zero.

Peter Senge points out that causes and effects are often not close together in time.[40] The results of the activity and decisions on the part of workers often take time to produce results, both positive and negative. The supervisor needs to be able to determine whether activities and decisions are likely to produce the required results, often well before the results materialise.

At the end of the day, a competent supervisor knows the worker's role well enough to know which result data matters. They also pay attention to activity – not just the quantity of the activity but the qualitative characteristics. Supervising either of those reps well would require their boss paying attention, hearing a couple of the stories behind the data, and perhaps understanding the rep's thinking behind their behaviour.

Managing by outcomes

In the face of COVID-19's impact upon working environments, and the rise of ubiquitous internet access and cloud computing, the workplace has become a bit of an ambiguous term. I can write and submit a proposal to a client from my backyard, a café or an airplane. Thanks to video conferencing applications I can do most of my job from just about anywhere. During the pandemic we found ways to undertake even typically office bound roles like accounts from home.

This means bosses may need to supervise staff they can't easily observe and about whom it's hard to form casual assumptions. For some supervisors this has triggered a troubling sense of lost control.

In this environment it's all the more important to manage by outcomes, not clock punching. The bottom line is, simply attending the workplace adds no value to the organisation in and of itself. We pay people for the contribution they make. In some jobs, that contribution can only be made in the context of attending the workplace. This includes a huge range of jobs, from a ward nurse to a barista. Other jobs can be performed just about anywhere or

---

[40] Senge, P. M. *The Fifth Discipline: The Art and Practice of the Learning Organization,* rev. edn (Currency, New York, 2006).

require the worker to be on the road. I tell my staff that I'm not buying their time, I'm buying their contribution. I pay them for outcomes, not attendance.

Managing by report

Probably the best way of determining whether your expectations are being met is to have your workers report against pre-determined criteria in a regular basis. This report might be written or verbal. Typically, the report would include a balance of both activity and outcomes and cover a spread of measures so that no one KPI can be easily 'gamed'. The frequency and content of the report will vary with the level of responsibility and autonomy of the role you're supervising.

The call centre operator taking those inbound calls might have a brief verbal with their boss at the end of a shift, and their immediate performance against KPIs might be tracked automatically. But the chat still reinforces the outcomes that matter and might give opportunity for the worker to mention a sore wrist or a misogynistic comment from a colleague. Proper attention from the supervisor could ward off a lost time injury or worse.

An exec might report to a general manager once a month and be required to put together a written report comprised of a detailed scorecard of metrics, including budget variance, an outline of activity against strategy, and a summary on HR issues in their team.

It's generally preferable for the worker to report their performance to their supervisor. In my time working on total quality management projects, I heard time and again how simply measuring and reporting something saw performance almost magically improve in that area – without even setting a target or making changes to processes. Simply asking workers to measure and report the percentage of reject product will often see the number fall over time (provided there are variables the workers can affect to improve the score – if there's a fundamental flaw in the process, the number may not move, or it may go in the opposite direction).

You may have seen the same dynamic at work in your own experience. If you have to record every purchase you make and report it (even to yourself) at the end of the week, you'll almost certainly spend less. The first step in losing weight is to keep a food diary. The same thinking is behind people wearing fitbits. If we make ourselves pay attention to something, we'll start to direct our intention toward it as well.

Getting your staff to pay attention to results for themselves – rather than you gathering the data and confronting them with the numbers – is a key step toward them taking responsibility for results and directing their efforts toward higher achievement. It worth noting that 'Inattention to Results' sits at the pinnacle of Lencioni's pyramid of team dysfunction. And right underneath it is 'Lack of Accountability.'[41]

Before we leave this topic, it would be remiss of me not to mention the power of shared goals and mutual accountability. It's a tad beyond the scope of this book, but it's well addressed by a number of authors, perhaps none with a more elegant simplicity than Lencioni in *The Advantage*.[42] When team members report their progress and achievements to their peers as well as their boss, the sense of a shared destiny is fostered that is both challenging and supportive. Elite sporting teams have over recent years been paying increasing attention to the power of peer accountability to impact player performance.

---

[41] Lencioni, P. *The Five Dysfunctions of a Team* (Jossey-Bass San Francisco 2002).
[42] Lencioni, P. *The Advantage: Why Organizational Health Trumps Everything Else in Business* (Jossey-Bass San Francisco 2012).

Summary

- In order to fulfil your responsibility as a boss, you need to objectively determine whether your expectations are being met.
- Ignoring results or relying on casual perception are common and ineffectual strategies, while using KPIs and measuring activity have their limitations.
- Measuring outcomes and managing by report are much more effective ways of determining whether your expectations are being met.

Discussion

- How does your organisation measure performance? How would you rate its effectiveness?
- How confident are you that you can reliably determine whether your workers are meeting your expectations?

Action

- Identify one practice you could abandon and one you could adopt to improve the way you measure worker performance.

Chapter 11
The breakfast of champions

Feedback relative to expectations

As a teenager I attended a technical school – a boys only secondary college that taught a basic academic curriculum of English, maths and sciences, plus subjects like technical drafting, woodwork, and engineering. It was designed for boys who wanted to be engineers or carpenters, rather than doctors or lawyers (or writers). For reasons that never became clear, the school catered for years seven to eleven (rather than the usual seven to twelve), and the drab, battleship grey uniform with black leather school shoes was compulsory only for students in years seven to ten.

A guy in my year ten class decided to simply stop wearing the uniform, showing up dressed however he pleased. Surprised, I asked him if he was ever confronted by a teacher or vice principal about his flouting of the rules. "Never," he replied.

The next day I showed up in blue jeans, a t-shirt and a pair of Adidas trainers. I did the same the next day, and the next. For most of my time in year ten, I ignored the uniform rules and never once did any of the teachers confront me. For all intents and purposes, the uniform rule was merely a suggestion that could be safely ignored.

It's been said that the standard you walk past is the standard you accept. Some people – including me – will play this to their own advantage.

We've just spent a pretty good chunk of time getting a line of sight on employee performance and whether it meets expectations. Now it's time to talk about providing feedback.

As a former colleague of mine loved to remind us, "Feedback is the breakfast of champions." In the world of supervision, it's often the defining factor between 'okay' performance and performance beyond expectations.

Let me open with the central tenet of feedback. No matter how clear you try to be, no one will 'get it' when you define your expectations for the first time.

Even reading the previous chapters very carefully, and diligently putting them into practice will not eliminate discrepancies between your expectations, and your worker's understanding of your expectations. This is true in just about every facet of life. So often spouses think they're going to absolutely delight their partner only to be met with a vaguely disappointed look. Later we'll look at some of the emotional processes that get in the way, but for now, let's just assume that no matter how explicit and unambiguous the PD, no matter how detailed the strategy and no matter how many times you ask, 'Have I made myself clear?' the person you're supervising will – to one degree or another – misunderstand what you expect. It's no one's fault, it's pretty much unavoidable, and life as a supervisor is so much easier if we just assume it to be the case.

This of course begins with some real basics. Let's assume the letter of appointment for your new worker clearly states that their working hours are from 7:30 AM to 4:00 PM Monday to Friday. I'm pretty sure any boss would think that means being on the job ready to begin the first task at 7:30. Some workers just don't interpret it that way. They might think these times are just guidelines, with a degree of flexibility. They may be surprised to learn that wandering in at 7:40, making a cup of coffee, having a quick glance at their social media feed and eventually settling in at their desk at 7:55 is not what you expect. What are you going to do?

The standard you walk past

I've lost count of the number of times I've had supervisors complain to me that young people these days are slack and unmotivated. I would counter that supervisors these days are even more slack and unmotivated, because, instead of doing their job and telling their younger workers when their performance is not up to scratch, they just find a consultant or coach or colleague with whom they can have a bit of a bleat. Let's be unequivocal – it's your job to address behaviour and performance from your workers that does not meet your expectation. If you don't, the problem lies with you, not the worker. There, I said it.

Most workplaces have rules about safety, sexual harassment, discrimination and privacy, designed to make the workplace safe, fair, harmonious and legally compliant. If the managers of an organisation ignore instances of these rules being transgressed in the same way my teachers ignored my snubbing the uniform rules, the organisation will sooner or later find itself in a court or tribunal being ordered to make a significant compensation payment. In the meantime, workers' respect for management will erode, and it's likely that turnover will rise as performance falls.

The standard you walk past is the standard you accept, and you could be walking directly toward trouble if you ignore people ignoring the rules.

If a teacher had simply asked me, "Mate, why are you out of uniform?" I would've had no good answer, and I may have received a detention slip. Even a warning of a detention would have been enough to persuade me to get with the program. That simple question is a form of feedback. Of course, employees not meeting your expectations are not always trying you out to see whether you'll follow through. Sometimes it's simply a case of them not understanding what you were saying when you explained your expectations. Either way, to get the performance you're after, you'll need to provide clear and frequent feedback as to whether your expectations are being met.

Sometimes this feedback will come as part of your regular supervision meetings. Sometimes it needs to be given on the spot.

Providing immediate feedback

Where a worker is clearly breaching the 'rules' – either in the form of failing to follow company policy or flouting the terms of their employment, it's important that the feedback is as immediate as reasonably possible. As soon as you allow the behaviour to go on by failing to address it, you've given your tacit approval and suggested to the worker that whatever 'rule' they've broken is only a suggestion. You're now part of the problem.

That means if one of your workers is late, talk to them the same day. If you see a person failing to follow a safe work practice, intervene immediately. If someone tells a joke that would not pass muster in front of an equal opportunity commissioner, let them know immediately, "That's not okay here."

Let's go back to our coffee-sipping, social media-checking worker who thinks a 7:30 start time actually means 7:55. If you were their boss, how would you handle it? Why not take a minute to jot down some thoughts?

Here's my best shot.

I would approach the worker that morning, greet them and ask for a quick chat in a private place – probably just a spot that's visible but out of earshot of the other workers – this is a low key, informal, gentle clarification kind of conversation, not formal performance management. The conversation would go something like this...

"So (worker's name), I noticed you got in today about ten minutes late, and then took a good chunk of time on other things before settling in to work."

Await response.

Presuming there's no valid reason for their behaviour: "I just want to remind you that I expect you to be at your desk at 7:30. If you want to get a coffee before you start, you'll need to roll in early enough to make it before start time. Okay?"

Await response.

Presuming it's not rage or tears: "Thanks." Followed by your perfunctory sign-off of choice and an encouraging smile. (Mine is "Knock 'em dead!" It may not work for you.)

Then, I would go straight to my own desk and note the particulars of the conversation in my diary. It's not formal corrective action, but it's nonetheless corrective action and it will be admissible as evidence if things go awry.

The following day I would note the worker's arrival and commencement time. Assuming they've got the message, I would find some reason to stop by their desk and offer them some small but meaningful encouragement about something unrelated. Perhaps something like, "Hey (worker's name), I noticed how you turned around that cranky customer yesterday; kept your cool, stuck to the facts, showed a bit of empathy. Nice work."

What happened above was feedback – being clear about where the workers conduct or performance is not up to your expectations, then balancing it with feedback about where it exceeded expectations.

Stephen Covey uses the idea of an 'Emotional Bank Account' to get people thinking about their positive and negative impacts on those around them.[43] The corrective conversation above would be a 'withdrawal' on the account I have with the worker. The praise for their work with the cranky customer would be a deposit. Various people have proposed a minimum ratio for withdrawals versus deposits, since one withdrawal can cancel out several deposits. The consensus seems to be about 1:5. You might want to bear this in mind as you provide feedback to your people. Try to catch them doing the right thing, notice it and express your gratitude. It actually gives the corrective conversations more force without you being forceful.

If you really want to take feedback to the next level, you could embark on the journey that Kim Scott calls 'Radical Candour'.[44] The idea is to tell people the information they need to know to excel, even if it will cause them discomfort. It's not a licence to tee off on people, but a commitment to provide guidance (Scott prefers this to the term 'feedback') that will help them become aware of their shortcomings and blind spots in order to reach their potential.

Scott's concept of radical candour calls for both caring personally *and* challenging directly. Challenge without care she calls 'obnoxious aggression' – which is what we fear being accused of should we tell people the uncomfortable truth. Care without challenge she labels 'ruinous empathy'. You'll no doubt see the parallel between Scott's theory and the support/expectation balance I introduced earlier. In avoiding the discomfort of radical candour, we subtly deny people the information they need to succeed. C. S. Lewis said "If you look for truth, you may find comfort in the end; if you look for comfort you will not get either comfort or truth only soft soap and wishful thinking to begin, and in the end, despair." [45]

Our society places so much emphasis on empathy and on avoiding saying anything that might hurt people's feelings that we have abandoned telling the

---

[43] Covey, S. *The Seven Habits of Highly Effective People: Powerful Lessons in Personal Change* (Free Press, New York, 1989).
[44] Scott, K. *Radical Candor: Be a Kick-Ass Boss Without Losing Your Humanity* (Pan, London, 2017).
[45] Lewis, C. S. *Mere Christianity, Part 12* (Harper Collins, London, 2001), 32

truth. We conflate hurt feelings with ideas like trauma and harm. No one will ever become a grown-up without getting their feelings hurt.

Feedback in supervision meetings

The primary context for giving feedback is in the regular supervision meeting. While the immediate ad hoc feedback we discussed above is about a single issue, the supervision meeting covers the worker's performance more generally. If the worker is a volunteer who does as simple job once a week, there may not be a lot of feedback required. Even so, a ten-minute intentional conversation to give them a sense of how they're doing and to get their feedback on the experience of work is valuable.

For a worker with broad and diverse responsibilities, the refocusing opportunity that feedback provides is essential to ensure their area of responsibility does not gradually drift off course.

We'll talk about frequency of supervision conversations in the next section. For now, let's look at the theory of giving feedback. Feedback follows the processes of clarifying your expectations, communicating your expectations, and gaining information about the worker's efforts to meet your expectations.

Let's pick up where we left off in the previous chapter – figuring out how you'll get a line of sight on your worker's efforts. This might be a mixture of you own observation, data you can access from the organisation, and the worker's report. This report might be written, or verbal. The criteria for the worker's report should be set out in advance.

For example, my current staff are field workers, and although I lead the team, I also carry a significant field-based workload. We work with people and teams scattered across a wide geographic territory, almost none of whom work in the central office (affectionately known as 'The Death Star').

Reporting takes a couple of forms. Every month each member of the team completes a dashboard that maps out their activity and other key statistics in three of the four categories that make up our business model. It tracks the interaction of clients with our service at the developmental stages of *Engagement* (one-off or short-term client relationship), *Participation* (longer-term client relationship) and *Capacity-building* (where the client is becoming a service delivery partner). There will also be some brief commentary around key activities for the month. It takes a team member about thirty minutes to complete the dashboard.

In addition, each member of the team meets one-to-one with me for ninety minutes once a month to work through their key responsibilities as set out in their PD. These are reflected and quantified in the team strategic plan. A few days before each supervision meeting, I send an agenda with the major headings of the PD and the actions the team member agreed to tackle under each heading for the previous month. There is no doubt in anyone's mind that I expect to see each of those actions completed.

When we sit down to talk, I work through the agenda asking, "How did you go with..." at each heading. Usually, the response will be along the lines of, "Yeah, that went well," or "Y'know, I thought it over a little more and decided to go with..." We'll talk things over from there.

Here's the moment of feedback. If I'm happy with the work and the outcomes, I'll offer affirmation to confirm they're on the right track. If I'm concerned, I'll simply say, "I'm a little concerned about..." and there will be more conversation. Supervision conversations with my team are generally fairly collegial, even if we're dealing with tough topics.

If the team member misses a goal, I'll wait for their explanation. Some team members commit to a lot and may overestimate what they can achieve. Sometimes there will be extenuating circumstances (illness, unplanned requirements that blew out the plan, roadblocks from clients, or colleagues within the organisation). Once all things are considered, if I think I could've expected better, I'll gently say so.

As far as routine supervision of my team goes, that's the primary feedback mechanism: simple, personal, and based on both dashboard data and the worker's own verbal report.

We end each session with me recording the team member's goals for the coming month. Those goals are set collaboratively, with reference to the timelines set out in the strategic plan. And thereby, my expectations for that worker are clarified and communicated for the following month.

There's always a heading on the agenda for 'your stuff', where the team member can raise whatever they want, be it good ideas, advice, problems, or feedback for me. We'll confirm the date for the next conversation and I'll thank the team member for their time and their efforts.

This example demonstrates how the basic elements of supervision work together:

1. Clearly communicate expectations
2. Gather information to measure performance
3. Provide feedback as to whether expectations have been met

As a supervisory relationship develops, it will take on its own unique character: a conversation co-created by you and your worker.

With longstanding supervision relationships, I relax the process a little, especially with self-contained team members who consistently hit their goals and have a good handle on managing themselves. Those conversations generally deal with the reporting stuff quickly and then move more to collaboration on current projects or working through challenges.

Supervising CEOs as a chairperson will take a different tone, as they report officially to the board, not exclusively to the chair. The CEO's report to the board should cover the major headings of the CEO's PD, including strategy, risk, money, people, operations, projects, sector relationships, etc. Rather than laboriously stepping the CEO through each of these, I'll touch on the areas that are currently mission-critical and use the majority of time dealing with any that stand out – both for reasons of delight and concern. I'm there to represent the board's expectations, not just my own. The process tends to be more about helping the CEO get clarity about priorities and outcomes and clearing roadblocks. I'll only hold the CEO's feet to the fire in any sustained fashion if the board has expressed concerns or I anticipate that the board will have concerns.

Now that we've set feedback into context and worked through an example, let's pull apart the process of delivering feedback (the third step listed above) in a little more detail. My description above may have looked like a fairly casual conversation, but it worked through a sequence of four components:

a. Determining performance in quantitative and qualitative terms
b. Considering contextual factors
c. Making an evaluation of performance

d.   Communicating the evaluation of performance

Determining performance

This means using the line of sight we discussed earlier to get as clear a picture of your worker's performance as is reasonably possible. You'll notice in the example I used a couple of devices, both of which set out the reporting criteria: a dashboard and a meeting agenda. The implied questions these two devices ask are directly pertinent to what I expect.

The dashboard is based on the organisational business model. The meeting agenda references the worker's PD and the team strategic plan. I want to emphasise how important it is that the supervision conversation directly and explicitly addresses the key ideas that pertain to the worker's job.

The worker's job is to do their part in the overall strategy, so it makes sense to reference the document that sets these out. Because I supervise my team members monthly, the agenda addresses the worker's part in executing the strategy in the *current month*. The tasks that make this up will vary month to month. I need to know enough about my worker's role to have a good idea of this month's key milestones, according to the strategy.

In other contexts the supervisor may reference documents like a project plan, or reports that flow from a project management process. The supervisor may use reports like customer feedback summaries, production data, sales performance, on-time delivery etc. Other reports like budget variance or staff turnover will contribute to supervision of management staff.

When using data as part of the supervision conversation, the two key questions are whether the data measures something for which the worker is responsible (in whole or in part), and whether the worker knows they will be asked to give account of their performance based on a particular data set. This is crucial   it's profoundly unfair to ambush your worker with data for which they did not know they would be held accountable. Ideally the worker should have access to all the information that will be used to measure their performance ahead of the supervision meeting.

If you're using quantitative data, it's important that the worker knows in advance what number constitutes a good job. Think back to our conversation about KPIs. It's not much use if our friend the call centre operator is blissfully unaware that you expect them to take 120 calls per shift.

If the numbers are more of a cumulative nature or are based on strategy milestones (i.e. a particular number achieved by a particular date, with an improvement or progression by the next date), the targets should be made explicit.

Whatever your measures, be careful not to use too many. If you're a team leader supervising shop floor personnel or entry-level operators, you may have only a couple of KPIs. The person supervising our call centre operator might only routinely measure calls per shift and an average customer feedback score.

For a mid-level manager, I would expect perhaps 2-3 departmental output KPIs, perhaps 2-3 risk management KPIs, budget variance, and perhaps 2-3 strategy milestones, plus whatever tasks that were discussed in the previous supervision meeting. A more senior manager will likely have more,

If you're supervising a manager, they will likely measure and monitor more granulated performance indicators with the staff they supervise, especially in-process indicators – the things that you can measure part-way through the process that predict the eventual process outcome.

As a supervisor, you may need to dig into these finer slices of data if the output numbers don't meet your expectation, but I would counsel against routinely drilling down and analysing loads of data in regular supervision. The key is to find the very small number of metrics that will give you a reliable indication of overall performance.

Making an evaluation of performance

If you've been abundantly clear about the targets to be hit and the tasks to be completed, your worker will probably have a pretty good idea as to whether they've met your expectation even before the supervision meeting.

If you've set out targets, getting a baseline idea of your worker's performance is as simple as figuring out the difference between your expectations and the information you've received, both from the worker and from other sources. It's likely that you'll form a reasonably clear view on the worker's performance as you discuss the worker's report and the various pieces of information we've discussed earlier.

Considering contextual factors

Our efforts to set clear expectations and get a clear means of observing and determining performance are important and necessary, but they're not the final determination of acceptable performance. I like to say, "No battle plan survives the first shot." Your worker may have marched from their previous supervision meeting with a clear and reasonable plan, but in the intervening week or month, the circumstances of life and work may well have had other plans.

It could be as simple as an IT glitch that takes a day to fix, paralysing your worker by locking them out of their diary, contacts and documents. It could be your worker or one of their team getting sick, having a family crisis, or a key person quitting to take on a new job. It could be supplies held-up, business processes messed-up, or an industrial dispute stirred-up that throws your worker's plan and performance into disarray.

Then the question becomes, 'What kind of performance would be reasonable to expect given the contextual factors at play?' Just how extenuating *are* those extenuating circumstances? There's no guaranteed means of determining what degree to which expectations should be adjusted for unforeseen circumstances. This is one of the vast array of situations where, as a supervisor, you'll need to exercise your judgement.

It's perhaps easier to describe what poor judgement would look like than what sound judgement might be. Easiest to describe are the extremes – if you expect the worker to deliver top-level performance in the face of personal, organisational and technological challenges, you can be pretty sure yours will be one of the companies or departments that people find reasons to leave, or that experiences absences and workers compensation claims above your sector average.

Conversely, if you're consistently handing your people a free pass even for relatively minor unforeseen challenges, you can expect poor performance and entitlement within your team, and awkward questions from your boss. Think back to the theory of balancing support and demand we considered in chapter seven. This is one of the contexts where it most obviously plays out.

When seeking to arrive at a reasonable adjustment of expectations, you might want to consider what capacity your worker retained over the week or month, rather than what they lost. One day lost to a computer glitch may explain a missed deadline or a small decline in performance, but a full-time worker would have had another twenty-or-so days in the month that were not so disrupted. I would expect that the overall outcomes for the month would be close to normal.

Conversely, a worker whose child suffered a serious acute illness may have had their performance plummet for the week or month. Even when they were at work, they were probably so worried that they were scarcely productive. In that case I would consider anything they achieved for the supervisory period to be a bonus. I wouldn't allow things to go on like that if the condition were to become chronic, but in the acute phase, I'm not going to expect much.

In your week-by-week experience as a supervisor you probably find your workers dealing with things that fall somewhere on the spectrum between trivial and catastrophic, and you'll need to figure out what's fair and reasonable to expect. If you're unsure, you may need to take some time to think it over, to consult your boss, an HR specialist, or a trusted colleague.

In the next section, we'll talk some more about the supervisor as coach. When the week or month hasn't exactly gone to plan, it often presents a valuable learning opportunity.

If you're near the end of your supervision meeting and you're not sure whether the worker has met your expectations or not, it's likely that you've not had it straight in your own mind what your expectations are. You may need to open up a 'reasonable expectations' conversation with the worker to seek clarity, and save the feedback for the next supervision conversation.

Communicating your evaluation

If you've gathered your data, discussed the contents with your worker, and taken into consideration extenuating circumstances (got all that?), you should be ready to give that all-important feedback. If you've executed the preceding steps well, this should be the easy part, but there are some exceptions.

Dealing with tricky issues: non-compliance and misbehaviour

Sometimes providing feedback includes dealing with the more general expectations you have of your worker: expectations like their obligations involving health, safety, and equal opportunity; like being careful to tell the truth, or even maintaining basic courtesies.

If the problem is clear-cut and sufficiently serious to have likely harmed an individual, directly put personnel at risk of harm or put the organisation at risk, or if the workers actions may be considered criminal, you'll need to get some advice and commence corrective action as soon as the problem comes to your attention. This is your duty of care. Don't put it off until a routine supervision appointment.

Where these issues are more complex or nuanced, or don't need to be dealt with using immediate feedback, they'll likely come up in supervision, and they represent an important part of your feedback to the worker. A worker who blitzes their KPIs each month but leaves a trail of emotional destruction is going to be a source of ongoing problems for you, and in time, for your boss. If my worker acts inappropriately once, it's probably their fault. If they get away with it and act that way again, it's my fault.

Dealing with non-compliance and inappropriate conduct is never easy but dealing with such behaviour at the first report is in everyone's best interests. If it's a pattern in its infancy, early communication encourages your workers in the right direction. If it's an entrenched habit, that first report might be an indicator that you're sitting on a time bomb. Ignoring a reported incident in the hope that it's an isolated aberration is running an incalculable risk.

Generally, minor non-compliances and behavioural infractions can be dealt with in three steps: Firstly, raise the issue directly and unambiguously. For example, "I have a slightly tricky issue to raise with you. Another manager mentioned to me that they overheard you telling an off-colour joke in the lunchroom a few days ago. Do you recall anything like that?"

Secondly, wait for their response. They may blush with embarrassment and acknowledge they acted inappropriately, they may defend themselves, they may flatly deny it.

Thirdly, respond to them with a reiteration of the standards expected of them. If they acknowledge their failing you can simply say something like, "I'm hoping it's just a once off. Please be careful to keep jokes and off-the-cuff comments within the bounds of the code of conduct and the Equal Employment Opportunity policy. It's important that our humour doesn't cause problems for other people. If in doubt, leave it unsaid."

If the worker is defensive or denies the allegation, there's no point pushing for an acknowledgement or a confession. A response like, "I'm hearing that you don't think anything like that happened. I'm not here to try to prove who's right or wrong. I do need to emphasise to you that the code of conduct and the Equal Employment Opportunity policy require us to make sure our humour is not offensive to people. I've said what I need to say, and I'm happy leave it there."

If there was no substance to the complaint, your worker will likely be a bit miffed, but will probably get over it soon enough. If there was any truth to the complaint, hopefully they will get the message and mind their manners. If the behaviour becomes a pattern, you've got your supervision notes to show that you addressed the issue with the worker, and that may be important evidence later on.

It cuts both ways

We'll deal with the issue of worker feedback to you in more detail in a later chapter. For now, it's important to note that your worker providing you with thoughtful feedback is a rare gift. Given the inherent power imbalance of the supervisor/worker relationship, it's likely taken some decent courage on their part to share some uncomfortable truth with you.

Even if your worker's feedback appears to be a deflection of criticism relating to their performance or behaviour, it's important to listen carefully and take it seriously. You may need to ask them to hold the thought while you deal with the issue at hand but do whatever it takes to ensure you come back to their feedback and give it your attention. It's important to model maturity in handling negative feedback, otherwise we're holding workers to a higher standard than we hold ourselves.

While I've encouraged you to carefully gather data to provide a factual basis for feedback, supervision is fundamentally a human interaction, requiring you to take broader and more personal issues into consideration. Being a relational process rather than merely a transaction, you'll be required to exercise good judgement in evaluating performance, and be thoughtful in how you communicate.

Summary

- It all begins with clear expectations.
- Immediate, ad hoc feedback is important to reinforce desirable behaviours and to discourage undesirable behaviours.
    - Try to make the positives outweigh the negatives.
- Feedback in formal supervision is about communicating whether your expectations have been met.
    - Clearly communicating your expectations and how performance will be measured is prerequisite.
    - Prepare by gathering performance data, which may include a report from the worker.
    - Provide a supervision agenda that reflects guiding documents like the PD, the organisation's business process and the strategic plan.
    - Talk over the performance data with the worker before reaching an evaluation.
    - Take contextual factors into consideration.
    - Be clear as to where your expectations have been met.
    - Deal with tricky issues promptly.

Discussion

- How does your supervision practice compare with the steps outlined above?
- What indicators might suggest areas for improvement in your supervision practice?

Action

- What will you do in your next supervision meeting to improve the quality of your feedback processes?

Chapter 12
The support side

We've spent quite a while talking about expectations: figuring out what to expect, communicating what you expect, ascertaining whether your expectations are being met, and finally giving feedback to your worker about how well they're meeting your expectations. As you'll remember from the first section, it's important to provide workers with support proportionate to your expectations.

What support might look like

You might be wondering what I mean when I say 'support'. Think back to the example of the elite athlete. Successful athletes tend to surround themselves with people who contribute to their elite performance. They might have a coach for strategy, one for skills and one for conditioning. They might consult a dietician, a physiotherapist, a massage therapist and a doctor. All of these are supportive relationships that assist the athlete to achieve their best.

Support is what you offer the worker to help them achieve at the expected level. Some kinds of support might seem so routine as to be assumed, others you might think are a bit over the top. Remember, your challenge is to get the level right. If your workers are complaining, conflicting, resigning or engaging in various kinds of subterfuge, there a good chance you've got your support levels out of whack. The dilemma lies in determining whether you're giving too little or too much – most of the symptoms listed above could be signs of either. More on that a little later. First, let's look at what support might mean in the organisational setting.

Performance enhancing strategies (WADA-approved)

Your time and attention
I'm kind of an old guy now. I'm supposed to be self-defined, self-contained and self-directed – too old for other people's opinions to matter much to me. Yet when I'm candid with myself, the attention of my boss matters to me. It means something to me when they take up a cause that's important to me and

provide sponsorship. When they cancel or postpone a supervision appointment with me, something inside me interprets their choice as devaluing and dismissive.

Chances are, your time and attention mean a lot to your workers, be they infrequent volunteers, close colleagues or more independent reps and executives. When you set aside time to give them your full attention, you're communicating that your worker and their work are important to you.

Don't skimp on supervision or prioritise other meetings over time with your people. We spent a lot of time in the first section detailing how important supervision is as a responsibility to the organisation – don't forget it's also important to those who work for you.

When I say 'attention', I mean it. I love Susan Scott's phrase, "Be here, prepared to be nowhere else."[46] Time and attention means being fully present and fully interested. For the time you have allocated for supervision, it's important that your behaviour and your choices convey to your worker that they are your only priority. Turn off the phone, kick the door shut or go off-site.

Team time

I used to love the opening sequence of the 1980s cop show *Hill Street Blues*, where the beat cops and undercovers of the precinct gathered for a quick daily briefing. When I worked at Pacific Dunlop, we held our own version with the production team. The stand-up meeting was just that – the team all stood, spoke in bullet point phrases and were careful to keep to the bare minimum information everybody needed to know to get their job done that week. All done in less than ten minutes.

That's not what I mean by 'team time'. Team time is when your team get the opportunity to know one another: their backgrounds, their stories both personal and professional, their quirks and foibles, their hopes and triumphs. Most teams won't have these conversations because of a lack of trust. Yet having these conversations builds trust like no other activity (even more than

---

[46] Scott, S. *Fierce Conversations: Achieving Success at Work and in Life One Conversation at a Time* (Berkley New York 2002), 91.

high-ropes courses). For more on this, check out Lencioni's *The Five Dysfunctions of a Team*.[47]

The sense of community, of belonging, of being known and being valued are powerful supportive factors. As a leader you have the opportunity to foster these dynamics. In an elite sporting club, this interaction on the deeply personal level often happens every week. In high-performing exec teams it might be at a quarterly off-site gathering. I aim for team time on a monthly basis, even if it's only for twenty minutes or so.

Technology

Some of you are groaning as you read this. The sales rep who wants a top-of-the-range hyper-powerful, super slim, eye-wateringly expensive computer so they can do demos and create orders in real time from Timbuktu has almost become a cliché. That's not what I'm talking about.

Let me tell you a true story. Someone close to me works for a company that's a household name in Australia. The company retails to the residential building and renovation market. The company has been using the same computer software for decades – patching and tacking on functions in an ad hoc kind of way. Some commands are text-based, some arrow-key-based and others point and click. A transaction that on modern systems would be scan-and-swipe seamless from point of sale to warehouse dispatch to stock replenishment report takes up to half an hour to complete. A new showroom staff member takes an average of six months to sufficiently master the digital monstrosity to be able to complete sales independently. Oddly enough, one of Australia's major telcos uses the very latest version of the same software and it works like a Swiss watch.

Not only does this system cost the company hundreds of thousands in lost sales due to poor stock control and the inability to report staff making random discounts, it costs thousands of staff hours in inefficiencies and is a major source of staff dissatisfaction leading to turnover. The management of this company simply ignores complaints from their staff. The company cannot accurately estimate what the antiquated systems costs them in lost opportunity or staff turnover. It doesn't even know what it costs in terms of lapsed orders because the software does not have the functionality to produce

---

[47] Lencioni, P. *The Five Dysfunctions of a Team* (Jossey-Bass San Francisco 2002).

the reports required. This scenario is the antitheses of what I mean by using technology to support staff.

As I'm writing this paragraph, the planet is being gripped by the COVID-19 crisis (I guess that really dates the book). The only way I can conduct the coaching and training that makes up the lion's share of my job is through online video conferencing. The office is a ghost town, with most of the staff working from home. Over the weekend one of my staff ran a tutorial on the use of a video conferencing platform for training and governance meetings. People from all over the state participated. My team member was working from his study in suburban Melbourne. One participant was sitting up in bed, two hundred kilometres away.

The current challenge has demonstrated the incredible flexibility that technology affords us. Organisations that have been quick to embrace the advantages and efficiencies of communications technology have been able to respond quickly to the restrictions forced upon us by the COVID-19 pandemic. The technological laggards will probably not survive.

Empowering your workers with appropriate technology could afford them greater efficiencies, greater flexibility to juggle the demands of modern life, and the ability to adapt to challenges that the globalised world throws our way from time to time.

As a supervisor you should have enough knowledge of your worker's job to have a fair idea of what technology could do to make them more effective and efficient. Who knows, you may even make their life a little easier. If you can't determine this, you would do well to have the conversation with your worker.

Listen, and don't make excuses. Sometimes an investment of a few thousand dollars can lead to tens of thousands in improved performance. In the case of the company described earlier, a new integrated Enterprise Resource Program (i.e. company-wide computer system) with multi-site functionality would probably cost north of $200k to implement. I'm guessing the return-on-investment period would be under a year.

Training
Given that HR is my professional field, you would expect me to commend the value of training to you as a supportive mechanism. But not all training is

helpful or supportive, and some of what passes for training is quite simply a colossal waste of time and money.

Most large organisations have some kind of program of training for risk management, most of which is about exposing the worker to a mind-numbing quantum of content for the purpose of mitigating risks in relation to health and safety, equal opportunity, workplace bullying and the like. That kind of training is not supportive. It might be necessary for the covering of the collective managerial posterior, but your workers will grind their way through it while accumulating resentments, or simply refuse to do it and wait to see if their boss has the ticker to confront them on it.

At the other end of the scale is the cushy conference trip or specialised training retreat. Curiously, these are usually held at resorts in places like Port Douglas rather than, say a suburban community college during term break. The value of these events is usually estimated in terms of 'networking' and 'staying current'. Somehow these two outcomes are facilitated by immoderate consumption of top-shelf booze and enough time to get in eighteen holes of golf – every day.

That kind of training is not supportive either. It might be a reward or an entitlement, but the likelihood of such an experience genuinely advancing your worker's development is in most cases a little above nil, other than they might get headhunted to another organisation. Meanwhile, the litany of risks doesn't bear contemplation.

Supportive training does two main things. Firstly, it helps your worker do their job. In the current environment, I was super keen to learn how to run training events on a teleconferencing platform. I'm due to have my first go with about sixty participants in two days' time. The seminar that my team member ran was timely and helpful training. It means I'll do a better job.

Doing a better job is not just about getting more return for the money and resources you invest in your worker. It's about your worker feeling more competent, more confident and therefore, less anxious. We'll further unpack anxiety and its influence on performance a little latter. For now, let's think about your worker's experience of their role. Anxiety is an unpleasant emotion. All of us experience it and we all take steps to avoid it. It steers us toward self-preservation. That's how it works.

As we discussed earlier when we looked at burnout, anxiety comes from a wide variety of sources and it's almost impossible to apportion which anxieties come from where. To be human is to be anxious to some degree. That doesn't mean it's okay for work to be unduly anxiety producing.

Feeling incompetent or ill-equipped to do what's expected is a major source of workplace anxiety. If work is an unpleasant experience due to the anxiety it creates, your employee or volunteer will likely struggle to maintain their commitment and motivation. (Unless of course they're acutely dependent on their job and have no other options, in which case the anxiety associated with leaving might just be greater than the anxiety generated by staying). Ensuring your people are appropriately trained can help to keep anxiety to a sustainable level.

Skills-based training doesn't need to be long, expensive or off-site. Most employees benefit from some polishing up on self-management and personal effectiveness. I worked on this with my team by reading a book together – we discussed a couple of chapters each time we met as a team. The cost of a book is cheap professional development, and it helped my team use their time and energy more efficiently.

Some people spend a lot of time using programs like Microsoft Word and Excel with amazing inefficiency (we've all read those documents with a bazillion spaces and carriage returns because the author didn't know how to set tabs or force a page break). A few ten-minute micro lessons to correct a gap in expertise can result in hours saved. Often the expertise to provide these micro lessons is already resident in your organisation. You just need to be intentional about it.

Train your people to be good at what they do. Everyone wins.

Secondly, supportive training can be developmental. Some supervisors will assign a worker a responsibility for which they're not quite competent, then support them with some mentoring and training as they stretch to grow into the new dimension of their job. While this carries a bit of risk and needs to be done carefully to ensure the worker is not pushed beyond their capacity to grow and adapt, it can lead to workers blossoming into levels of expertise and contribution well beyond their starting point. It's an example of raising the expectation and making the corresponding increase in support.

140

Developmental training is not so much about being good at your current job as much as it is about growing into your next job – be it a step to a more responsible gig or an expanded version of your current one. People express reservations about developmental training, worrying that it means training people up for the job with your competitor they'll resign to take. Let me assure you, high potential people will invest in their own development no matter what. If you invest in people, they will be more likely to seek opportunities with your organisation – out of loyalty, convenience, a sense of the-devil-you-know, or a complex interplay of all three.

If your organisation can't make space for people to grow and advance, the most proactive and ambitious will eventually move on. There may not be much you can do to keep them. However, if your organisation develops a reputation for developing great people, high potential people will be attracted to join. Good development is part of the price you pay to attract talent. Meanwhile, a culture that encourages people to develop and to realise their potential fosters a sense of optimism that is in itself supportive.

Coaching

Coaching has become a bit of a buzzword over the past decade, and like many other buzzwords, it's in danger of being stripped of meaning. So let me define the term and then we'll get into applying it to the supportive side of the supervision relationship.

My best attempt at a definition is: 'Coaching is a relational process to facilitate a person improving their performance'. John Whitmore puts it this way: "Coaching is unlocking people's potential to maximize their own performance. It is helping them to learn rather than teaching them."[48]

Coaching, for this part of the conversation, is not remedial in the sense that it's not directed toward underperformers and underachievers to correct their deficits. I like to explain it this way: "How many support staff do you reckon Ashleigh Barty has?" (At the time of writing, Ash is the World No 1 in women's tennis). Most people could list off a main coach, perhaps a conditioning coach,

---

[48] Whitmore, J. *Coaching for Performance: GROWing Human Potential and Purpose: The Principles and Practice of Coaching and Leadership* (Nicholas Brealey, London, 1992), 11.

a masseur, a dietician, a physio, perhaps a mentor and a psych. They may not be exclusive to the Barty Party, but there would be people playing these parts in Ash's success. Then I ask, "Gee with all that help, do think she's in the remedial group?"

Then I ask, "How many support staff does a Wednesday afternoon hit-and-giggle player have?"

People who are serious about their performance seek out the best supportive relationships, and the most obvious one is a coach. Coaching is for those committed to being their best.

As a supervisor, providing a suitably qualified coach for your staff is an investment both in their immediate performance and their long-term development.

In the final section we'll talk about using coaching as a supervisory technique.

Access to experts

The knowledge economy is not confined to the corporate sector and Silicon Valley. Just being open for business, whether for profit or purpose, requires a huge diversity of applied knowledge. Even small, grass-roots community organisations now have a vast array of compliance obligations ranging from financial and taxation compliance to public safety and family violence reporting. Each compliance area comprises several subsets of specialist knowledge.

Many small businesses have all the above obligations plus a range of prerequisite skill sets in marketing, IT and HR in addition to whatever specialist knowledge is inherent in delivering the organisation's products and services.

Most smaller organisations don't have dedicated specialists in these essential fields, let alone subsets like website development, databasing, OHS, or employee relations. Most people in small businesses just do their best and hope they're more or less compliant.

Even in larger organisations, it's not uncommon to lack the specialist expertise needed to deal with the predictable and perhaps even unavoidable challenges that crop up within the business. (I've come across organisations with north of five hundred employees and no HR function – mind boggling).

For an employee with little IT expertise, trying resolve a tech problem in an organisation with no IT department may waste days at a time or several hours per week over a period of months, trying to solve or work around their challenge. This is not only terribly inefficient (and therefore costly), but also a stress-inducing morale-killer.

Likewise, a first-line team leader trying to deal with one of those play-the-system workers will probably be losing hair and sleep trying to get them to do as they're expected. In an organisation without resident specialised HR expertise, that team leader is on their way to becoming ill, resigning or simply giving up and letting aberrant workers have their way.

In various ways it makes sense to support your workers with specialist expertise, even if you need to buy it in from a consultant, employer group or industry body. Sure, those services can be expensive on an hourly basis, but they generally pay for themselves in multiples once you calculate all the knock-on costs of not providing them.

When a worker can have their IT issues quickly resolved, get the advice and reassurance needed to deal with thorny people problems, or more generally engage a short-term specialist to do specialised work, their sense of reassurance grows, their well-being is protected and they have more time and mental bandwidth available to do their core functions.

Helping staff – executive and research assistants

Providing ongoing support staff is an obvious way to ramp up support for a worker. It's also a somewhat vexed issue. Everyone would love to have a gopher to whom they can flick their tedious tasks. But it's not always the most efficient use of financial resources. Let me say upfront I've had staff ask for an assistant only to be met with my flat refusal and a recommendation that they read some of the aforementioned books about personal organisation and productivity. I don't have an executive assistant (EA) and I've never asked for one, despite having a reasonably demanding schedule of appointments and a decent spread of responsibilities. An assistant must clearly deliver measurable value for money, and that's usually possible only in cases where workers have very broad or highly specialised roles.

All that said, if you're paying an executive a package of $200k and they're spending a good chunk of their time on tasks that could be undertaken at the same or a better level of efficiency by an assistant on $80k, you might wonder if you could pull some higher yielding activity out of them if they could shed some of the mundane stuff.

So, when is it smart to provide an assistant? Here are some situations to think about.

Some jobs have a lot of personal logistics and administration involved. Jobs with a lot of travel or with a high number of meetings involving people from outside the organisation bring a lot of tiresome juggling to get everyone in the same physical or virtual space at the same time. There are apps that help cut down the complexity, but they don't eliminate it. In these cases, an EA shared amongst a team of execs might be worth considering (especially if they're charged with finding some savings on travel costs; it's amazing how much you can save when the person booking and the person travelling are not the same person).

Some general management (GM) jobs have a lot of disparate domains of activity that need to be coordinated, especially if there's a major project or change intervention being initiated. General management can really consume an executive's mental resources, because it requires working in a range of disciplines where the executive has a passing knowledge while they interact with department heads who specialise in their respective disciplines. There are a lot of ideas and concepts to integrate and coordinate into a functioning whole.

Add to that the seemingly endless list of small tasks and details to be tracked, scheduled and executed. Some will need to wait for information or triggering actions from outside the GM's office. These may not be rocket science, but they need to be attended to. They usually don't require the absolute pinnacle of the executive's intellectual prowess, but the sheer volume of details can be draining. An EA might provide a GM with the support they need to more efficiently and effectively do what only they can do.

Flipping to the specialist field, disciplines like engineering, law and the sciences are usually a curious combination of the acute and the tedious. A leader in one of these fields may devise brilliant solutions, formulate scintillating arguments or achieve breakthrough discoveries that bring to bear cerebral capabilities of stratospheric amplitude. Yet their brilliant achievements rely on information that can only be acquired by tedious, methodical and disciplined research.

It doesn't make a whole lot of economic sense to have your very best talent doing mundane work. Just bear in mind that sometimes mundane work is a bit of a mental break for the intense intellectual rigour in which a specialist might otherwise be engaged.

Also bear in mind that the communication processes and supervision requirements an assistant will bring introduces a degree of inefficiency to the management process, on top of the additional expense.

When considering an assistant, it's worth seriously interrogating the question, 'What will I get for the extra cost?' If you have in mind tasks that nobody is currently doing, it's fairly easy to figure out what the value of these tasks being completed might be. If a GM or specialist is currently performing these tasks, you'll need a pretty clear idea of what that they might do instead.

If you have an exec who's starting to show some signs of being under too much demand (just make sure that *is* the cause) an EA for a couple of days a week might bring the balance back. What you get for your money is an exec who gets their creative energy back, and is less likely to resign, take extended sick leave, or mentally check out.

If you provide a research assistant to a lawyer, they might be able to run more cases simultaneously. It would be worth putting in some metrics to measure it. An assistant to a specialist like a biochemist or a demographer might mean they can oversee more projects, or the assistant might be writing their research grant applications while they execute on their current grants.

Whatever the situation, make sure there is a clear and measurable benefit, and if possible, put in place the mechanisms to measure it before you agree to appoint an assistant. People tend to be overly optimistic in projecting the benefits, so be prepared for some ambit. I've seen too many cases of people taking on assistants and finding things for them to do, with no measurable benefit to the organisation. It's one of the primary ways bureaucracies become bloated and processes become convoluted.

Celebrations and acknowledgement

Acknowledging and celebrating achievement can do wonders for a worker's sense of being recognised and appreciated. At the same time it can foster resentment, rivalry and even sabotage on the part of others. For people of a particular temperament, public acknowledgement at a company town hall meeting could be all their Christmases come at once. For their more introverted colleagues, being made the focus of attention could literally make them throw up.

Sincere encouragement can be balm for the soul. But if a worker suspects the encouragement is insincere or manipulative, it can have the opposite effect. Some cultures respond well to pep rallies. Others – including Aussies – are more likely to meet unbridled positivity with a degree of scepticism.

So how do you do encouragement in a way that's actually encouraging?

I'm going to restrict the answer to personal encouragement and acknowledgement. As I outlined above, public acknowledgement is kind of fraught. I believe it should be reserved for special occasions, like the end of a huge project or the achievement of a milestone. Personal recognition can be tailored, immediate and much more relational.

To begin with, figure out how well you know the person. As their boss, I'm hoping you know them reasonably well, but I'm not assuming so. The better you know a person, the more you can take into account their temperament, tastes and life circumstances.

Now let's look at some options. The most basic is the 'catch 'em doing the right thing' treatment. You can do this immediately or in the routine supervision meeting. Something like, "I saw you taking extra time with that elderly gentleman at the service desk today. I saw in his face how much he appreciated your care. Thanks for putting in the extra effort with people who need it."

Another might be a simple email along the lines of, "Just got through talking to your client (name them). They really appreciated your attention to detail in your last interaction. It means a lot. Thanks heaps." I got a text a bit like that (but even briefer) from my boss just this week. I tend not to respond much to encouragement, but it really made my day.

I had a team member who was battling some really significant challenges in their personal life, as well as their work responsibilities which required a high degree of initiative. This team member was a bit older and before joining my team had been for years isolated and left to their own devices.

They saw me as a bit of a tough customer. (I'm reasonably tall, bearded and, being a Melbournian, tend to wear black most of the time. I've been told I look like a biker). My team member often came to supervision worried I was going to roast them for not getting through everything on their work plan. I never did, but one time they seemed particularly nervous.

As I worked through the points of the plan, there were undoubtedly a few things left incomplete. Yet the team member had made good progress on most of the key points, especially those that impacted progress on the strategy and the metrics on their dashboard. I took time to point out how much the team member had achieved, and that the big-ticket items were more-or-less on track.

I paused, looked them in the eye and said, "I realise you're up against some tough challenges at home, and that must take up a good part of your mental energy. You've done better than I had hoped."

The team member's shoulders dropped from their position of hunched tension. They let out long, noisy breath of relief. I watched the anxiety subside in their facial expression. I think I saw a twinkling of tears. From there we could talk through the work plan for the coming month, setting some useful goals and targets.

For this worker, the balance of support and expectation meant being quite overt and explicit with my affirmation, very brief and gentle about the missed targets (recognising that they were already beating themselves up) and redirecting the conversation toward goal-focused thinking.

Less recommended

Company-wide gifts and bonuses
Some organisations use gifts or money as a way to say 'thanks' and offer support. Like public recognition, this option is fraught. If the company has had a good year and made a tidy surplus by all means share it around, provided you can agree on a fair and equitable way of calculating it – which is where the

complexity comes in. If you opt for a simple percentage of salary (e.g. everybody gets a bonus that's 2% of their annual remuneration), the people at the top (who probably get the best of all the other perks anyway) will get the biggest bonus, triggering resentment in those at the bottom of the organisational chart. The rich get richer and the poor get the picture. The net impact is that the people at the bottom feel less support and the impact on motivation is negative.

I once chaired the board of a not-for-profit that had a couple of years of surprisingly large surpluses, thanks largely to a sector-wide shortage of suitable staff to support our steady expansion. This made recruitment difficult and slow. Our funding steadily increased while our payroll stayed more-or-less stable. Our staff stepped up and carried the extra load until we finally found the right staff to fill our vacancies. The board decided to give every full-time worker on the payroll the same bonus, from CEO down to the office assistant. Part-timers received pro rata, and new hires received pro rata based on how much of the financial year they'd been with us.

The CEO held a town hall meeting to announce the bonuses and explain the pro rata rationale. She used the opportunity to acknowledge that the surplus was the result of the people's effort and diligence, pointing out the specifics of organisation-wide performance like careful cost control, increased quality assurance compliance, and smooth adoption of a new IT platform. She emphasised her appreciation and admiration for her people. Then she assured the whole staff of two things. Firstly, there was an ongoing and concerted effort to keep recruiting to alleviate the high workload, and that the bonus was a one-off, not the 'new normal'. Although there were a few murmurs about who deserved more or less, overall, the impact was positive.

Many organisations offer a Christmas hamper or bonus. Do this two years in a row and from then on it's an entitlement, meaning its supportive value is reduced.

Performance bonuses
Other organisations offer financial bonuses for hitting performance targets. While a widespread practice at the executive level, these become just part and parcel of the remuneration package rather than a supportive mechanism. They also have a tendency to incentivise unforeseen and sometimes unconscionable action.

At the more basic levels of the organisation, financial incentives are generally pretty small and often seen by workers like a carrot dangled before the gormless donkey to make it go faster.

Performance bonuses might be motivating, but they're not supportive.

Thoughtful gifts
Personal gifts are another tricky area. Lavish gifts are really another means of performance bonus, but with less obvious tax implications than cash.

When it comes to gifts, it's the thought that counts. Small but thoughtful gifts can be incredibly supportive, especially if it shows the boss really knows and 'gets' their worker. I once worked with an American woman who had been invited to keynote a conference my organisation was running. She asked to be driven to a couple of different thrift shops (or op shops as we Aussies call them – shops that are run by charities selling donated goods). She was on the lookout for quirky little trinkets to give to the important people in her life – things that reflected their interests and personalities.

An inexpensive gift that shows real thought goes a lot further in expressing support and appreciation than a bulk-purchased gift card. Such gifts are best confined to smaller, tighter-knit teams where the gift is an expression of appreciation of the person rather than a reward for performance.

The risk with personalising things is the possibility of being accused of favouritism. Proceed with caution.

Support that feels like expectation
I've worked with a few organisations that have recognised their tendency to be higher on expectations than support, and have sought to correct the balance by putting on events or functions to say 'thank-you', or offering 'development opportunities' – often outside of work hours or in addition to the time expected of volunteers. For some (often younger people without family commitments) these are valuable and positive. To those who are already under the pump with workload and other commitments such as kids or study, it's just another obligation, and is perceived as exacerbating the imbalance of expectation and support.

If you ask someone to turn up at something, even if it's to be nice to them, you're still adding to expectation. Think carefully before opting for this means of support.

Remedial or therapeutic kinds of support

Extra contact

I'm writing this chapter from home isolation due to the COVID-19 crisis. All of my team are in similar confinement. The general level of anxiety in my organisation, like the rest of society, is quite elevated. I'm really pleased with how my team has stepped up, taken initiative and adapted their various service offers both to comply with social distancing requirements, and also to provide additional support to our clients.

I've doubled the frequency and shortened the duration of team meetings, providing extra time in the meeting to just catch up, and also being mindful of the need to keep my team goal focused. I've also made a point of calling each of them regularly to just check in and make sure they're doing okay. Extra contact is reassuring. It helps maintain calm so people have maximum mental bandwidth (we'll see in the next section how anxiety interferes with intellectual functioning).

If a worker is under particular challenge, whether from their work responsibilities or issues outside of work, increasing the frequency of contact can be a helpful way of supporting them through a tough time. This simple tweak lifts the supportive side of supervision in a number of ways.

If supervision is more frequent, your worker will likely be dealing with a shorter list of items to follow up. There are fewer things to cover off before they meet with you again, which means more opportunity to provide a little 'steering and brakes' if they're heading off track, or provide reassurance if they're mostly meeting expectation.

More frequent contact means you'll have a more accurate picture of your worker's state of mind, their capacity and vulnerabilities. You can adjust your expectations and tailor your supportive effort accordingly.

If you can take a coaching approach to your supervision, your extra contact is an opportunity for your worker to 'borrow your brain' to help them think through their challenges.

Counselling

Many organisations in Australia have an Employee Assistance Program (EAP) that includes a small number of free, confidential counselling sessions. While an EAP is a good start, there's not much evidence that 3-4 sessions with a general practice counsellor will do anything more than provide some temporary emotional support. (Most of the studies that validate psycho-therapeutic frameworks like Cognitive Behaviour Therapy stretch for a minimum of twenty sessions. The highest determining factor in the success of psychotherapies is the quality of the therapeutic alliance – the relationship between the client and the therapist. It's pretty hard to build a sufficiently productive alliance in three sessions).

When one of my team or a client has shown some warning signs that they could use the assistance of a counsellor, I'll usually speak plainly and directly with them about their vulnerability. Often, I'll let them know that my current coach is also a registered psychologist (I try to practice what I preach). I'll sometimes observe that the sanest thing to do when one is vulnerable is to get a little help.

I would rather spend my professional development budget on some psychotherapy if I think it will be supportive, rather than an expensive training event where an anxious team member won't be able to fully engage.

Coaching and mentoring

We spoke before about coaching as a means of building a worker's capacity and performance. That kind of coaching is about maximising potential. Here I want to spend a little time thinking about coaching and mentoring for workers who are just struggling to keep up.

As a supervisor, it's your job to keep the expected standards of performance in the worker's field of view. You might amend your expectations to accommodate challenges faced by the worker, but for the most part it's your job to gain the contribution from your worker that represents a good return on the time, money and other resources invested into the worker. As a boss, you have an agenda; you can't be entirely neutral.

A coach or mentor from outside the organisation can play a supportive role separate from the organisation's expectations. The worker can tell their coach things they may not want to tell you for fear of repercussions. An outside coach is in a better position to help your worker calm down and become thoughtful about their challenges, because the coach has no power to fire them, demote them, overlook them for promotion, wall them off from resources or squeeze their budget.

In the safe and neutral third space your worker has a better shot at becoming more objective, developing a greater awareness of themselves and their circumstances, and taking more responsibility for their own part of their challenges.

Some bosses get a bit nervous about their team talking to a coach. "What if my worker says stuff that's critical of me and makes me look bad?" They almost certainly will, but in the case of an external coach, you have little to lose, and a lot to gain.

How much could you gain? Perhaps more than money can buy – and we'll talk more about that the next chapter.

Summary

- The primary means of support to your worker is your time and attention, and a positive team culture.
- Support mechanisms for optimal performance include:
  - Access to appropriate technology
  - Training and coaching
  - Access to expert counsel and assistance
  - Support staff
- Personal acknowledgement and celebration can be very supportive if tailored to the worker's temperament.
- Less effective mechanisms for support include company-wide bonuses and gifts.
- Support for struggling workers includes:
  - Extra supervisory contact
  - Counselling
  - Coaching and mentoring

Discussion

- What's the one means of support that would deliver the most value in helping your workers move toward optimal performance?
- Would the cost of delivering that support be returned in the value of the performance improvement?

Action

- What will you do in the next 30 days to ensure your workers experience the support necessary to perform to expectations?

Chapter 13
The holy grail – discretionary work effort

The effort money won't buy
What's the difference between the worker who does barely enough to avoid getting performance managed, and the worker who brings all their energy, creativity and perseverance to work every day?

It's not about the money – well, not exactly. You can have a clock puncher and the eager beaver who get paid the same. Research by Edwin Locke found that money can be a powerful motivator to higher performance, but only when a series of specific conditions are met, such as the employee being motivated by money (not everyone is, especially once their basic needs are met), the performance gain and the financial benefit are directly linked, and the amount of extra money on offer is significant to the employee.[49] On top of that, to put these factors to work for you, you'll need a fair bit of budgetary and human resource policy discretion. Most of us don't have that.

It's possible, legal and ethical, to elicit superior performance from your workers without any change to their pay and without coercing them. It's about creating an environment where they choose to contribute a greater effort at their own discretion.

Everyone's a volunteer
So far, I've used a number of different terms for the people you supervise: employees, volunteers, staff, workers. I've very intentionally avoided making too much distinction between those whom you pay and those who volunteer. Both kinds of worker are serving in your organisation because it serves some kind of purpose for them – to make a living, to make a difference, to feel a sense of belonging.

---

[49] Locke, E. A. *Toward a theory of task motivation and incentives* Organizational Behavior and Human Performance Vol 3 Edition 2 1968.

Because I spend most of my time in the not-for-profit sector, I've had dozens of conversations about the difference between paid staff and volunteers. People tell me how hard it is working with volunteers because you can't expect much of them and you can't make demands of them the way you can an employee.

Now it's true that the work-for-pay bargain means a boss can bang the table and insist a worker does as they say. A boss can hold the prospect of a worker's ongoing employment over their head like the sword of Damocles, forcing them to comply. But to use that approach any more than rarely is a failure of leadership – it's pushing from the back rather than leading from the front.

The real genius of supervision lies in treating everyone like a volunteer. Yes, you read that right. Any boss with a modicum of management acumen can extract the bare minimum work effort out of a worker. The boss worth their salary is the one who can consistently gain the extra effort that the worker voluntarily gives because they choose to do so.

Engagement

Right at the outset I introduced you to the Gallup organisation's research on worker engagement. Gallup spends a lot of resources on demographic and organisational research: matters pertaining to politics and business. However, they also do a lot of work in the not-for-profit space. Gallup's research points to constituent engagement – whether employees, volunteers or members – as a consistent success factor across both for-profit and not-for-profit sectors.[50] Engagement carries the idea of a sense of partnership, of shared understanding and goals, and of mutual benefit. Engagement, according to Gallup is fuelled by clear and positive mutual understanding between the constituent and the organisational leadership along four dimensions:

- What can the constituent expect from the organisation? – What do *I* get out of this?
- What's does the organisation expect of the constituent? – What's my contribution here?

---

[50] Cited by Winseman, A. L. *Growing and Engaged Church* (Gallup, New York 2018).

- Does the constituent have a sense of belonging here? – Do I matter, can you see me as a person beyond a unit of labour?
- How can both the constituent and the organisation grow? – How can we become more than they already are?

We've already spoken at length on expectation, and we'll talk about it some more in the next section. We'll talk a little more about belonging in a minute, and we'll address growth in detail in the final section. According to Gallup, engagement is crucial to gaining discretionary work effort. Engagement makes for a far richer and more mutually beneficial relationship between the worker and organisation.

This discretionary work effort is not about the extra unpaid hours many workers put in nowadays because it's prerequisite to being made permanent instead of casual or short-term. Neither is it 'discretionary' if it's what's expected to gain a promotion, or to avoid being top of the list when 'rightsizing' or 'restructuring' means a cut in headcount. That kind of extra effort has an element of coercion about it. I believe it's simply unethical for employers like legal firms and retailers to use these kinds of tactics to squeeze extra effort out of their people even if there's a promotion or a partnership on offer a few years down the track.

'Discretionary' means the effort beyond the minimum, given as a choice without coercion and without expectation of being repaid or rewarded with security, tenure or advancement. The discretionary work effort is the work an employee *volunteers* to their employer.

For the supervisor, the critical question at this juncture is one of motivation: why would a worker voluntarily put in extra effort with no prospect of recompense?

The answer will be as unique as the employee. In the not-for-profit space, lots of people forego the much higher salaries they could command in the commercial sphere for the sake of a cause about which they're passionate. Most nurses I know go above and beyond because the needs of vulnerable people are right in front of them and it seems right to do. Similarly with teachers. In these cases it's more about the cause than the boss.

Yet I've worked in manufacturing environments, retail companies and consultancies – all of which existed to return a profit to their investors – and where people put in much more than they had to. Conversely, I've seen workplaces where the workers observe a strict 'work to rule' policy and do as little as they must to avoid getting fired.

It comes down to culture. Culture comes down to leadership and that's where we get back to you, the boss. We spent a fair bit of time talking in the first section about being a leader worth following. A boss needs – at least to a certain degree – to have their own act together in order to have credibility and congruence. Not many people will volunteer their discretionary work effort to the boss who says, "Do as I say, not as I do."

Care

Earlier in this section I spoke about the boss who's a gift to their organisation because they make working there a great experience. You'll remember Deb who lit up the work environment at the RSPCA. Now let me take that one step further. This will be a 'duh!' for some and a revelation to others. The boss who consistently elicits the discretionary work effort is the boss who cares. Not just subscribing to the idea that people are unique and valuable and perhaps even sacred, but who actually makes an effort to build the conviction in the minds of their workers that they actually matter to their boss.

For some bosses, care comes so naturally that they're only partially aware of their day-to-day actions that communicate to their people how much they matter. For the rest of us – and I would put myself in the remedial class here – communicating care requires effort and intentionality – perhaps even planning a fair way ahead.

To explain what I mean, let me first give you glimpse of my natural tendencies. When I complete temperament surveys like Myers-Briggs Type Indicator or DiSC, the picture that emerges is of a task focused, impatient introvert. I'm not all that much fun at parties. I have a strong internal regard for people, but I'm not naturally inclined to express it.

I have to work at showing my team that I care. I'm not trying to pretend to care, I'm trying to become better at communicating that care in ways that speak to them. This is how it plays out.

Today is Easter Monday 2020. It's the last day of a short period of annual leave for me. The COVID-19 crisis still rages, so I've been stuck at home, trying to get ahead of my writing goals and chip away at the house renovation that will probably never end. My diary tomorrow is littered with the tasks and meetings typical of a manager with a small team and a handful of projects to manage.

At 9:00 AM tomorrow, the time when isolated workers are expected to open for business, I've slotted an hour for pastoral care calls: first to my team members and then to some of my clients whom I know are single and will be finding the forced isolation of this time really challenging. I really do care, but I have to be quite mechanical to prioritise showing it.

Now the reason I've given you an insight into the weird way I function is because, in times of high anxiety, even people who are more naturally inclined to communicate their caring can lose the habit. We can get so preoccupied with the things that make us anxious that we forget those simple gestures that communicate care and appreciation. What follows runs the risk of being like teaching your granny to suck eggs, but I'm writing it here because, particularly in the midst of the current crisis, I've watched leaders simply forget. I know it seems basic, but I encourage you to take some concrete steps to show care – schedule it in your diary if you have to.

- Say 'Thank you' – it's so obvious yet so uncommon. Every time you have formal supervision or a significant interaction with any of your team, or anyone who serves your team, be thankful. Martin Seligman's work on authentic happiness suggests that being thankful is as good for your wellbeing as it is for the person you're thanking.[51]
- Notice when your workers *do* put in the discretionary work effort and acknowledge it. Any time a worker goes above and beyond (and I do this with people who are not my staff as well as my own team), specifically point out what you saw them doing and say how much you appreciate it. For example:
    - "Mate, I noticed how hard you pushed to get that clearance through in time. I really appreciate the effort and persistence you put in."

---

[51] Seligman, M. *Authentic Happiness: Using the New Positive Psychology to Realize Your Potential for Lasting Fulfilment* (The Free Press, New York 2002).

- "Hey Jen, I watched you deal with that cranky customer just now. You really kept your cool and managed to be kind even when he was being obnoxious."
- Make contact just for the purpose of finding out how your worker is doing. Get to know the things that put them under particular pressure and inquire about them specifically – not framed as an accountability question, but as a pastoral care question. For example:
  - "Hey Tommy, just calling to see how you're going." (And, after a few more general wellbeing questions), "I know your mum's been in and out of hospital over the past few months, how's she faring?"
- Be particularly attentive to the emotional tone of your worker's communications. If you see a shift from their normal style, or if there's emotional content that suggests things aren't going well for them, make personal contact to check in with them – soon. If you have a worker who's normally calm and business-like who suddenly starts using words like 'frustrated' or 'sabotaged', they might be just having a bad day or they might be on the edge of a meltdown. Don't make assumptions, call them immediately, even if it makes you a few minutes late to your next meeting.

I know the above actions are not exactly breakthrough management techniques, and that spelling them out might seem a little redundant – except the majority of bosses forget to do them, so busy are they with the rest of their preoccupations. Remember your people *are* your job; if you're too busy to do the above, you're just too busy. You'll either need to grow your capacity or get some of your current tasks off your plate.

Involvement

People commit to what they're involved in, not the other way around. Read that last statement again and think about it for a minute. We're hoping our workers will volunteer their discretionary work effort, meaning we're wanting them to increase their commitment to the organisation. The simplest way to gain greater commitment is to invite greater involvement.

The more of a person's capacity you can involve, the more committed they'll become. This may require a shift in your thinking. Most of us assume people don't want to be asked to help. Yet, the evidence seems to point the other way.

Asking for help carries the implication that you think the person you're inviting has something valuable to contribute. Imagine asking a man to show his strength by loosening the lid on a pickle jar. As a bloke I can assure you that any invitation to show my strength will be enthusiastically accepted.

Now imagine your workers and the members of your community organisation all have their particular 'pickle jars' they're good at 'opening'. For some people it's cooking up a banquet, for others it's interior aesthetics, for someone else it's digital communications, and yet another it might be creating systems to organise things. You need to be thoughtful here, but I encourage you to assume people like to be invited to use their knowledge and skills. Keep an eye and an ear out for the things people like to do and see if you can invite them to use what they have to serve the organisation. If they decline, you've lost nothing. If they accept, you've given them a chance to shine, a chance to be thanked and you've deepened their commitment to you and the organisation.

Ownership

'Ownership' has become something of a buzzword in contemporary leadership and management theory. Organisational systems and learning guru Peter Senge uses the terms 'enrolment' and 'commitment' to describe the idea of people wanting the vision of the organisation to come to pass and being willing to do whatever is required to bring it to reality.[52] Another way of thinking about it is 'internalisation' – the vision of the organisation making the transition from an externally applied idea that needs constant reinforcement to an internally held conviction that's 'owned' personally. Once a person owns the vision, all they need is resourcing and guidance.

Yet ownership goes beyond simply internalising a vision as one's own. It also includes the idea of power to make decisions. Let me illustrate. By now you've probably guessed that I'm a bit of a car buff. On the weekend I like to drive my 1963 Holden around the nearby hills. This car is mine. I removed and repaired, cleaned, painted, polished or replaced every piece of it. I just don't have the same sense of ownership for the rental car that I pick up at the airport, drive around to my appointments and then hand back at the end of the day. Sure, I'm careful and responsible with the car (have you seen what

---

[52] Senge, Peter M. *The Fifth Discipline: The Art and Practice of the Learning Organization* rev. edn (Currency, New York, 2006).

rental companies charge if you so much as scratch a hubcap?), but I have no sense of ownership. No one waxes a rental car.

I can choose what I do with my Holden. If I'm not happy with how a panel has come up, I can decide to strip it to bare metal, massage it into shape and repaint it. I'm not sure the rental company would let me do that with their car and I'm not sure I would want to.

M. Scott Peck uses the word *cathexis* to describe internalisation of an idea or a person or an object,[53] as one would fall in love with a person or a pet or their garden (or a car). He pulled the concept from Freudian theory, which links it to human drives originating in the libido (that's Freud for you). The Merriam-Webster dictionary defines *cathexis* as '...investment of mental or emotional energy in a person, object, or idea.'[54] It comes from a Greek word meaning 'holding' or 'retaining'. Peck uses term *'cathect'* to convey the idea of taking a representation or even an idealisation of a person, object, or idea into oneself. If you've ever fallen in love, you know what I mean. While you can't own your beloved, you have a sense that they're *yours.* If you really want to elicit your worker's discretionary work effort, you need them to own their job, to *cathect* the job (although falling in love with their job is a bit too much to hope for).

Workers are more likely to invest mental or emotional energy into their jobs if they have the ability to influence their job – if there's scope for their emotional investment to lead to a decision for change. Think of a worker investing sufficient mental and emotional energy in their job that they begin to imagine how they could be more efficient or more effective. Imagine they approach their boss to discuss the possibilities. When you think about it, it's not all that different to the worker asking the boss on a date. How that boss responds could crush the worker's soul or make it sing. The worker is taking a risk by putting themselves out there.

Imagine the boss hears enough of the worker's thinking to register that this will involve their own mental effort, and bushes them off with, "Nah, that'll never work. Just do your job and everything will be fine." The worker's heart sinks. Like the jilted suitor, they return to their tasks, deflated and

---

[53] Peck, M. S. *The Road Less Travelled: A New Psychology of Love, Traditional Values and Spiritual Growth* (Simon & Schuster, New York 1978).
[54] https://www.merriam-webster.com/dictionary/cathexis.

demotivated. At lunchtime they pull out their phone and start browsing Seek.com.

Now imagine if the boss listened carefully and fed back to the worker that they appreciated their thinking and commended them for putting their heart into their work. Even if they went on to point out some difficulties and barriers, the acknowledgement of the worker's effort and initiative would probably result in the worker going away determined to find a way around the barriers, just like the awkward young kid who thinks they might just have a shot at coaxing their crush into going with them to the school dance.

We can nurture cathexis, or we can squeeze it out of our workers. One way to nurture cathexis is to invite your worker to reflect on how their job could be improved in terms of efficiency, sustainability or effectiveness. (Do this personally, in supervision, not through a suggestion box). Another is to figure out the extent to which you can give your worker power to make decisions about their work, to put their stamp on things.

Even in tightly regulated, quality-controlled environments, bosses can invite and reward thinking, initiative and courage. A nurse I know recently recounted an experience where they had gone from their ward to pick up a patient from post-op. The post-op team were getting some pressure from the surgeons to clear out some space so they could accelerate their operating list. The ward nurse arrived and checked the patient, especially their op-site which required specialised knowledge and treatment. The ward nurse was not satisfied that the patient was ready to transfer to the ward (uncontrolled bleeding is a bit of a give-away). They stated their case to the post-op team. Soon there were five post-op team members gathered around the ward nurse seeking to pressure them to take the patient anyway. The nurse held their position, repeated their clinical reasoning and told the team to call them back when the patient met the proper release criteria. The patient ended up going back to theatre to have the op-site repaired.

When the nurse arrived back at their ward, they got a sincere standing ovation from their in-charge nurse and the nursing unit manager for their sound clinical reasoning, attention to detail, and courage under fire. Do you reckon that nurse takes their job to heart? You bet.

It sounds counter-intuitive, but giving people some say about their role, respecting and rewarding their initiative and courage, and asking them to use their best thinking to solve problems actually has a supportive effect. It tells workers their thinking matters, that their ideas are valuable, that they – even if they're an entry-level hourly hire – are valuable.

Belonging

You'll remember right back in the introduction I cited Gallup's research showing how belonging contributed to employee engagement, which in turn predicted better productivity, higher quality and less turnover. People perform better and hang around longer when they feel a sense of belonging.

People love to be a part of a team that achieves something. There's something compelling about working together to achieve a goal. I marvel at amateur theatre companies that exert extraordinary effort to put on a show – costumes, sets, endless learning of parts and rehearsals, bumping everything in and tearing it out again in super-tight time frames – all for a season that may only be three or four shows.

The possibility of pooling one's own effort with the effort of others to do something that makes an audience laugh and cry and applaud wildly at the end is worth all the sweat and worry and frustration. Being a part of a team that accomplishes something great is one of the finest experiences in life. It creates a sense of meaning, of being valued, of belonging. Humans are social mammals. We have a deep and innate need to belong.

A sense of belonging will generally trump the value of the cause of a particular organisation (although the two factors may reinforce one-another). Imagine a technician working for the Mercedes-Benz Formula One racing team. That tech will go all out for Mercedes, working crazy hours in the lead-up to race day, all for the sake of getting the win for the team. The next season that same technician could be poached over to Ferrari. You can bet they'll put in the same herculean effort to get the win for the very people they were trying desperately to beat the previous year. Why? It's all about with whom you belong.

As a boss, building a sense of belonging among your staff is a key dimension of providing a supportive environment that will encourage excellent performance. Yet it seems so hard to pin down. How do I foster a particular 'sense' in another individual (and still get all my other work done)?

Let's begin with the idea of place. We like to think of things having their own place so we know where to find them. We don't generally think this way about people, but place can be a powerful way to foster a sense of belonging.

To understand how important place is to some people, just watch what happens when a 'shared workspace' philosophy is introduced to an office environment. Theoretically, this system works by a principle of no one having their own space. Each day everyone chooses a generic, vacant workstation, sets up their stuff and gets to work. At the end they pack it all up and leave the space blank. You might work at a different desk each day. It's a nice theory except it almost never works that way.

My workplace recently attempted the shared workspace idea, setting out a generalised office area where three teams all have access to 'unallocated' workstations. Within a week a pattern established itself. The staff who regularly work in the office each claimed a workstation as their own, marking out their territory with pictures and whimsical items and bits of stationery.

To sit at one of those desks feels like wearing someone else's clothes. Humans are spatial creatures. We tend to build our habits and customs around spaces. We mark out our spaces in ways only slightly more sophisticated than other territorial species. My space is where I belong.

Humans have other 'spaces' that we mark out as our own. These might be spaces in the little rituals that we tend to create, especially in families. Dad always carves the roast or cooks the barbecue. Mum always organises the social calendar. The youngest son always starts the singing of 'happy birthday'.

People having a particular and peculiar role grants them a sense of belonging by playing a part in the rituals and rhythms of the shared life of the family or workplace. As a boss, knowing your people well enough to assign them incidental responsibilities that reflect their uniqueness – even if they're a little quirky – helps them to know that you see them, not just as a unit of labour, but as a person.

Knowing your people well enough to know their particular 'pickle jar' is an extension of that idea. One of my friends thinks of these as 'superpowers'. Of course, you'd hope that the people on your team have unique skills that pertain specifically to their core responsibilities. I'm thinking here about the non-core responsibilities that you could give to anyone but would be a delight to one person and a burden to another.

In a manufacturing plant where I worked years ago, the annual Christmas lunch had morphed into a bit of an extravaganza. It was overseen by the maintenance manager, who had possibly missed his vocation as a restauranteur. In the days leading up to the lunch, he seemed to undergo a personal metamorphosis from mild-mannered engineer to a MasterChef judge on steroids. This was not really his 'day' job, but he seemed to take on the responsibility with an inexplicable passion.

The food was always amazing, and our engineer turned restaurateur was always showered in praise. This was his superpower and the one time of year when, more than any other, he knew he had a unique and valued place in the company community. Belonging is about cathexis flowing both ways; it's the feeling of being embraced by the person, or the group we've taken to heart. It leads to a sense of ownership and investment that performance pay could never achieve.

The validation cycle
Belonging is not something you can arrive at by rational argument. Nobody's going to gain a sense that they're a part of the team just because the boss sets out a series of convincing propositions that are designed to lead a worker to conclude that they belong. It happens in a much more intuitive, osmotic kind of process combining elements of care, involvement and ownership which we looked at earlier.

A lot like falling in love, belonging follows a pattern of risk and validation. We spoke earlier about the supervisor extending trust to the worker by giving them some responsibility and seeing how they handle it. If that goes well and the supervisor continues to give responsibility to the worker, it's easy to see how the worker can gain a sense of being valued and trusted, and hence a sense of belonging.

Also, like falling in love there's a reciprocal cycle that's initiated by the worker. It begins with the worker's impulse to give a little more of themselves than meeting the bare minimum expectations. Unless organisational culture or part experience directs them otherwise, most people are keen to give of themselves to whatever it is they're involved in. I've seen this at play even in low-end kinds of jobs. That impulse might take the form of a suggestion to improve a process, an offer to help with something, or staying after knock-off time to finish whatever it is they're working on. Whatever the action, they're sticking their neck out a little bit.

Now here's the critical point. You can either kick the cycle of validation into play by responding positively and with warmth, or you can stop the cycle stone dead by being dismissive. Let's play out an example.

Imagine it's 5:25 PM. The rest of the staff finish at 5:00 PM and you think you're the last person in the office (clearly this is not a legal or accounting firm, but stay with me). You're just about to hit the lights when you hear the familiar clattering of someone typing at a keyboard. You follow the sound to the new employee who's still beavering away at the pile of accounts payable to be entered into the accounting program.

"Still here?" you query.

"Yeah, there's a payment run tomorrow and I think it will be a bit tight, so I thought I'd get these entered before I go home."

Now imagine you're already late to pick up your kids from after school sport, so you're in a bit of a hurry. In your mind you're thinking, "I coulda locked this kid in here, set the alarm and ended up with a security call out! We keep pretty short accounts anyway – these payments could have waited."

So, what are you going to do? (Just to build the tension, let me make it clear that what you do next could see you gain or lose thousands of dollars in discretionary work effort). You could say, "Hey look, you need to check first if you're going to stay back! I could have locked you in here! Anyway, I'm really late so grab your stuff, we've gotta go." That response will go a long way to turning a motivated volunteer of discretionary work effort into a cynical clock watcher, because it de-validates the worker's effort and motivation.

Another option is to say, "Hey, I really appreciate your effort to stay on top of things. It's great to have someone so committed to the task. So here's the thing: everyone is pretty much gone by 5:15 each night – there's not much of a culture of working back around here, because most of us have kids to pick up. Speaking of which, I really need to lock up and go as I'm late to get my own kids. Can you grab your stuff and walk out with me?" On the way to the car park, there's warm conversation about plans for the evening and reiteration of thanks and appreciation for the worker's commitment.

This response validates the worker's mindset and motivation and goes a long way towards earning that worker's ongoing cooperation and effort. Even though their enthusiasm caused a bit of inconvenience, they showed the right attitude. As a boss, that attitude is almost as good as cash in your hand. You would do well to nurture and cultivate attitudes like that.

Validating your workers' attitudes makes them feel, well, *valued*. They'll probably feel a sense of being appreciated and a sense of approval, and those are pleasant feelings. If a person has experienced those feelings in response to what their boss says, they'll be very motivated to do something to get their boss to validate them and make them feel the same way again. The cycle of validation has begun. If you can sincerely validate your employee's discretionary work efforts, there's an excellent chance they'll continue to offer them.

Of course, knowing how to use the cycle of validation is power, and with power comes responsibility. In a neurobiological sense, when you validate an employee, you activate a centre in their brain called the *caudate nucleus*, which is associated with expecting and detecting rewards, and the *ventral tegmental area*, which is associated with motivation to pursue and acquire rewards and the pleasure that those rewards activate. These in turn engage other parts of the brain including the *limbic ring*, which is associated with motivating behaviour that induces pleasure, like eating and sex. (The limbic ring has some other less pleasurable functions too, but we'll get to those in the next section). This is pretty much the same set of neural circuits that light up when someone is in love, and when someone is indulging in their addictions.[55]

Activating these parts of the brain leads to a heightened sense of wellbeing, and because that powerfully motivates a person to seek more of whatever generates those good feelings, the cycle of validation makes people vulnerable to being manipulated. This goes some way to explaining how and why romantic internet scams operate.

I want to caution against the insincere or careless use of validation as a way of getting what you want from your workers. Some bosses have used validation to get a whole lot more from their workers than would ever appear on their position description.

When using validation as a kind of emotional reward (that's how the brain processes it), make sure you are mindful of the pattern that could be set up. Be careful not to be too frequent in your validation, and if you notice a worker getting caught up in validation-seeking behaviour (it can become an addiction like any other reward structure), you have a duty of care to apply the brakes. This might take the form of a frank conversation, or putting some limits on how many hours they work or how much extra responsibility they take on themselves. Be careful – if the cycle has been operating for a while, you may get some disproportionate reactions.

To counter this, maintaining good supportive contact regardless of how much discretionary work effort is offered means there's not an abrupt end to the sense of being appreciated. Conversely, bosses who only offer thanks and appreciation when workers go above and beyond are setting up for validation cycles that will likely end in resentment.

So ends our theory section. In the next section we'll look at the process of putting it all to work.

---

[55] Schwartz, R. and Olds, J. *Love and the Brain* Harvard Medical School Newsletter Spring 2015 https://neuro.hms.harvard.edu/harvard-mahoney-neuroscience-institute/brain-newsletter/and-brain/love-and-brain.

Summary

- The discretionary work effort is the work volunteered by a worker.
    - It's an outcome of the worker's engagement in their workplace.
    - It's not coerced or linked to incentives.
- Engagement that leads to a worker contributing discretionary work effort is fostered by:
    - A sincere belief that the boss cares about them
    - Involvement in shaping the work and the workplace
    - Ownership – taking the job to heart
    - Belonging – a sense of being embraced by their work group
        - Belonging can be reinforced by careful and ethical use of the validation cycle.

Discussion

- To what extent do you put in a discretionary work effort?
    - What does that tell you about your engagement at work?
- Where do you see your workers offering a discretionary work effort?
    - What do you think is motivating that behaviour?

Implementation

- What can you do with your work team to foster a greater sense of involvement, ownership and belonging?

What we've covered

Section 1: A boss worth working for

- Your first responsibility is to be the boss of yourself
- Your next responsibility is to your organisation
- You are responsible for the stewardship of humans
- Your workers are your job
- Exercising responsibility requires authority
- Supervision is a working relationship

Section 2: The task of supervision

- There are several prevailing theories of optimal performance
  - Theories X and Y have shaped management theory for the past 100 years
  - Fad theories are too simplistic to be really useful
  - Supervision is an adaptive challenge
- Supervision is about expectations and support
  - High expectations and high support produce high performance
  - Find the right level for your workers
  - Problems arise when the balance is lost
- Define your expectations
  - Document your expectations using a Position Description
  - Translate the Position Description into actual performance using a Work Plan
  - Adjust your expectations and approach to fit the circumstances
- Determine if your expectations are met
  - You need an intentional, reliable, factual means
  - Most methods by themselves have limitations.
  - Measuring outcomes and managing by report is generally effective
- Give workers feedback as to whether they meet your expectations
  - Use immediate feedback to reinforce positive and discourage negative behaviours

- Use formal supervision to clearly communicate whether your performance expectations have been met
- You may have to adjust your expectations to suit circumstances
- Provide support to facilitate performance
  - Invest your time and attention
  - Provide appropriate training, tech, counsel and people
  - Be careful with public acknowledgement, bonuses and gifts
  - Support struggling workers with appropriate time, coaching and counselling
- Encourage a discretionary work effort
  - Engaged workers are more likely to volunteer extra work effort on top of their required minimum
  - Engagement is fostered by feeling cared for, involvement, ownership and belonging

Section 3
How to effectively supervise

In this section we'll go through the whole supervision process step by step, beginning with some basics around recruiting (that's where you first get to communicate your expectations), then moving forward through what's recently been termed 'onboarding'. From there we'll look at routine supervision and how to build a growing alliance with your workers.

Later in this section we'll tackle some of those juicy bits you've been so eager to talk about. We'll look at things like burnout, managing poor performance, dealing with pushback and conflict.

In the process we'll pay a brief visit to some basics in human neurophysiology and social patterns, using family systems theory in particular.

We begin with recruitment and selection. While involvement in these activities helps to establish a good working relationship and clear expectations, I recognise that a lot of readers have little or no involvement in the recruitment and selection of their workers. If you can negotiate some access to the process in your workplace, all the better. If you can't, you may want to skip to chapter 15 which is an introduction about onboarding. Even if you don't control the onboarding process, as a boss you'll play a vital part.

Warning: self-proclaimed expert ahead

This section at times takes on a prescriptive tone. I'll talk sometimes about my own practice, preferences and rationales. Which leads me to give you my rationale on being prescriptive. Most management books, including some of the excellent volumes quoted throughout this work, set out principles and concepts, leaving the reader to figure out the specifics of translating the abstract and generalised into the concrete and specific. Having worked as a coach and trainer in various guises for most of my adult life, I've formulated this hypothesis: *most people struggle to translate the abstract and generalised into the concrete and specific.* I've coached dozens of leaders who've read Stephen Covey's *Seven Habits* and who have not put even one of those habits into practice. So, I'll share my practice. At times I'll even tell you straight out what I think should be done in particular settings. Feel free to disagree.

Hegel's *dialectic* advocated that the process of an idea being posited (*thesis*), then countered (*antithesis*) would lead to debate that produced a third and better apprehension of the truth (*synthesis*). While it virtually became his philosophical calling card, he attributed the process to Kant.[56] Anyhow, treat the following as my best thinking and counsel, and consider this an invitation to counter it with better thinking.

---

[56] Kant, E. *Critique of Pure Reason* (1781).

Chapter 14
Recruiting and selecting

Don't be President Kirkman

As I'm writing this chapter, my hometown of Melbourne is enduring its third month of a second lockdown due to the COVID-19 pandemic. We've all given up baking our own sourdough bread and cooking elaborate recipes. All of our plans to learn to play new instruments, learn to code with Python and develop a killer set of abs have fallen by the wayside. What's left is Netflix. In an effort to find something reasonably well-written without gratuitous titillation and depictions of graphic violence, I've settled on *Designated Survivor* where virtual (and virtuous) nobody Tom Kirkman (played by Kiefer Sutherland) finds himself dropped into the oval office as President of the United States.

Over the course of the series President Kirkman makes a succession of hiring decisions based on first impressions and single critical incidents. It's great television. It's terrible human resource management practice. By the end of the second series some of Kirkman's captain's calls are dead, others he's fired and one has become a bitter rival. In the real world, you don't have script writers to save you.

Recruiting

There are whole volumes written about recruitment and selection. Some of them are worth reading, some are selling snake oil and some make the process seem a whole lot more complex and expensive than it needs to be. Set out below is not a finely detailed procedure for recruiting – there are other places to find the nuts and bolts. It's more of a design brief for recruiting, describing the important considerations of the main steps and hopefully helping you to avoid some of the all-too-common mistakes.

Consider the context

Do the hard work of following due process. I recall a consulting job I undertook a few years ago with an educational institution. Their principal had recently stepped down and the board were considering engaging me to guide them through recruiting and selecting a replacement.

The circumstances of the previous incumbent's departure had been uncomfortable, and the directors were a little rattled. It became clear that they were anxious to get another principal in place as soon as possible to calm themselves and the rest of the organisation. I cautioned them. "What kind of principal do you want?" I wondered out loud.

The response was a kind of confused silence accompanied by facial expressions that conveyed, "What kind of idiot question is that?" I went to inquire as to whether they wanted an administrative type to maintain and strengthen the institutional aspect of the organisation, an entrepreneur to take the organisation to new places, or a scholar to boost the academic standing of the college. (I resisted asking about a grandparent type to make everyone feel comfortable). Any of these emphases would fit neatly under the generic title of 'principal'.

The frowns changed subtly from questioning my sanity to concern for the organisation. It was clear that they were unsure as to what the organisation needed. So we agreed to retain the interim principal for six months while we went through an organisational and environmental review. With a clear picture of the organisation and its context, we could design the role of the principal for this organisation at this juncture.

You don't need to put the whole organisation under the microscope to recruit more junior roles. You should, however, think carefully about that actual role in the actual context, and avoid the temptation to jump straight to advertising.

Design the role – position descriptions
By this stage, you might be sick of hearing about PDs. Yet the PD is the most fundamental resource for the recruiting process. Do the careful job analysis to create a PD that clearly sets out what's expected of the role, clearly identifies the individual to whom the new role reports, and which roles report to the new one.

You'd do well to research what kind of remuneration is required to attract the right candidate. A number of HR consultancies publish salary surveys, which give an indication of the salary range for various roles in various sectors and sizes of organisation. You'll have to pay for the information. It's worth pitching the right salary range to ensure you're not lowballing the market, wasting money or setting up a golden handcuff. All of this is tedious and it slows the process. It will save you months of heartache later.

From the PD you can create selection criteria: the competencies and characteristics required for the role. The competencies should relate directly to the expectations set out in the PD. Characteristics can be specific to the job (e.g. salespeople require intrinsic motivation, researchers require perseverance, curiosity and meticulousness, HR managers need to be good with process) and some will be drawn from your organisational values. In more senior roles you'll also need to take into account organisational strategy. Be thoughtful about these. Don't confuse behavioural characteristics like meticulousness with personality traits – but more on that later.

Most jobs have some prerequisites: these include qualifications, experience and availability. Be careful here. In the actual execution of a job, broad qualifications and years of experience don't count for as much as you might imagine. In some gigs, certain things almost go without saying – it's reasonable to want a senior accountant to be a CPA, or for a welder to have trade certificates in welding. Just be careful you're not setting yourself up for getting an academia nut (unless that's what you want) or paying for a lot of criteria you don't really need. Avoid including 'nice-to-have' criteria that are not necessarily needed for the role.

Likewise, years of experience could be very useful, or it could just make a person stuck in their ways or in possession of a redundant knowledge base. You'll want enough experience to demonstrate the prerequisite competence – and that's likely to take less time than you think. Be thorough and considered in setting out your selection criteria. They'll serve you well in your advertising and in your selection process.

Hit the market
Now you're ready to go recruiting. Be thoughtful about where you advertise and how you advertise. Contemporary recruiting generally involves advertising online. Making the most of the possibilities of online hiring technologies is well beyond the scope of this book, but we can tree-top some basics.

Some jobsites assist you with application management functions. If you're recruiting a generalised role like a receptionist or accounts payable clerk, you may well get a gazillion applications – so making use of the targeting and filtering functions may be well worth your while.

You may also want to become acquainted with the sites where particular professions are recruited, or where your industry tends to advertise – sometimes trade journals or other sector-specific publications are worth a shot. You could also get on the front foot with more proactive search possibilities through sites like LinkedIn. The key question is, "How do I get my ad in front of the kind of person I want to employ?" Jobsites tend to attract only jobseekers. Your ideal candidate may not be 'in the market' right now – until they see your ad and become curious. If all this is causing you to glaze over, you may choose to use a recruitment consultancy – but beware, they're expensive and they may not take as much care as you would like.

On top of all this is the burgeoning number of apps that are designed to automate much of the recruiting process. Some are associated with job websites, some not. Most importantly, they're handy for managing large numbers of applications, from filtering by keyword to assigning status and managing correspondence. If you're doing a lot of recruiting or anticipate a large number of applications, or if you're planning a multifaceted advertising campaign, investing in an app and taking the time to learn its functions may be the way to go.

Let's just assume you've figured out your recruiting strategy. Now for the advertisement. You're advertising on at least three levels:

1. The Person
2. The Organisation
3. The Role

Let's begin with the final one, because that's likely to be your ad headline. I'm a fan of using the least ambiguous headline as possible. It's become a little bit cool and funky to come up with unconventional titles, like 'Organisational Excellence Catalyst' when what you want is someone to design and implement a QA system. A headline like 'Quality System Implementation Lead' will more likely get you what you're asking for. Ambiguity is an enemy of effective recruiting. Be very clear, right from the headline. We'll come back to the role in a minute.

Now let's get the right person interested. Assuming your ad is in the right place at the right time, I encourage you to pitch for the right person. My favourite opening line is what I call the 'Why, yes!' line – you want your ideal candidate to read a question (actual or implied) about themselves and answer, 'Why, yes!' Here's the kind of opening line that would get me interested…

"Can you coach leaders to perform to their highest potential?" to which I (modestly) exclaim, "Why, yes!" Bingo! You've got me reading.

You might instead use a summary subheading with the question implied: "Build a world-class leadership pipeline," to which I respond, "I'd love to do that!"

Here's where you're trying to build a link between the ideal candidate's best aspirations and the core purpose of the job. The opening hook should communicate the essence of the job and be an important motivator for the ideal candidate. Once you have their interest, you can go on to talk a little about the role. Make it clear what the role involves doing and what might make it attractive: things like the kind of status or influence involved, the geographical territory (implies travel), the kind of people the role relates to etc. For example, I would be attracted to a job that reports to the CEO or a senior GM, that involves a broad geographical area, that works on strategy, and that involves developing leaders. You'll also need to give a clear indication of the key responsibilities.

By this time, I'm really interested and now I want to know about the organisation. This is an acid test of what the positives actually boil down to. Here you're selling the organisation, so put your best foot forward – but make sure you're scrupulously honest. Any candidate worth their salt will investigate your bona fides.

If the role and the organisation are all triggering green lights for your ideal candidate, now's the time to let them know what it will take to get an interview. This is the paragraph that usually begins with, 'The successful candidate will be…' and then goes on to list qualifications, experience, competencies and qualities you so carefully set out in the selection criteria. You don't need to use that exact opening phrase. You could say, "The person we're looking for is…" or whatever you think conveys the 'feel' of your organisation.

Got all that? Add the key details like salary, tenure and application process and you're done. Proofread it and post it up!

Selecting

Here's where your apps can be a great help if you're getting a huge number of applications. But beware – candidates are learning to game the apps. Savvy candidates will use the wording of your ad as a template to write their cover letter and sprinkle their resume with terms from your ad. Other well meaning applicants may write a sincere response to your ad but use synonyms for your terms and may therefore be cut by the app's algorithm. So be thoughtful about how you set the filtering criteria in the app. If you only anticipate 20 or so applications, I recommend bypassing the app and reading each one.

Initial shortlisting (whether you've got the whole list of applicants or the initial cut from your app) is about quickly scanning the applications to see how well they fit the selection criteria. Some people create a quick checklist and evaluate each against it. I tend to have three categories: 'yep', 'nope' and 'maybe', and each application gets about 90 seconds of my time to be allocated to one of these. Then I review the 'maybe' group a little more closely and allocate them either to 'yep' or 'nope'.

If the 'yep' group is still too big, I start getting picky, weeding out any that seem a little thin in meeting the selection criteria. At this stage I want to emphasise, that it's the selection criteria that determine the application's progress – not whether they have other attractive characteristics outside those criteria. Don't fall for the candidate that seems to be a superstar but can't demonstrate the characteristics you need.

I tend to prune my list to about seven or eight, then consult with my selection panel (if I use one) and work with them to get the list down to about five. At this stage the 'nope' applicants get a quick email from me saying, "Thanks for applying but on this occasion your application has not been successful." Nothing more. Then I set up phone screens with the remaining five.

A phone screen is a telephone conversation of about 30 minutes with the candidate that addresses 3-5 key selection criteria that can't be concretely determined via the resume. For example, if you want a person with a minimum undergraduate degree in their field, that should be set out in the resume. Getting an academic transcript will verify it. That's not what the phone screen is about.

The phone screen is about what the candidate means by what they say in their application. By that, I mean it's time to go beyond general descriptions like, 'I thrive in a high-pressure situations' or 'I have ten years' experience in pharmaceutical sales' to actual behavioural descriptions.

This leads us to a quick diversion into selection theory.

Predictive validity
There seems to be a lot of mystique around selection, as if it's some mind game or black art. While TV shows like *Game of Thrones, House of Cards* or *West Wing* depict all kinds of intrigue and manipulation – using people like chess pieces and clever strategies to catch people in their words – let me make something clear: selection interviewing is not like that. Neither is it about making assumptions and diagnoses about a candidate's psychology or motivation, so cage your inner Freud at this point.

Selecting a candidate is all about making a prediction regarding how they will perform in your workplace in the role in which you seek to engage them. The aim is to make a reliable prediction, based on evidence you can gain through the selection process. The prevailing theory is that past behaviour is the best predictor of future behaviour. We use this logic all the time. We wouldn't buy a dog with a history of biting people, we wouldn't employ a person with a conviction for embezzlement as an accounts payable clerk, and we wouldn't employ a person to manage corporate data security if they'd never done that kind of work before.

Various methods of selection have varying degrees of predictive validity, i.e. the degree to which the information you gain will provide a valid basis for predicting future behaviour. Asking, "Are you an honest person?" has obviously low predictive validity. Providing a person with a scenario that involves honesty at a cost may give you something to go on (although scenarios have proven to be pretty unreliable too). You might set up an elaborate lab-type experiment with actors, secret recordings and hidden cameras like some kind of FBI-based TV show (there actually are assessment centres that will do this for you, but the cost is eye-watering) – and even then, the predictive validity is not necessarily super.

Selection is about actual behaviour

The most reliable method of predicting future behaviour is a technique called behavioural interviewing. While there are all sorts of tools and techniques out there claimed to improve your strike rate in selection, behavioural interviewing remains the bedrock of a good selection process. It works on the idea of behavioural consistency – that a behaviour that is consistent across time and contexts will very likely be replicated into the future.

Put simply, behavioural interviewing involves asking candidates to give you examples from their previous experience where they demonstrated the behaviours you've identified as necessary. You're not asking for the candidate's evaluation or asking them to tell you what they would do – you're asking them to describe what they have *actually* done.

Let's work on an example. A fairly common behavioural category sought in selection is 'resilience'. Now, you could ask the candidate, "Are you resilient?" and of course they will give you the 'correct' answer of "yes" accompanied by nodding and a sincere facial expression. This gives you absolutely zero useful data upon which to make a predictively valid selection.

Or you could say, "We're looking for a candidate who demonstrates resilience. Describe for me a time in your life where you showed your ability to endure adversity." They may respond by telling you about a terrible experience, which is useful backdrop information, but still not much about their actual behaviour. However, if you probe further, you'll get to the gold (or the gravel, depending on the candidate).

You might ask a follow-up question like, "I can see that would have been pretty tough. Describe for me what you did in response to the challenge." This will begin to give you a line of sight on the candidate's actual behaviour. You could follow up with further questions like, "What strategies did you use to maintain your wellbeing and resolve?" or "How did you deal with the staff who were actively opposing you?" or "What did you do to keep clear-headed under pressure?" The answers to these will provide a rich picture of how your candidate behaves in a tough situation.

Remember that behavioural interviewing is based on the idea of consistency over time and context. If the candidate tells you a story from ten years ago, you might follow with a request for something more recent to show consistency over time. If they talk about a situation from their current workplace, you might ask for a second example from a different context. Unless the behavioural category is specific to the job for which you're interviewing, you could invite examples from volunteer or community contexts. If the candidate consistently behaves a particular way, it will show up across contexts.

Let me provide a personal example. I pay pretty close attention to my finances. I'm not the kind of person who runs a personal general ledger, but I make sure I have accurate information upon which to make financial decisions. I review statements to pick up unauthorised transactions. I have a financial plan stretching forward several years.

Twenty years ago, I took over corporate services responsibility for a small NGO. The finances were opaque and inaccurate. I immediately set about making sure we had accurate, meaningful and timely reporting each month. That involved rebuilding the general ledger, setting up simpler reporting for field staff and inboarding the accounting functions for more immediate and transparent control. Three years later I had accurate accounts with commentary on my desk by the third of the month, every month.

A year ago I took on chairing a small not-for-profit. The accounts were vague and certainly did not meet accounting standards. In the process of rebuilding the board I ensured we took on a very competent treasurer and kept pushing from the chair until I was satisfied we had an accurate balance sheet alongside profit and loss statements that reflected the actual activity of the organisation.

There you have three contexts – one personal, one from my employment, one from my community engagement – over 20 years. What do you reckon I might do if I took on a GM or chairing role of an organisation with substandard accounting practices?

In a phone screen I'll generally ask for one account per category. In an interview I'll ask for two or three.

Knowing what to look for
It may seem obvious, but a great deal of selection failure comes down to not knowing what you're looking for. That means the person doing the selecting needs to know the required behaviour when they see it.

With our 'resilience' example above, I would be looking for evidence to show:

- Consistently holding their position in the face of opposition or influences that would push them to waver from their convictions
- Maintaining meaningful contact with other players in the context and not withdrawing
- Engaging in appropriate debate and even conflict without it descending into quarrels, personal attacks and turf wars
- Ability to repair inevitable relationship ruptures
- Willingness to identify and mobilise extra resources, including appropriate support and counsel
- Maintaining their personal disciplines

Good interviewing drills down to these levels. The more concrete the behaviours identified, the higher the predictive validity.

Knowing what to look for does not come from thin air – it comes from experience, observation, study and application of sound theory. As I write this, I'm in my mid-fifties. I have some personal experience of dealing with adversity. I have seen both inspiring and disturbing examples of people under pressure. I'm not a particularly resilient person, but I know what it looks like. I could not have accurately interviewed for resilience when I was 21. Sure, I had by then toughed-out a couple of instances of leadership backlash, but I had handled them mostly by sheer determination with a dash of depression. I did not then know what genuine, sustained resilience looked like.

Some jobs have highly technical or specialised aspects where a general-purpose recruiting manager could not reasonably recognise appropriate actual behaviour from bluff and bluster. I would never get a gig as a management or financial accountant, but I am pretty confident I could select for one. I would need expert help selecting a forensic accountant.

While you might glean from a resume that a candidate was involved in a particular project, it does not give you a clear view of what they actually did. Titles can be confusing. An assistant editor on a film might spend a good deal of time in the edit suite making decisions on whole scenes, choosing shots and duration, keeping in mind issues like tension, overall run time, detail reveals and continuity. They might be only a small step from lead editing responsibility. An assistant *to* the editor might spend most of their day running cans and making coffee. The titles of the job sound the same, but the actual behaviour and experience are a world apart.

Selecting using behavioural data

So let's get back to phone screening. The purpose of the phone screen is to determine whether it's worth your while interviewing the shortlisted candidate. To put it another way, I want to know if this person can provide enough relevant behavioural data to explore in detail at interview. To do this I will typically create a screening interview proforma with about five questions.

Let's look at a couple of examples. Going back to our film editor example, let's presume I want someone with experience working on making actual editing decisions with a high degree of autonomy (not someone working as a gopher for an actual editor). I might say, "Think of a recent project where you had significant involvement in the editing process – take me through the activities of your typical day."

I might follow that up with shorter questions about the technology and technique they were using, the other roles with which they were interacting, etc. Unless they're a particularly skilled liar, I'll get a pretty good idea of their level of involvement.

Or imagine I'm looking for a sales manager with experience in developing effective sales campaigns and an emphasis on innovation. I've got a list of applicants all with ten-plus years of experience as sales managers. I'm worried some of the candidates actually have one year of experience repeated 10 times. I could ask a question like, "Describe for me a theory or concept you've learned about recently and how you used that to enhance a sales strategy."

Using the same example, imagine the role will be managing a sales force of eight reps over a national territory. My selection criteria includes demonstrated ability to optimise sales team performance. I'm a little worried that I may have applicants in the mix who have spent most of their 'sales manager' time as sole functionaries rather than leading sales teams. I might ask a question like, "Share with me your best example of getting the best out of a sales rep working for you." You can imagine the wealth of useful behavioural data their response might bring.

In phone screening I'm not going to drill down to fine detail or ask for multiple examples – I'm just looking to ascertain which candidates have the best shot at providing the kind of data I'm looking for at an interview. Five questions like that will usually give you sufficient data to shorten your list down to the two or three people you want to get in front of an interview panel.

The interview

There are short courses you can do in behavioural interviewing, and if you're new to this I recommend you consider taking one. Courses tend to concentrate on the technique for the actual interview. To this point we've been looking at the prep-work that sets you up for applying that technique to best effect:

- Analyse the job
- Write or update the PD
- Use the PD to develop selection criteria
- Use the selection criteria to build your recruitment strategy, including a killer ad
- Use your selection criteria to longlist
- Use your selection criteria to phone screen the longlist and reduce it to a shortlist.

Before we get into the nuts and bolts of the interview, I need to debunk a ubiquitous misnomer. You've probably seen webinars and books and teaser offerings promising lists of 'most effective interview questions'. These lists are attractive because they promise to give you some kind of advantage or short cut, or the assurance you're asking the 'right' questions.

Let me give it to you straight – there are no generic 'right' questions. The best questions are the ones that will elicit the necessary data to enable you to predict whether the candidate will perform as you expect. The questions for each role will be unique to the role. You need to do the hard work of analysis and formalising criteria, then ask questions geared to those criteria. There are no short cuts. Offering lists of great questions is like offering a list of great tennis shots – the best shot is context specific. There is no generic killer shot.

Most interviews nowadays are conducted by a panel. I've been a candidate in interviews with a panel of ten people (I'm not kidding). It turns out that all of the various factions and facets of the organisation needed to be represented. Translation – the organisation has internal trust problems. The panel needs sufficient expertise to make a valid prediction of the candidate's performance. I honestly cannot see any good reason for more than three. If you can't find that expertise spread across three people, how can you expect to find all that you're looking for in just one candidate?

Typically, a panel would include the immediate supervisor of the role being hired (I'll explain why in a minute), a person with particular expertise in the field of the role being hired, and perhaps a senior manager or an HR specialist who has a good handle on the selection process. The panel should be based primarily on knowledge and skill, not representing particular factions and special interests.

Your panel should include the immediate supervisor of the role being hired (presumably you). The supervisory relationship begins with the first contact, and the interview is a great opportunity to set the tone for the relationship. It also gives the incoming candidate a sense of their prospective boss; remember, they're also interviewing you. If you, through your demeanour and competence in the interview demonstrate to the candidate that you're a great boss to work for, they're more likely to say 'yes' to your offer and 'no' to the offer of your competitor.

There is sometimes a subtle difference in priorities between the immediate supervisor and others – particularly us HR-types. As a direct supervisor, you want to appoint someone who's going to meet all your expectations, be an asset to your team and not give you any grief. You want someone who'll bring that discretionary work effort we spoke about earlier. As much as the people in HR will say we want all that as well, we're probably recruiting dozens of roles each year, and frankly we also want this thing off our desk. An okay candidate is usually okay with us. As far as possible, be fully engaged with your own hiring, establish a great working alliance right from the get-go and don't settle for just okay.

It's worth seeking the assistance of technicians and specialists when you're recruiting technical and specialised roles. You'll need the expertise of people who know the required competencies when they see them. Otherwise, you're allowing the candidate to make the assessment. If your organisation does not have people with a good idea of what the required competencies might look like behaviourally, borrow someone from another organisation to sit on your panel. Industry groups and training institutions are a good place to find them.

Now that you've got a shortlist and a panel, it's time to conduct the interviews. I like to create an interview questionnaire that I use as a standard template for each interview for a given recruiting job. That questionnaire will include a place to record the date, panel members' names and the candidate's name. Then comes some bullet points to open the interview which serve as prompts to cover the setup thoroughly. Let me step you through those:

- Introduce the panel members and why they were chosen (if you haven't advised this earlier, which is also common practice)
    - E.g. I'm here because, if you're successful, I'll be your boss. We invited Claire Bloggs onto the panel because she serves as chair of our industry peak body. Jenny Che is part of the panel because she heads up the HR function for the group.
- Introduce the interview process
    - E.g. This is a behavioural interview so we're going to ask for accounts of past behaviour that demonstrate certain competencies and characteristics. What we're after is behaviour about what you've actually done – so try to keep that the focus and minimise detail about the context and what other people did or said.
    - We will take what you say at face value. If we ask you to recall an event where you dealt with a particular issue or demonstrated a particular skill – that's what we're looking for. We're not here to play mind games or psychoanalyse you.
    - We've got a lot to get through and our time is limited, so sometimes we'll interrupt you either to focus the question more narrowly or because we have enough data to move on. Don't take an interruption as commentary on how you're doing. We interrupt everyone.
- Confidentiality
    - This interview is like a footy trip – what happens in this room stays in this room. Your answers will be confidential and not shared outside this context.
- What we're not assessing you on
    - We're not here to evaluate how well you interview. Sometimes behavioural questions trigger memories that carry a bit of emotion. That's fine. If you need a break or a minute to settle, that won't be something that counts against you.

The questionnaire will then set out the behavioural categories for the interview. If you have a lot of categories, you'll need to be thoughtful about which ones to interrogate thoroughly. If they're all considered mission-critical, you'll need to set aside a decent chunk of time and allow some breaks. For CEO-level roles with 10-12 categories I'll bat for a three or four-hour interview (seriously). Sometimes my clients won't agree, but the more thoroughly you can examine the candidate's behavioural data, the more reliable the outcome. For a mid-level manager, I'll generally go about 90 minutes with perhaps seven categories. First tier supervisors will be five or six categories and take about an hour. The more senior the role, the deeper I want to drill down, and the longer the interview.

Prior to the interview I'll generally have a planning meeting with the panellists and we'll share out the various parts of the interview, so each person takes an active role and we don't fall into interrupting one another.

I encourage the panellists to write down their opening question for each category where they're leading the questioning. This is a good discipline for people who are relatively new to behavioural interviewing, and it ensures sharp, unambiguous and efficiently worded questions. Sometimes going off the cuff leads to questions that are vague, complex, wordy or even unintelligible. They inevitably need to be recast after the candidate stumbles around them for five minutes. Time is of the essence.

The closing part of the interview is when you clarify referees and inform the candidate of what's next. We'll talk more about referees in a minute, but in the interview it's prudent to seek the specific names and contact details of the candidate's referees. If there's a particular person you think it's important that you speak with and the candidate does not volunteer their name and details, ask specifically for the person's details and express permission to contact them. Sometimes candidates will only provide the sugar-coated referees. Contacting former supervisors and colleagues without the candidate's permission may put you on the wrong side of privacy legislation.

I'll give the candidate some idea about the process ahead and when they'll be contacted. I never, *ever* offer the candidate a job on the spot. The candidate that's too good to be true probably is. Keep calm and follow the process (you could print that on a coffee mug).

Conducting the interview is then simply a matter of following the plan. The more senior the role, the more is at stake so the more thorough the examination of each behavioural category. For a CEO-level role I will generally seek three examples of each particular behaviour across at least two contexts. The opening questions for each category will take the same general form as the examples I provided earlier. However, the follow-up probing will be more detailed and drill down to the point where I can clearly visualise the candidate in action. Pushing for this level of clarity generally thwarts any attempts by a candidate to bluff their way through. If the descriptions become generalised or the tense moves from 'I did this' to 'I would do that' I know their story is thin.

If a line of questioning leads to the candidate describing a situation where I can't see them demonstrating the behaviour I'm looking for, I'll start with a new opening question and try again in the same category. For example, imagine I ask, "Describe for me a situation where you have effectively resolved a conflict," and the candidate relates an experience of overruling someone by force of personality, or firing a subordinate with whom they disagreed, or being avoidant until the situation blew over. These are not the behaviours I'm looking for, but it's only one instance, so I can't with a high degree of validity predict that this is their typical conflict management style. So, I'll try again with something like, "I'm looking to get a clear picture of how you bring resolution and reconciliation to a conflictual situation." If, after two or three attempts the candidate is not coming up with accounts that show the competency and characteristics required in the category, I'll move on. When it comes to scoring the behavioural data, the candidate won't rate well in that category.

As the interview goes on, you'll be able to draw on earlier accounts where you've already seen the behaviour you're looking for in later categories, so while it might take 20 minutes to thoroughly examine a category earlier in the interview, you might only need five minutes to fill in some blanks toward the end of the interview.

Which brings us to scoring. Immediately after the interview I'll work through each category with the panel and we'll agree on a score for the candidate in each category. Common practice is to use a scale of zero to five, where zero equals none of required behaviour observed in the category, three equals behaviours demonstrated to the required level, and five equals exceptionally high levels of competence demonstrated in this category.

Sometimes there will be a debate among the panel as to how to score a candidate in a particular category. Such debates are usually settled by focusing on the actual behaviour the candidate described, rather than guesses or hunches about the context surrounding the answers during the interview. Then compare the behavioural data with the required behaviour. My mantras are, "Show me the data," and, "What does the selection criteria say?" You can't entirely eliminate subjectivity from your evaluation, so try to maintain as much objectivity as you can. Hunches, intuitions and impulses are not objective processes. Don't recruit like President Kirkman.

Numerical scoring is helpful in a few ways. If you have two strong candidates, their scores will shape the final choice. If all of your candidates score poorly, you have good reason to go back to the market or to rethink the role. A candidate needs to score three or better in most categories for me to consider progressing with their application. The few times when I've let a low scorer through due to pressure to fill a role, I've always regretted it.

If your selection decision is ever questioned, or if you find yourself in a court or tribunal defending a discrimination claim, you will be able to show an objective selection process.

Temperamental tools

Some recruiters advocate the use of instruments that measure temperament as recruiting tools; commonly used instruments include the Myers-Brigg Type Indicator, CliftonStrengths and DiSC. The Myers-Briggs Foundation states straight-up, "It is not ethical to use the MBTI instrument for hiring or for deciding job assignments."[57] Yet if you Google 'using MBTI for recruitment', there are a number of people only too willing to offer MBTI as part of their recruiting process. Likewise, Gallup states, "...there are serious and dangerous pitfalls if we mistakenly use the CliftonStrengths assessment as a selection tool."[58] Yet scroll down your Google search and there are consultancies advocating its use in making hiring decisions. It's the same story with DiSC. Use only as directed.

While there is a very large body of job analysis based around the Sixteen Personality Factor Questionnaire (16PF), even it has some limitations. For

---

[57] www.myersbriggs.org.
[58] www.gallup.com/workplace.

example, there is a solid 16PF research base showing the temperamental traits more common in successful accountants. But these are necessarily generalised by the very nature of the large data set. You probably don't a have a statistically valid, peer reviewed analysis of the accountant you need in your organisation right now – and the variation could be significant enough for you to reject a highly suited candidate for one who scores better against a general profile.

If you really must use a temperamental test, spend the money and use a test that's validated for use in recruitment and is administered by suitably accredited practitioners. Regardless, I would be wary about using a temperamental tool as your primary means of selection.

Check references

Before you make that magic phone call to offer a candidate a job (I love making those calls) and the corresponding calls breaking the bad news to unsuccessful candidates (I hate making those calls) it's important to do a spot of reference checking.

Reference checking is a bit of a bone of contention in HR circles. Some organisations have a policy of refusing to provide references for former employees (incredibly, their recruitment policy will often insist on ref-checking candidates before contracting). Others do their ref-checking by email or cloud-based app. Others claim it's all too hard and risky.

My personal preference is to use phone calls for ref-checking. Providing a reference can be a little delicate if the candidate did not fully meet expectations in the previous job, so there is often a lot of information conveyed in the subtleties of language. Most referees will be reticent to provide explicit information that might harm a candidate's chances of landing a job. It's important to word your questions so that the referee can give you sufficient information without exposing themselves to legal ramifications later on. Sometimes referees will convey information 'not in so many words,' but clearly enough for you to get their meaning. You don't get those nuances with anything that requires the referee to write a response.

I will generally call at least two referees and speak with them for about 20 minutes. I'll do the usual confirmation of employment and position for the dates set out in the candidate's resume, ask for a general outline of the role and clarify the relationship between the referee and the candidate. The closer the working relationship, the more valid the information provided.

I'll check some character basics like honesty and integrity, with questions like, "Are you confident that the candidate was honest in all their dealings while in the employ of your organisation?" I may also ask about their relational 'wake' with questions like, "In your opinion, did the candidate have harmonious and constructive relationships with their colleagues?" If I get a less than reassuring response, I may ask carefully, "Without telling tales out of school, should I be concerned about their relational style in considering them for this role?"

I will also ask some general performance questions like, "Did you have any concerns with the candidate meeting their deadlines or achieving their performance targets?"

If I was unsure of any of the information shared in the behavioural interview with the candidate, I may ask a referee to clarify (that's why I sometimes request referees not on the standard list provided by the candidate).

If the referee has a less-than-flattering take on the candidate, they will usually be hesitant in their response and use a lot of qualifiers. If I have a conversation where the referee is guarded or reticent, I may seek a third referee.

Contracting

I'm going to assume you'll either have the confidence and expertise to nail down the contracting stage of the recruitment journey, or that you'll get solid legal advice. In Australia you can't contract out of your statutory obligations under workplace relations legislation like the Fair Work Act. Save yourself the pain of legal problems by doing your homework in setting up the employment contract or letter of offer. Wage theft is a significant problem in Australia. Do the right thing.

All that said, and for reasons we'll get to in the next chapter, you would be well advised in your letter of offer or employment contract to stipulate a trial or probationary period. This is especially valuable in jurisdictions where there is solid workplace relations legislation to protect workers against unfair dismissal. Just bear in mind that you'll need to have good reason for a probationary period of longer than about six months. If the period is unreasonably long, it's vulnerable to legal challenge.

In Australia, most workers are covered by the Commonwealth Fair Work Act, which precludes employees of less than six months continuous employment (or employees of less than twelve months continuous employment in small organisations) from pursuing a claim for unfair dismissal in the Fair Work Commission. Before you rely on these exclusions, get some professional advice. Setting a trial period where the contract can be terminated by either party simply makes things unambiguous.

Summary

- Recruit for the specific job in your specific organisation at this specific time.
    - As the successful candidate's boss, get involved in the process as much as you can.
    - Carefully put together a PD.
    - Use the PD to develop selection criteria.
    - Use the selection criteria to design your advertising strategy and write a killer ad.
    - Consider using an app if you anticipate a high volume of candidates.
- Select based on actual behaviour across time and contexts – this has high predictive validity.
    - Use a basic behavioural phone screen to reduce your longlist to a shortlist.
    - Use careful behavioural interviewing with numerical scoring to select your candidate.
    - Check references to confirm information and manage risks.

Discussion

- How does the process described in this chapter compare to your recruiting experience?

Action

- What's the one change you could make to your recruiting practice that will improve your effectiveness?

Chapter 15
Onboarding

Induction

Induction is the process by which you orient your new worker to their new workplace and make them aware of the more generalised expectations contained in company-wide policies.

A thoughtful induction establishes your worker in the relationships they'll need going forward and helps them harmonise with the organisational culture. A thoughtfully planned and smoothly executed induction builds the worker's confidence in you and in the organisation.

It's good practice to develop a specific induction plan for every new hire. Your HR department (if you have one) will no doubt have an induction checklist and will often provide a package of policies and procedures for your new hire to wade through.

True to form so far, I encourage you to take a look at the position description (PD) for your new worker's role and make note of any particular items you'll want to address in the induction process. The Australian Fair Work Act and Regulations require you to specify the award or agreement under which the worker is employed. You'll also need to direct the new employee as to where they can access the award or agreement. Best if you cover these things off.

Some PDs list key relationships. If so, make sure introductions to these people are included in the induction plan. If there's union representation on site, show good faith by ensuring you introduce your new worker to their on-site union rep.

In Australia you can download an induction checklist from the Fair Work Ombudsman,[59] or state-based workplace health and safety instrumentalities (the checklist from Worksafe Tasmania is very clear and simple).[60]

---

[59] www.fairwork.gov.au.
[60] www.worksafe.tas.gov.au.

Induction done badly

Regrettably, most companies have allowed induction to become a box-ticking and butt-covering exercise on a grand scale. The apparent goal is to jam into the new worker's head all the dos and don'ts of the workplace so that they have no excuse when they're reported for bullying or sexual harassment or selling the organisation's intellectual property to a foreign power.

Most organisations either dump a bunch of documentation in a new worker's lap (literally or virtually) and insist they read through it all, often on their own time. Then they're required to sign off that they've read and understood it all. Now let's be honest. They're no more likely to read those documents than to read the terms and conditions that come with downloading a new app on a personal device. Nobody's signature on an induction form is big enough to cover anyone's butt. If it's challenged in court, it's likely that the box-ticking will be seen for what it is, especially if you ask the new worker to do it on their own time.

A little better than the ream of documents is the induction video. These can be a useful and engaging way of stepping new workers through things like preventing workplace bullying, harassment and discrimination, or general safety information like housekeeping, workstation setup or storage of dangerous goods. But be careful.

One organisation with which I'm familiar purchased a large suite of induction videos from a consultancy that allegedly 'tailored' the content to their new client. The organisation wanted to 're-induct' their entire workforce to improve their risk management. The videos all told had a cumulative run time of something like 30 hours. Workers would receive an email reminder every couple of weeks to complete another two or three hours' worth. The videos were repetitive and at times factually incorrect, especially when referring to legislation and regulations. The videos made mention of company officers who did not exist and policies that were yet to be introduced. At the end of each video was a short multiple-choice test, and each employee had to score 100% in order to sign off the unit as completed. Sometimes the questions were ambiguous or offered a clearly incorrect option as the correct response. When a worker 'failed' the test they had to repeat the module.

When even members of the senior management team started to jack-up about being bombarded with the mind-numbing training videos, the re-induction program was put on ice.

A team sport

A more thoughtful and productive way of introducing new people to your team is to break the induction process up into pieces and assign those pieces to members of your team and other key functionaries in the organisation.

You might ask the HR people to take the new hire through the terms and conditions of their employment, and the forms to use to apply for leave.

It's probably best if you step them through your expectations about punctuality, breaks and what to do if they're late or otherwise can't get to work.

You or a team member may take them on a site tour, pointing out things like emergency assembly points, facilities like toilets and the meal room, and where the various departments are located. On the tour, introduce the new worker to people as you encounter them. Make a point of introducing them to the people with whom they'll likely need to interact as part of their day-to-day work.

Issues like evacuation and site safety could be handled by the evacuation warden. Policies and procedures designed to prevent bullying, harassment and discrimination could be handled by a contact officer (i.e. the person to whom they would need to report any such problems).

Breaking the induction process up into bits and sharing it around gives the worker time to integrate the information and connect the information with the people to whom they'll need to relate when they put that information to use. It reinforces and legitimises the roles of people like evacuation wardens and contact officers and establishes relationships that the new worker may need to draw upon later. Sharing induction around also saves your worker from getting a bunch of policies dumped on them. It also saves you, their immediate boss, from spending hours going over things personally.

Navigating culture

One of the most helpful aspects of induction is also one of the most overlooked, and that's culture. Whether the new worker is a CEO or a volunteer, helping them know the unwritten rules and expectations that make up the culture of the organisation will help them be thoughtful about the choices they make. If they're a CEO, they may decide to directly and explicitly counter those tacit norms, but there's a world of difference between intentionally seeking to shape culture and getting blindsided by it.

If you visit a country with a culture that's very different to your own, you would do well to get a hold of a cultural guide like those offered by Lonely Planet. They'll help you avoid cultural *faux pas* and possibly save you from embarrassment or arrest. Think of a person joining your organisation as someone entering a slightly foreign country. Every organisation has its own set of norms and expectations, but very few put them up on a warning poster in the foyer. As a boss, you'll do your new worker a huge favour if you let them in on the way things roll in your team, your department, your site, your organisation.

One of the things to consider is how your new hire should address people. In some organisations, anyone senior to you is addressed as sir or madam, and those junior to you by their first name or possibly their surname. In other organisations people senior to you are addressed by title, or by a salutary 'Mister' or 'Madam' before their title. For example, US politicians are addressed as 'Madam Vice President' or 'Mr Speaker' even outside of the houses of congress and in private conversations. In Australia parliamentarians are addressed by formal titles in the formal chambers (e.g. 'Mr Speaker') and less formally outside. Our Prime Minister might be addressed as 'Prime Minister' in a media interview, but may also be addressed as 'Mr Morrison'. The general public might address the PM as 'Scott' or 'Scomo' and no one would think twice about it. In many Aussie organisations everyone is on a first name basis and using formal salutation would be out of place.

In some organisations on time is late and five minutes early is on time. In others ten minutes late is on time and on time is being a suck-up. In some organisations every email should be responded to reasonably quickly, even if it's with a brief 'acknowledged', in others it's okay not to respond at all.

One of the ways to really get off on the wrong foot is with clothing. Trying to define policy around clothing, especially female clothing, is a minefield. If you can let your workers know what's generally expected and acceptable, what might raise eyebrows and what will definitely create a stir, you can then allow them to make informed choices. Formally enforcing dress codes for reasons other than safety is generally a good way to land yourself in the Equal Opportunity Commission or the equivalent jurisdiction in your setting, but most people will appreciate a little guidance.

Different organisations have different ideas on quitting time for employees. In many legal and chartered accounting firms, knocking off before 7:00 PM is a guaranteed way to ensure you will never be made a partner. In some public service organisations, working later than the prescribed quitting time is frowned upon because there is no budget for overtime and allowing a person to work back without being paid for it will trigger industrial action.

Try to think through the quirks of your organisation and let your new worker in on them. It builds confidence, reduces anxiety and decreases the possibility of your boss asking you to have a little chat with your new worker because they've unwittingly offended someone.

Summary

- Induction is a great opportunity to get your worker off to a great start.
    - Plan thoughtfully.
    - Don't treat it as a butt-covering exercise or resort to a data-dump.
    - Induction as a team sport is more effective and less arduous.
    - Include culture .

Discussion

- What was your entry into your organisation like?
- From what you've read just now, what would you do differently?

Implementation

- What can you do in the next few weeks that will set you up to provide a more effective induction next time you hire someone?

Chapter 16
Establishing a supervision relationship

Now for the brass tacks of routine supervision. There's a common leadership maxim, sometimes attributed to nineteenth century Baptist preacher Charles Haddon Spurgeon: 'Begin as you intend to go on'. In the supervisory sense, it means starting out as the boss you intend to be six weeks, six months and six years into the supervisory relationship.

In the first section we talked about getting your priorities and attitude sorted. In the second section we looked at the importance of making your expectations clear. It's important to pull all of this together from day one.

In this chapter, we'll begin with the commencement of supervision with a new worker. In the next we'll switch and talk a little about starting out when you're the new boss of an existing worker.

Supervision is generally conducted in two ways: by routine interaction and by structured supervision meetings. In establishing the supervisory relationship, those first structured meetings are critical, so we'll deal with them before we talk a little about routine interaction.

You'll note that we begin with fairly highly engaged supervision before settling into the normal frequency of supervision meetings. This serves two purposes. Firstly, it gives the worker a much better chance of beginning well and quickly establishing themselves as a productive contributor to the organisation. Secondly, if you've made a recruiting blunder, you'll realise it early before too much damage is done to the organisation and your reputation.

Clarity and preparation

In the US military, they drill the rule of six Ps into every new officer recruit: Prior Planning and Preparation Prevents Poor Performance. (Actually, the military version uses slightly more colourful language, but we're in polite company so I'll keep it nice). This is where many supervisory relationships fail

– the supervisor lacks clarity as to what they expect from their worker and fails to adequately prepare for supervision meetings.

I encourage every boss to prepare thoughtfully for each supervision meeting. I send an agenda to every person I supervise a few days before our scheduled appointment. I do the same with all my coaching clients. If there's information that the worker needs to collect, or I suspect that they'll still have some actions outstanding from a previous meeting, I'll send the agenda a little earlier. It's amazing how much of the work that was set out in a previous meeting gets done in those few days between receiving the agenda and attending the next supervision meeting.

I want every supervision or coaching appointment to be an hour of calm and clarity no matter what kind of chaos people may be facing for the rest of the month. I therefore need to prepare in a calm state and with clarity. That means taking the time to get clear in my mind what I'm trying to achieve through my supervision, and what my expectations are of the worker. In supervision meetings I hope to:

- Build a strong working alliance, characterised by respect and trust
- Give the worker a clear idea of who they're working for – my character, values and priorities
- Make it clear what I expect of the worker
- Give the worker a clear understanding as to whether they've met my expectations
- Reassure the worker that I am a resource to them – a source of guidance and support.

It's important to conduct your supervision meeting in a place where your worker has your full attention and there is little chance of being interrupted. If you have an office – great. Kick the door shut. (Back when I had an office, I wanted it to be an obvious routine that I would meet with individuals with the door closed. If you only meet with a worker behind a closed door when there's trouble, it fuels the office rumour mill). If your workplace has bookable rooms, you could use one of them. I'll often take a worker to a nearby café. If you're working remotely, do what it takes to keep the cat, kids and other interrupters at bay. Put your phone on silent and your calls on hold. Your worker needs to know that this is important.

Starting supervision: the first meeting

With the immediate essentials of induction out of the way, the first supervision meeting with a new worker should be as early as possible. Unless your organisation has an extensive and formal orientation program, that meeting should be on day one or two. I would go so far as to say that it's a higher priority for a new worker to meet with their boss than for them to meet with the people the new worker will supervise. Remember our discussion back in chapter two about the organisation (represented by you, their boss) having priority over the individual needs of workers? Begin as you intend to go on – and as you intend your new worker to go on.

There's a part of me that hesitates to write this paragraph, but I've seen too many bosses epically fail here – especially senior management types. If you're starting a new worker and they are your direct report, you should clear out a decent chunk of time in your diary on their first day to get them started well. I'm thinking a couple of hours, not a couple of minutes. If you're too busy to do that and want to flick it to someone else, then perhaps your new hire should report to someone else. Workers are not little clockwork monkeys that you can wind up and set going for your amusement. Take up your responsibility, invest the time.

Define yourself

By now you might predict that I'll hold out the position description (PD) as the first point of reference for that opening supervision meeting. A well-informed guess. But there's something even more important: you. Remember Gallup's research I cited earlier – the single most important determinant of your worker's enjoyment and productivity in their work is their relationship with you. It's important that your new worker establishes a trusting and productive relationship with you. This meeting is an opportunity to start this off well.

I've already given a little lecture on the importance of giving this meeting a good chunk of time. To that let me add, give it a good chunk of yourself. I like to summarise that in three big ideas. Who I am, what I'm committed to, and what you can expect of me. Let's break those down.

There's an excruciating group therapy scene in the film *Anger Management* where a therapist played by Jack Nicholson asks the newcomer played by Adam Sandler to, "Tell us who you are." The therapist rejects every response as 'hobbies' or 'occupation' or 'personality' as if to say 'who' this hapless therapy seeker might 'be' is something deeper, more fundamental or esoteric.

I prefer to think more in terms of that great philosopher-ogre Shrek: "Ogres are like onions." So are humans. Sociologist Tony Campolo once asked, "What if you're like an onion? What if once you peel away all the layers [of interests and occupation and family and education and culture], there's nothing left? What if you're just the sum total of your layers?" Indeed.

In saying who I am I might tell a new worker how long I've been in the gig, what I've done previously, my marital and parental status. I usually look for something that came up in their resume, the phone screen, in the job interview or other conversations that might lead to a point of connection. It might be a sport or a musical instrument they play, a hobby they have, where they live or went to school. I'll usually lead with a question, draw the new worker out a bit about themselves, then reciprocate with a snippet of information about myself. I'm not giving them the whole onion, just enough to build a sense of resonance.

If I notice that they're familiar with a particular behavioural style or temperamental model (some people actually put these in their resume!), I might ask them a question or two about their preferred style, temperament or strengths, before sharing a little about my own.

Define commitments

Next comes my commitments, in a job-specific sense. I'll be as frank as I can be about the big-picture things I'm pursuing. Some of those will be headings in my personal work plan (which in a general sense may stretch up to a decade ahead) and some will be about the kind of culture I am personally seeking to create in the team and in the wider organisation. For example, in my current employment I'm seeking to instil a value of intentionality (i.e. if you want something to happen you'll need to do it on purpose: you'll need a thoroughgoing plan). I'm also trying to model accountability and to foster a commitment to best practice. Each of these I weave into my conversations and I intentionally model them in how I conduct myself and how I lead others. This helps my team understand some of the whys and wherefores of what I do and what I ask them to do.

Then there's my specific commitments to my new worker, or put differently, what they can expect of me. I state up front I'm committed to their success, to their development and to their enjoyment of their work. I want to be the kind of boss that they will want to work for. I mostly work remotely so an 'open door' policy is a bit passé, but I will state that I'm committed to taking their ideas and concerns seriously. I look them in the eye as I say it (or down the camera if we're working over Zoom).

Define expectations

The PD sets out what you expect of the worker, and your primary job as a supervisor is to ensure your worker meets your expectations. Some of the info in the PD has already been addressed in the induction process. In this meeting you're most interested in the responsibilities and outcomes. Initially I'll step through the PD fairly quickly, simply going over the main ideas for emphasis. I won't drill down too much until it's time to create a work plan. In some cases, the PD will get more attention in the second work plan than in the first – but more on that in a minute.

The next point of reference is the organisation's current strategic plan. The more senior the role, the more critical this is. Yet even the most junior call centre worker would benefit from knowing that, for example, the current strategic theme is 'customer enrichment', especially if they've just come from another call centre that was all about 'maximising new customer acquisition.' To the extent that a worker makes decisions – even if it's choosing a turn of phrase or when to terminate a call – is the extent to which the worker needs to understand the bigger picture.

If the job is a fairly basic one, or if there are procedures that detail the work more specifically, you may be able to go through the PD and strategic plan fairly quickly and then get down to the tasks that make up the job. Entry-level or lower skilled jobs may need only a relatively short opening supervision meeting before you move to the actual context where the work is to be performed.

A new worker can quickly be deployed in simple tasks using the well-known, four step process set out below. You may take the worker through this basic on-the-job training, or hand it off to a suitably trained and suitably briefed co-worker. (Don't dump the new worker on a more experienced worker and presume the more senior worker will know what to do).

1. Demonstrate
   - Allow the worker to watch the task being completed at normal speed and using the normal process. For a call centre worker, that may mean having them observe as you make or take a couple of routine calls. For a retail worker that may mean serving a customer or two as the new hire watches.
   - Then explain tasks step by step including the various aspects to take into consideration. Use procedures and work instructions to guide the process if you're in a quality-assured environment. Be very clear and specific about the quality standards required.
2. Collaborate
   - Give the worker a chance to try completing the task. That may mean role playing if there's a risk of them annoying a customer or allowing them to practice before going live with real people or real products.
   - Talk them through the task as they undertake it, and work toward them completing the task seamlessly and at the speed expected. Don't underestimate the importance of meeting your expectation for speed. Unless you're clear on the pace you expect, you could end up with a worker who thinks being ponderously slow is okay. That will eventually cost you in terms of poor productivity, annoyed customers and resentful co-workers. To achieve efficiency, there's a need for (safe, reasonable, appropriate) speed.
3. Observe
   - Watch the worker complete the task a few times. Provide whatever pointers and reminders might be helpful.
4. Supervise
   - Allow the worker to operate without direct or constant observation and check in with them from time to time to monitor the speed and quality of their work. If it doesn't meet your expectations, let them know immediately and specifically. If necessary, repeat the overall process again.

If the job has more autonomy and responsibility, you'll probably need to spend a little more time in your first meeting developing their first work plan. We've already spoken a little about work plans back in chapter 10. You'll remember that the work plan is the explicit plan for getting done all the responsibilities on the PD as they present themselves in current tasks and challenges. It's more than a to-do list because it translates into what will be done when. You might want to go back and refresh your memory.

Personally, my work plan is my calendar, which I maintain using Microsoft Outlook. Every task that I plan to do is scheduled as an appointment in my diary.

The content of your new worker's first work plan will be different to the content of their plans once they've been up and running for a while. There will be the various induction activities we spoke about earlier, along with things like product familiarisation, training on the enterprise information system, and perhaps introductions to their client or customer base. This is why the PD may do more to inform work plans once they're through most of the familiarisation and orientation activity.

In your first meeting, discuss with your new worker all the activities they will need to undertake in their first two to four weeks in order to establish themselves well in their role. There may be some immediate challenges to address or there may be a chronic problem they need to appraise. If you've done your preparation, you'll probably bring a decent list of items you believe will need to be included in their work plan. If your newcomer is anything beyond completely green, they'll likely have some ideas too. My preference is to ask the worker for their thoughts and draw out as much as I can before I fill in any blanks with my thinking. As far as possible I want my workers to be thinking and planning for themselves to the extent that their responsibilities allow.

Once the list of activities is shaped up, I will usually ask a new worker to schedule them into a work plan or calendar app and talk me through it. I won't do this on an ongoing basis, but I do want to instil in them the idea that I'm serious about planning the work and working the plan.

If you have other people doing roles similar to that of your new worker, you may be able to assign them a buddy they can shadow for a few days. This approach uses socialisation rather than overt instruction, and while it may seem a bit homey and inefficient, it's how you learned most of the knowledge you now use every day, including your first language and the protocols of basic human interaction in your culture. It's often used to get sales reps up and running while they cram product knowledge and familiarise themselves with ordering procedures.

Fairly early in the piece you'll want to address KPIs, milestones and any other means you have for measuring performance and progress. Given that the first meeting is all about getting the new worker up and running (and there's a lot to go through), you may wish to simply flag with the new worker that you intend to go through their performance metrics with them in the next meeting. There's usually so much induction and orientation to get through in the first meeting in the first couple of weeks on the job that any routine reports on KPIs or other result areas will probably be meaningless. As we discussed back in chapter 10 these are usually set out in the 'results' section of the PD so it should come as no surprise to the new worker.

Monitoring though software

I've briefly touched on workflow planning software and performance monitoring software as a means of gathering hard data on employee performance. Such programs are practically ubiquitous in work environments like call centres. If your workplace uses any kind of automated system to allocate and schedule tasks, or to monitor and measure employee performance, it is imperative that you make your new hire aware of this practice, what will be monitored and how the information will be used. Failure to do so is ethically doubtful and legally contestable.

Next conversation

It's vital to ensure that the next supervision meeting is inked in the diary before you end the first one. It's worth considering forward planning all your routine supervision appointments for the coming year. Allow me to remind you that it's not good form to postpone or cancel supervision appointments unless it's absolutely unavoidable. If you want your worker to take their responsibilities seriously, you should take your supervision responsibilities seriously. When supervision appointments are regularly moved or cancelled, it communicates that your worker is not that important, and that supervision is perfunctory. Don't be that boss.

The following supervision meeting will usually be a week or two after commencement, even if you plan for routine supervision to be monthly. I encourage you to prepare an agenda, and make sure you follow up on the key points of their work plan. That means making an appointment with yourself to prepare and send an agenda.

I take notes in every supervision meeting and every coaching appointment. I always include points for action and the timeslot for the next appointment. With some people I'll send them the calendar invitation for the next appointment as soon as I make it.

At the end of the meeting, I email the notes to the worker or client.

Summary of the first meeting

- The first meeting is mostly about establishing your relationship. Look to make a solid personal connection with your new worker. Be clear about yourself and your commitments.
- Be clear about their role and responsibilities by stepping them through the PD. Get them working in their role as early as is practicable.
- There will probably be a number of induction and orientation tasks for your new worker to complete. Get them all into their work plan.
- Be clear about accountabilities like KPIs, targets and milestones and how they will be measured.
- Get the next supervision appointment into the diary.

The second meeting

To my mind the second meeting is a hybrid of the opening meeting and the kind of meeting that will become the norm as the supervisory relationship settles into its own rhythm. In this meeting I'll retain some aspects of the first meeting (define self, define commitments, define expectations) and introduce the general format of meetings to come.

It's in this and subsequent meetings that the PD and the organisational strategy become primary reference documents for the supervisory relationship.

In planning the agenda for supervision, I'll typically follow the format set out below:

- Connect with the worker and gain a general sense of how they are going. This is where I'll do a little more self-disclosure and make reference to my commitments.
- Follow up specific issues from the previous meeting, especially if they're not captured under Strategy/PD. This could be a pretty long list in the second meeting, because it will include following up all the induction and orientation actions. Make reference to your notes from the first meeting to ensure effective follow-up.
- Work through PD Strategy headings. The more senior the role, the more emphasis on pure strategy. I'm not going to routinely step a CEO through each of their PD headings in each supervision meeting, but I probably will for a less experienced or more junior worker. Address performance milestones, targets and KPIs under the appropriate heading from the PD and strategy. You'll either ask your worker to report them to you, or you'll have sourced them and will be feeding them back to the worker. Either way, this requires preparation before the meeting.
- Remember to include opportunity for the worker to raise questions or issues they wish to discuss.

With workers doing less complex jobs, this second meeting may only be 20-30 minutes. With more complex and independent roles, I recommend you allow 60-90 minutes. That time will fly by so you may need to be thoughtful about how much detail you explore in each of the strategy/PD headings. For the second meeting, I'll generally think through which of these I want the new worker to make a more immediate priority and concentrate there.

Because the first supervision meeting is usually so jam-packed with the details and logistics of induction and orientation, the second meeting is where a boss really gets an opportunity to set the tone of supervision. While the difference in responsibility and authority is obvious, I want as far as possible for each supervision meeting to be an adult-to-adult conversation about both parties fulfilling the responsibilities of their job. Unless there are serious problems to address, I'm aiming for a more peer-to-peer posture. I want my people to be frank and fearless with me, willing to tell me the truth, even if it's awful and even if it's about me.

Connecting

In the first two sections of the book, I emphasised the importance of the supervisory relationship as the major determinant of the quality of the worker's experience of work and of the worker's performance. I've encouraged you to be involved in the recruiting and onboarding process, and to invest significant time and effort into your first supervisory meeting.

In the second meeting it's important to continue to invest in the relationship. I encourage you to intentionally cultivate understanding and trust by connecting on a personal level – showing interest in the worker as a human being, not just a unit of labour. I also encourage some thoughtful self-disclosure, so the worker feels like they're working for a person, not just the organisational machine.

I'll begin the meeting with a few open-ended questions, usually with something innocuous like, "So, how are you settling in?" Followed by something a little more focused like, "What are you most pleased about?" or "What stood out for you in your first week?" If I've heard any positive feedback about them or noticed them going above and beyond the call of duty, I'll let them know and express appreciation.

Most people, when asked how they're going, will reciprocate. I use this opportunity to give the worker a bit of an idea of what I'm working on or what I'm pursuing strategically. I won't blurt out all my hopes and dreams and fears and triumphs. I'll just tell them enough to create a sense of mutuality, and to help the worker get a sense of what they're dealing with in reporting to me. The better a worker knows their boss, the more easily they will trust them (unless of course that boss proves to be untrustworthy, but that's not you).

Follow–up

This will likely be the first real opportunity for the worker to gauge how much you really mean what you say. In the first meeting you'll have set some tasks for the worker to complete. This is the juncture where the worker discovers how serious you were in expecting those tasks to be completed.

I'll transition into this part of the meeting by saying something like, "Last time we spoke we agreed on some tasks you would tackle, so let's step through those now." Then I'll go through the list of actions from the previous meeting to ensure they were completed. If a task is not completed, I'll inquire as to why. Unless the task was time critical, I'll usually let it pass if there's a reasonable explanation. I will however, let the worker know that we'll carry over that task to the 'Actions' list from this appointment.

If a time-critical task is not completed, or if there are a number of tasks still to be completed, I'll want a good account from the worker as to why. Sometimes there are circumstances beyond the worker's control, or they're waiting for other people to do their part. If the uncompleted tasks are simply a case of the worker not being sufficiently organised, I'll ask questions about how they might manage themselves differently so that they get their tasks completed.

This can be pretty tricky territory. It may be that the worker lacks the competence to get the work done on time. They may have a lousy work ethic. They may be slow to adapt to a new environment and need a little time to find their feet. They may have issues outside the workplace that are making them anxious and distracted.

Stephen Covey's counsel, 'Seek first to understand, then be understood' is helpful here.[61] Understand what lies behind your worker's disappointing performance (seek to understand) and then make it abundantly clear that you expect things to improve (be understood). That doesn't mean banging the table with your fist. It does mean ensuring your worker understands that you're serious. It's possible to manage all of this while remaining warm and supportive. You might consider saying something along the lines of, "I genuinely want you to succeed here, and that means completing your tasks each month. If there's something you need or you're being blocked, let me know."

Given we're talking about the second meeting in a new supervisory relationship, I'm not suggesting you dwell too long on the performance deficit, unless it's a case of very significant underperformance. Often a mismatch between the worker's performance and your expectation is simply a case of the worker not being clear that you expect tasks on the work plan to be completed. In many cases the simple reality check of your clear feedback will be enough to get them performing to expectations.

---

[61] Covey, Stephen. *The Seven Habits of Highly Effective People* (The Business Library Melbourne. 1997), 235.

If there are concrete reasons for the worker failing to meet your expectations, it's important that you and the worker consider some steps to resolve the situation. They may need some training or some extra coaching in order to get up to speed. Some people are just a little slow to get with the program – with a good balance of support and clear expectations, they'll often flourish into highly productive workers.

It may be that you're simply expecting more than is reasonable and you'll need to adjust your expectations.

If your worker's performance is significantly below what you expect, it's important that you're very clear that you won't accept their current level of performance. I would recommend scheduling your next supervision appointment fairly soon (e.g. perhaps in a week or so). Letting poor performance continue can be construed as acceptance.

Strategy/PD headings

The seniority of the role and how closely it's linked to strategy will determine how much strategy informs your supervision agenda. For a point of sale retail worker, strategy may only go as far as a KPI linked to a current sales campaign. For a CEO in a young company or in a high innovation environment, the supervision conversation may be predominantly about strategy.

This section of the meeting is a little like the previous one, but it includes items that will become the regular touchpoints for the supervisory conversation. It also includes conversation about goals and targets going forward.

In chapter 10 we talked over the four main ideas in the PD, the last of which is 'results'. When you designed the job and either developed or updated the PD, you would have done well to think through the tangible results you expect for a worker in this role. You may have even considered the exact metrics you will use and how the data for those metrics will be gathered and reported. If you didn't go to that level of detail at the job design stage, now is the time to think it over.

In chapter 11 we spoke about getting a line of sight on your worker's performance. We spoke about how not to do it (like relying on perception), and some of the pitfalls of KPIs and measures of activity. This part of the supervisory interview is where you put all of that thinking to work.

In planning this part of the meeting, you'll need clarity on the information you will either gather yourself or have the worker report back to you. Even in the most basic volunteer role there's likely to be some way to objectively determine whether your expectations are met. In an employed role, you may be drawing on variations of the following examples:

- For a personal care attendant in an aged-care facility, check 'clock in' data gathered from the organisation's security or time-recording system.
- For a retail worker, sales data like upsell value, gathered from the point of sale system.
- For a call centre worker, customer rating reports, inquiry clearances or sales closures.
- For a sales rep, data from the customer relations information system about new leads, lead development, number of sales, average value of sales (the possibilities are pretty much endless).
- If your team uses a workflow management system like 'Monday', you can pull out reports on tasks completed or outstanding.

You may also rely more on data provided by your worker. Just remember, you're looking to measure results or activity and other indicators that will lead to results.

Some roles may not be easily measured by data you can dump out of a system. While some workplaces have all their workflows and projects set up in electronic management systems, many others are still fairly manual – including most community-based organisations. While plans and processes may be developed or even performed using technology, the meta-view of their progress and completion will only be gained by the worker actually reporting their progress against a plan or towards a target.

If your worker's job has a project component to it, and it's not being coordinated with an application like Microsoft Project, you'll need to refer to the project plan, figure out where you expect the worker to be up to, and determine whether the worker is meeting that expectation.

In the second meeting, you may or may not work with actual data. You may simply use this meeting as the time to introduce the range of measures that will be addressed in supervision and make clear how you expect the worker to report them (for example, many organisations have a dashboard). If possible, it's helpful to show the worker how they can access data about their performance for themselves.

If you do choose to address actual data in this meeting, it's important that you allow the worker time to gather whatever information you want them to bring – this is why I have a monthly dashboard-reporting routine and why I send a supervision agenda to each worker a few days before we meet.

When addressing the performance data, be mindful about whether the worker will have had time to settle in and complete their onboarding tasks. Otherwise presenting the data could be perceived as making unfair demands. Behavioural data like punctuality is meaningful from day one. If your worker is turning up late, you'll need to address it at this meeting if not sooner. But you may need to be a little more thoughtful about performance standards that could take a little while to attain. Remember the principles and processes for feedback we talked over in chapter 12.

If you choose to present data like upsell rates from a point of sale system, or KPIs like tasks completed, you'll need to make it clear as to whether you think their current performance is reasonable at this stage of the new worker's tenure, and the expected timeframe for the worker to achieve stated performance targets. This can be done in a collaborative, friendly and reassuring tone while still making clear your expectations.

Being directive

You tend not to hear the rejoinder, "...and that's an order!" around workplaces anymore. Giving orders is nowadays seen as being unenlightened, so 'last century', very 'theory X'. (You'll remember our discussion about the theories alphabet back in chapter seven). Directing a worker doesn't need to be conducted with the tone of a drill sergeant. However, it's part of your job as a supervisor to give instruction, be directive, and tell the worker what you expect them to do.

As you work through the headings of responsibilities and strategy in your agenda, you'll need to be clear about what you expect the worker to prioritise and accomplish over the next supervision interval. As you address each heading, be clear about what you expect the worker to do next, or do more, or do differently. Record these carefully in your meeting notes. You may not necessarily record a directive under each heading. If the worker is performing to expectations, you might simply encourage them to stick with it and move on.

Be careful to match the level of detail to the worker's level of responsibility and autonomy. Workers with little experience in entry-level roles may need quite specific instruction. That might go down to the level of, "Take some time before you log on to organise your workspace so you have the information you need at hand," or "Check the upsell offers at the start of every shift." More senior and independent workers may only need to be instructed in broad descriptions like, "I'll need a cost-benefit analysis on that initiative by the end of the week."

Your stuff

This is the part of the meeting where I invite the worker to raise any questions, feedback, ideas, problems or whatever else they may have on their mind to talk over. It may surprise you that I put this heading last. My thinking goes back to the idea I unpacked in chapter two that we're here to serve the organisation's purposes first, with the intention that we will simultaneously be able to serve the interests of the worker. I wouldn't set this order in stone, but I think it generally makes sense in light of the theory discussed earlier.

At this early stage in the relationship with your worker, it may be helpful to have a few prompt questions that will help draw out the worker if necessary. Possible questions might be:

- Is there anything you need me to explain further or clarify?
- Are people treating you kindly?
- Do you feel confident you'll settle into the role and get up to speed?
- Are there any issues left over from induction and orientation that we need to clear up?

If the worker raises anything that needs your involvement to resolve or follow up, it's imperative that you make a note of the matter and prioritise giving it some attention. If you demonstrate good follow-through at this stage it goes a long way to build trust in you and confidence in your leadership. Fail to follow-through and the worker's trust in you is undermined. They may begin to suspect that you're not all that interested in their welfare, and your prospects of gaining the discretionary work effort we discussed in chapter 14 begin to look doubtful.

Make sure you lock in the next supervision appointment. This will probably be on the timeframe of the supervision interval you intend to maintain going forward (i.e. weekly or monthly). This might be a good time to lock in a regular meeting schedule for the coming year.

A note on notes

I've already emphasised the importance of taking notes in each supervision meeting. My habit is to use the agenda as the notes template, then record facts and observations from the worker in blue type, and actions to be undertaken in green type.

I send meeting agendas and record all my supervision and coaching appointment notes as emails in Microsoft Outlook. I have a separate folder for each worker or client. At the end of the supervision meeting, I tidy up the formatting of my notes and send them as an email to the worker, BCC me. Then I shift the incoming copy from my inbox to the worker's folder.

How you record your notes and whether you send a copy to the worker is up to you. Some would say it's important that the worker takes responsibility for making their own notes. Personally, I like the idea that the worker has my expectations expressed to them verbally and then again in writing. It decreases the opportunity for ambiguity.

Summary of the second meeting

- Connect with the worker relationally, help them get to know you by telling a little about yourself and being clear on your commitments.
- Follow up specific issues from the previous meeting. Offer encouragement and appreciation for tasks completed. Deal directly with incomplete tasks.
- Work through PD and strategy headings as appropriate for the role. Discuss performance data and give the worker clear feedback as to whether they've met your expectations.
- Provide opportunity for the worker to raise questions or issues. Make absolutely sure you follow through on commitments you make.

- Set a date for the next meeting, or better still, block in meeting appointments for the rest of the year.

Third and subsequent meetings

By the time the third supervision meeting rolls around, your worker should be largely through with their induction and orientation program, and in most cases will have a sufficient handle on their role to start delivering on the result areas of their PD.

Preparing for the regular supervision meeting will follow a similar pattern to the process outlined for the second meeting. There will likely be less follow-up to do with onboarding tasks and greater focus on the regular rhythms of the job.

Connect

I encourage you to come up with thoughtful connecting questions beyond a simple, "So, how're things going?" A question that encourages a little reflection helps to set the conversational tone to go beyond the superficial. You'll need to tailor this question a little to the context. Asking a newly minted 16-year-old retail assistant what they've observed about the organisation's culture is probably asking a little too much. Asking them what they're finding easy and what they're finding hard might be a better place to begin.

Conversely, inviting people who already have significant work and life experience to be reflective, to be observant and to be curious can be a gift, especially if you take their responses seriously.

Follow-up

It's important to maintain a solid discipline of following up on commitments and directives from the last meeting, both yours and theirs. You may choose to list them in a separate section or raise them as you work through the headings for responsibilities and strategy. Either way, it's imperative that you close the loop of commitment *to* action and accountability *for* action. This is a fundamental aspect of the rhythm of clear expectations and clear feedback that underpins good supervision.

If you neglect to follow up on commitments, you're tacitly sending the message that commitments are just suggestions that can be taken up or left undone at the worker's discretion – in which case you're not fulfilling your basic responsibility of supervision.

If a worker does not follow through on a commitment (or if you don't!), it's important to figure out the contributing factors. When a worker answers, "no" to your question as to whether a task from the previous meeting was completed, it's helpful to respond with calm and curiosity. I'll say something like, "That's not what I expected. Why do you think this didn't get done?" This invites the worker to consider the contributing factors behind the uncompleted commitment, rather than triggering a defensive reaction.

I once had a worker look at me blankly and say, "I just didn't think it was important." I managed to stifle my impulse to respond with, "WHAT?" took a breath and asked, "What gave you the sense that this was not important?" The worker's answer revealed that they and I had very, very different ideas as to the job at hand and how the relationship was going to work. It became clear that I needed both to calmly emphasise that directives given in a supervision meeting were not mere 'suggestions' and to pay closer attention to the worker's follow-through.

In unpacking the reasons behind tasks uncompleted and directives unfulfilled, there's opportunity to understand the working environment from the worker's perspective. If there's a genuine commitment to understand, the conversation will rarely get to, "Lift your game or you're fired." That conversation we had back in chapter eight around balancing support and expectation is relevant here. There may be good reasons as to why your expectations were not met. Sometimes there are steps the supervisor can take in terms of providing some extra training, some extra resources like IT, or just using a bit of positional clout to clear blockages.

All that said, sometimes it just comes down to the worker needing to apply themselves more diligently. If that's the case, that's pretty much what I'll say to them. If their performance is a long way shy of what I expect, I'll be clear about that too.

When a worker comes to a supervision meeting and reports a large number of completed tasks, or reports enduring some really difficult circumstances or facing up to tough challenges, I'll offer measured and sincere appreciation for their work. I try to be as clear and specific as I can on this, and look especially to show understanding of what they've endured and the effort they've put in.

I'm not particularly quick to offer praise. I've worked with some organisations that have sought to create what I like to call a 'Lego Movie' culture, where 'everything is awesome' all the time and everybody is showered in compliments no matter what. Its apparent insincerity makes me wary. Part of this may be cultural – we Aussies tend to understate things and reserve our praise for sporting heroes. But I'm also aware that hyper positivity creates a culture where people cannot tell each other the plain truth. Being more measured in praise means an exceptional contribution is recognised as just that, and a 'good enough' contribution is not elevated to the realm of stratospheric. Performance that is below expectation can be dealt with honestly and fairly without being glossed over or seen as catastrophic.

PD and strategy

I tend to routinely treat this section of the supervision conversation as a kind of 'check progress and plan for what's next' segment. I usually adopt more of a coaching approach here (we'll talk more about this in Section 4), checking that targets are being met and milestones reached on time and, where appropriate, in budget. In contexts where a dashboard is used, it's easy to do a quick overview and then pay attention to the outlier indicators, seeking to learn from and capitalise on the better-than-expected results and figuring out the drivers of and possible responses to lower-than-expected results.

Without a reporting dashboard, it's a matter of working through the key results from the PD and milestones from the strategy and checking that they're on track.

Where a worker exceeds your expectation, simply acknowledging the fact and offering sincere thanks is usually enough to make the worker feel appreciated. It's not uncommon for new hires to push themselves hard to create a good impression. If you suspect the worker is pushing themselves to unstainable levels, you might want to ask some gentle sustainability questions.

If the worker's performance is less than your baseline expectation, it warrants an approach that's a little more pointed. If the PD or your previous supervision conversations have set clear targets that have not been reached, it's important to be abundantly clear that you expect things to improve. We talked a little about this earlier when walking through the second meeting.

If you get to your fourth or later meeting and the worker's performance is still below what you would reasonably expect at this stage, it's time to ask some serious questions. It's beyond the scope of this book to try to play out all the various possible ways the conversation could go, but here are a few principles to keep in mind:

- Suspend judgement – before deciding that hiring this person was a grave mistake, commit to examining the situation from a variety of angles. Assume that there's a reasonable way to rectify the poor performance until that assumption becomes untenable.
- Get curious – poor performance can be driven by simple things like not understanding certain processes (this is particularly likely where good performance requires adept use of computer software). Sometimes poor personal organisation or a disruptive workmate can be factors. Be prepared to think laterally in figuring out what stands between your worker and your expectations.
- Be (a little) patient. Without rehashing too much neurobiology, some people are vulnerable to elevated anxiety when they start a new job. Anxiety interferes with intellectual processes, making people seem less clever than they actually are. Getting forceful and heaping pressure on them will only make it worse (and set your hiring journey back to square one). Be calm, be supportive, and be clear.
- Provide adequate resources and allow adequate time for your new worker to get up to speed, but no more. Avoiding the unpleasant task of performance-managing or firing a poorly performing worker by accepting less-than reasonable performance or providing more than reasonable assistance is a dereliction of supervisory responsibility. It's also a surefire way to demotivate the rest of your workers and foster resentment toward you.

Very occasionally, by the third (or perhaps fourth or fifth) meeting, it becomes clear that the worker is simply not up to the job and is unlikely to reach stated expectations any time soon, even with your careful application of the advice set out above. Or, in the same vein, it may become apparent that the worker's values and attitudes are not compatible with those of the organisation. In either case, as soon as you're not optimistic that a worker will settle into being a productive and harmonious contributor, I strongly encourage you to look at quickly ending the employment relationship (this advice comes out of some painful personal experience).

You'll remember back in chapter 15, I advocated writing a specific probationary or trial period into the contract. Because no selection process is absolutely goof-proof, it's important to have a means of quickly reversing a bad hiring call. In terminating a worker, it's important to clearly establish their rights and entitlements and ensure they're fully satisfied. Once you're clear on what's required, act promptly.

Celebrate the little things

Even when working with fairly mundane aspects of performance, it's worth bearing in mind how small steps, or subtle nuances in a worker's way of handling things can add to longer-term strategies. Reminding a worker how the small things that they do are a part of achieving much bigger things helps provide a sense of importance and value to their work.

For example, I'm currently chairing a small not-for-profit that provides training and consulting services, mainly in the healthcare and community services sectors. I'm working with the CEO to develop a client pathway model. Recently, she piloted a series of short webinars, which applied the organisation's approach to particular contexts, like recovery from drug and alcohol addiction. The webinars were run by grads from the organisation's training program. The immediate aim of the webinar series was to raise a little cash to ease the financial pressure on the organisation. The webinars attracted modest registrations and made a corresponding return to the organisation – they weren't a failure, but they didn't raise a motza either. In our supervision conversation, the CEO was a little deflated at the result.

The conversation turned to considering the value proposition of running the webinars to our grads: here was a chance to leverage the organisation's brand to build their own personal profile. At the same time, they were deepening their involvement and connection with the organisation. Thus, they became more avid ambassadors for the organisation in their spheres of influence. At the same time, those registrations represented new people at the entry step in the organisation's customer journey. Those people are now on the mailing list and may respond to an invitation to engage in further services offered in the coming months. In addition to those benefits, the organisation learned a little more about promoting and running webinars, something that will help improve customer experience into the future.

The webinars may not have been a huge financial win, but they provided a series of small but important wins at both 'ends' of the customer pathway – new people became aware of the organisation, and long-term partners expanded the organisation's reach and capacity.

That short detour in our supervision conversation provided some encouragement to the CEO, and also reinforced in her mind the kind of 'pathway' thinking that I wanted to permeate the whole organisation.

Forward vision
One of the pitfalls of supervision is to fixate on the forensic (i.e. just looking at performance for the period leading up to the supervision conversation). It's equally important to look forward to the next set of milestones in the strategy, challenges lying ahead, and to possible improvements in key result areas.

Looking forward encourages the worker to plan their allocation of time and other resources. It also helps to identify where financial resources or other contributions from other parts of the organisation will be required. You may need to use you influence to line up these resources so they're available when needed. Getting on the front foot in your supervision can sometimes avert delays and avoid problems.

A little stretch
A good supervisor will usually encourage workers to steadily improve performance in key result areas, even if their performance is already meeting expectations. In doing so, it's important to maintain some perspective. Performance has natural limits determined by personal and organisational capacity. Sooner or later the law of diminishing returns will kick in (usually sooner). Like an athlete, as a worker gets closer and closer to their peak, the increased effort yields smaller and smaller gains. If an athlete shoots for too much they risk injury and a significant setback – the law of diminishing returns can quickly give way to the law of decreasing returns.

There's a prevailing doctrine in the Australian public sector built around the somewhat elusive concept of a 'productivity dividend.' As far as I can tell this is the idea that, as systems are improved and automated, organisations (i.e. government departments and agencies) can maintain their service levels with fewer and fewer staff. Going further, it implies, in a somewhat Darwinian fashion, that cutting back staff will force the remaining staff to find more efficient ways of working. In practice this usually translates to staff figuring out the aspects of their role they can neglect without immediate consequences (and often it's compliance and risk-management activity that get ignored). The consequence of that neglect sometimes takes years to come to light, and occasionally does so in the form of spectacular failure. The productivity-dividended-to-death Victorian Department of Health and Human Services Communicable Disease Section discovered this when their appallingly under resourced department was comprehensively overwhelmed by the onset of the recent COVID-19 pandemic. Cue parliamentary inquiry and political recriminations.

Now that we've guarded against the insidious evil of relentless work intensification and pointed to an illustrative horror story, we can cautiously consider the possibility of encouraging a worker to stretch a little to make incremental lifts in their performance.

This may be as simple as a statement along the lines of, "You hit twenty closed sales last month with a total value of nearly forty grand. I wonder what it would take to nail a couple more sales and push it over the $40K mark."

Or you might see how far the simple process of an ongoing feedback loop could take you. (Remember back in Chapter 11 we talked about performance data feedback having a motivational effect in and of itself). Simply plotting performance data on a graph and asking the worker for their thoughts may be enough to get them thinking about possibilities for pushing the numbers a little higher.

In encouraging your worker to deliver a little more, be open to their feedback and suggestions as to what it may take. Often worker's productivity is held back to antiquated or unreliable computer software, by unnecessarily complex or convoluted systems, or poorly designed workflows. If you suspect any of these may be contributing, ask questions and listen carefully to the answers.

Principal roles
Often a CEO or managing director will report to a board, but that reporting relationship should go through the chair or a person delegated by the board to

supervise the CEO. Otherwise, the CEO effectively has no boss except when the board is convened.

If you're chairing a board, it's your job to ensure adequate supervision of the person delegated by the board to operate the organisation, whether their title is CEO, principal or senior minister.

In supervising CEOs, I take the same overall approach that I do with my other staff: define myself, define my expectations, and work them through development of a work plan. Some chairs may baulk at the insistence on a work plan. I would argue that it's even more critical for a CEO than for a first-line supervisor. The work plan keeps the focus on the important and the strategic when a CEO will face considerable pressure to be diverted by the anxiously urgent and the tactical. Tactics only have meaning in light of strategy – otherwise they descend into expediency.

In working with a CEO, I won't necessarily step them through all of their routine responsibilities, especially once they're up and running in the role. The board should have suitable reporting parameters to gain a decent line of sight on routine management issues through the CEO's regular report to the board. Neither will I ask them to granulate their plan down to diary slots. At this level they should have that kind of discipline nailed. If they don't, I'll get the clues soon enough.

As a chair I'm interested in what's getting the CEO's attention and energy, so I'm interested in their work plan from that perspective. I'm also wanting to get an idea of whether they're asking too much or too little of themselves and the organisation, so I'm keen to see how many different projects and innovations they're trying to keep running all at once. Some CEOs manage their anxiety by getting distracted by shiny new projects and possibilities. Others just get lost in the day-to-day rigours of business as usual. The work plan will give you a line of sight as to which end of the spectrum they're heading toward.

Other considerations

Sponsorship
Sometimes the improved productivity conversation with a worker surfaces issues that are much broader than the scope of supervisory relationship. Issues like IT systems or customer care policies are often organisation wide.

It's easy to throw up your hands and say, "I'm hearing you, but it's out of my hands." The issue may be outside of your scope of authority, but it may not be beyond your sphere of influence.

Promising to relay the worker feedback up the chain of command is a small thing you can do. If you hear similar feedback for multiple workers, you might want to write a discussion paper, which includes some estimates of what the poor system or policy is costing. Putting in some effort and engaging your worker's help in developing such a paper shows you're taking their feedback seriously. Even if you're unsuccessful in influencing the thinking higher-up, you've built a stronger allegiance with your workers.

Pay attention to the whole team

While we're thinking about establishing the supervisory relationship with a new worker, it's worth thinking briefly about engaging the rest of the workers in the new recruit's immediate work area. Co-workers can do a great deal to assist or inhibit a newcomer establishing themselves as part of a team. This is especially tricky if a team has been together for a long time. A quick story will help you see what I mean.

A graduate nurse I know decided to specialise in renal nursing – it's an aspect of nursing that's highly technical and involves a fairly broad spectrum of specialist knowledge. In many ways it's one step back from intensive care (lots of renal specialist nurses progress to becoming ICU nurses). To broaden their knowledge, the young grad decided to do a rotation in a dialysis unit. Dialysis is highly specialised and takes quite a while to learn. But once mastered, it's fairly routine, and can become a bit monotonous. For this reason most grads try to avoid dialysis. The grads that do end up in a dialysis unit rotation are often not all that thrilled to be there.

The unit to which this young grad was assigned was populated largely with staff who'd been in the unit for quite a number of years (a few years in a dialysis unit may cause a nurse's general ward craft to atrophy, so these units tend to accumulate people who stick around until retirement). The existing staff were used to grad nurses who weren't really interested and had developed the habit of doing most of the grads' work for them. Hence the grads never really became independently proficient. A presupposition developed among the long termers that new grads just weren't up to it and weren't interested, and their behaviour set up a self-reinforcing cycle.

When our young grad started, they were driven bananas by the old hands constantly interfering and taking over their work, as was the custom. The young nurse kindly requested they back off and allow some space for learning. The old hands kept on taking over.

The young grad spoke to the senior nurse. You would think that the senior would be happy to have a grad who was engaged, committed and keen to learn. Yet, in response to the young nurse's request for some space, the senior did... nothing. Zip, nada, zilch, zero. Even after several conversations, it was largely left to the young nurse to muster their own assertiveness and push hard to get the existing dialysis unit staff to back off. This created waves and the young nurse felt disliked and marginalised.

The young nurse spoke with the unit manager who reluctantly took some steps to intervene. It helped a little, but in the end the young nurse was relieved when a place back on the renal ward was offered and they could exit the dialysis unit before the official end of their rotation.

A newcomer in any group has the inevitable effect of disrupting the relational homeostasis of the group. If there are cliques and rifts in a team, the newcomers may be pulled in various directions as people either seek to recruit the newcomer to their corner or defend themselves against the threat the newcomer poses. If you want an excruciating example, just watch the 2000 American rom com *Meet the Parents*.

Some really stuck teams simply keep newcomers at arm's length so their comfortable relational rut remains undisturbed. The newcomer eventually gets the hint and moves on. This is especially prevalent in volunteer organisations like service clubs and churches.

The lesson here? Pay attention to team culture and the behaviours by which the culture is expressed. If you have a longstanding team where newcomers tend to come and go while the core of old hands remain, you've probably got some cultural issues to address. You'll need to show more courage and commitment than the senior nurse in the story above.

Supervision in groups

In my consulting practice I'm often asked by managers with board spans of control (they're probably supervising more staff than they can optimally manage) whether they could supervise staff in groups. Or some managers assure me that their staff are well supervised because they have a team meeting first thing every Monday.

The idea of group supervision comes from the field of professional supervision – the kind of supervision where therapists and social workers discuss cases in small groups in order to support good practice. You'll remember all the way back in the introduction I differentiated *professional* supervision from *positional* supervision. This book is about the latter. You can do professional supervision in groups. Team meetings are useful and compliment positional supervision, but they're not in themselves adequate positional supervision. Remember, supervision is about making individuals aware of your expectations and providing feedback as to whether those expectations are met. In a group, poor individual performance can be obscured within the overall team's results. It's only through one-to-one conversations that you'll learn about who's carrying whom and what resulting resentments may be simmering.

If you don't have time to adequately supervise your staff individually, your job, and perhaps your organisational structure requires redesign. We'll talk some more about this when we deal with spans of control in the final section.

Supervision by routine interaction

In a great many workplaces, including much of retail, hospitality, healthcare, construction, logistics and manufacturing, the most common form of supervision is conducted through routine interactions. The supervisor and the worker tend to work in the same area, often at reasonably close quarters, and have opportunity to interact many times during the day. For many people in these industries, routine interaction is the only form of supervision they will ever receive.

If you're the front of house supervisor in a restaurant, or a leading hand on a building site, it makes sense that you'll be providing direction and instruction to your staff multiple times every shift. This is normal and necessary, and I'd like to emphasise a couple of key ideas. Firstly, routine interaction should not replace structured supervision meetings. These meetings might only be twenty minutes, and they might only be monthly, but the discipline of sitting down and talking about your worker's contribution to the organisation will deliver in spades, especially when the worker is just starting out with you.

Some people might argue, "But I tell them what they need to know each day as we work. They're doing what I expect. Why waste time with another meeting?" I would respond, "The discipline of structured meetings is as much about the relationship as it is about performance, and it's as much about your performance as a supervisor as it is about theirs as a worker." Structured meetings push the supervisor to pay attention, to notice the workers strengths and challenges, and to show appreciation and concern as appropriate. These topics may never find their way into the conversation in the immediate hustle and bustle of, "Reset table thirteen for six and a high chair" or "Give me a hand standing up these wall frames."

Secondly, even in your routine supervision, applying the disciplines of good supervision is just as important: make your expectations clear, give unambiguous feedback as to whether your expectations are being met, provide the resources necessary for your worker to do their job, take an interest in the person as an individual, and commend the efforts that go above and beyond (i.e. all the stuff we've been talking over since the contents page).

Routine interaction is the context where immediate instruction and direction are given, often under time pressure and when the boss is in the middle of other tasks. It's all too easy for communication to be rushed and unclear. To reduce the possibility of unclear communication resulting in disappointing outcomes, it's worth developing some basic habits for clear communication:

- Stop whatever it is your doing
- Look directly at the worker and ensure you have their full attention
- State what you want them to do in short, direct sentences. Be careful to give them the information they need to fulfil your expectations
- Check that they have understood. If in doubt, ask them to tell you in their own words what it is you want them to do.

Using good supervision practice in the often time-pressured context of minute-by-minute interactions is not easy. It requires another level of self-awareness and intention, often stacked on top of the pressure of the immediate. It's much easier in the planned and structured context of the formal meeting than it is to do on the fly.

One way to improve routine or ad hoc supervision is to seek to build in the disciplines of good supervision one habit at a time. This might begin with figuring out the one aspect of your supervision that, if you improved, would most positively impact your worker's performance. That will likely take some self-observation, some reflection or perhaps a conversation with your coach.

You could ask yourself, "Do my workers consistently do as I expect, or am I regularly surprised, disappointed or even frustrated with them or their work?" If you workers are not showing up on time, not following safety rules or other procedures, or not doing the stuff you want them to do, either you're not being clear in communicating your expectations, or you're not following through on feedback, which means they've concluded your directions can be safely ignored. If any of this paragraph rings true, you could commit to a course of action to change your part in the dance of disappointment.

Or you might ask yourself, "Do I let my workers know that I value their work?" That might lead to a commitment for you to seek to develop a habit of saying, "Thank you."

Whatever you decide to work on, habits that go against your natural instincts can be pretty hard to form. People use all kinds of devices to prompt and remind themselves to do what doesn't come naturally. Putting a daily reminder in your phone calendar or setting a daily reminder alarm five minutes before you begin work is a good way to keep new habits front of mind.

From time to time I've used a five-minute review checklist, which I'll complete after every coaching appointment to rate how I've performed on the criteria I'm seeking to change. I might do the review for three months then stop and look over the results. I find that any mechanical reminder or review system starts to lose its power to influence after two or three months.

Summary

- The chapter looked at the first, the second, the third and subsequent supervision meeting with a new worker. Each meeting followed a roughly similar pattern:
    - Prepare thoroughly
    - Connect relationally
    - Define yourself
    - Use the PD and Strategy documents to clarify your expectations
    - Make clear how performance will be measured and give an evaluation based on those measures
    - Encourage creation of a work plan
    - Give opportunity for the worker to provide feedback or raise issues
- In conducting supervision meetings:
    - Celebrate the successes and commendable behaviour
    - Directly address performance and behaviour that's below expectation
    - Take opportunity to challenge a small stretch in performance
    - Pay attention to how the worker is relating to the rest of their team
- The disciplines of scheduled supervision apply in routine interaction:
    - Make expectations clear, especially when giving instructions
    - Provide unambiguous feedback
- You may need to work on this one habit at a time.

Discussion
- What aspect of your supervision are you already doing well?
- If you were to improve one aspect of your supervision, which would likely produce the most improvement in your worker's performance?

Action
- Identify one habit you would like to cultivate and create a plan to imbed it into your practice.

Chapter 17
A new boss with an established worker

In the previous chapters we've walked through the important initial stages of what businesses term the 'HR life cycle': designing the job, recruiting and selecting, inducting the new worker and getting them established. But that's not the only way supervisory relationships begin. Sometimes it's the supervisor who's the new kid on the block, starting a new role with the organisation and inheriting a pre-existing worker or group of workers who've previously been under the supervision of someone else.

Another variation is the aftermath of a restructure, where both the supervisor and worker have been around for a while, but changes in the organisational structure means that the worker has been assigned a new supervisor, and for the purposes of our discussion, that new supervisor is you.

These two scenarios are similar in that the worker is already established in the organisation before you find yourself as their boss. That means you're effectively stepping into a role in your worker's life that someone else has occupied. The worker will bring some backstory in the form of habits, expectations and assumptions that they probably won't tell you about – you'll need to uncover them as you go.

Sometimes your worker's previous supervisor was the 'ideal' boss – they were a friend and a mentor and a sponsor and a cheerleader – the Goldilocks boss who was not too demanding and not too chill, not too close but not too distant, involved without micromanaging, empowering yet supportive and like Mary Poppins, practically perfect in every way.

Conversely, the previous supervisor may have been a lousy boss: perhaps impossible to please, maybe disinterested, possibly too chummy, perhaps too distant. Perhaps they threw Trumpian tantrums, or were Machiavellian, or palled up with the team members they liked to the exclusion of those they didn't.

Whether you're following the perfect boss, one who was perfectly awful, or a supervisor that was somewhere in between, the previous boss was not you and inevitably you'll do things differently. It's predictable that there will be a mismatch of assumptions and expectations, which will likely lead to some gear grinding as you and your worker recalibrate the supervisory relationship.

Consistent with the theory we've been discussing from the outset, starting an effective supervisory relationship well means being clear about two things: what you expect of the worker and what the worker can expect of you. In this way it's very similar to starting off a new recruit, but the dynamics will be different. A worker who's already established some history with the organisation has already developed a set of presuppositions about their job that you may or may not see the need to challenge. These include what exactly is within their range of responsibilities and what isn't, how their work is to be done, how they will relate to their co-workers (including you), what rules do and don't apply to them and what a reasonable day's work might look like.

This can be complicated territory. Marching in and announcing bold, sweeping changes may make for a great movie script, but it comes at a cost you may want to weigh up before you take action. New brooms may sweep clean as the saying goes, but your efforts to push on a prevailing system will almost certainly trigger a response of that system pushing back. You may be surprised at the creativity and tenacity a worker can muster when their equilibrium is threatened.

Conversely, simply letting sleeping dogs lie while you try to figure out what's going on risks you appearing to tolerate behaviours, attitudes and performance levels that you probably shouldn't. You may not rock the boat, but you won't be fulfilling your responsibilities either.

A 'third way' is not so much a compromise between the new broom and the passive observer, as an effort to be thoughtfully self-defined. Let's work through some of the points upon which you could chose to define yourself and in so doing, make clear what you expect of the worker and what the worker can expect of you.

The first meeting

First port of call is to get a hold of the worker's position description (PD). This will likely be a useful resource both on being clear on the actual parameters of the job, and as a reference point for your conversation. While you're there you would do well to get a hold of the worker's personnel file, either in hard copy or as a digital report dropped out of your payroll system or HRIS. Depending on what your organisation retains on file, you should be able to get things like the worker's start date, other roles they've had in the organisation and training that they've done. You might even get a copy of their resume, which will tell you their prior work history and qualifications. If your organisation does performance appraisals, the records of these should be available too. You may not make use of this information straight away, but it's worth knowing before that first formal meeting.

Connecting

Most people want to know a bit about who they're dealing with, so at the introduction stage of a meeting I'll usually give a worker a bit of a personal potted history. I don't mind telling people a bit about my professional background, the suburb I live in, where I went to school and what I'm into. This models a bit of openness and fosters a bit of trust. I want people who work for me to know me as a human who probably has some things in common with them. Then I'll invite the worker to tell me a little about themselves without specifying the criteria.

The PD

Next point of self-definition may go like this: "In order to supervise your work well, I need to understand your job. I'd like you to step me through your PD and give me an idea of your job day-to-day." Now this may sound mundane if you're supervising jobs more at the entry level like retail assistants, wait staff or call centre operators. But if you pay attention, your worker is about to give you a wealth of useful information about the job, the organisation and their place in it as they see it. What's on the PD may not bear even a passing resemblance to what they tell you.

I'm assuming here that a PD exists for your worker in their role. If it doesn't, you can use this opportunity to begin creating one. Working together on a sketch pad or a whiteboard can be a helpful way of mapping this out collaboratively. It's a bit time consuming but well worth the effort, both for the information you'll gain and for communicating to your worker that you genuinely are interested in them and what they do.

I've spoken a little earlier about work plans. If the job has any degree of autonomy or agency, I'll ask the worker, "So what do you have planned for the coming week?" (Or the coming month, depending on their seniority). If they have a work plan, they'll possibly pull it out to show me. If they don't, it can be useful to ask, "So how do you plan and track your tasks and responsibilities." Be prepared for some interesting answers.

Strategy

If there's an organisational strategic plan and your worker has some responsibility in its implementation, it's also helpful to raise it in the first meeting. This conveys to the worker that the strategy is important and will play a significant role in shaping their work. Since our overall scenario here is a worker who has been around longer than their boss, asking for the worker's understanding of their role's place in the strategy will probably be more useful than simply setting out how you see it.

Don't be surprised if your worker comes back at you with cynicism about your organisation's strategic statements, or simply shrugs as if to ask, "There's a strategy?" To be frank, organisational strategies are a dime a dozen, and a significant proportion of them never filter down much below the board or the senior management group. Some never go beyond slogans that nobody believes. (I'm still waiting for one of the big four banks in Australia to be sufficiently authentic as to admit that their actual mission is to build fabulous executive wealth through bonuses, share price increases and dividends – and that all else, including compliance with the law and service to customers, are inconvenient necessities to that end). If you draw a blank or get a cynical response, it might be wise to leave the issue for the time being and do some sleuthing to find out what exposure the worker has had to the strategy and what implementation efforts have previously been undertaken. The worker might have very good reasons for being unaware or less than enthusiastic.

If the worker has some knowledge of the strategy, it's valuable to tease out how it's expressed in their work. They may not be able to draw a direct link. It may be necessary to pick the strategy apart a little, to find where it might inform the worker's priorities. Some organisational strategies are 'whole of organisation' in scope and are intended to influence every worker's contribution. Some are more limited. If your worker's role seems untouched by the strategy, you may need to think through whether their role needs some re-design, or whether to accept that their role is simply outside the scope of the strategy.

However, if you can make the direct link between the worker's role and the organisational strategy, it's useful to get the specifics of how the strategy informs their practice and their priorities. This will tell you a great deal about how well the strategy is embedded in the organisation. It's particularly illuminating to draw links between stated outcomes in the strategy and the metrics by which the worker's performance is measured.

Clarifying expectations

If your worker is in a fairly low-responsibility role, you could at this stage move straight to clarifying expectations. This is especially important if the conversation with your worker has flagged some things that you think should be changed as soon as possible. So here comes another piece of self-definition. It might go something like this:

"I'm committed to this organisation being effective and successful. I'm also committed to you being effective and successful. That means sooner or later we'll probably have conversations about changing things to improve our efficiency or to improve your experience of the workplace."

Depending on the worker's demeanour and your own confidence, you may go on to ask, "Is there anything you think we should change right away?"

Chances are they'll answer in the negative, or request things you simply aren't in a position to deliver, like, as my dear old Dad likes to say, "Ten grand a week and time to spend it." Sometimes these requests will be simple ambit claims, and sometimes they will be sheer optimism. Treating either with good humour and non-reactivity is important.

However, you may occasionally strike gold – the simple request for a change that is deliverable, that will mean a lot to your worker. If, perchance, your worker offers such an idea, making every effort to see it delivered will earn you trust and confidence that may have otherwise taken months and years to accrue.

When to go with the status quo

There's a reasonable possibility that your discussion with your worker about their PD, their current work practices and their integration of the strategy will leave you with the impression that their current practice and performance is close enough to your expectation, at least for the time being. By this I mean the worker is performing at a level acceptable to you.

If the worker is performing to reasonable expectations, it's important to communicate that to them; to give them a clear idea of where their performance stands. In the absence of clear information, people generally make stuff up, and the stuff they make up is often based on their worst fears. Remember the principles – clear expectations and clear feedback as to whether those expectations are being met.

And when not to....

Now comes the part where judgement is required. If, as you talk with your worker and observe the workplace, you see things that you believe should be changed, there's a decision to be made as to whether it's best that you insist they change immediately, that you raise them with the worker (or in some cases, workers) for their consideration and comment, or that you observe and research for a while.

There are rules and standards that are simply your responsibility to enforce, such as company policies regarding safety, harassment and bullying, equal opportunity and proper management of finances, just to name a few. Breaches of these should be raised with the worker at the first opportunity, which may be before your formal supervision meeting. The same goes for matters like tardiness, taking too much time with 'watercooler chats', being poorly presented and the like. These should be dealt with directly, specifically, personally and no later than the first supervision meeting (or the supervision meeting immediately after you become aware of the problem). Behaviours like this don't change through general statements to the work group, subtle hints, memos, emails, signs or any other methods of avoiding a frank one-to-one conversation. The longer you put off the uncomfortable conversation, the more you're subtly communicating that you are willing to tolerate poor conduct. I gave some examples back in chapter 12 illustrating how you might have these conversations, so I won't replicate them here. These conversations don't need to be adversarial. You can be kind, personable and assertive all at the same time.

Other issues like poor productivity or poor work quality may require a slightly different approach. These kind of performance issues should be dealt with promptly (again, you don't want the worker to think you're okay with poor performance) yet may take a little more work to rectify than a simple insistence that the worker 'pull their socks up'.

Since this is a new relationship and you can't necessarily claim to know the worker's job, leading with an observation and then a question is often a useful technique. For example, let's imagine that you're a supervisor in a call centre, and there's been a team rationalisation. You've had a couple of workers who previously worked for another supervisor added to your team. They're doing the same job as before; they just have a new boss: you. In preparation for the first supervisory meeting with one team member, you run a KPI report and find that they handle about 25% fewer calls per shift than the average for your team. There could be any number of reasons for the apparent poor performance, and not all of them suggest an uncommitted or disengaged worker.

Let's assume you've already made it clear that you're committed to the organisation's efficiency and success, and also to theirs. Your next statement might be along the lines of, "So, there is one issue I would like to make progress on straight away. I've looked through the KPI reports they suggest you're handling fewer calls per shift than the average for the team. It looks to me that it's around twenty five percent less. I'm interested in your thinking as to what might be causing that number to be low."

From there the quality of the conversation will depend on your worker's reaction. A worker whose call clearance rate is low because they just don't care may be defensive, may just shrug, or may seek to deflect to another issue. The worker's numbers may be poor because they take a long time expressing care and concern for the caller, or because their language is indirect, or any number of other reasons. The worker may be genuinely surprised that their numbers are low and may have no idea why.

You may choose at this stage to simply ask the worker to pay attention to their practice and see what they might observe, then pick up the issue in the next supervision meeting. If you have some idea on why the call clearance rate is low, you may want to offer your thoughts. However you choose to proceed, the summary message is that you expect clearance rates to improve and this will be an issue for attention in supervision. Often, the simple awareness that there is now some accountability for productivity will be enough to motivate a worker to make the necessary changes. Sometimes there are logistical or technological issues to be resolved that are beyond the worker's control. The conversation may uncover a need for some training or some other kind of intervention.

I'm guessing by now some readers may be uncomfortable with the idea of raising conduct and performance issues in the first meeting. It seems like a 'new broom sweeps clean' approach that's inconsistent with the relational and collaborative supervision advocated earlier in the book.

I accept that such an immediate and direct approach may come as a bit of a shock. However, immediate and direct doesn't mean harsh, abrasive or aggressive. I'm advocating being calm and clear with as much warmth as one can manage while remaining congruent. You'll also remember our conversation way back in Chapter 8 about balancing expectation with support, hence the reference to logistics, tech and training in the previous paragraph.

In my experience, while you may get a bit of pushback early on, workers will come to trust and appreciate you being clear, consistent and fair. Conversely, if you don't make your expectations clear from the outset, you'll need at some stage to get around to it. The longer you leave it, the harder it is, and the more it seems to your workers like you're being inconsistent. It's easier to loosen the reins a little after a while than it is to tighten them.

Most of our discomfort with taking up our responsibilities from day one is our anticipation of a negative reaction from our workers. If you ask workers to change their behaviour, even if it's slightly, you'll likely get some degree of pushback. You might as well get it done with at the outset. Remember, supervision is difficult because it requires us to tolerate unpleasant feelings both in ourselves and others.

Reimagining the role
Sometimes changes are required that are not so much about improving a KPI or meeting a compliance standard as coming to a new understanding of the role. I'll give you a common example to illustrate.

Most CEOs or equivalent roles have an executive assistant (EA). Common responsibilities include managing schedule (including appointments in the CEO's calendar), managing communication (including first line filtration of emails) playing host to the CEO's guests and doing administrative stuff like travel bookings, putting together PowerPoint decks, and preparing reports.

Now an EA could do all those things and be exactly what the CEO wants or precisely not what the CEO wants. It comes down to how the role is imagined. I've worked with EAs who imagine their role as a kind of organisational 'mother', who mediates the relationships of the 'kids' (i.e. all the rest of the staff and possibly other constituents) with the 'father' (i.e. the CEO). This sounds unforgivably 1950s sexist because it is – both in terms of corporate culture and familial archetypes – yet there are CEOs out there (and yes, they are mostly old guys) who want and expect that, and there are an equal number of EAs (yes, predominantly middle-aged women) who are only too pleased to deliver.

Other EAs function like a general manager while their boss plays 'president'. These EAs typically know a lot more about what's going on than does their boss, and they carefully curate the information flow from the boss to the outside world ensuring their role is both powerful and indispensable. The bonus for the boss is that they can pretty much do as they please because their image, ideas and directives will be 'nuanced' by the EA.

There are probably a bunch of other EA archetypes out there (and I need to acknowledge most EAs are awesome people who do a great deal to keep the C-suite running efficiently). The point being, you could use the same PD to describe the role, yet the decisions and information flow, and actual 'how' of the job as distinct from the 'what' could vary immensely. (This goes some way to explaining why managing their support staff is a recurring topic when coaching CEOs).

A boss 'inheriting' their predecessor's EA, or a rookie CEO with a veteran EA could be up for an interesting tussle.

A CEO at cross purposes with their EA could work through endless iterations of the PD and still find themselves dissatisfied, over-managed, in the dark and misrepresented. In working this issue through with CEO-types, it's generally come down to taking a more right-brained approach by providing an overall simile or metaphor for the role. One CEO put it to their EA like this: "Currently your role seems to function like a counsellor, calming and reassuring people by absorbing their anxiety, then passing that anxiety on to me. What I need is for you to be a firewall – redirecting the people and issues that are not my problems to solve, and arranging the people and issues that are, in a way that I can deal with them appropriately." What followed was an ongoing learning curve as to what should and shouldn't get to the CEO's office and inbox and in what order.

You'll notice that even in the use of a simile, the CEO was nonetheless clarifying their expectations. The earlier in the relationship that this kind of meta-definition can be articulated, the better. If an executive can have a pre-prepared metaphor that provides an overarching motif for their assistant's role, and introduce it in their first meeting, it will help to press the 'reset' button in the assistant's mind, and challenge the assumption that their new boss will just want the same as the previous one.

Back in chapter 10 we dealt with position descriptions in detail. You may remember I encouraged PDs to begin with a purpose statement. If you suspect your newly acquired worker's role needs to be re-imagined, I encourage you to spend some time working with them on defining a clear overarching purpose for their role. It can be helpful to include a metaphor or simile in the purpose statement to clarify the purpose.

Once you've settled on the amendments to the PD, you'll need to be rigorous in giving feedback: both when the worker delivers what you want and when they don't. It will likely take a while for them to settle into the required mindset, and until they do, frequent feedback gives the basis for which to adjust.

Work plan

While it might seem a tough ask to introduce formal work planning at the first meeting, there's good reason to consider doing so. My general rule of thumb is to ask for a work plan unless there's a good reason not to. This meeting is mostly about helping the worker get a bit of a bead on you and what their role is going to be like going forward. I'm encouraging you to cultivate the habit of regular work planning with the people you supervise, so you might as well introduce them to that discipline right from the get-go. Begin as you intend to continue.

To this point the conversation with the worker has covered:

- A bit of a get to know you.
- A look at the PD and how it translates into day-to-day work.

- Consideration of the organisational strategy and how it informs the worker's role.
- Areas where immediate change or improvement is required.

All of that should provide a pretty solid basis for developing a work plan. I am reluctant to go through the mechanics of creating a work plan in the supervision session, unless it becomes clear to me that the worker has no idea how to proceed. I will, however, summarise the key points from the earlier conversation that need to be included in the plan.

I've spent a fair bit of time on work planning in earlier chapters, so I won't rehash it all here. However, there are a couple of key points that are particularly salient in this context.

Firstly, work to define the issues for the work plan to a level of concreteness and specificity that it can both be scheduled into a calendar and signed-off as completed when it's done. While you may not be able to nail down some of the improvements or changes to this degree, it's surprising how many issues can be addressed, whether scheduled directly or at least supported by a concrete action.

Let's work on an example. Remember the call centre worker we talked about earlier? Let's imagine that after some discussion, you and they agree that they need to be more succinct and more structured in taking their calls, spending less time canvassing the details of each customer's problems. You can't schedule 'be more assertive.' However, actions for the work plan could include:

- Create a list of phrases that you can use to pivot the conversation from problem to solution and post it up in your workspace.
- Review your statistics at the end of each day and take a minute to reflect on what may have contributed to your improvement or decline (assuming those stats are automatically generated and available to the worker).
- Contact HR and book in some refresher training in call management techniques.

Second, bear in mind the seniority of the role and the degree to which the worker initiates the work, or the work comes to them. An entry-level role that's mostly responsive may only need a few items to slot into their calendar. Adjust your expectations of the plan's sophistication to suit the role.

Third, err on the side of supervising a little too closely at the outset. Even with a CEO, I might ask to see their work plan in the first few meetings, and then relax the visibility as I become confident that they're executing as expected. Nobody wants to be micromanaged, but it's a recipe for disappointment to assume that anyone – even a senior exec – has a functional planning discipline.

Access to you

One of the last pieces to address with your worker who is new to you, but well established in the organisation, is the idea of access. Some bosses have blanket policies like 'I'm always available to my staff.' I'm not sure anyone with management responsibility would want to be constantly open to interruption. In my current role (and when we're not in lockdown), I'm physically in the same building as my team members no more than about once a week. We communicate by phone, email and Zoom. I encourage my team members to use email for information, phone for personal and sensitive stuff, and Zoom for meetings where there are multiple agenda items or more than two people present. I'm happy for team members to take their chances calling me pretty much any time, but to recognise that I have a decent coaching and consulting load and I'm not going to take a call while I'm with a client.

It's important for you to figure out the general expectations and protocols around contact and clearly communicate them to your worker – otherwise they'll likely assume it's the same with you as it was with their old boss – and that's probably not what you want.

The worker's agenda items

Before you close out the meeting, give the worker a chance to air anything they want to discuss. I put this on the agenda I send to the worker a few days before we meet, so they have time to think over what they might want to raise. While it's the supervisor's prerogative to set the agenda, it's important to give the worker sufficient time to bring their issues.

Meeting schedule

It's useful in this first meeting to map out your supervision meeting schedule for the year. If you can't do that, at least nail down the date for the next meeting.

Second and subsequent meetings

From here you can probably follow the same routine set out in the previous chapter under 'Third and subsequent meetings'. An established worker will have a somewhat different on-ramp to your supervision schedule, but once they're there, it's not too different to supervising a new hire who's had a chance to find their feet.

That said, one important difference is the established worker's knowledge, both the technical nous they've gained in the role, and the organisational intel they've picked up just by being around. If you can build a trusting relationship with some of those 'old hands' they can be a wealth of useful information as to what's been tried and failed, the context within which decisions were made, policy practice and expectations in previous eras etc. Especially in long-standing and highly unionised environments, tapping the collective corporate memory can help make sense of what might otherwise be completely bewildering.

This is particularly important for younger managers who inherit older, longstanding workers. Doing them the honour of hearing their recollections and respecting their experience will go a long way to earning their trust and loyalty.

An established worker with an established attitude

Sometimes as a supervisor you'll 'inherit' a worker who just seems to have the wrong attitude to you, to the organisation, to the world in general or any combination thereof. As an HR manager, coaching supervisors to manage workers with challenging attitudes was a reasonably frequent task for me.

Let's get to the most fundamental mistake straight up: it's a mistake to try to fix a worker's attitude. Attempts to do this will almost certainly have the opposite effect, galvanising the worker's indifference, hostility or passive resistance. There is no Australian case law or regulation that will give you safe grounds for terminating an employee for a substandard attitude (if you live in the US where labour laws are generally more pro employer, you may have a shot). Attitudes are subjective and almost impossible to establish in fact.

So give up on that idea. Instead of seeking to fix the worker, seek to work on your response to the worker and your relationship with the worker. After all, that's what you have capacity to influence.

Frequently, when supervising a worker with a problematic attitude, you'll find them 'living in your head and not paying any rent'. I have lost count of the number of coaching conversations I've had around this. Supervisors recognise that one of their workers seems intent on opposing them, making their life hard, or just being difficult. (This is surprisingly common in volunteer organisations and not-for-profits, where one might assume everyone was values-driven). As supervisors, we find these people a source of angst, and so we find ourselves focusing on them and ruminating about them. As soon as we're in that rumination pattern, we've lost our objectivity and we're vulnerable to projecting the worst intent on their actions and inactions.

If a boss doesn't like a worker's attitude and suspects them of opposition or sabotage, they're extremely vulnerable to treating the worker according to perception rather than the fundamental principles of good supervision. This will be experienced by the 'difficult' worker as being unfair, inequitable, harsh or just plain old mean. As soon as the worker perceives this, they'll almost certainly respond in kind. Together, the supervisor and the worker have co-created a self-reinforcing cycle of resentment, mistrust and friction.

Meanwhile you can bet your 'problem' worker will be busy recruiting other workers to their point of view and justifying their way of behaving. The supervisor faces the danger of mutiny, even if it's tacit. If you have a worker taking up a lot of your mental bandwidth, it's worth engaging a coach or psychologist to help you get some objectivity.

Enough with the mistakes now. Let's think about how to handle this well. Firstly, the line of approach needs to be based in fact. If a worker does their job as expected, does not impinge upon others and keeps to whatever standards of conduct are commonly required in the workplace, their attitude is irrelevant. They are free to secretly desire to marry you or murder you in their heart of hearts, so long as it does not translate into unacceptable performance or behaviour.

Second, if you find the worker living in your head, it will take care and attention to be absolutely scrupulously fair with them. That means treating them as you would your most willing and cooperative worker in terms of the appreciation you express and the encouragement you offer (even if it's shrugged off). Going further, it's important to give the same supervisory attention (no less, no more) and the same opportunities. There's an old Jewish proverb that goes, "If your enemy is hungry, give him food to eat; if he is thirsty, give him water to drink. In doing this, you will heap burning coals on his head..."[62] Now I would prefer to do what is right and fair because those are my principles, but sometimes the idea of vengeful kindness is the best I can manage. Either way, it beats getting into the doom loop of discrimination.

Thirdly, think contact. This is a concept drawn from Murray Bowen's Family Systems Theory.[63] According to Bowen, the two-person relationship or 'dyad' (in this case, you and your worker) is too unstable to weather the challenges of ordinary life. Sooner or later, one of the parties will draw another person into the relationship frame to steady themselves. We all do this. Think of the last time someone upset you and how strong was the impulse to tell a third person about the other person's unfair/bizarre/outrageous (or whatever) behaviour. As soon as you have a bit of a strained relationship with one of your workers, they will probably begin 'triangling' other people by telling them their side of the story. If those people are a part of your team, it will instantly alter their relationship with you. Remember, this is not some diabolical, Machiavellian scheme to destroy you – it's just what upset people automatically do.

How adversely your relationship with the rest of your workers is impacted will depend to a certain degree on what you do. The trick, according to Bowen's theory, is to be in calm, thoughtful, individual contact with each member of the team. That's *individual,* one-to-one contact. These relationships can be characterised as 'open, equal and separate'.[64]

Being open means relating with as much transparency as is wise. A great first step in this department is being honest about what you don't know or are unsure about. It's counterintuitive, but this kind of honesty actually engenders

[62] From the Jewish Scriptures, Proverbs 25:21-22a.
[63] Bowen, M. *Family Therapy in Clinical Practice* (Jason Aronson New York 1978).
[64] Roberta Gilbert's Summary of Bowen's idea of well differentiated relationship, set out in Gilbert, R. M. *The Cornerstone Concept: In Leadership, In Life* (Leading Systems, Falls Church 2008).

trust rather than undermining it. Consulting people on decisions that may affect them, or seeking to draw on their experience and expertise, communicates trust and value.

An equal relationship means relating as much as possible adult-to-adult rather than master-servant or parent-child. Just because I'm someone's boss does not mean I am superior or have a right to better treatment. My authority is simply a function of the responsibility attached to my role. Provided that is not undermined, we can otherwise relate as peers.

Being separate in a relationship means welcoming the other person having different beliefs, priorities and convictions, without there being an effort to achieve some form of groupthink. Provided our thinking and priorities are sufficiently aligned for us to get our respective jobs done well, the differences can be seen as either advantageous or at least peripheral. Don't underestimate how difficult it is to avoid the instinct to get everyone in your team to agree with you.

Putting this into practice in the orbit of your worker with an attitude means seeking to be in regular contact with each of your workers, and talking about the regular issues that affect you and them. It's absolutely *not* about trying to swing anyone to your side, warning people about the toxicity of a 'problem' worker or doing anything to try to sway allegiances or opinions. It works best if you can find ways to talk about yourself, your commitments and your thinking, and inviting the other person to talk about their thinking, their goals and commitments. If you can avoid talking about third parties at all, so much the better.

Routine contact and maintaining personable small talk with a difficult worker is essential to taking the heat out of the relationship. If every conversation is about points of contention, the intensity will only increase and the capacity to listen will decrease accordingly. This is counter to our instincts with a person that arouses our anxiety. The automatic human impulse is to go straight for the jugular of the contested issue (a 'fight' response, even if it's measured and factual) or to keep our distance (a flight response). Being calmly present without the anxious need to 'sort things out here and now' will yield a more relaxed and trusting relationship in the medium-term. It's important to deal with contested issues, but doing this in a thoughtful, timely and considered way in a well chosen forum is far more productive than fighting running battles or putting up the sandbags.

All of the forgoing notwithstanding, when your worker's bad attitude spills over into bad behaviour or poor performance, it's your responsibility to deal with it. All you can legitimately address is the facts of their behaviour and performance. It's imperative that you address these promptly, clearly and specifically, without the conversation spilling over into generalities that you can't establish in fact. We've already spoken about the techniques and process for doing this in chapter 12 and in chapter 17, so I won't rehash it here. If dealing with the issue requires formal performance management, it's important that you make reference to your organisation's performance management policy and engage the counsel of your HR department. If your organisation doesn't have a specialist HR function, I strongly recommend you seek some professional counsel from your legal advisor or your peak body organisation.

Now be warned that if your 'difficult' worker actually does have a bad attitude, addressing specific, factual instances of bad behaviour or poor performance will in all likelihood appear to make that attitude worse. That in turn is likely to motivate them to engage in more undesirable behaviours that are a product of the bad attitude, and it's your job as their boss to deal with that, too.

Before descending into a spiral that will inevitably cost someone (hopefully not you) their job, let's take a step back and think about this for a minute

If you've inherited a worker with an ugly attitude, it's possible they've had a previous boss in the organisation who's been confronted with that same attitude. The very fact that the worker and their attitude have remained in the organisation and are now a problem for you suggests that their previous boss may not have taken an optimal approach. Perhaps they found the worker intimidating and distanced from them by minimising contact and pretending not to know about their behaviour. It may be that the previous boss continually clashed with this worker. (I've had workers transferred to my team because their previous boss struggled to manage them). The previous boss may have marginalised this worker by recruiting their teammates onto the boss's side. (Supervisors have an unfair advantage in their capacity to treat some workers favourably and others less so). Perhaps the boss tried to make peace by giving the difficult worker whatever they wanted.

You'll notice that the supervision patterns outlined in the paragraph above reflect the four basic patterned responses to anxiety we discussed back in chapter nine: conflict, distance or cut-off, functional reciprocity (over-functioning and under-functioning), and projection to a third person (triangling). Watching for the presence of these patterns, both among your workers and more importantly in your own behaviour, will help you take emotional temperature of the situation.

Whatever the backstory, chances are your supervision is a change to the kind of leadership to which the 'problem' worker has become accustomed. Change creates anxiety, anxiety tends to fuel reactivity and reactivity is sometimes expressed in bad behaviour and poor performance. It's worth paying some attention to this before you head down the track of three-written-warnings-and-you're-fired.

Bear in mind that, while you're probably losing sleep over the angst this worker is causing you, there's a good chance they're not a happy camper either. You may choose to sit down with the worker and observe something along the lines of, "You know, I'm not sure either of us is enjoying this working relationship. I'm interested in thinking with you about what might be done to improve things." Be prepared for responses ranging from a simple and cynical grunt to a fully-fledged-rendered-in-Technicolor-blow-by-blow rehearsal of all of your sins and the sins of the company, the world, the universe and everything. Deep breath...

Rather than engaging too much with whatever content they've just given you, a summary response like, "I'm hearing you're not enjoying this either," or "Wow, there's a bit to unpack there," is probably your best bet. Picking apart their statement for its validity and accuracy is most likely a hiding to nothing. Instead, you can open up the possibility of exploring some of the facts of the worker's employment experience before they were assigned to you.

Questions about the bare-bones facts of their previous supervisory relationship both help to get the worker thinking rather than reacting (we'll go into the psychology of this in chapter 21). It will also give you some useful information about the kind of supervision they've experienced previously and how it might contrast with the supervision they're experiencing with you.

It can be illuminating to discover when the 'attitude' began to show up. Sometimes the worker will tell you. It may be helpful talking to people who've known the worker for longer than you to see whether their dissatisfaction is a recent development or whether it's been brewing for years.

I'm inclined to ask an unhappy worker, "Was there a time when you enjoyed this job?" If the answer is 'no', you're probably in for a long haul. If the answer is 'yes', finding out what the job was like back then can reveal a great deal and possibly give you some clues as to what you might be able to do to improve things. I once asked that question to a worker I inherited and discovered that there was a time when their job was a joy – they had been part of a team and felt a sense of community. Some brutal budget cuts and a restructure had left them working for several years in isolation for a boss who was entirely disinterested. This was my cue to invite more collaboration with the other members of my team, lengthen the 'connect' segment of our team meetings and increase my pastoral contact. I also slightly shifted the support-expectation balance in our supervision. I didn't lower my expectations – I just raised the support a little. The transformation over the coming year was like watching a wilted plant burst back to life with a little water and sunlight.

I'm not advocating you bend your whole supervision approach to suit a grumpy worker. I am inviting you to consider the possibilities of taking a curious and flexible approach to see what you might be able to do. I'm guessing a significant part in the change of heart in the worker I just described stemmed from someone making the effort to take them seriously, listen carefully and make some small changes in an effort to make their job more enjoyable.

Once you've got a bit of the worker's backstory, asking some questions around the source of their annoyance can open some windows of opportunity. A statement like, "I'm interested to know specifically what bothers you about your work here, and to hear your thoughts on how we might improve things."

Before I go on, let me put a few caveats. Firstly, don't ask this question unless you're prepared to put in the effort to address their concerns, and this may require some significant time and effort on your part. If a worker gives you their thinking and you ignore it, blow it off or simply fail to do anything with it, you'll only add to their cynicism.

Second, a cynical attitude is one of the symptoms of burnout. We look more at burnout in the next chapter. You may want to ask some questions or even use a burnout inventory to gauge that. We've already looked at sources of anxiety. The unhappy worker may have a whole range of other challenges outside of work, and the anxiety from those challenges may be leaking into their workplace demeanour. They might tell you about these, but if their trust in you is low, they probably won't and will resist and resent any attempts to inquire.

Third, if the worker with attitude is particularly hard-boiled, it may take a few attempts to get them to trust you enough to offer their thoughts. Your initial attempts may simply be met with a "You're just trying to… and I'm not going to play your … games and you can go shove …" (you can fill in the blanks from your experience or imagination). You may respond with something like, "I was asking an honest question, and I am interested in your thinking – but I'm not going to try to force you." Define yourself, don't defend yourself.

Sometimes your question will roll around in the worker's mind for a while, and your opportunity could come up incidentally. The next time the worker complains about something, or a challenge arises in the workplace, asking for their thinking may just give you the opportunity to show them you'll take their thinking seriously and will seek to act on what they say.

Sometimes the worker with an attitude is actually a case of mismanaged talent. Remember our conversations a few chapters back about Deming and his continuous improvement process? Deming's genius lay in recognising the latent possibility of expertise and insight in the worker who every day operates a particular process. That call centre operator earning a minimum wage will over time develop a body of tacit knowledge and expertise, not just in dealing with calls, but also on the quirks and limitations of the computer system they're using, the reliability or otherwise of the various staff and departments with which they interact and a whole range of other organisational idiosyncrasies. Because they're human they'll adapt to these to suit their own needs and goals. Therein lies a body of knowledge you can leverage, if you can just gain access to it.

Occasionally you'll find a person who can not only lament the problems but provide valuable insight into solutions – they may very well be your grumpy worker, driven to distraction by systems and processes that could be

252

improved if only someone in the upline would pay attention. If you, their boss, can tap that reservoir of knowledge, you'll not only have a happier worker who's easier to supervise, but a more effective and efficient organisation.

In the last few pages, we've gone over the approaches and steps you can take to give a worker with a problematic attitude opportunity to begin having a change of heart. Remember that any effort on your part to improve the relationship with your worker runs the risk of making things worse in the short-term. If the relationship with the worker is to improve, it will take time, consistency and regular contact on your part.

All that said, even if you are the perfect boss and your supervisory approach is exemplary, there are some workers who are just stuck in their oppositional and unproductive ways. Even while you're working to gain their trust and demonstrate fairness, if a worker fails to meet the required standards for performance and conduct, it's your responsibility to address the issue. I've had the unpleasant duty of firing workers of whom I have been quite fond, because they repeatedly chose behaviours that they knew were out of line.

Entering as the leader of a new team

Whole books have been written on team leadership and team dynamics, so we'll only touch briefly on how the principles we've already discussed might apply when taking on leadership of a team.

Much of what we've covered in taking on new supervisory relationships applies when taking on a new team. It's just that you'll need to be working through the individual process with a number of workers simultaneously.

The temptation at this point is trying to do too much of the individual supervision work in the group setting. Working with your team as a group is important, but it's not a substitute for working with each team member in individual supervision.

Just as you would in the individual setting, as the leader of the team it's critical that you're clear about your goals, priorities, values and commitments – making clear what the team can expect from you. You'll need to state and restate these with your team as a group, and then again in individual supervision.

Further, in the team setting it's important to be clear about what you expect. Not in a table thumping, drill sergeant kind of way, but simply making clear what's required in terms of performance and behaviour. Being calm and clear about this may be a bit of an emotional workout, because we anticipate resistance. However, clarity and consistency are actually reassuring for the team, removing the need to second-guess what it is you want.

If you're about to start with a new team, it's worth taking the time to figure out what you want to communicate to them in terms of what they can expect of you and what you will expect of them. Then figure out how to consistently communicate it at every opportunity.

When we talked earlier about starting a new worker, I recommended a little bit of self-disclosure: information about your background and interests, then inviting the new worker to share a little of their own. In the team setting, you can take this a little further if you have the time and resources. Patrick Lencioni recommends taking the time to have each team member tell their story (this usually takes place in a team retreat or off-site).[65] This will include where they grew up, went to school, sports or interests they pursued, and what led to their choice of career. Some would go further and talk a little about their family of origin or even their family background. I don't mind telling people most of my family lines come from England. The two major streams from my mother's side came here in the mid nineteenth century, seeking fortune and a better life in Melbourne, which at the time was the world's richest city. Dad's side came here in the first quarter of the twentieth century, either side of the First World War. They came fleeing political persecution and the ravages of the war.

I've used this technique in team formation and have been amazed at how quickly self-disclosure establishes trust and builds cohesiveness through shared understanding. That said, all it takes is one immature or bigoted person to turn the activity into an opportunity for practicing your performance management and relationship repair skills.

Just as you would provide feedback to an individual worker in the form of performance data and observations on behaviour, the same goes for teams. Having a team strategy progress chart or dashboard as a regular feature of

---

[65] Lencioni, P. *The Five Dysfunctions of a Team* (Jossey Bass, San Francisco 2002).

team meetings keeps the team focused on achieving objectives and performance targets. When things go well, you can facilitate a discussion about the contributing factors that you might be able to repeat or even increase.[66] When things don't go to plan, you can ask a very similar set of questions about contributing factors and how you might change things to prevent or decrease those factors replicating. Focusing solely on the drivers of problems or solely on the drivers of success lead to missing important information. Great leaders look at both sides.

Frequency

Once the supervisory relationship is established, the question turns to how often a supervisor should meet with their individual workers, and what might be a typical length of meeting.

If the worker has a relatively simple role like our friend the call centre operator, their boss will have opportunity to provide ongoing feedback through daily interaction on the office floor. In this case, a 10-minute chat every couple of weeks will likely suffice for giving feedback, and a longer conversation may only happen every couple of months.

For a worker with broad and diverse responsibilities, a monthly 90-minute meeting may be needed, simply because there will be a range of issues to canvas.

Road, field and remote workers

For workers who are 'on the road' like sales reps, or consultants who spend a lot of their time in other workplaces, consider looking at a fairly regular schedule of contact, simply because there's far less opportunity for those five-minute chats in the stairwell or the lunchroom that happen naturally in a workplace where everyone is under the same roof. Similar considerations may

---

[66] Figuring out the contributing factors to your success and seeking to repeat and replicate them in broader settings is a fundamental principle of appreciative inquiry, an approach formulated by management consultant and academic David L. Cooperrider. See https://www.champlain.edu/ai-home/about-us/who-is-david-cooperrider/david-cooperrider-biography. A similar way of thinking was formulated as 'net forward energy ratio' by Doug Krug and Ed Oakley in their classic *Enlightened Leadership: Getting to the Heart of Change* (Simon and Schuster New York 1993). We'll revisit these two a little later.

apply for workers who operate remotely and may only visit the office infrequently.

Regular contact needn't be a formal supervision meeting on every occasion. I've been a field worker or a remote worker for most of the past twenty years, and I've had staff scattered across the city and sometimes across the country throughout that time. I've generally settled into formal supervision with each of my staff about once a month for workers in more independent roles, and a little more often with people whose roles are more highly integrated with the day-to-day operations of the organisation.

But that's not to say our only contact is in formal supervision. Phone calls to simply be in touch are an important part of maintaining the supervisory relationship. Sometimes it's as simple as broadening a call, to solve a problem or answer a question, into a quick wellbeing check. Occasionally I'll use time in the car to make a series of quick check in calls with each of my staff.

In the post-COVID distributed workplace, supervisors may consider holding a 5-minute video conference meeting at the start of each workday just to give everyone a sense of being 'at work' and connected. This also provides some structure to the worker's day, knowing they need to have their game face on at a set time.

The critical idea in managing a dispersed workforce is meaningful and efficient contact. The key to making this happen is intentionality. If you just 'try to be in touch a little more', chances are the tyranny of the immediate will keep you from those brief but important moments of contact and before you know it two weeks will have elapsed without you having a one-to-one chat with some of your staff.

You'll note I used the word 'chat'. By that I mean a phone call, video conference or face-to-face dialogue. Email and text exchanges are better than nothing, but are vastly inferior to a verbal conversation. We'll develop the concept of engagement in the next section, but the key to maintaining that sense of belonging in your workers is to talk with them.

We've spent the last few chapters looking at the mechanics of the supervisory relationship, applying the central concepts of expectation, support and feedback. In the next three chapters, we'll examine the supervisory relationship in managing challenges like burnout, pushback and conflict.

Summary

- A new relationship with an existing worker will almost always mean challenging some presuppositions. In initiating supervision:
    - Prepare by researching the worker's history and role
    - Listen carefully to their understanding of their job and how it relates to the PD and strategy
    - Be clear on your expectations, which may mean:
        - Maintaining the role mostly as it has been
        - Making changes to practice and performance
        - Reimagining the role
    - Ask the worker to create a work plan if they have a multi-faceted role
    - The second and subsequent meetings will be more like routine supervision
- Sometimes you'll inherit a worker with an 'attitude'.
    - Get some supportive help if they're 'living in your head'.
    - Challenge behaviour, not attitude.
    - Cultivate an equal, open and separate relationship.
    - Seek to collaborate on improving their experience of work.
- If you take up supervising a team
    - Don't substitute team process for individual supervision;
    - Seek to build a culture where people know each other.

Discussion

- If you've inherited a pre-existing employee, what are some of the presuppositions you needed to challenge?

Implementation

- What could you do to cultivate more equal, open and separate relationships with your workers?

Chapter 18
Burnout in the age of anxiety

A conversation about workplace expectation is apt to lead to a conversation about unrealistic expectations and burnout. While this book is not primarily about preventing burnout, I've so far counselled bosses to be fair, reasonable, clear, appropriately supportive and to have reasonable expectations. This will steer you in the opposite direction to creating the kind of conditions where burnout proliferates.

However, burnout is a complex phenomenon, and one you're almost certain to encounter as a boss – even if you're an excellent boss. You may have been surprised that the support vs expectation diagram in chapter eight does not state 'burnout' as a result of high expectation–low support environments. Burnout is certainly a term that's gained momentum since American psychologist Herbert Freudenberger coined it in the 1970s.[67] For a while burnout was a hot topic in human resources management circles, then waned in the early twenty-first century as the more positively-framed terms of 'wellbeing' and 'flourishing' became more prominent. It seems we were worried about the possibility of suggestion-induced onset, so we would talk about 'promoting wellbeing' or 'developing resilience', rather than 'preventing burnout'. Then came the pandemic and the management literature has since exploded with articles about burnout.

Burnout is...

In the latest revision of the International Classification of Diseases (ICD-11), the World Health Organisation (WHO) defines burnout as an occupational phenomenon resulting from unsuccessful management of chronic workplace stress, characterized by feelings of energy depletion or exhaustion, increased mental distance from one's job, or feelings of negativism or cynicism related to one's job, and reduced professional efficacy.[68]

---

[67] Freudenberger, Herbert with Richelson, G. *Burn Out: The High Cost of High Achievement. What it is and how to survive it.* (Bantam, New York. 1980).
[68] https://www.who.int/mental_health/evidence/burn-out/en/.

Since the term 'burnout' first gained currency, American social psychologist Christina Maslach has emerged as the preeminent authority on the subject. The Maslach Burnout Inventory (MBI)[69] has become the standard instrument for measuring an individual's burnout status.

The MBI measures the three characteristics listed in the WHO definition, summarised as exhaustion, cynicism and reduced professional efficacy – or "I'm tired, no one cares and what's the use?" While widely used and accepted, the instrument commonly scores individuals who report reasonable energy, engagement and efficacy as experiencing some degree of burnout. With that in mind, it's no surprise that, according to recent research by the Gallup organisation, 76% of workers sometimes experience feelings of burnout.[70]

Burnout is driven by...

Workplace factors
A little later we'll look at the variety of factors outside the workplace that may correlate with a vulnerability to burnout, or exacerbate the experience of stress in the workplace. For now, let's work with WHO presumption that burnout is driven by workplace factors. Christina Maslach and her colleagues identify six workplace-based drivers of burnout:

1. Workload beyond sustainable capacity
2. Not having sufficient control to moderate and schedule workload
3. A sense that the reward doesn't match the contribution
4. A sense of community or belonging, where the worker enjoys supportive relationships
5. A sense that the worker is being treated unfairly
6. A mismatch of values [71]

A recent study by the Gallup organisation identified five factors that correlate most highly with employee burnout:

---

[69] Maslach, C. *The Maslach Burnout Inventory Manual* in Zalaquett, C. P. and Wood, R. J. (eds) Evaluating Stress: A Book of Resources (Scarecrow, Lanham, 1997).
[70] Wigert, B. *Employee Burnout: The Biggest Myth*
https://www.gallup.com/workplace/288539/employee-burnout-biggest-myth.aspx.
[71] Michel, A. *Burnout and the Brain* Association for Psychological Science January 29, 2016
https://www.psychologicalscience.org/observer/burnout-and-the-brain.

1. Unfair treatment at work
2. Unmanageable workload
3. Unclear communication from managers
4. Lack of manager support
5. Unreasonable time pressure [72]

No doubt you can see the similarities. You'll note that workload is *a* factor in burnout, but not *the* solitary cause.

Challenge

The burnout literature, consistent with the WHO definition above, generally thinks of burnout in terms of unmanaged chronic stress. Stress has attracted a pretty negative valence which may not be helpful in understanding the dynamics of burnout. A more objective consideration can be made by thinking of stress and stressors in terms of challenge.

Workplace stress can be understood in terms of the challenge experienced by the worker. It's not that we should shy away from challenge per se. Facing challenge is a normal part of everyday life. To build physical fitness and strength, we subject our bodies to challenge – growing stronger is a natural adaptation to challenge. However, if we over challenge our muscles, we risk injury. When a worker does not have the resources to consistently meet the overall level of challenge they experience, they feel symptoms of stress – or more correctly, over-stress. Over-stress is the result of challenge beyond capacity.

Drawing on some of the factors identified by Maslach and Gallup, let's have a look at some burnout drivers framed in terms of challenge.

Challenge beyond capacity could simply be a matter of asking for more than can be reasonably given. If a call centre worker's role requires them to handle calls that take an average of ten minutes to adequately resolve, they can manage about 45 calls in a standard 7.6-hour shift. All else being equal, that would be a reasonable challenge. Expecting them to handle 80 calls a shift,

---

[72] Wigert, B. *Employee Burnout: The Biggest Myth*
https://www.gallup.com/workplace/288539/employee-burnout-biggest-myth.aspx.

creates a risk of over-stress. The same goes for a lawyer operating more files than they can adequately handle in a reasonable work week.

Challenge can be understood in terms of the degree to which demand can be moderated and managed. A worker who has multiple people all making competing demands of them may at times feel like a ninja fending off attacks from all angles. That might be okay occasionally, but not for 38 hours a week. They may experience their work as a more manageable challenge if they have scope to prioritise and schedule their tasks.

Sometimes challenge is more to do with difficulty or ambiguity than the time it takes to complete tasks. Tasks that can't be handled by routine use of procedural memory are more challenging than those that can. If a task requires a degree of adaptation, the task feels harder because there's usually a series of little problems to solve embedded in the overall task. Problem-solving requires assessing the problem, identifying and evaluating options for a solution, then trialling solutions until one works. It's part of the reason it takes twice as long to do an unfamiliar task for the first time than it does for the third or fourth time. Further, with repetition we build a little repository of tacit knowledge about the task: it can be as simple as knowing which function to use and where the command for it is located in a software application. A job with a high proportion of adaptive tasks will present more challenge than one with tasks for which there is a known and well-practiced procedure.

Sometimes challenge comes in the form of uncertainty: a lack of role clarity, tenuous or inadequate access to resources, or ambiguity around the outcomes expected. Some uncertain situations are exacerbated by people feeling vulnerable or upset – as might occur when a restructure is announced.

A further variable in challenge is the impact of success or failure. I like to tinker with old cars. If I overtighten a bolt and it breaks, it may take some time, effort and expense to rectify, but it's unlikely to change the course of my life or anyone else's. A mistake by a nurse in an emergency department could result in the permanent disability or death of a patient, with all the implications that entails. The tasks may not be observably hard, but when a decision must be made and the stakes are high, it ratchet's up the degree of challenge experienced.

Challenge may also take the form of a pressure to compromise integrity. A worker may find themselves involved in things that cut across their sense of what is right, good and fair. Or perhaps they're on the receiving end of a perceived injustice, which generally combines with a sense of powerlessness. Sometimes it's simply being aware that the organisation of which they're a part is engaging in unethical conduct. Challenges to integrity may illicit anything from a generalised sense of unease to utter outrage.

At the extreme end, challenge may take the form of threat or confrontation. This might be risk to personal safety, such as an armed combat situation, or the emergency services personnel who frequently work in the face of hostility, even from the people they're trying to help or protect. Or it may be context where the threat is experienced vicariously: medical personnel, lawyers and investigators working on child abuse cases. It's upsetting to be exposed to upset people. It may not be necessarily harmful per se, but it adds massively to the overall load of challenge. Recently, a worker at Victoria's Office of Public Prosecutions sued her employer for damages after she was diagnosed with PTSD attributed to her work requiring her to observe graphic images as evidence and to interview complainants. [73]

Perhaps the least recognised and yet surprisingly common form of challenge is the tendency or humans to take responsibility for matters over which they have no real control. Ed Friedman observes: "Stress and Burnout are relational rather than quantitative and are due primarily to getting caught in a responsible position for others and their problems."[74] A teacher who tries to influence a parent to change their approach to parenting, a sports coach who frets over a protégé frittering away their opportunities through ill-discipline, and a boss trying to motivate their unmotivated workers will all experience the stress that we compare to bashing one's own head against a brick wall.

---

[73] https://www.abc.net.au/news/2022-05-25/zagi-kozarov-psychiatric-injury-at-work-law-report/101081728.
[74] Friedman, E. H. *Failure of Nerve: Leadership in the Age of the Quick Fix* (Seabury, New York, 1999), 202.

Chronic exhaustion

Feelings of ongoing fatigue or chronic exhaustion are probably the most telling indicators of burnout.[75] We're not talking about acute exhaustion, which you might feel at the end of a gruelling week directing a theatre production, moving house, or after running a marathon. Acute exhaustion is cured by a bit of a break and some decent sleep.

Chronic exhaustion is that feeling of being tired all the time for weeks on end. Not all chronic exhaustion is a sign of burnout. Parents of a newborn feel exhausted from sleep deprivation. More recently we've seen chronic exhaustion associated with 'long COVID'.

Chronic exhaustion related to burnout is sometimes described as a chronically depleted battery. The demands of the day draw down more than the recharge of sleep at night replaces, the week at work takes more out than the weekend puts back in – and so a sense of continual and increasing deficit emerges. Others have likened burnout to an overdraft. [76]

When a battery runs flat, the device it powers stops. However, some workers – particularly those in fields where their work is seen to be 'essential' (e.g. in healthcare, where the term 'burnout' originated) – continue to force themselves to function even when experiencing all the indicators of pronounced burnout. In their severely depleted state, they borrow resources they would otherwise commit to other spheres of life: their interests outside of work, their health and their relationships. Life becomes unbalanced and their minds, bodies and families begin to react.

When all of a worker's spheres of life are overdrawn, eventually their being puts them on 'stop credit' and a whole-of-person collapse may ensue.

---

[75] Nortje, Alicia *Warning Signs of Burnout: 11 Reliable Tests & Questionnaires* https://positivepsychology.com/burnout-tests-signs/.
[76] Drummond, Dike *Part I: Burnout Basics – Symptoms, Effects, Prevalence and the Five Main Causes* Missouri Medicine, 2016 Jul-Aug; 113(4): 252–255. https://www.ncbi.nlm.nih.gov/pmc/articles/PMC6139917/.

Burnout Brain

Research over the past decade has discovered observable changes in brain structure and function correlating with people who score highly on burnout tests like the one devised by Maslach.

One study found that subjects experiencing a high degree of burnout were more easily startled by loud noises and reported greater difficulty managing strong negative emotions than those in the control group. It could be that burnout sets us more on edge and may contribute to us being more reactive. The researchers looked further and discovered that the centre in the brain that generated the fight-flight response (the amygdala) was enlarged in those experiencing burnout. [77]

Another study found that the medial prefrontal cortex, a part of the brain that's involved in executive functions, deteriorates or thins out in those experiencing burnout. This happens naturally with age, but it appears that burnout may accelerate the normal process of decline.[78] Executive function is essential to managing strong emotional reactions, calming oneself and making thoughtful adaptations to challenge.

The first study also found that the connectivity between these two centres was significantly weakened in those reporting a high degree of workplace stress, meaning the ability of the medial prefrontal cortex to have a moderating impact on the upset amygdala was reduced. This appears to set up a vicious cycle where the stressed person becomes increasingly vulnerable to being upset, while their capacity to calm themselves is steadily reduced.

The news is not all entirely bleak. One study found that the mental processing difficulties associated with acute stress subsided when the challenge was removed.[79] Other research has suggested that some of the neurobiological

[77] Golkar, A., Johansson, E., Kasahara, M., Osika, W., Perski, A., & Savic, I. *The influence of work-related chronic stress on the regulation of emotion and on functional connectivity in the brain*. in *PLOS ONE 9*: e104550. doi:10.1371/journal.pone.0104550 (2014).
[78] Savic, I. *Structural changes of the brain in relation to occupational stress*. in *Cerebral Cortex, 25*, 1554–1564. doi:10.1093/cercor/bht348 (2015).
[79] Liston, C., McEwen, B. S., & Casey, B. J. *Psychosocial stress reversibly disrupts prefrontal processing and attentional control*. Proceedings of the National Academy of Sciences, *106*, 912–917. doi:10.1073/pnas.0807041106 (2009).

changes correlated to burnout may be reversible through the practice of meditation.[80] Just bear in mind, the anxious, ruminating, fatigued burnout candidate's first impulse is unlikely to be meditation.

The complicating factor: anxiety leaks

The WHO definition of burnout works nicely in the diagnosis-driven medical sphere where everything is neatly categorised. The problems facing the psychological sphere is that, while it's related to the medical sphere, its primary area of concern – mental and emotional processes – are almost impossible to objectively measure in terms of causation.

Nonetheless, the prevailing understanding of burnout is that it's caused by things that happen in the workplace, as described by Maslach and the Gallup organisation above.

This might be okay if our brains worked like pocket calculators, dealing with immediate inputs, performing prescribed functions and producing outputs with no consideration of wider relationships. While we try to encourage people not to bring family issues to work and not to take work issues home, humans simply don't function that way. It's reasonable to expect that, if an employee's partner is hospitalised following a nasty road accident, that worker's thinking capacities won't be fully directed toward their work for a few days. Their functioning will be impaired by their worry about their partner.

Conversely, if there's a huge project with tight deadlines looming at work, an executive might be a little snippy or emotionally distant at home. The centres in our brains that drive emotional responses simply don't have separate modes for 'work' and 'home'. If something in one sphere of life is causing us concern, our minds will tend to be a little preoccupied with it, even when we're in a different sphere. An enlarged and overactive amygdala does not shrink back to normal size and settle down at the stroke of 5.00 PM.

---

[80] Hölzel, B. K., Carmody, C., Vangel, M., Congleton, C., Yerramsetti, S. M., Gard, T. and Lazar, S. W. *Mindfulness practice leads to increases in regional brain gray matter density* Psychiatry Res. 2011 Jan 30; 191(1): 36–43. doi: 10.1016/j.pscychresns.2010.08.006 (2010).

Variable resilience

Martin Seligman, the catalyst for the contemporary movement for positive psychology, has worked extensively on the issue of resilience with major corporations, schools and also with the US military. Post Traumatic Stress Disorder (PTSD) in US veterans has skyrocketed, and Seligman, in his book *Flourish* recounts his work to build resilience in serving personnel.[81] I was struck by his observation that personnel serving in or close to combat often reported increased symptoms of anxiety after contact with their partners back in the US. (A quirk of modern warfare is that a soldier can be dodging fire from AK47s and sheltering from an onslaught of RPGs in the morning, then chat to their partners and kids on facetime in the afternoon). Seligman wondered whether absorbing the worry of their partner might just be adding to the stress of dealing with a hostile force. The military introduced some pastoral care and coaching with the partners back at home, ensuring that their worry didn't leak into their interaction with the partner serving on foreign soil. The soldiers' anxieties abated accordingly.

Seligman's work in resilience was fuelled at least in part by the variability of response among veterans who experienced similar traumatic incidents. It's not as if PTSD coincides one-to-one with surviving an attack. Seligman observed that for some, such an experience would lead to an array of debilitating symptoms, while others would emerge more resilient.

Several decades before Seligman, American Psychiatrist Murray Bowen was asking similar questions about variability.[82] Bowen's subject of study was schizophrenia, and the prevailing theory of the time (the late 1950s) was that schizophrenia in a teenager or young adult could be attributed to certain characteristics of their mother's parenting style (Theorore Lidz's notion of a schizophrenogenic mother was widely held in the psychiatric community.[83]). However, Bowen observed similar phenomena in mother-child interactions *without* the child developing schizophrenia that he had observed in mother-child relationships where a child had developed schizophrenia. While certain dynamics between a mother and child seemed to correlate with a child

---

[81] Seligman, M. E. P. *Flourish: A Visionary New Understanding of Happiness and Well-being* (Free Press, New York 2011).
[82] Bowen, M. *Family Therapy in Clinical Practice* (Jason Aronson, New York 1978)
[83] Lidz, T., Fleck, S. and Cornelison, A. *Schizophrenia and the family* (International Universities Press, Madison,1965).

developing schizophrenia, those dynamics did not *account* for the emergence of schizophrenia, especially when the same family might produce one child with schizophrenia and others entirely without symptoms.

Bowen's observation led him to look more broadly at the nuclear family, then broader still at the multigenerational family. In formulating his theory of the family as a multigenerational system, Bowen posited that symptoms emerging in a family member was one of a range of observable phenomena that might emerge in a family when the system was faced with challenge and change. We'll be revisiting Bowen's Family Systems Theory from time-to-time throughout this book.

Later researchers like Brent Bezo have coined the phrase 'generational trauma' to describe the influence of traumatic events across generations.[84] When you have a person showing signs of stress in a workplace, there are a number of theories and a growing body of research suggesting the contributing factors could trace back a long way beyond your line of sight as a supervisor.

Burnout, stress and anxiety

Let's bring all this back to burnout, because it will eventually come up in your supervision conversations. Burnout, by the definition cited earlier, is caused by stress in the workplace, which is pretty hard to isolate from other stressors in our lives because our brains don't delineate the way medical diagnosis would like them to. There are instruments that claim to make the delineation, but they rely on subjective attribution.

Linear causation or even multifactorial causation does not do justice to our neurobiology. Sure, we can see that one stimulus here will trigger an apparent response there, but the processes in between are multi-systemic and we're still trying to understand them.

Stress or Anxiety?

The psychological world defines stress as "the pattern of specific and nonspecific responses a person makes to stimulus events that disturb his or her equilibrium and tax or exceed his or her ability to cope". Anxiety is defined

---

[84] Cited by DeAngelis, T. *The Legacy of Trauma* (American Psychological Society Monitor on Psychology February 2019, Vol 50, No. 2).

as "the apprehensive anticipation of future danger or misfortune accompanied by a feeling of worry, distress, and/or somatic symptoms of tension. The focus of anticipated danger may be internal or external."[85]

While stress and anxiety can be differentiated in terms of their causes, our actual neurophysiological response to either cannot. Psychologist Alicia Clark, makes the following observation:

"At their most intense, they share the almost reflexive 'defensive survival reaction', commonly known as fight-or-flight, that sets off a cascade of physical changes along the hypothalamic-pituitary-adrenal (HPA) axis preparing the body for threat. Attention is sharpened, energy is boosted, while oxygen and immunity are heightened readying the body for action. While the intensity of the threat response can vary, the experience of stress and anxiety in our bodies is almost indistinguishable physiologically."[86]

Earlier we briefly looked at the amygdala, that little structure in the brain that's been shown to enlarge and become more sensitized in those who score highly on burnout scales. The amygdala plays a central role in kicking off the cascade of effects along the HPA axis.

We can measure things like cortisol which is produced when the HPA axis is triggered. We can measure extremity temperature (it drops when the HPA axis is triggered) and we can measure skin sweat response (it increases when the HPA axis is triggered) but we can't say for sure what the actual trigger is, unless we get you wearing biofeedback electrodes all day, spitting in a cup every fifteen minutes and assaying it for cortisol, and correlating all that data to your minute-by-minute thought processes and experiences.

Chronic emotional arousal may eventually lead to the symptoms we associate with burnout. However, while we might attribute those symptoms to workplace stress, we can't with any certainty assign causation to stress versus

---

[85] The Diagnostic and Statistical Manual of Mental Disorders, Fifth Edition (DSM-5) American Psychiatric Association.
[86] Clark, A. H. *Curious About the Difference Between Stress and Anxiety? key facts you need to know.* Hack your Anxiety Psychology Today March 2019 https://www.psychologytoday.com/us/blog/hack-your-anxiety/201903/curious-about-the-difference-between-stress-and-anxiety.

anxiety, or definitively isolate the source to the workplace. Anxiety 'leaks' into the work sphere from other spheres as we saw in Seligman's example. It can also leak into the present from the past, and as Bowen observed, perhaps even across multiple generations.

Freud seemed to regard dealing with anxiety as a kind of holy grail of psychoanalysis, observing: "There is no question that the problem of anxiety is the nodal point at which the most various important questions converge, a riddle whose solution would be bound to throw a flood of light on our whole mental existence.[87]

Building on Freud, attachment theories attribute a good proportion of human troubles to 'anxious attachment' flowing from early experience of parental figures. As we saw earlier, Bowen located the roots of human dysfunction in chronic anxiety transmitted through the multigenerational process.[88]

Further complicating matters, vulnerability to burnout has been linked to a range of personality factors.[89] The burgeoning new field of epigenetics has added even further considerations, showing that childhood stressors can impact the way genes are switched and copied, predisposing the child to certain responses to stress later in life.[90]

To summarise this little section, what looks like workplace stress can be a whole lot more complicated than it appears. Let me add a final aspect of complexity.

History of angst

Since Danish philosopher Søren Kierkegaard published *The Concept of Anxiety* in 1844, Western society has become angsty about, well, angst. Kierkegaard argued that while animals are driven by instinct, humans have the capacity to choose right or wrong, producing a profound anxiety. Later existentialists

---

[87] Freud, S. *Introductory Lectures of Psycho-Analysis* (Norton, New York 1933).
[88] Bowen, M. *Family Therapy in Clinical Practice* (Jason Aronson, New York 1978).
[89] Alarcon, G., Eschleman, K.J. and Bowling, N. A. *Relationships between personality variables and burnout: A meta-analysis* in Work & Stress: An International Journal of Work, Health & Organisations Volume 23, 2009 – Issue 3.
[90] Zannas, A. S., West, A. E. *Epigenetics and the regulation of stress vulnerability and resilience.* Neuroscience. 2014;264:157–170.

built upon Kierkegaard's work, leading to the emergence of the notion of existential despair.

English American poet W. H. Auden entitled his lengthy 1947 eclogue *The Age of Anxiety*, and since then it's become a popular description for the contemporary era (even Pete Townsend, legendary lead guitarist of The Who, used the term to title his first novel).

The data seems to suggest that Kierkegaard, Auden and Townsend are on to something. According to the Anxiety and Depression Association of America, anxiety disorders affect 18.1% of the US adult population every year.[91]

If those statistics hold for the population in which you work, that means you've got a one in six shot that the person across the table from you in a supervision meeting will have or develop an anxiety disorder sometime soon.

A range of psychological theories and some solid neurobiological research all point to previous experience (especially in early childhood) contributing to the present-day experience of anxiety (which differs in presentation from stress only in the attribution of its cause, which is always subjective). Add to that anxious responses to societal and family stressors and it's pretty clear that attributing a person's burnout symptoms solely to their workplace experience might just be a little simplistic.

Now, all of that said, in Australia your organisation can still be whacked with a nasty workers compensation claim if a worker can successfully claim that a stressor in their workplace was a significant contributing factor to their burnout symptoms (or more accurately, if you fail to prove otherwise, since the system is necessarily more protective of the worker). By 'significant' the law does not mean 'predominant'. You can read this chapter to the judge if you like, but I'm pretty sure it won't help your chances.

Total psychological load

I use the term total psychological load to describe the cumulative challenges from all our spheres of life – this could be the chronic anxiety instilled through

---

[91] Anxiety and Depression Association of America *Anxiety Disorders – Facts & Statistics* https://adaa.org/understanding-anxiety/facts-statistics.

our family of origin and multigenerational processes, the vicissitudes of life in a family and a broader society, along with the stresses of work.

If we take all the foregoing together, we could describe burnout as the result of prolonged experience of a total psychological load that exceeds our capacity to adapt in healthy and sustainable ways.

We talked a little earlier about metaphors for burnout – a flat battery, or an overdrawn account. Robert Creech comes at it from the opposite direction, thinking in terms of overwhelm rather than depletion.[92] Imagine a glass that is your receptacle for containing your total emotional load – it represents your ability to productively adapt to challenge. At the bottom is the stuff that's pretty much always there: the anxieties that come from your family of origin and prior experience. You might be able to reduce the volume through therapy, but it's slow, had work and you'll always have some sensitivities.

Next is all the anxiety that comes from your life, your family and society: health worries, finances, marriage, kids, extended family, community involvement. These vary according to circumstance – a cancer diagnosis or a kid going off the rails could just about fill the rest of the glass – maybe even cause it to overflow.

Now pour in your workplace challenges. So long as the sum of all these challenges – your total emotional load – remains within your capacity to adapt in healthy ways, you will be able to live and work without anything 'spilling over the top of your glass'.

So what does 'spillage' look like and how can we tell when we ourselves, or one of our workers, is close to capacity?

Reading the emotional process of the system

Despite the broad range of processes driving anxiety and stress, there are some identifiable behavioural patterns that point to them getting close to the top of the glass. These are worth watching out for, not so you can stamp them out, but as indicators of how your workers are doing. To define these patterns, let's return for a few minutes to Bowen's Family Systems Theory.

---

[92] Creech, R. *Family Systems and Congregational Life* (Baker, Grand Rapids 2019).

Bowen observed four general patterns of behaviour when a relational system (a collection of humans who are somehow interdependent) is under stress.[93] More specifically, these patterns become evident when a relational system is less able to respond to challenge by productive adaptation (i.e. the system's collective glasses are getting close to full). The more the relationships are depended upon for survival and wellbeing, the greater the propensity for these patterns to emerge and the greater the intensity with which they're expressed. That means these patterns appear most commonly or intensely in families, because families are the primary unit for survival and wellbeing in social species like us. But because workplaces also play a fairly important role in survival and wellbeing, the patterns emerge fairly commonly at work.

Before I outline the four patterns, let's explore productive adaptation a little further. A productive adaptation is a way of changing plans, priorities and behaviours in order to meet a challenge without impinging upon the functioning or development of members of the system. Imagine a family comprising two parents and two teenagers and two cars. Now imagine one of those cars suddenly has a catastrophic engine failure as a parent is driving home from work. What would good adaptation look like? You can probably list off a series of helpful responses:

- Calling ahead to alert the other parent to what's happened.
- Calling for a tow truck.
- Calling a grandparent to ask them to pick up one of the teenagers from ballet class.
- Doing a cost-benefit analysis about whether to repair the car or replace it.
- Talking to the bank about a financial plan to cover the unexpected cost.
- Arranging to borrow a relative's spare car.

There would be perhaps a dozen more adaptive responses required to deal with the various facets of what is a reasonably unremarkable challenge. Adaptation usually requires mobilizing resources from within and around the relational system. It also means members of the system showing some flexibility while still maintaining their overall responsibilities and life course.

---

[93] These four patterns are described throughout Bowen's two major works: Bowen, M. *Family Therapy in Clinical Practice* (Jason Aronson, New York 1978), and Bowen, M. and Kerr, M. *Family Evaluation: The Role of Family as an Emotional Unit that Governs Individual Behaviour and Development* (North, New York 1988).

Most families have sufficient adaptive capacity to take these kinds of challenges in their stride.

Now let's change the script a little. Let's assume the family has just moved from interstate and is yet to develop relational networks. They're hundreds of kilometres from their extended family. They've just bought a new house and they're financially stretched. One of the parents is a nurse working rotating shifts and cannot use public transport to get to work. In this situation the family has less flexibility and less capacity to draw on resources outside of their system. Their adaptive capacity is reduced.

Put enough challenge on a system and instead of thoughtful responses, its members will start displaying instinctive reactions that are more automatic and less thoughtfully considered. This is not about pathology. It's just about ability to maintain function under challenge.

Anxious patterns

Now let's take a look at those four generalised patterns that Bowen observed as reactions to anxiety.

Conflict is perhaps the most predictable reaction in a situation like the one just described. Imagine the phone call: "Waddaya mean it just blew up? Did a red light show up on the dashboard? I told you to pay more attention."

"Well, you were supposed to get it serviced last month and you put it off. I said delaying it was a bad idea, but you knew better…"

"Yeah, well we couldn't afford to get it serviced last month."

"We might have if you hadn't pushed for this huge great dream home that we can't afford."

"And the service would have been cheaper if we'd bought a Hyundai, but you insisted we get some overly complicated European thing that has to be serviced by a dealer."

And so it goes. This is not a debate about how to solve the problem, but a quarrel about who's to blame. Conflict like this is not productive in terms of adaptation, but it still serves a purpose – as a way of blowing off all those stress hormones that are aroused by the challenge. For many relationships, conflict is the main pressure relief valve.

Distance often follows conflict, or sometime precedes it if conflict or other intense interaction is anticipated. Distance in this situation could take a variety of forms. Perhaps the parent driving the stricken car decides that the issue cannot be discussed and determines to deal with everything by themselves. Perhaps after the initial call to their partner gets heated, they decide to head to the pub instead of going home. Maybe the couple argue and then give each other the silent treatment for a couple of days. If the intensity gets high enough, one may threaten to leave or actually physically distance from the other.

All of us use distance to manage intensity. Used judiciously it can be a helpful intensity moderator. When it becomes prolonged, or weaponised, it tends to interfere with the responsible functioning of both parties.

Functional reciprocity is a kind of technical way of describing one-up and one-down relationship situations. It's a pattern where one person doesn't live up to the level or responsibility to which they could reasonably be expected, while another takes more than their own share of responsibility. It's sometimes difficult to tell where it starts.

In our blown-up car scenario, perhaps the partner at home responds with, "Oh, you poor thing! That's terrible! Don't you worry about anything, leave everything to me and I'll get it sorted out. I've just ordered a cab for you, and I'll have a tow truck come and collect the car." A clear case of what Bowen called being over-responsible or 'over-functioning'.

It would take some careful diplomacy for the partner with the dead car to take up their responsibility here. Much easier to just let the other person do everything. Alternatively, being under-responsible might take the form of getting drunk or throwing their hands up and saying, "I can't get to work now, so I'll just quit!"

Projection to a third person is perhaps the most common yet the least understood of Bowen's four patterns. He observed it initially as overfocus on a child, whereby a couple found a sense of togetherness and unity by agreeing on the need to put a great degree of their energy and attention into their child. Of course, kids need parental attention, but too much can impinge on a kid's development (we've all cringed at instances of helicopter parenting). As Bowen's theory developed, he saw projection to a third person (or 'triangling') as going well beyond the primary parental triangle to being a ubiquitous pattern of human interaction.

For our hapless couple with the broken car, any number of anxious triangles could be activated. The partner at home could hang up the phone and turn to one of the teenagers with an exasperated sigh: "Your father has blown up the car – trying to win the green light grand prix no doubt. I guess that means no footy training for you tonight." If not the kid, the partner could always call one of their own parents and complain about their partner. Alternatively, the couple could find solace in agreeing that the relative who recommended they buy the now deceased car was an imbecile and recite all the other instances of that relative's stupidity. They could equally avoid dealing with their anxiety over the blown-up car by directing all their attention and worry toward the threat it might pose to their son's football career and his fragile sense of wellbeing.

We've all fallen into all four of these patterns in one form or another. They're what we humans do when we lose our capacity to think, or we choose not to. We conflict, distance, over-function, under-function and triangle because they serve to reduce the immediate, acute feelings of anxiety.

You'll no doubt be able to think of examples of these four patterns in the workplace. As an HR Manager, I was everybody's favourite to be pulled into a triangle, and sometimes that triangle also involved conflict. Distancing often shows up as absenteeism, or just missing commitments.

Over-functioning deserves a special mention, heeding Friedman's counsel I quoted earlier, and also reflecting on my experience as a leadership coach. A significant proportion of my coaching conversations centre on employee management, whether it's a denizen of the C-suite or a recalcitrant casual hire.

So often out impulse when dealing with an underperforming worker is to offer them support. This may by appropriate and even highly advisable, or it may be the beginning of a spiral into a reciprocal relationship of over- and under-functioning. When we go light on accountability and heavy on support, we risk facilitating more underperformance. When we take on responsibilities we should be leaving with our workers, we risk adding move to our own glass and inching toward overflow.

The four patterns are unhelpful simply because they divert energy away from solving problems and pursuing longer-term goals. If they are transitory and only moderate in their intensity, they're not a cause for alarm. However, the supervisor should be concerned about them becoming entrenched: perpetual conflict, distancing becoming frequent and widespread, over- and under-functioning becoming rigid and marked, projection to a third becoming a preoccupation or manifesting as scapegoating.

Treat these as you would lights on your car's dashboard. They're signs of the system struggling to adapt to challenge. If the challenge becomes chronic or intensifies, the glass can spill over into symptoms, including burnout. So let's take a quick look at the symptoms that show up when an individual or a system's collective glass begins to overflow.

Symptom development
Physical Symptoms We've already explored what happens when the HPA axis is activated and the body prepares to deal with an acute challenge. When the amygdala is chronically aroused and the HPA axis chronically active, some knock-on effects will begin to show up.

Being perpetually prepared for action sometimes results in chronic muscle tension, often around the neck and shoulders, which in turn can lead to recurrent headaches as well as generalised pain. Poor ergonomics will sometime exacerbate or replicate this condition. This may show up as an uptick in repetitive strain injuries.

Persistent anxiety has also been associated with inflammation which contributes to a broad array of human diseases, both acute and chronic.[94] To the supervisor's observation, this may show up as a vulnerability to conditions involving joint inflammation. Other inflammation-related conditions like hypertension turn up in medical examinations.

While the exact mechanisms are not well understood, there's a growing body of research pointing to the correlation of stress/anxiety and autoimmune

---

[94] Yun-Zi Liu, Yun-Xia Wang, and Chun-Lei Jiang *Inflammation: The Common Pathway of Stress-Related Diseases* Frontiers in Human Neuroscience.2017; 11: 316.

diseases.[95] This may be related to the response of the immune system of the activated HPA axis. It may be observable as flare-ups of episodic conditions like psoriasis or arthritis (which also involve inflammation).

Psychological Symptoms Persistent anxiety that impacts an individual's functioning is likely to be diagnosed as an anxiety disorder. While there are numerous subtypes, the common factors are a persistent rumination about and/or a disproportionate fear response to the object upon which the anxiety is fixed.

Anxiety's correlation with depression has been well established in the psychological literature.

While anxiety and depression are both normal human responses to particular challenges, the supervisor would do well to look for disproportionality, and where the worker's capacity is reduced.

Social Symptoms We often call these coping mechanisms – anything that will give us a shot of dopamine to make us feel better in the moment. As Anna Lembke points out, we're all vulnerable to the lure of dopamine, and some of the ways we might pursue our natural dopamine hit can be good for us – e.g. exercise.[96] Unless it's taken to an unhelpful extreme, this is not generally regarded as a social symptom. Other ways of getting the dopamine fix are less constructive: addictions or compulsive behaviours toward anything from romance fiction to purchases (like my tendency to buy another project car when I'm feeling unhappy) – through to gambling, porn, alcohol, drugs, and extramarital affairs. Psychologists might assign them separate categories, but they all share the same neurobiological marker – dopamine.

Other social symptoms are less about the pursuit of feeling good and more about maladaptive reactions to feeling bad. These generally show up doing harm to self and/or others. Often these pair up with coping mechanisms like alcohol. If they show up in the workplace, swift action is required.

---

[95] Shmerling, R. H. *Autoimmune disease and stress: Is there a link?* Harvard Health Publishing Oct 2020 https://www.health.harvard.edu/blog/autoimmune-disease-and-stress-is-there-a-link-2018071114230.
[96] Lembke, A. *Dopamine Nation: Finding Balance in the Age of Indulgence* (Headline, London 2021).

To summarise, four patterns of anxious emotional process and the three types of symptoms that emerge when the total emotional load is close to or beyond the capacity to adapt. My encouragement is for you to become a keen observer of your people and the systems they form, and to treat your observations as information about the system. It's not a call to become the fixer, rescuer or therapist. Now let's take a look at some ways of managing yourself and leading your people in the face of burnout risk.

Reducing the risk of burnout

As a supervisor, being observant of these behavioural patterns serves as a kind of emotional dashboard for the systems in which you participate. Firstly, observing your own behaviour in terms of the four patterns will give you an idea of the available capacity in your own glass. If you see yourself being a little more conflictual than normal, feeling the impulse to retreat, falling into being the super-supervisor, avoiding your responsibilities or habitually talking about people who aren't in the room, it may be that you're close to or exceeding your own capacities, especially if you're employing these behaviours more than usual.

Also watch yourself for physical, mental and social symptoms. Be a little tough with yourself. These issues are easy to explain away until they mess up your life.

When you observe an uptick in the frequency or intensity of any of the four patterns among your workers, it's your cue to become curious as to the sources of anxiety that produce the patterns. Be aware that the inherent power imbalance in the supervisory relationship means that you're more likely to be invited into a conflict or to be held at a distance, to be the object of projection, and to be expected to take more responsibility than is yours to take.

Remember, systems interlock and anxiety from one system, such as a worker's family, can 'leak' into their workplace. Anxiety in the workplace can also leak out into the various families represented. If the various triangles in which the patterns occur seem to feature one particular person, it's a fair bet that there's a whole lot more going on for that person that you can immediately see. Rather than seeing them as a troublemaker, it's worth moving toward them.

Without trying to turn you into an organisational psychologist, let me suggest some helpful strategies for working in anxious systems, drawn from Bowen's theory.

A low-stress boss

As a supervisor, workplace stress will be a significant issue for you to manage, both in yourself and in your team. For the reasons I outlined above, you can't simply reduce it to an issue about workload or expectations.

In 1985 Ed Friedman gave us the term, 'non-anxious presence'.[97] I hear it quoted so often in so many quarters that it's become a bit of a cliché. To put the strapline into context, Friedman observes that being calm enough to be curious and thoughtful, while being sufficiently self-defined to be clear, is in and of itself therapeutic. But it's only beneficial if you're present. As a boss, being in regular contact and in a calm frame of mind is a resource to your people.

If you're worried about stress in your workplace, think over the things we discussed in the first section: being personally well-organised and disciplined, being clear on your own responsibilities and treating workers as valuable. If you can bring some of that thinking to your supervision practice, it will serve as a protective factor against workplace stress. A good deal of what we'll cover in the rest of the book is how to put that philosophy of supervision into practice.

Put another way, being a responsible, consistent boss is one of the most important contributions you can make to reducing workplace stress and the risk of burnout – more than employee assistance programs and wellness interventions that might temporarily relieve the symptoms.

Remember Maslach identified six general causes for burnout, and only one of them is about high workload. It's common for supervisors to see the signs of burnout and reflexively reduce workload expectations. Yet, if other causes are the primary drivers, reducing workload will only put more pressure on the

---

[97] Friedman, E. H. *Generation to Generation: Family Process in Church and Synagogue* (Guildford, New York 1985).

supervisor as they try to meet the expectations to which their boss holds them accountable.

A research posture

In managing an anxious system, let's talk about your posture, or how you understand your role. As far as your responsibilities will allow, adopting the posture of a curious researcher will help you stay neutral – viewing the various behaviour as phenomena to examine and understand rather than threats, crimes, pathologies or Machiavellian attempts to take over the world. The researcher's posture is reticent to assume things, is likely to form hypotheses but hold them lightly, and is slow to form a definitive judgement.

Of course, evidence that a worker has engaged in clearly prohibited behaviour or has been significantly irresponsible will require your more direct and authoritative intervention. Just bear in mind, a lot of workplace tension is not about such clear contraventions.

The anxious system will invite you, as the boss, to jump in and fix things. If you can tolerate the weight of expectation and be more about questions than about quick-fix solutions, you may just help the system to grow up a little.

Contact, contact, contact

Calm contact, regardless of the content of what is said, has a stabilising influence on anxious systems. So often, when an organisation is under challenge, the senior leaders bunker down in their offices and hold lengthy, worried meetings. Actually, getting out among the workforce and just being present and curious will do more to calm the organisation than just about anything else.

If your team is under challenge or showing some of the four patterns, make a habit of being in more frequent contact, even if you don't always deal with 'the issue'. If there's tension between two workers, you can bet one or both will seek to draw you toward their side to set up a kind of two-against-one scenario – this is how triangles work. Staying in equal contact with both sides and resisting the invitation to agree with one party or the other will tacitly encourage them to sort things out for themselves.

In response to invitations to join one person in a coalition against another, I've sometimes said things like, "I'm hearing you. I can see this is bothering you. I want to be careful not to take sides here. I wonder what the other person

281

would tell me about this if they had the chance." There are always at least two versions of events, and the parties sometimes sound like they're describing two entirely different incidents. Unless you're investigating a formal complaint, it may not be your job to get to 'the truth'.

Stating and demonstrating your own position

Being clear about your responsibilities and commitments is pretty useful when anxiety is high. Anxiety has the effect of focusing the mind on the immediate and narrow considerations of the individual. It's important not to allow yourself to be recruited to its cause. Keeping in mind the following commitments can help keep you in a neutral position:

- Your commitment to the longer-term objectives of the organisation
- Your commitment to your responsibilities as a supervisor
- Your commitment to staying out of things that people can resolve by themselves
- Your commitment to avoid stating an opinion about things that don't require your opinion (just be careful not to give the impression of tacit agreement)
- Your commitment to reserve your formation of an opinion until you have sufficient information

If you can maintain a researcher position and state your observations about the emotional process rather than getting embroiled in the content, it encourages others to become curious too. Sometimes I'll wonder out loud about the things that make me curious.

A coaching approach

When you observe that the total emotional load is nearing a person's capacity, taking the approach of coaching is often more helpful than charging in with swift solutions. Coaching is about using thoughtful questions to raise a person's awareness and to clarify their personal responsibilities. Coaching presumes that a person is competent to manage their life if they can just think clearly about it. A coaching approach treats everyone as a responsible adult, and most people respond by acting as a responsible adult.

None of us want to infantilise or patronise our workers. Yet many of us are vulnerable to an impulse to step in and fix things where no direct help is required, or to respond to a person's upset feelings as if they have no capacity to soothe themselves. On the whole people have more capacity to think their way through challenges than we imagine. What often derails them is the intensity of their feelings. If our responses to their difficulty summon or reinforce their feelings of upset, we may be encouraging them to dive deeper into their upset state. Elton John may be right that "...it feels so good to hurt so bad,"[98] but that's not necessarily helpful. As a boss we can get pulled into tacitly taking sides by being too quick to empathise.

Assuming that people have the emotional maturity to calm themselves and the resourcefulness to solve their own problems is actually calming and empowering. As Edwin Friedman says, clarity is more important than empathy.[99] Asking questions based on this assumption tends to flip people into a more thoughtful space. A response like, "Wow, there's a lot going on there. What have you done to steady yourself and stay on track?" has the effect of getting people to think about things to steady themselves. You could follow it up with, "What else do you think might help you to keep your equilibrium in the face of this?" Further questions like, "What sort of resources will you need to draw on to meet this challenge?" will get your worker thinking about what they need and they'll probably even start to identify where they can get it. These questions carry the assumption that the worker has the resources to manage, and that you believe in their abilities. Herein lies the paradox: when we ask those sorts of questions, the worker will almost certainly feel cared-for and respected. They'll more likely walk away from the conversation in a more optimistic frame of mind than if you just empathised with their difficulty.

In a 2005 article about recovering from burnout, Christina Maslach and Michael Leiter[100] cover two case studies of people experiencing all three indicators of burnout, and their path to recovery. It's interesting to note that in both cases the way forward was not for the management of the organisation to alter their expectations or provide more support. Rather the workers themselves changed their own expectation, assumption and posture toward their work context. If burnout is the result of chronically unmanaged stress (as

---

[98] From *Sad Songs (Say So Much)* from the album *Breaking Hearts* Music by Elton John, Lyrics by Bernie Taupin (Geffen Music 1984).
[99] Friedman, E. H. *A Failure of Nerve: Leadership in the Age of the Quick Fix* (Seabury, New York, 1999).
[100] Maslach, C. and Leiter, M. P. *Reversing Burnout: How to rekindle your passion for your work*. Stanford Social Innovation Review Winter 2005
https://ssir.org/articles/entry/reversing_burnout.

the definition states), then one live option is to help the worker improve their management of their stress and stressors, by changing their perceptions expectations, work processes and patterns of relating. Coaching is a useful way to help workers explore these possibilities. We'll talk more extensively about the mechanics of coaching in section four.

And all that said, it's important that you make a careful evaluation of the worker's circumstance and take reasonable steps to ensure that their work expectations are reasonable, and consider modifying work expectations where appropriate. Just be careful not to invite them into an under-functioning position.

Managing workers with burnout

Once a worker is showing significant symptoms or has received a diagnosis of burnout from their GP, you'll need to balance your desire to be an empowering, thoughtful boss with the risk management obligations of the company. That means accessing the appropriate mental health care for your worker. If your organisation has an Employee Assistance Program, this may be a useful place to begin. Just bear in mind that the 3-5 sessions offered by an EAP are usually only sufficient to provide some support and some stress management techniques. Sometimes this is enough, often it's not.

If your worker is showing the three signs of burnout and/or showing symptoms of ongoing anxiety described above, but is yet to receive a diagnosis, you may consider making a professional coach or external supervisor available to them. A more neutral outsider can sometimes be more helpful than a boss with some coaching questions.

If you have a worker experiencing diagnosable burnout, it's important that you maintain fairly frequent contact and keep an eye on how they're travelling. If the worker is seeing a therapist such as a psychologist on an ongoing basis, you may consider seeking permission to set up a three-way meeting with the worker and the therapist to better understand how you might be a resource. Just be aware that workers and therapists will often refuse.

Getting to know your workers

The better your relationship with your workers, the more they will entrust you with information about their life outside of the workplace, and the more amenable they will be to you taking a coaching approach when they present difficulties. We'll look more at building that relationship when we consider the mechanics of the supervisory relationship in the next section.

Being mindful of the overall weight of challenge

If you can get a decent line of sight on the overall load of challenge a worker is carrying and keep an eye on their capacity to manage, you can be thoughtful about when and where to add a little stretch challenge to induce some growth and development, and where to dial back the overall level of challenge if the worker is showing some early signs of burnout risk.

We've spent a bit of time in this chapter looking at the various ways you can observe patterns and symptoms in your workplace system as a form of feedback about the system's capacity to adapt to challenge. In the next chapter we'll look at feedback coming from our workers as information about the supervision relationship.

We've also looked at stress, anxiety and their various associated brain functions. In the chapter after next we'll take a deeper dive into one of those anxious patterns – conflict. And we'll think a little more about how anxious brains turn conflicts into quarrels.

Summary

- Burnout is a recognised condition characterised by exhaustion, cynicism and reduced professional efficacy.
- The stress that is by definition the cause of burnout, is biologically indistinguishable from anxiety.
- The actual contributing factors for stress and anxiety are difficult to accurately determine, because attribution is subjective. Factors outside the workplace may predispose a worker to an anxious response to challenges in the workplace.
- Burnout can be understood as a chronic depletion of resources, or as total emotional load overwhelming the capacity to productively adapt.
- There are predictable patterns of behaviour that indicate a system under stress.
- There are mental, physical and social symptoms that emerge when people experience ongoing elevated anxiety.
- Being a responsible, curious and non-reactive presence can do a great deal to moderate workplace anxiety and serve as a protective factor against burnout.

Discussion

- When have you experienced challenge in one sphere of life contributing to you being more sensitive or reactive in another?
- When have you noticed any of the four anxious patterns becoming more prevalent in a workplace?

Action

- Based on what you've learned in this chapter, what's one action you could take to help reduce burnout risk in your workplace?

Chapter 19
Worker response and reaction

For several chapters now, I've been encouraging you to be thoughtful about how much you expect of your workers, how much support you offer and how you might adapt your approach to them based on their unique characteristics as individuals. In the previous chapter we spent some time exploring patterns and symptoms in the relationship system of your workplace that provide information about your workers' capacity to adapt to their current challenges. It may read as if I've assumed you can, by careful analysis and observation, figure out the perfect fit for each worker and each work team. It would be nice to be able to do that if it were possible. However, supervision is more of an adaptive challenge than a technical one, so there will be a degree of trial and error.

Just as your workers need feedback from you as to whether they're meeting your expectations, you would do well to take heed of the feedback you receive from your workers. I'm not talking about putting on your 'psychologist face' at the end of every conversation and asking, in a slightly worried tone, if the supervision met all their felt needs for affirmation and validation. But neither am I talking about assuming we always get it more-or-less right and the workers will need to suck it up if they're unhappy. Your workers are already giving you feedback in the form of their responses and reaction. It's simply a case of seeing it for what it is.

Feedback: ready or not

Feedback comes in various forms. Sometimes its's explicit, sometimes implicit. Sometimes we seek feedback. We'll talk more about that in chapter 21. Workers' responses and reactions are feedback that comes to us whether we're ready or not. Direct feedback in the form of a straightforward, reasonably objective statement delivered in a calm tone is a rarity. Even then, we might find it hard to take, especially if it catches us by surprise.

I've had workers tell me I move too fast and they feel a bit jangled and overwhelmed. I have had workers tell me that I assume too much and don't communicate in enough detail. Having read this far, by now you know me well enough to know that these are my besetting sins. By temperament I am fast paced and intuitive, and if I'm not mindful about these tendencies it can rankle with people. When I get that kind of feedback I find it pretty easy to sigh, give the worker my *mea culpa*, and commit to slowing down and communicating in more detail.

Conversely, when a worker looks me in the eye and says they believe I don't care about them, I find it hard to take. I value people. I have a track record of supporting workers who are having a hard time of life. I've invested time and training in underperforming workers to help them get up to speed rather than opting to quickly 'manage them out'. I want to trot all of these defences out to prove I'm not that guy. And all that will do is prove the worker's case.

When a worker responds or reacts to me in a way that blindsides me or seems at odds with the kind of boss I'm trying to be, I have a responsibility to engage the worker at face value. At my best, I'll pause and say something like, "Wow. That's certainly not what I'm trying to be/do. Help me to see more clearly what it's like from your point of view." It's almost certain that I will not agree with much of what comes next. At my best I'll keep asking and inviting the worker to tell me more until I've got a reasonably clear idea of their point of view. That's me at my best.

I had a conversation years back with a volunteer leader who operated as my kind of 2IC in a community-based organisation we served. She was younger than I and less experienced in leadership (not that I had that much in the bank either at that stage). Still, she summoned up the courage to make a time to talk, and in our appointment she clearly and sensitively laid out some home truths I was not prepared to hear. It felt like a gut punch. It seemed so unfair. I felt so misunderstood. I knew some of it was a bunch of 'bullets' someone else had handed her to fire. I knew who that guy was and I knew he had his own 'issues'. I countered. I protested. I whined.

My colleague stayed with me, listened to my protests and held her ground. She knew she was right, but she didn't bulldoze. Over the hour or so that we spoke, I came to accept the inescapable, unpleasant truth. She had exposed a major blind spot for me. The ancient Hebrew King Solomon, a collector of proverbs and wise sayings, noted this: "Wounds from a friend can be trusted, but an enemy multiplies kisses."[101] Sure my colleague drew a little emotional blood, but her courage and sincerity were an act of leadership and an act of love. I'm a better leader today thanks to her.

When people give you feedback, it pays to listen. Thoughtfully engaging with the feedback you receive will make you a better person and a better boss, even if it firstly makes you miserable.

However, feedback doesn't always come thoughtfully packaged from people who have your best interests at heart. Mostly it comes implied, wrapped up in phenomena like dissonance, resistance and even hostility. Over the next few pages we'll unpack these before we look at the anatomy of a thoughtful response. Let's begin with the more subtle forms.

Resonance and dissonance

In every conversation there are more than just the words and ideas of the topic being discussed: there's implicit information about the relationship. Daniel Goleman's book *The New Leaders* develops the idea of 'resonant leadership' which literally means to be on a similar wavelength.[102] A musical chord works on the idea of notes being complimentary as the frequencies of their vibrations harmonise. A major chord is made up of a root note, plus a third that vibrates at one and a quarter times the speed of the root, plus a fifth that vibrates at one and a half times the root. The three notes resonate. When a note is off key, the maths don't work neatly (a note that's vibrating at seventy-nine forty-sevenths of the root will not harmonise). It sounds discordant or dissonant.

We've all been in conversations that feel dissonant; those times when it feels like neither party really understands what the other is meaning. Each person might be comprehending the individual words, but not getting the message. If I'm in a conversation like that with someone I've just met I might try to find an excuse to wriggle out of it – I find discordant conversations excruciating.

---

[101] From the Book of Proverbs in the *Mishlei Shlomo*, or **The Proverbs of Solomon** in the Tanakh (Hebrew Scriptures).
[102] Goleman, D., Boyatzis, R. and McKee, A. **The New Leaders: Transforming the Art of Leadership into the Science of Results** (Sphere, London 2007).

If your supervision conversations feel dissonant, that feeling is feedback about the quality of the relationship. Like a red light glowing on your car dashboard, you ignore such feedback at your peril.

As the boss, you're the leader of the conversation. While your dissonant conversation is a co-creation of you and your worker, as the leader it's your responsibility to get things in tune. Instinctively, when a conversation is dissonant, we tend to talk more, hoping more words will make things clearer. Actually, the opposite is true.

When band members arrive for rehearsal, after setting up and warming up, it's time to tune up. When you're tuning, you want everyone else to stop playing so you can hear. I play bass, so when it's time to tune up I want everyone else to be quiet and the pianist to play a low E. One note. Not a chord. Not a Rachmaninov concerto. One single low E. I'll respond with one note, the open E string. I'll adjust the tuning key for that string until it's in perfect resonance with the piano note. I may need the piano to sound the note several times before we move to the A, then the D and G.

If your supervision conversation is off key, filling the air with more notes will only turn the conversation into a cacophony. Stop playing, stop talking. You might want to observe out loud, "I'm not sure we're on the same wavelength here."

As the leader, you get to take the initiative and put aside your agenda for the moment. Ask your worker for a single point that they think is important to the conversation. Ask them to explain it as clearly as they can. That's their low E. Then do your best to offer your understanding of what they just said. Not your interpretation, not the implications, not your brilliant insight. See if you can play an E in tune with theirs. Ask them if you heard it right. You may need to get them to state their point again and then have another go at feeding it back.

From there try their next point, using the same pattern.

Pushback

Sometimes feedback will come to you in a more oppositional form. Usually this comes in the form of your worker arguing with your ideas and opinions, or resisting your direction. In a more extreme form it comes as accusation and even threat. We'll tackle the more strident pushback in a minute. For now, let's just go with relatively calm apparently rational opposition.

Regardless of the content of your worker's resistance, the process of pushback – the very fact that the worker is resisting your thinking and instruction is telling you something. Pushback is information you can use, provided you can make some sense of it.

Typically, the conversation will go one of two ways – either concentrating on the content of the conversation, or a contest of power in the relationship. Very occasionally the conversation will deal with the process of the pushback itself, and this is where the real information is likely to reside. But let's for a minute go back to contests of ideas and power.

Sometimes (and it's less common than you might think), the pushback is purely a contest of ideas. You might want to move ahead with implementing an idea, the worker might want to slow down and consult with stakeholders. The ensuing conversation might try to balance considerations about urgency and efficiency, with the risks of resistance and disenfranchisement. A healthy supervisory relationship will be able to contain even a quite robust debate without people becoming upset. As long as the pronouns stay in the first person singular – "I think…", "I'm concerned about…", "My priority is…" – the conversation is about ideas and you'll likely end up with a useful outcome.

Occasionally when leading a meeting I've paused, looked around the room at my colleagues and observed, "I'm not going to get my way here, am I?" In the contest of ideas, other people in the room frequently have better ideas than mine. Because it's a contest of ideas, the idea that emerges as the best usually wins. Sometimes it's not that simple but we'll come back to that in a minute.

As soon as the pronouns turn to second person – "You're trying to…", "You just want to…", "You keep saying…" – it's stopped being a contest of ideas and become a contest of personalities. The *con*tent may look like ideas, but the *int*ent shifts from 'May the best idea win' to 'I'm determined not to lose'. Notice it's generally not as much about winning as it is about not losing. Once you're there, the conversation seldom recovers without someone putting aside their personal agenda and being willing to do something like the 'tune up' described earlier, or the person with the most power bulldozing their idea through.

As a boss you can reduce the likelihood of a conversation descending from a contest of ideas to a contest of personalities by holding your own ideas lightly, maintaining a posture of curiosity and listening carefully to the other points of view. Slow down. Ask questions.

If you find yourself frequently using the power of your position to deal with worker pushback, you can pretty much forget their discretionary work effort. The best you're going to get is their 'good-enough-to-not-get-fired' work effort. The worst is various forms of subterfuge.

Sometimes, in order to do your job and fulfil your responsibilities, you just have to say, "My way or the highway." But it's an option you don't want to be going to very often.

The disproportionate response

Sometimes feedback comes in the form of disproportionate responses – those times when what you think is a fairly routine issue attracts a surprisingly strong response. It pays to notice these.

Last century, back when I had a lot of hair, it was all black and mostly on my head, my wife and I were foster parents. One girl was with us through most of her teenage years. Prior to coming our way, she had lived in various housing commission homes and caravan parks, dragged about with her steadily increasing number of siblings by a mother who struggled with an acquired brain injury and a tendency toward destructive relationships.

About six months after our foster kid came to us, we bought our first home – a modest little weatherboard cottage in desperate need of some TLC. We worked hard to get the place liveable and settled in. Our foster kid was able to continue at the same school. I finished my study and got a real job, and then a promotion. We had a little money for things like holidays. For the first time in her life, our foster kid had genuine stability. Life was predictable. She could form friendships and make plans confident that there was unlikely to be a screaming match followed by a late-night taxi ride to a new beginning on the other side of town.

Another year or so later we began to have children of our own. Two doors up from us a larger, brick veneer house was put up for mortgagee's auction. Sure it needed some work, but it had an extra bedroom and two living areas. I suggested to the family that we consider buying it. Our foster kid went apoplectic. I was blindsided by the reaction. We're talking about a move two-doors up the street – to the house on the other side of the next-door neighbour's house. We could carry our stuff from one house to the other by hand.

That's what I mean by a disproportionate response.

I figured there was a bit more in play, so I dropped the idea. Years later it dawned on me what was actually going on. (You probably figured it out as you read the story, but I'm a bit slow on the uptake). In the mind of our foster kid, her stability and security were fragile. Even the smallest change could topple the delicate edifice of her new life into the tangled chaos of her past. In her experience, new babies and house moves correlated to disruption, unpredictability, loss and anxiety.

You've likely seen this in the workplace. You propose a small change to a shift roster and get a reaction more befitting mass redundancies. You talk about introducing of a bit of new technology to improve efficiency and it's as if you were asking everybody to drive on the other side of the road and speak Swahili.

This kind of reaction is providing you useful information. It might be feedback about your relationship with your worker (or your overall workforce), or it might be telling you something about your leadership style, or it might be largely about your worker and their backstory. Your mission is to find out which.

I don't have a guaranteed formula for success here, but I do have a pretty certain prescription for failure. Unfortunately, that prescription is the strategy most leaders follow: argue. I don't mean quarrel, I mean trying to convince the unconvinced person or persons of the benefits of your position. While you may be brilliantly persuasive, it's unlikely that your worker will be persuaded. In fact, they're more likely to galvanise their position. And the reason for that gets back to our earlier discussion about content and process.

Arguing the rationale is a question of content. If you're dealing with a disproportionate response, the issue is unlikely to be with the content of your proposal per se and going in harder with the content will most likely result in the worker coming back harder with their resistance. Arguing content often leads to the distance between you and your worker widening.

More likely to be at play here is emotional process where the disproportionality or intensity of the response is driven by emotional loading that's leaked into this issue from somewhere else. You're not going to find out by arguing.

At this point there's a choice to be made. You could just tell the worker to go buy themselves a vacuum cleaner and suck it up, because this change is just going to happen. Using your positional authority like this is sometimes necessary, especially if the change is time-pressured and you resign yourself to making some relational repairs later. Or it might be that the dissenting worker has a long and colourful tradition of imagining themselves to be leader of the opposition, and you're not willing to reward their bad behaviour. That may be the case – but remind yourself that throwing your weight around comes with a price tag, even if you don't have to pay straight away.

Alternatively, you might choose to slow things down and become a student of the emotional process. Your greatest asset in the sphere of emotional process is your curiosity – noticing the intensity of the disproportionate reaction – asking yourself, "I wonder where that's coming from?" Sometimes the worker will tell you directly if you ask.

Becoming curious helps to get your posture right. Scott Peck, in his classic *The Road Less Travelled* uses the term 'bracketing' to describe suspending your opinions and agenda for a minute and genuinely seeking to understand the other person.[103] Stephen Covey's fifth habit of 'seeking first to understand, then to be understood' carries a similar idea.[104]

Remember, pushback is a form of feedback. The benefit to you is the insight you can gain about your leadership and supervision skills. Don't waste the opportunity by simply seeking to win the day, when what you could win is both your own growth toward maturity and the heart of your worker.

---

[103] Peck, M. S. *The Road Less Travelled: A New Psychology of Love, Traditional Values and Spiritual Growth* (Simon & Schuster, New York 1978).
[104] Covey, Stephen *The Seven Habits of Highly Effective People* (The Business Library Melbourne. 1997).

Your workers may just be honest with you if you can create an environment where they believe you're genuinely interested in what they have to say, are open to receiving some critique and are willing to take responsibility for your part in whatever difficulties arise. Asking questions that invite critique and responding non-defensively will help to create a climate of trust where people can be frank.

Once you've listened carefully you may need to take some time out to weigh up the information you've been given by your worker. It's unlikely you'll agree with everything they've said. The most valuable part may well be the insight it provides into your character and leadership. Personally, I find I'll get the most out of this kind of evaluation if I engage the help of my coach. I'm seeking to figure out my contribution to the challenge or problem at hand.

If you make a habit of seeing people's responses as feedback, you'll probably find the same issue coming up over and over again. For me it's usually about my impatience, my eagerness for results, my assumption that everyone is as intuitive as I am and will therefore just 'get it' based on the few scraps of information I've given.

Once you've given good consideration to your part in the issue, you might want to wonder about whether the disproportionate response is fuelled by reactivity to something else.

Even more helpful to a calmer, more enlightened conversation is to pick up on Immanuel Kant's reasoning process of 'thesis, antithesis, synthesis'.[105] This means the conversation is not about *your* idea winning per se, it's more about the *best* idea winning, and that idea may as yet be unarticulated. Being open to the possibility that the most helpful way forward may yet lie undiscovered helps you be a little more neutral, rather than just pushing for your ideas. Being open to the possibility that your worker's opposing view – even if it's fuelled by all sorts of irrationality – may just contain a valuable trace of genius. It can pique your curiosity. This in turn calms the conversation down, shifting it from a battle of wills to a search for a solution.

Having taken a deep breath and assumed the Peck-Covey-Kant curiosity posture, let's return to thinking about framing our response to the resounding

---

[105] Kant, E. *Critique of Pure Reason* (1781).

'No!' from your worker. You might be tempted to ask, "Well, why not?" While that's a fair question, it may be seen as a challenge, which takes you back to inadvertently galvanising their position. You may be able to observe, "I can see that you feel strongly about this." That might be enough to elicit more from the worker. Or you may need to follow up with, "I'm interested in understanding your thinking on this." Or possibly, "Help me to see the bad outcome you're trying to prevent."

Whatever comes next will be rich with information, if you can pay attention and keep yourself from reacting.

If they come back with, "I'm just not doing it and that's final" or they clam up, you may need to revert to the vacuum cleaner option (perhaps in less inflammatory terms), or you may want to leave it for a little while and come back once they've settled a little. Even this tells you a lot about your worker and your relationship with them.

Provided they're willing to give you something, your mission at this point is to listen very carefully and take notice of a few things. Firstly, watch for the pronouns. If the worker is using first person singular pronouns, there's a good chance that you'll be able to use the tune-up approach, giving back to them exactly what you think they're saying (no interpretation or evaluation), then responding with your thinking, couched in the same, 'I think...', 'My goal...' kind of language. It may be a tortured conversation and it may take a few attempts. Be prepared to take their thinking into consideration and modify your position – the final synthesis of thinking may well be a lot better than your initial thesis.

You might get some backstory information: "When we tried this at my last workplace, it was a disaster." You might get some information about their fears and sensitivities: "If you change the roster it will stuff-up my weekend access arrangement with my kids."

In such cases it's wise to stick with the worker's concern or objection. "Okay, tell me what went wrong" or "So I'm hearing your concern about juggling your access visits. What are your constraints?" Be careful to ensure you've heard them out before you get to the solution side or resume selling your idea. Sometimes, if you listen patiently, the worker will relax a little and offer you a workable solution, or perhaps even accept your position unamended.

If your worker comes back at you with those second-person pronouns, it can be really tough to stay calm and curious and keep the conversation about the ideas. If you respond in kind with second-person pronouns, the conversation is likely to turn into a game of accusation poker, where each side keeps raising the stakes until someone has had enough and folds. Not the route to a productive outcome.

Unless you're really up against a deadline, if the pushback doesn't abate fairly quickly, it's worth taking some time between the emergence of the pushback and seeking to resolve it. I know the ambiguity of an unresolved issue may mean you spend a few days with your worker 'living in your head and not paying any rent,' but if you can manage your anxiety, slowing things down gives everyone time to reflect on what's at hand and have conversations with themselves and with others.

If your worker is upset, you can pretty much guarantee that they'll share that upset with others, and most likely with their co-workers. While we would all prefer that this didn't happen, it's just what humans do. Sometimes those conversations will stir up a bit of a storm, but just as often they serve to stabilise things.

If your worker 'triangles' a co-worker and they get close and comfortable by agreeing that they are 'right' and you are 'wrong', at least you can take solace in the fact that this will usually help your worker calm down. In calming down they will regain their thinking capacity and may just begin to think over what you've said. Any efforts to stop triangling or to try to convince the third person of your side of the story almost always have the opposite outcome to what you intend. Meanwhile, hopefully you (and your coach if you have one) can go over your part in the interaction.

One of the key strategies to moderate the impact of triangles activating throughout your team (and the wider organisation) is to thoughtfully and intentionally maintain calm contact with as many of the players as you can manage. Anxious triangles tend to distort perceptions. Just being in touch with people helps other individuals to maintain their own estimation of you, rather than having their perceptions shaped by another anxious person. In maintaining contact, you don't necessarily need to try to address or fix anything, just be in touch and be yourself.

If the pushback is just reactivity with minimal hostility, your effort to slow things down, stay relatively calm, be patient and think over your own part in the problem will usually result in you gaining some useful insight into your own leadership and maturity, and it might just get you to some increased trust with your worker and some better decisions being made.

The hostile response

Sometimes the disproportionate feedback comes wrapped up in a layer of hostility. In my research for this book, dealing with conflict was one of the major challenges for which supervisors were seeking help and counsel.

Dealing with conflict with your workers is such a crucial subject that it deserves its own chapter. So turn the page…

Summary

- Your workers are giving you feedback, even if you don't recognise it.
- Attending to the feedback you receive will make you a better person and a better boss, even if it makes you unhappy for a little while.
- Dissonance is feedback.
    - You may need to do a 'tune-up' to resolve it.
- Pushback and disproportionate responses are feedback.
    - Make understanding your priority, not winning.
    - Patience and curiosity will get you further than force in the long run.
    - Keep contact with other team members to minimise the impact of triangling.

Discussion

- Recall your last piece of difficult feedback.
    - What could you have done more, less or differently to gain more benefit?

Implementation

- How will you remind yourself to be patient and curious in the face of feedback you may prefer not to hear?

Chapter 20
The conflictual worker

Most people hate conflict – or at least would prefer not to be involved in conflict. People who love conflict and look for combative opportunities would probably receive some kind of diagnosis were they to visit a psychologist. Conflict arouses a range of unpleasant emotions.

Faced with aggression, even the most calm and reasonable person will find themselves emotionally activated. Assuming you're not the kind of character Tom Cruise would play in a *Jack Reacher* or *Mission Impossible* flick (i.e. coldly calm and rational no matter the threat), the hostile environment is one that's unlikely to bring out your best or the best outcome for the organisation.

Given its potential, one would think conflict is something to be avoided. Yet Patrick Lencioni identifies fear of conflict as a significant inhibitor to team cohesion and performance.[106] As we have discussed earlier, conflict is one of the normal human responses to anxiety and challenge. In a minute we'll consider some strong evidence to suggest that behind the conflictual attitude may be some very substantive issues that require our careful attention.

Dealing with conflict is a normal and important part of supervision. Avoidance of conflict is the enemy of good supervision.

Having said all that, let's dive into the world of conflict with your worker.

What goes before

So much of how conflictual conversations play out is dependent on the state of the relationship before the difficult issue arises. That's why this little section is here, toward the back of the book, rather than up front, even though conflict is one of the most commonly reported areas of difficulty for supervisors.

If you have a solid, trusting collegial relationship with your worker, and they have solid reasons for trusting you and believing that you'll treat them fairly, most difficult issues can be addressed, even if the conversation gets pretty

---

[106] Lencioni, P. *The Five Dysfunction's of a Team* (Jossey Bass, San Francisco 2002).

intense. If the relationship is distant or strained, it will be more likely to descend from debate around an issue into a conflict about personally winning or losing.

It's worth the effort to cultivate working relationships strong enough to hold the pressure of tough conversations. Regular, open conversations, where the balance of support and expectation is maintained and reinforced will go a long way to creating a working alliance that will bear the strain. If the relationship is not in a good state of repair, there's no time to straighten things out when the difficult issue arises.

It's not uncommon for potentially conflictual interactions to emerge early in the supervisory relationship, especially when you find yourself supervising a worker who's been around the organisation for a while. If a worker has been poorly supervised and you initiate appropriate and responsible supervision, it's not uncommon to get some pushback. In the face of this, some bosses lose their nerve and choose to tiptoe around the worker's resistance. Do that early in the relationship and it's likely you'll keep doing it.

Susan Scott points out that just about everything we do and don't do has a self-reinforcing effect.[107] Anyone who's tried to lose weight or get fit knows this. Cave-in and eat the cream bun once, and it's just a little easier to do it again – and it's just a little harder to hold your resolve faced with the next cream bun. Drag your sleepy body out of bed a 5:00 AM and pound out those five kilometres one morning, and the next day it's a little easier. Surrender to your reticence to define yourself with that crusty worker, and you're likely to find it harder next time. Keep giving in and that worker has got you on a string. Take the pain now. You'll be happier later.

If the supervisory relationship is new, you won't have had time to build trust and establish some relational capital. Most people in this situation will be more anxious in the face of resistance, and therefore vulnerable to caving-in, avoiding the issue, or using the inherent power of the supervisory position to shut the worker down. All of these are options likely to be regretted later.

---

[107] Scott, S. *Fierce Leadership: A Bold Alternative to the Worst "Best" practices of Business Today* (Broadway Business New York 2009).

In dealing with a worker who is combative, and with whom you're yet to establish a resonant relationship, it's essential to prioritise dealing squarely with the issue, maintaining standards and expectations, and avoiding compromising your personal integrity. This may make things harder in the short-term, and it may mean a rupture in the relationship. However, relationship ruptures are easier to repair than your integrity. Don't let your own anxiety keep you from being the boss you know you ought to be.

Turn up

In considering dealing with potentially conflictual conversations, let's get it straight right up front. Deal with this personally. If things are tense with your worker (i.e. they report to you), it's your job to be the first conversation. A lot of supervisors will try to flick these conversations to someone in HR (cue exasperated sigh and eye roll from any HR types reading this).

Other supervisors will distance themselves from the potentially unpleasant conversation by resorting to email, or even worse, a text message or something via a messaging app. Text-based communications are for information. If there's likely to be any kind of emotional overlay, don't chicken out with an email or text. Make an appointment and show up personally. If you're working remotely or have a dispersed workforce, use video conferencing or, if all else fails, the good old phone.

A lot of leaders will simply not abide hostility and will refuse to continue a conversation if a worker becomes angry or accusatory. There's good reason to be wary of walking into a conflictual situation, provided it's not an excuse to avoid an uncomfortable situation that has low probability of causing actual harm.

Unsafe and uncomfortable are not the same thing

No one likes dealing with a worker who is angry, especially if that anger is directed at you. Unfortunately, as a supervisor it's pretty likely that sooner or later you'll be confronted with a worker who is angry at you. Recently, the idea of 'psychological safety' has become a bit of a mantra, and I've noticed people using the phrase in their explaining why it's okay to avoid engaging in an uncomfortable conversation.

Lately there's emerged a prevailing notion – largely unsupported by research – that any kind of unpleasant experience carries the risk of trauma (i.e.

unpleasant experiences present an unacceptable risk of long-term harm). Harm should not be confused with hurt. Harm will actually impair your functioning. Hurt is just an experience of an unpleasant sensation like emotional upset or physical pain. When I push myself to swim a little harder, it hurts. I recover quickly. No harm done. If I try to lift a 200 kilogram engine block and prolapse a disc, I'll be out of action for an extended period, and perhaps be permanently impaired. That's actual harm. Going to the dentist is usually unpleasant. But it's worse if you don't go.

I'm not advocating that you should put yourself in actual harm's way. I am saying you will in all likelihood recover quickly from a difficult conversation even if it's a painful experience. Don't conflate discomfort with trauma.

That said, I acknowledge that my viewpoint may not be the most objective. Growing up in the neighbourhood I did and going to the schools I went to, I have a little more tolerance for aggression than most. I still get the physiological signs of threat when someone gets angry with me – but I am sometimes willing to put up with some antagonism, provided there's not an outright threat, and provided I think I have a shot at talking-down an upset person. You'll need to figure out your threshold.

The win is not trying to win

Before we get into the finer points of dealing with an angry worker, let's get the main point clear right from the outset. This is not about winning an argument. Facing an angry person certainly feels like an adversarial situation, and the supervisor's fight or flight instincts will undoubtedly be aroused. However, unless you're actually in harm's way, as a boss it's important to think beyond the simple instincts of conflict, and to take up your responsibilities while bringing to bear your best thinking.

If you're in a highly unionised environment, the discourse from the union about the worker-management relationship will likely be couched in the language of struggle, which is inherently adversarial. This flows from the very foundation of trade union ideology. Any boss who gets drawn into this adversarial paradigm is inadvertently allowing an outside philosophy and agenda to shape their employee relations.

The win is not about defending yourself, defeating the worker or winning an argument. If you treat this as a fight, you can kiss the discretionary work effort goodbye. And you may inadvertently book yourself an illuminating field trip to a court or a commission.

Tone

In seeking to conduct a constructive conversation in the face of emotional intensity, your tone will be a significant contributor to whether things calm down or heat up. In tricky conversations with upset workers, I try to keep in mind that I'm here to be a resource, not a warrior. In terms of observable behaviour, that means trying to slow down my speech. When I'm passionate about something, my pace increases, and words pour out of my mouth like rats from a burning building. In a potentially conflictual situation, it's just not helpful.

When I feel like I'm facing opposition, my instinct is to speak with greater volume. While this may be a useful tactic in parliament, it's only going to escalate things in the workplace. Making a conscious effort to speak at no more than normal conversational volume – even if it means dealing with frequent interruptions – may seem slower, but it does wonders to moderate the intensity of the conversation.

One of the ways chauvinistic men dismiss women is to accuse them of being 'shrill'. It's generally an unfair and unkind description, and belittles the substance of their argument by mocking their tone. However, there's a little bit of insight behind the bigotry. If you listen to female news readers, you'll note that they generally have fairly low-pitched voices. Several studies have found that people perceive lower pitched voices as more authoritative.[108] When we're emotionally activated, our pitch naturally goes up, and it unconsciously undermines our credibility with the other person. Keeping your speech slower, fairly quiet and in your lower register helps to sound credible while de-escalating the upset.

While I'm confessing my failings, I may as well own up to my worst shortcoming when it comes to difficult conversations – my choice of words. When I'm anxious my instinct is to try to make my argument more forceful. I

---

[108] For example: Cheng, J. T., Tracy, J. L., Ho, S. and Henrich, J. *Listen, Follow Me: Dynamic Vocal Signals of Dominance Predict Emergent Social Rank in Humans* (Journal of Experimental Psychology Epub Mar 2016).

can resort to colourful and even dramatic metaphors and similes, use absolute language about my opinions as if they were unassailable facts, and resort to overstatement to the point of hyperbole. Phew, there I said it. I feel better already. Inevitably I pay for my sins. Be careful with your words.

If you suspect things could become reactive, you may need to practice your tone with someone you trust before going into the conversation. A little while ago one of my team had a very difficult issue arise between him and a colleague in another department. Their responsibilities interfaced at several points and my team member was finding his colleague pretty uncooperative. So, before scheduling a meeting to sort things out, he role-played the conversation several times with his wife, just to ensure his tone and choice of words weren't going to add to the reactivity. You may want to find someone with whom to workshop your tough conversation: your coach, your boss or someone from HR might be helpful in this regard.

The jewel behind the dragon

In the face of upset turned to aggression, the key is to stay calm enough to keep your thinking and to try to get to the worker's intent. Sometimes behind that less-than-helpful demeanour is a heart filled with good intention and some vitally important information – if you can just get past the initial onslaught. To draw on Tolkien's imagery from *The Hobbit*,[109] imagine the worker's anger is like the evil dragon Smaug, presiding over a treasure of unknown substance and value – you'll just need to get past the dragon to get to the gold, which is the worker themselves, and their good intentions. The anger is the dragon, the person is the treasure. Have at it, Bilbo.

If you're fairly certain your worker is just spoiling for a fight, there's not a lot of point volunteering to be their verbal punching bag. You may need to state you're not willing to talk with them while they're aggressive and postpone the conversation until things have calmed down. Sometimes rescheduling the conversation and inviting a couple of support people to stabilise things can prevent things spiralling into a career-ending exchange.

If you're confident you can keep reasonably calm, reasonably neutral and that the situation is safe (i.e. the worker is not going to get so aggressive as to do

---

[109] Tolkien, J. R. R. *The Hobbit* (HarperCollins, New York, 2012).

you actual harm), there's opportunity to build some real credibility and trust into the relationship if you can stay present with a worker who's clearly a long way from their best. Let me emphasise again, this depends on your ability to stay calm and keep your thinking. If you're feeling sufficiently threatened or intimidated that you're unlikely to retain a neutral posture, it's best to pull out and come back to the conversation when the heat has dissipated.

Park the car, hold the keys

When working with an angry person, the most important thing to attend to is your own presence. Forget your hope of getting the worker to calm down and agree with you for a minute. That means setting aside your side of the story and any desire to convince the worker of anything – for now. I call this parking the car – i.e. stop driving your agenda and instead commit to serving the worker.

But that doesn't mean you hand over control, abandon your principles or even change your position. Holding the keys means retaining your responsibility as supervisor and not allowing the worker's upset feelings to be the determinant of your decisions.

Your first goal is to be relatively unruffled and to stay present. One of the best ways to do this is to set yourself the goal of getting to the basic facts of the other person's issue. You're going to get a whole lot of information about how upset they are, how hurt/afraid/enraged they are, how unfair it all is, how you, the management of the organisation and a range of people are responsible for their suffering, etc. The volume likely will be on ten. It's important to take notice of the intensity, but not engage it.

Before you even consider giving your side of the story, see if you can pick out some facts – not opinions, not interpretations, just bare-bones facts – in what the worker is saying. When you get a chance (you may need to wait a while before the worker draws breath), offer them your best shot at the facts they've given you, minus all the reactivity.

"So, let me see if I'm hearing you correctly. The shift roster was changed and the new shift arrangements will cause significant problems for you. Is that right so far?"

Be prepared for another tirade. Remember, when a person is upset, they generally don't have good access to their more sophisticated thought processes (we'll go into a bit more detail on this in a minute). You may need to do a few rounds of rant-summarise-rant-summarise before your worker's emotional storm has dissipated. Remember, most important is your calm presence; that in itself communicates your commitment to your worker and what's important to them.

If the worker's upset escalates you may need to call a halt. I encourage taking personal responsibility for the halt, using first-person pronouns. You might want to use an approach like, "I can see how important this is to you, and I genuinely want to help. And I'm just not at my best with this level of intensity. I need to take a break and allow things to calm down a bit." From there it's important that one or both of you leave the room. I suggest taking some time to breathe and get your thinking back before you decide on your next move. Having a couple of other people in the room for the next attempt is probably wise. It's best if you can schedule to resume the conversation pretty soon – within 48 hours if possible. Otherwise, it looks a bit like a fob-off.

Rather than escalating, if your calm presence is helping the worker calm down, you can probably persevere with offering periodical restatement of the facts as you hear them until the worker seems satisfied that you've heard them.

A couple of things to point out here: There's a lot of material around in the field of counselling and psychotherapy that will encourage you to focus in more on the emotional content than the facts. If you've read any of the thinking based on attachment theory you've probably heard the term 'validate their emotions'. This theory encourages you to 'reflect back the feelings they're expressing'. You'll note I'm advocating reflecting back the facts. Minus the exaggeration and intensity, minus the interpretations and implications, and minus the emotional valence. Calm facts, not feelings – here's why.

As a person's boss, you're not their parent and you're not their counsellor. You're not there to fix, heal or reparent anyone. You're not there to nurture their 'inner child'. Playing counsellor is not only a confusion of roles, it's a little dangerous. It's not that hard to draw out a person's hurts and vulnerabilities. Anyone with a bit of curiosity and a willingness to listen can probably do that. However, working appropriately with a person in such an exposed state takes real care and expertise. As a worker's boss, but not their therapist, it's inappropriate for you to go there. Further, unless you have specific and thorough training in a psychotherapeutic discipline, there's potential you could do them harm.

Facts are inherently neutral, although people will impose meanings and implications on them that are more emotional and subjective. Bare-bones, objective facts do not take sides or by themselves apportion blame. Facts are external to the person. To the extent that they can be verified, facts tend to be stable over time. Feelings, on the other hand, are inherently subjective, influenced by a number of factors including everything from nutrition to endocrine balance to priming from experiences in one's family of origin. Emotions are notoriously hard to pin down.

Further, recent research by neuroscientist Lisa Barrett suggests that emotions are constructed depending on a complex and almost instantaneous interplay of sensory inputs, internal concepts and categories, mental simulations, instinctive goals and biosystem energy levels.[110] All these combine to generate an emotion experienced as a feeling. Many of these are contextually, biologically and experientially variable, making feelings (the consciously experienced aspect of emotion) a guide with a pretty high margin of error.

Talking about facts is the first step in a process I call 'talking to the inner grown-up'. While the upset person is likely to have lost their objectivity and perhaps some of their self-control, what they're presenting to you is not the sum of themselves. They'll be capable of being more thoughtful and reasonable when they're not upset. There's a reasonable adult in there somewhere, even if what you're getting just now shows no particular maturity, poise or nuance. For the time being, their brain is operating as if it's under threat. You can't fix them, but as their boss you can be a helpful resource. To understand how, let's do a quick dive inside your upset worker's head.

---

[110] Barrett, L. F. *How Emotions Are Made: The Secret Life of the Brain* (Pan, London 2017).

Neurobiology of upset

In the middle of the twentieth century, American neuroscientist Paul MacLean developed a model of the human brain that identified three levels of development and corresponding functioning. The *primal brain* is the most basic and takes care of most of the automatic functions to keep us alive. The *emotional brain* or limbic system is made of various centres that process things like fear and desire, dealing with drives that ensure survival, and responding to threat. It works in part by associating current stimuli with memories or prior experience to very quickly determine how to respond. It's where fight and flight responses are triggered, setting off stress responses through the endocrine system via the HPA axis. When you feel your muscles tense, your fingers chill, your hands sweat and your pulse increase, it's because your limbic system is aroused in response to a perceived threat. We talked about this earlier when we discussed anxiety. All mammals share the same basic limbic architecture.

By its sheer size and neuron count, the *rational brain* or neocortex separates humans from every other creature. The human neocortex processes stuff like complex language, abstract reasoning and sophisticated planning – things that other primates, despite their genetic similarity to us, are unable to do. It's why humans write symphonies and make iPhones, and baboons don't.

More recent science has distanced itself from MacLean's model, pointing out that it's not that simple and nowhere near as clear-cut. However, his model is still in widespread use as a generalised schema. Used as a mud-map to human functioning rather than a scientific blueprint for detailed research, it remains rather useful.

The neurobiology of the human brain under threat is complex, and it's way beyond the scope of this book to give you a finely grained analysis of all the various parts and functions. You can get a pretty good layperson's understanding by reading Daniel Goleman's *Emotional Intelligence*.[111] I recommend every leader read it. Goleman builds on MacLean's basic delineations to help us understand what happens when humans get upset.

---

[111] Goleman, D. *Emotional Intelligence: Why It Can Matter More Than IQ* (Bloomsbury London 1996).

The worker in front of you with exaggerated facial expressions, expansive gestures and hyperbolic language at a volume near the threshold of pain is experiencing a limbic system in overdrive. Because it works by association and does not process language, the limbic system is lightning fast but rather imprecise. It's not about careful calculation, it's about speed. Facing an oncoming train, humans tend not to patiently evaluate options – they just jump off the tracks toward whatever seems to be the safest place, just the same as any other animal would, because we share similar limbic functions.

By the time the neocortex cottons on to the limbic system's arousal, the rest of the body is moving to battle stations; there's already stress hormone being released, big muscles being readied, and non-critical functions being bypassed. In the midst of all the systemic reactions the neocortex is vulnerable to being dragged into the crisis. When that happens, thinking is forced to attend to the threat and attention becomes tunnel visioned. Goleman calls this 'an emotional hijack'.[112]

Under an emotional hijacking, a person's thinking brain is not doing its best work – it's been conscripted into the emotional crisis and is to some extent doing the bidding of the limbic system. When focused on the perceived threat, the neocortex can become preoccupied with interpreting every sign and detail in terms of its threat potential, setting up a self-reinforcing loop with the limbic system. To your worker in this state of upset, your words will be evaluated primarily in terms of their threat level. Complex reasoning, nuance and self-awareness give way to the survival instinct.

Sometimes a person reaches a state of upset so intense that they begin to experience serious impairments to their neocortical function – they struggle to find words or maintain a line of thought. Goleman terms this state 'emotional flooding'.[113] When a person is flooded, they're in no state to reason. It's unwise and unfair to expect them to. If you or your worker shows signs of flooding, the only productive way forward is to take a break and allow some time for the limbic intensity to subside. Doing some exercise is often helpful at this stage because it releases all that pent-up energy in the larger muscles. This is why people go for a walk to cool down.

---

[112] Goleman, D. *Emotional Intelligence*, 13.
[113] Goleman, D. *Emotional Intelligence*, 138.

However, if a person is upset but not flooded, they haven't entirely lost their ability to think straight. Their brain can rebalance the tussle between the limbic and neocortical circuits in favour of the neocortex. It does this by setting the neocortex to work on what it does best: working with facts, analysing, testing, and tracing out chains of logic. Lisa Barrett's research quoted earlier suggests that a person's internally held immediate goal is a crucial factor in the construction of emotions. Change the goal and the emotional state is constructed somewhat differently. The emotion experienced as feelings shifts with it.

This is why it's so helpful for you as the boss of the upset worker to be present, calm and unemotional, while asking moderately phrased, fact-based questions. In doing so you help to shift the focus of the worker's brain away from the sense of threat toward something more productive. You'll remember me paraphrasing Edwin Friedman earlier: *clarity is more important than empathy*.[114]

By being present and calm you're interrupting the threat-perception loop. If you 'get large' in your physical presence, tone of voice, or language, you'll only reinforce the sense of threat and stoke the limbic fire. If you're calm, quiet and moderate, the neocortex is less likely to be finding alarm triggers to send downstairs to the limbic system. By calling on the worker's neocortex to answer questions about the facts presented to them, or to evaluate what you've said for its accuracy, you're distracting your worker's neocortex from its preoccupation with the limbic system's upset. Do this for long enough and the neocortex will gradually gain the upper hand.

You'll know your worker's neocortex is beginning to emerge from the limbic hijack when they start to become less intense – they'll interrupt you less, their speech will slow down, the pitch and volume will be lower. As they continue to regain their thoughtful self, their facial expressions will be less extreme, their gestures more contained, their language more moderate.

Once your worker has regained their thinking, you are presented with a rare and precious opportunity. Be careful not to waste it.

---

[114] Friedman, E. H. *A Failure of Nerve: Leadership in the Age of the Quick Fix* (Seabury New York 1999).

Anger is not the core problem

The most obvious way to waste the opportunity is to view the worker's anger as the problem. Typically, supervisors making this mistake respond in one of two ways: The first is to believe that, since the anger is the problem and worker is now calm, the problem is solved. "Good job," they tell themselves, dust their hands off, smile reassuringly at their worker and go back to whatever they were doing before.

The second response to viewing anger as the problem roughly follows a chain of reasoning that goes like this: "My worker got angry, anger is a problem, therefore my worker has an anger problem." In my observation, supervisors most likely to fall into this misconception are rather sensitive to anger – being in the presence of an angry person makes them very uncomfortable, perhaps even afraid. There may well be something in their own backstory that's fostered such a sensitivity.

By designating the worker who became angry as a person with an anger problem, the supervisor creates what Edwin Friedman termed an 'identified patient'[115] – a person who has less capacity and credibility because they carry a pathology. A worker with identified patient status allows the supervisor to take a 'one-up' position.[116] Drawn from the field of transactional analysis pioneered by Eric Berne in the late 1950s, the idea of taking a one-up position equates to acting like a parent, subtly using the power imbalance of the supervisory relationship to push the worker into a 'one-down' or child-like position.[117]

A worker in a one-down position offers the supervisor an opportunity to boost their own sense of wellbeing by being over-adequate, offering the worker unnecessary comfort, support, help and perhaps even excuses to fail. If the worker plays along, their functioning and performance will likely deteriorate over time.

---

[115] Friedman, E. H. *Generation to Generation: Family Process in Church and Synagogue* (Guilford, New York 1985), 20.
[116] Friedman, E. H. *Generation to Generation*.
[117] Berne, E. *Games People Play – The Basic Handbook of Transactional Analysis* (Ballantine, New York 1964).

The greatest relief to the supervisor who relegates their worker to identified patient status is that they can safely ignore whatever grievances the worker may raise. Instead of taking their worker's anger as a possible indicator of a workplace problem or an opportunity for their own growth, the worker's anger can be dismissed as a pathology inherent to the worker.

Which brings us back to the opportunity that the angry worker represents. Recent research found that in nine instances out of ten, when a worker gets angry, it's because their rights have been infringed, their integrity violated or their sense of justice offended – not because they're a jerk, a bully or because they have 'a problem with anger'.[118] So when a supervisor ignores the content of a person's upset because they're uncomfortable with the process of their upset, they run a pretty high risk of ignoring a firsthand report of impropriety and injustice.

Let's take a moment to summarise our journey with the angry worker so far. An angry worker is tough to manage, and you should only seek to engage with them in their angry state if you can remain reasonably calm, are not feeling particularly threatened and it's unlikely any harm will come to you.

An angry worker is experiencing arousal of their limbic system (emotional brain) which can hijack the functioning of their neocortex (thinking brain). By being calm and curious, reflecting back the facts you hear and asking fact-based questions, you as the supervisor can be a resource in helping them calm down and regain their thoughtfulness. Once the worker has regained their better thinking capacities, an opportunity for learning, growth and insight presents itself.

You'll remember I mentioned earlier the idea of talking to the inner adult. Working with facts is one of the first steps. The next step is for you, the supervisor, to assume that your worker is an independent, competent, resourceful adult who can in all likelihood make reasonably good decisions for themselves.

---

[118] Geddes, D., Roberts Callister, R. and Gibson, D. E. *A Message in the Madness: Functions of Workplace Anger in Organizational Life* (Academy of Management Perspectives Vol. 34, No. 1 2020).

Your language and how you shape your questions should be consistent with that assumption. Questions like, "Is there anything else you think would be helpful for me to know?" treats the worker like a responsible peer. It invites your worker's own thinking about facts. Questions like, "Do you feel that I've listened to you?" have parental overtones and invite the worker to plunge back into the emotional current.

As I write this, I'm anticipating some of you will be reluctant to accept thinking that runs so counter to the way our culture currently gives primacy to feelings. I acknowledge that it goes against a lot of what is taught in counselling courses and in workshops on marriage and parenting. Experience has made me a little wary of positioning myself as the one who steadies and soothes a worker's upset by validating their emotions. I don't disagree with much of the observational research underlying attachment theory. In fact, on a number of occasions when I have, in my impulse to be caring and in my lack of self-differentiation, offered validation and soothing, attachments did indeed form, resulting in further hurt feelings when boundaries needed to be drawn.

Once your worker's limbic arousal has subsided sufficiently for them to regain capacity for productive thinking, you can work with them on the factual content you reflected back to them while they were upset. These facts are critical in you determining your specific responsibilities to the worker as their boss.

If the worker was upset because their legal rights were infringed (things like sexual harassment, assault, discrimination), you'll need to ensure that proper process is followed to take those issues seriously and address the matter appropriately. It's beyond the scope of this book to tease out all the possibilities here. If you're in a large organisation your HR department and/or your legal department should be able to guide you. There will almost certainly be policy and procedure set out for you to follow. If you're in a small organisation I strongly recommend taking counsel from your lawyer, your peak body or from the appropriate government instrumentality. In Australia most of the state and federal commissions that cover human rights, equal opportunity and industrial relations have advisory services, although they tend to be geared towards complainants. You may need to pause the conversation for you to get some advice or access the organisation's policy and procedure.

If the worker was upset because there was poor process or behaviour that caused them trouble (like the change to the shift roster in our earlier hypothetical example), sometimes the best response is to offer your best understanding of the situation as they've described it to you, and then ask, "What do you think should happen from here?" They may ask for someone's head on a plate, or they may offer you a surprisingly sensible way forward. It's not uncommon to be able to work collaboratively to find a solution, even with someone who twenty minutes earlier was furious.

Careful work here can build lasting trust between you and your worker. The trick is to stay neutral and curious and resist the impulse to defend yourself or the organisation. Responding to accusations about others that go to their motivation, character or intelligence can be redirected with, "I can see you're not happy with that person. But, they're not here to respond. I would like us to put our effort toward a way forward." If the accusation is about behaviour that is unpleasant or inappropriate without being the basis for a complaint outside the organisation, you might want to explore a conciliation process or the worker making a formal complaint. There may be call for you to thoughtfully take ownership of your part in the problem and offer them an apology.

Once the worker is calm and has had opportunity to talk thoughtfully about the issue, it may turn out that for various reasons there's not much that can be done, that there was simply a misunderstanding (we all grab the wrong end of the stick sometimes), or that anxiety from some other sphere of the worker's life has spilled over into the workplace. You'll get a clear sense of this if, after some calmer conversation, it seems like the worker's reaction to the stated problem was markedly disproportionate. If you know the worker well and there is a high level of trust, they may choose to confide in you. Beware of going on a fishing expedition just to satisfy your curiosity. You may never get a clear line of sight on the actual source of the anxiety.

Sometimes you'll come to a point where the worker realises that there's not much that can be done or that they want to be done. They simply wanted someone to pay attention to what was important to them. If you think this is the case, make very certain that you've given the worker every opportunity to consider their options. While you can't guarantee it won't happen, it is worth the effort of doing what you can to prevent the issue blowing up later.

Responding

As you're moving from understanding the source of the worker's upset toward finding a productive way forward, it might be time to offer your thinking. You may have some information that would be useful, some perspective that will give the worker opportunity to see things with some circumspection, or just some plain old wisdom. This needs to be framed carefully, respectfully, briefly and often with some qualifiers that keep the conversation adult-to-adult rather than you coming across as patronising.

I like to use phrases like, "My sense of it is…" or "My thinking on it is…" or even "I have some curiosity about…" You'll note that I'm using words that convey intellectual process rather than emotional process, avoiding phrasing like, "I feel…" I'm also stating it as my viewpoint, rather than indisputable and self-evident fact. This might lead to more conversation around understanding the situation before you move toward solutions.

If the worker reacts to your opinions, it may take the conversation back to the rant-reflect-rant-reflect pattern we explored above until the reactivity has diminished and a thoughtful conversation can proceed. If it goes on too long or gets too intense, you may need to call a halt and come back for another go in a day or two.

Right now, you might be thinking, "This seems all very lopsided. I'm expected to hold my tongue and discipline myself to attend the worker while they get upset." Yep, it is lopsided. The worker-supervisor relationship is inherently lopsided, where the supervisor has more power and commensurate responsibility. Being in the more powerful and responsible position obliges the supervisor to take the lead in establishing a productive conversation. It gets back to the servant-leadership we talked about way back in the first section.

Your position

So far in this progression of thought I have presumed that the worker has some kind of reasonable case behind all the emotion, and that you as the boss would do very well to do whatever you can to understand it. Hopefully I've laboured that point sufficiently. Just as important is for you to get clear in your own thinking about the issue, and at the appropriate time, to make that evident to your worker.

Now you might be thinking, "Finally I get to put my side!" Granted, it seems to be several pages ago that we began this journey with the angry worker, and only now do we get to the boss putting their case. Just to be clear:

- Before putting your case it's important to be pretty sure you've got a handle on what's behind the worker's anger – remember Stephen Covey's counsel to 'seek first to understand, then be understood'.[119]
- There may be some significant risk management issues to which you'll need to attend if the worker's rights or entitlements have been infringed, or if there's evidence of other illegal activity.
- There's no point putting your case when the worker's limbic system is sufficiently aroused as to significantly interfere with their rational thinking processes.

All of the foregoing notwithstanding, it may be that you simply don't agree with the worker, or perhaps have reached the conclusion they don't have a valid case to be pursued or complaint to be addressed. You may have a whole other side to the story that significantly shifts the weight of your worker's case.

Putting your position

Having been careful and responsible with your worker, now's the time to put your position: thoughtfully, calmly, moderately, and with appropriate qualifications.

Temperamentally, I'm a little on the combative side. I instinctively see tense interactions through a lens of a battle to be won, the angry person as an enemy to be defeated. I can be as much directed by my limbic system as anyone else, and perhaps more than most. On the outside I might be showing patience, forbearance and self-discipline, but in my mind I'm forming counter-arguments, as if I'm mentally slotting rounds into the cylinder of a metaphorical revolver, and waiting until I get a clear shot. I need to constantly remind myself that it's not about winning, it's not about defeating the worker and their arguments. If your temperament is anything like mine, we both need the voice of sanity instructing us to put the metaphorical gun down.

---

[119] Covey, Stephen. **The Seven Habits of Highly Effective People** (The Business Library, Melbourne. 1997), 235.

Stating your position is not about destroying your worker's arguments, exposing their ulterior motives or demonstrating their inferior intellect or character – even if you believe you have strong evidence for all of those things. Stating your position is not about winning. (Have I laboured that point sufficiently?)

Stating your position is communicating the plain and coolheaded information about your best thinking, your values and your commitments. These may not sit easily with the worker's thinking, values and priorities. Your position may be somewhat at odds with theirs. Remember your first responsibility is to the organisation that gave rise to the supervisor-worker relationship you're now trying to manage.

A statement of position might go something like this: "I hear that you believe you have been treated unfairly, and that you believe the manager who decided to change the shift roster should be fired. Here's my thinking. I don't know what led to the decision to change the roster. I haven't heard that manager's thinking or what circumstances led to the new roster. I think it's important that everyone is treated fairly, so I'm committed to taking this matter up with the management team. Fairness means that the manager who changed the roster should get a chance to explain. I can't guarantee you'll get what you want, but I can offer my commitment to take the matter up with management."

Your thinking, your values, your commitment. You may want to summarise this into a statement of what the worker can expect of you.

Stating your position may trigger the worker's anger, and we're back to where we were a few pages ago. I'm not one for endless cycles of upset. If the worker fires up and doesn't quickly recover, you may need to call halt. In calling a halt, it's best to take responsibility to the extent you can. "It seems that things have become heated again. I don't think there's much more productive work we can do at this stage. I will follow-through on my commitments as soon as I reasonably can and let you know as soon as I have progress to report. For now, I'm going to pause the conversation."

I recognise that it's pretty unlikely you'll find yourself in a situation where the above example provides you with a script. You may come to a position where you don't think there is anything you need to do to address the worker's anger: it may be a case where the worker has misunderstood what was going on, misunderstood their entitlements, or is simply projecting onto you a bunch of unresolved issues from another sphere of their life. While you may have pretty good evidence for all of this, there's no point shifting the dispute to matters of opinion where there is nothing to be gained.

If, after careful thinking, your position is that the worker has no valid case to put, your first responsibility is simply to give them the facts as you see them. "I've heard your case and I understand the new roster creates some significant challenges for you. However, my best understanding is that the process followed met the requirements of the industrial agreement that governs your employment." Pause, check for their reaction. If they're with you, continue. "I talked the new shift arrangements over with the leadership team. The changes are necessary to meet operational requirements. The agreement does allow you to negotiate to swap shifts with other workers. You may want to consider that option." Pause again, check for their reaction again. "Unless new information arises that would give me a reason to rethink my position, I don't intend to take this any further."

You'll note the example did not talk about the worker overreacting, misunderstanding their entitlements, projecting their unresolved 'parent' issues onto you or anything else subjective. You'll also note there was no mention of compromise or meeting halfway. As the supervisor, your responsibility is to uphold the agreements and obligations the company has entered into. While it's often implied, you have no obligation to pacify a worker's upset by going beyond the company's agreed commitment. Indeed, you may set a very expensive precedent and in so doing find yourself answering some very awkward questions from your own supervisor.

The worker may return to their angry state. Other than total acquiescence and dereliction of your responsibilities (and yes, some bosses choose that option), there's no formula for preventing a worker getting angry with their boss. At the end of the day the boss's job is to do what's right according to their own convictions, to fulfil their responsibilities to the organisation and to comply with the laws and regulations that govern the supervisory relationship. Some workers will simply be unhappy with you doing that.

That said, your tone and what you say and do next can make a difference in determining whether you get the entire workforce out the front of the workplace with placards (or more likely forming a frowning cluster in the corner of the tearoom, muttering obscenities with hushed voices) – or whether your worker stays reasonably calm and is willing to be thoughtful in what they do next.

Own your stuff

While it's not always possible and not always appropriate, if you've been able to keep your thinking through the process, you may have already spotted aspects of your part in the issue that you might want to do differently next time. If you can see those potential opportunities to improve, and your relationship with your worker is solid enough for you to trust them not to turn your words back on you, verbalising your thinking with them will do wonders for building your credibility as a trustworthy leader. You might consider something like, "You know, as we've been talking, I started to think about my part in all this. It seems to me that I could've been a better resource to you and the rest of the team if I had foreseen potential changes to the shift roster that would have logically flowed from the company taking on that new contract. In future, I'll try to keep in mind potential implications for your team when changes are on the horizon. I can't guarantee a different outcome, but I will try to create more lead time to give the team more time to plan and adapt."

Notice in the example,

- Prominent use of first-person singular pronouns
- Vocabulary about thinking, not feeling
- What the worker can expect going forward

If you think there might be some learning for you in the whole exchange, but you're not yet ready to verbalise it, you might want to express your commitment to reflecting on the events leading up to the conversation and then initiate another conversation. Modelling that you have a learning posture and that you don't assume that you always get everything right gives the worker the safety and encouragement they might need to do the same. People tend to view humble people more highly than they do proud ones.

None of us like a boss who never admits their failure or shortcomings, and who never apologises. Don't be that boss.

Getting perspective on your contribution to workplace tension requires a willingness to be brutally honest with yourself, and a good degree of self-awareness. I can't say I'm exactly top of the class on either of those criteria. My instinct is to find someone who'll sympathise and agree with me that it was all the other guy's fault. That may help me feel a little better, but it does me no good in my desire to become more of an adult and a more effective boss.

Going against my instinct to 'triangle' another person, I will often sit down with my journal and seek to get some clarity on the situation. When I'm upset, my journaling generally follows a predictable pattern. First, I'll describe the situation. Sometimes I can step back and be a little more objective in my description, sometimes it's more subjective, reactive and a bit of bleating self-justification. Then I'll look at my own actions, reactions, thoughts, fears and emotions. Again, sometimes with a good degree of maturity, sometimes a bit tinged with tantrum. No matter, it's all grist for the mill. Next is the critical bit. I ask myself the question, "What can I observe about myself and what can I do differently?" I don't always do a great job of this, but there's usually enough willingness on my part to learn and grow that I'll try to test my assumptions, check whether I'm looking at the facts of the actual situation or reacting to my fears, my conditioning or my hurt feelings. Often, I can see where I'm projecting onto the other person, where I'm ducking my responsibilities or where I'm just letting my ongoing frustrations bubble to the surface. In this exercise I try to be informed by theory I've learned, be it Bowen's Family Systems Theory, general systems theory from thinkers like Peter Senge, or some of the other ways of understanding to which I've already introduced you.

Occasionally my reflection leads me back to a person with whom I've interacted, and I'll try to own up to my part of the problem. Sometimes I'll develop a plan to do things a little differently.

Of course, the other resource I draw upon is my coach. My current coach is a psychologist trained in Family Systems Theory, so she doesn't let me get away with much.

Worker options

As the tricky conversation comes towards its end, it's worthwhile asking the worker where they think the conversation leaves them. They might be satisfied to have had their say and want no further action. You or they may have already committed to a course of action and it may simply be a matter of you, them or both putting into action the commitments you've made.

Frequently, the conversation doesn't end all neatly tied up in a bow, and the worker is left mulling their next move.

If you sense things have not resolved, it's important to give your worker opportunity to explore some options. There may be a range of resources and options available to them, even if you would prefer that they don't take some of them up. I probably wouldn't relish my worker bringing their union into a workplace dispute, but it casts things in a very different light for me to say, "Your union will have an industrial advisor and a legal team available to advise you. You may want to consider talking things over with them." It tells my worker that I'm not trying to hide something or infringe their rights.

By asking a few thoughtful questions you'll be able to offer some possibilities that can be useful to your worker. In addition to their union (if you're in a unionised environment), the worker may consider:

- Accessing your employee assistance program (if your organisation has one)
- Talking to a workplace contact officer (your workplace really should have one)
- Talking to someone in the HR department
- Talking to your boss (if your boss is amenable)
- Contacting the applicable industrial court or commission (in Australia the usual first port of call is the Fair Work Ombudsman)

Paradoxically, in my experience, a worker is less likely to pursue you and your organisation through legal channels if you let them know their options rather than if you try to discourage them.

The worker's learning

The final little nugget you may be able to mine from a conflictual situation is for the worker to learn from the experience. Generally speaking, attempts to help the worker reflect on their contribution to the difficulty and to gain insight into their own opportunities to grow will be met with defensiveness and a counter-accusation of victim-blaming or attempting to shift responsibility.

You're more likely to have a shot at helping the worker learn and grow by reflecting on a conflict with you, if you have a trusting, transparent relationship prior to the conflict. As the boss, leading the way by taking responsibility for your own shortcomings will help.

Without that solid pre-existing foundation of good faith, simply asking a worker to articulate their part in the problem runs a pretty high risk of reigniting things or driving the conflict underground.

Having noted the caveats, once a worker has fully regained their best thinking – which takes at least a few hours after a significant upset – there may be space to invite them to think over their opportunities for growth and maturity coming out of the conflict. Because I use Bowen's Family Systems Theory so frequently and my clients find is so helpful, it features in the professional development program of teams that I lead.[120] Family Systems provides a way of understanding and a vocabulary for describing human interactions that encourages maturity by becoming a more differentiated self. With team members who have a reasonable grounding in theory, I can ask questions about their reactions, sensitivities and responsibilities with a reasonable confidence that they'll take my questions as an invitation to grow and develop rather than an opportunity for me to pile all the blame on them.

If you want to build a culture in your team where people value personal maturity and responsibility, reading a book like *Growing Yourself Up* by Jenny Brown,[121] or *The Anxious Organization* by Jeff Miller together as a team can be a great place to start.[122] Make sure as the leader you show the way by talking about the things you're learning about yourself, the things that challenge you and your commitments to change. Allow other team members to make their own discoveries about themselves.

---

[120] A good summary of the Theory is available from the Bowen Centre: https://thebowencenter.org/theory/.

[121] Brown, J. *Growing Yourself Up: How to Bring Your Best to Al of Life's Relationships* (Exisle Wollombi 2012).

[122] Miller, J. A. *The Anxious Organization: Why Smart Companies Do Dumb Things* (Vinculum, Miami 2019).

Summary

- Conflict is a normal part of work life and avoiding it is counterproductive.
- Deal with conflict personally.
    - Accept the discomfort. It in itself won't harm you.
- Avoid trying to win.
- Watch your tone – pace, volume, pitch, moderate language.
- Park the car, hold the keys.
    - Set your agenda aside for a while, but don't relinquish control of the process.
- When a worker is upset, they will not be able to bring their best thinking.
- Anger is not the problem.
    - In most cases, an angry worker has a legitimate concern.
- Talk to the inner adult: facts, not feelings.
- When appropriate, define yourself, your values, your commitments.
- Own your stuff – treat this as a learning opportunity.
- Let the worker know their options.
- Create learning opportunities where appropriate

Discussion

- Which concept most surprised you? Which did you find hardest to accept?

Implementation

- What's your default style in conflict? What could you do differently?

What we've covered

Section 1: Be a boss worth working for

- Your first responsibility is to be the boss of yourself
- Your next responsibility is to your organisation
- You are responsible for the stewardship of humans
- Your workers are your job
- Exercising responsibility requires authority
- Supervision is a working relationship

Section 2: The task of supervision

- There are several prevailing theories of optimal performance
- Supervision is about expectations and support
- Define your expectations
- Determine if your expectations are met
- Give workers feedback as to whether they meet your expectations
- Provide support to facilitate performance
- Encourage a discretionary work effort

Section 3: How to effectively supervise

- Recruit and select with your supervision relationship in mind
  - Recruit for this role in this organisation at this time – set specific criteria
  - Select using valid, highly predictive methods
- Onboard thoughtfully
  - Go beyond butt-covering and get your worker off to a great start
  - Make it a team sport
  - Induct for culture, not just tasks and procedures
- Intentionally establish a supervision relationship
  - Plan and prepare thoroughly for routine supervision
  - Define reality, yourself and your expectations
  - Give clear and timely feedback
- Understand burnout
  - The stress that causes burnout is neurobiologically the same as anxiety

- Burnout can be understood as overall challenges exceeding one's capacity to adapt
  - Learn to read the anxious patterns and symptoms that predict burnout
  - Consistent presence and good leadership practice help reduce the likelihood and severity of burnout
- Worker response and reaction
  - Dissonance, pushback and disproportionate responses contain valuable information
  - Calm presence and attunement enable understanding
- Work with the conflictual worker
  - Work from a posture of understanding rather than winning or suppressing anger
  - Manage your tone: pace, pitch, language
  - Understand the neurological functioning behind the behaviour
  - Anger is not the problem: there's likely to be something substantive behind the upset
  - Respond by defining yourself and your commitments

Section 4
A vision for excellent supervision

This final section moves from the basics of supervision to the understanding and skills that underpin truly excellent supervision. Having narrowed supervision to its basic elements and developed each of these, here we broaden out to consider a range of aspects that contribute to being the boss people genuinely desire to work for.

Stewardship

Way back in the first section, I developed the idea that we're not just supervising units of labour purchased at market rates, but our fellow humans, who are priceless, perhaps sacred. I also talked about responsibility. In exercising authority over those we supervise, we have a responsibility for their wellbeing and best interests.

While I've spent most of this book talking about supervision as a discipline that applies equally whether we're overseeing paid employees or volunteers, let me take a minute to concentrate on the employment setting.

For most of us, paid work makes up a huge part of our lives: the average Australian spends 35.7 hours per week at work,[123] and a further 4.5 hours per week getting there.[124] Further, our work largely determines our purchasing capacity and connectedness for an array of the factors that impact our lifestyle: where we live, what we do for leisure, the people with whom we socialise. Work provides structure to our days and weeks and goes some way to shaping our identity and even our place in the world. Our work is a big deal. No wonder being unemployed can be so devastating.

---

[123] Research by University of Melbourne's Professor Mark Wooden
https://fbe.unimelb.edu.au/newsroom/push-for-longer-hours-makes-headlines,-but-more-australians-want-to-work-less#:~:text=While%20a%2037.5%2Dhour%20work,work%20shorter%20or%20longer%20hours.
[124] https://www.rmit.edu.au/news/all-news/2019/jul/increasing-commuting-times#:~:text=Average%20daily%20commuting%20times%20across,aged%2015%20years%20and%20older.

Remember we've touched several times on the concept of the discretionary work effort – that degree of a person's contribution to the organisation that they offer because they choose to, not because they have to. I mentioned too the Gallup organisation's research showing employee engagement as the key to gaining that discretionary work effort. Engagement not only predicts business outcomes like higher worker productivity and reduced turnover, it also points to workers having a good experience of the workplace. Engaged workers enjoy going to work.

Gallup's Jim Clifton and Jim Harter estimate that seventy percent of variance in employee engagement is determined by their direct supervisor.[125] More than anything else, you determine the quality of your worker's experience of work. And because work is such a substantial determinant of so many other factors in a person's life, your role as a worker's boss significantly influences their quality of life.

How you impact your worker's quality of life is to some extent determined by how you see your role. Are you like a remote commander-in-chief or a platoon lieutenant, a wolf pack leader or a mother hen? You won't know for sure unless your workers tell you, so we begin this section with a short chapter on soliciting feedback.

There's a growing consensus that to generate employee engagement and enjoy the associated benefits, the most helpful way of understanding your role is to think of yourself as a coach, so a chapter about coaching follows.

We then look at supervision at the various life stages of the worker before linking supervision to strategy, culture and organisational design. After a deeper dive into the emotional or instinctual side of organisation life, we'll conclude with chapters on appraisal and development.

---

[125] Clifton, J. and Harter J. *It's the Manager* (Gallup New York 2019).

Chapter 21
Seeking feedback and following through

Over the last couple of chapters we've been talking about feedback in the forms of dissonance, pushback and conflict. These 'coming, ready or not' kinds of feedback provide valuable opportunities to grow in maturity. They can help you to become more thoughtful and less reactive under pressure.

As supervisors we can also take some initiative in seeking feedback. I've put this second to the more reactive forms of feedback, because frankly, we're less likely to get unvarnished feedback when we seek it than when it walks right up to us and pokes its finger into our chest.

Occasionally I've sent our surveys to my coaching clients, asking for specific feedback on their experience of being coached. While I'd like to think I'm super-coach, the reality is that I still have plenty of scope to improve. However, I tend only to coach nice people, because their feedback is always nice. If the survey asks for an opinion on a seven-point Likert scale ranging from terrible to brilliant, I need to take an average score of five and a half as an unmitigated disaster. People seem to be reluctant to risk hurting my feelings.

There are a bunch of ways to seek feedback, ranging from the very simple to the mind-blowingly comprehensive. Whole books have been written on this if you want to dig into it deeply. For now, let's look at a couple of possibilities.

360-degree feedback
Typically 360-degree feedback involves a manager identifying people who are above them, below them and beside them in the organisational chart, and sometimes some outsiders like customers. Those so nominated complete a survey seeking evaluation of the manager's behaviour, competence and performance.

Broadly speaking, 360s come in two forms. One is a standard questionnaire linked to a statistically validated data set. These provide a reasonably objective and reliable evaluation of a manager based on the norms of the dataset. The other is the customised questionnaire based on whatever it is that the manager or their boss may be seeking feedback about.

As a rough guide, only use the customised style when you are seeking very specific feedback and in the form of qualitative, short answer responses. A seven-point Likert scale with no standardisation is not particularly meaningful. Otherwise, use a well validated standardised instrument.

A variation is to ask a neutral person like an independent consultant to conduct some short interviews with your staff and perhaps some others in the 360-degree radius. This is a useful strategy to gain specific feedback about specific issues. Avoid group discussions, as the herd instinct will inevitably bias the group's responses toward the views of the most powerful person in the group.

There's a more detailed discussion about 360-degree feedback as a tool for appraisal in chapter 28.

Just ask

Lately I've been asking my clients two basic questions at the close of each coaching conversation: "Did this conversation achieve what you hoped it would?" and "What's one thing I could do more, less or different to be a more useful resource to you?"

Often the answers are, 'Yes' and 'Nothing, it's all good', which is pleasant to hear but not much use. However, sometimes I hear really useful feedback that I can use to sharpen up my skills and better serve my clients. It's worth asking.

I recently read an online post by an organisational psychologist who suggested asking for a score out of ten. Since people rarely give a perfect score, their response can be followed with a question like, "What would I need to do to get closer to a ten?" If you have a trusting relationship with your workers, these questions or similar will serve you well as a routine or occasional addendum to your regular supervision conversations.

At the end of one of those dissonant, pushback or conflictual conversations you may have achieved a sufficient degree of repair to ask your worker to give you some feedback about how you handled the situation. Questions like, 'What do you find helpful?' and 'What could I have done differently?' may yield some very useful insight into what it's like to be on the other side of your effort to attend an upset worker. Just make sure the worker has well and truly calmed down before asking.

Following through

Difficult conversations often resolve with both parties committing to doing some things differently. Unless you seek feedback with others with the express purpose of learning how you can develop and mature, don't even begin to seek feedback. One of the most efficient ways to shred your worker's respect for you and destroy the trust in your supervisory relationship is to fail to follow through with your commitments. A close second is to seek feedback and then fail to take it seriously.

Because I'm kind of old, because organisations like to restructure, and because I like to have a few different roles going simultaneously, I've had quite a few bosses over the years and I've enjoyed fairly frank and open relationships with most of them. Let me share stories of a couple of exceptions.

At one time I'd become embroiled in a power tussle with another manager, more senior than me in another department. I'd become increasingly frustrated with the intransigence of the other person blocking my goals, and in my frustration put in writing a couple of statements that, while absolutely technically accurate, were not really offered in the spirit of collaboration and cooperation – a classic case of losing my best thinking in my upset state. Things put in writing tend to find their way up the chain of command. Inevitably, I had to eat some humble pie. It also gave me plenty to work on with my coach.

In the wash-up conversation with my own boss, I owned up to my part, and also made it clear how I had felt let down by some of their actions and inactions that had left me feeling like I was alone in trying to resolve the impasse. In the close-out of the conversation we each made commitments about what we would do differently going forward. Over the ensuing months my boss continued as they had previously, doing nothing to address the concerns I raised and not undertaking the specific action to which they had committed. My trust in them, already damaged coming into the conversation, slowly evaporated. Next stop was the jobs board on LinkedIn.

Years ago, I served a large organisation that decided there was enough muttering among the ranks about the 'dysfunctional culture' that it was time to take the bull by the horns. A consultancy was engaged to conduct a comprehensive, multimode workplace culture evaluation. There were interviews, focus groups and anonymous surveys. A couple of months later a fairly weighty report was distributed. To the consultancy's credit, there was broad agreement among the rank-and-file workers and middle managers that the report nailed the problems pretty accurately. There were six or seven key points of action that went right to the heart of how the senior leaders needed to change.

A couple of weeks later there was a town hall meeting where the CEO and their team would respond to the report. There was an air of anticipation (and some small degree of schadenfreude) among the staff. Most hoped it would be the dawning of a new day. It was not to be.

Of the key recommendations set out in the report, the CEO simply ignored all but one, which was about communication. Their solution was to employ a 'comms guy'. The sense of deflated hope in the room was palpable, quickly giving way to anger and cynicism. Here was an opportunity for real change, but it meant an admission of shortcomings and a commitment to personal change on the part of the leaders. Sadly, that opportunity lay untouched in the 'too hard' basket.

When a boss blows off the feedback they receive, especially if it's feedback they've solicited, or if they fail to follow through on their commitments, they'll lose the people who value maturity and integrity, and those who are sufficiently marketable to find another role where they can trust and respect those above them. Over time, what's left is a pool of people comprising an increasing proportion of those that just don't care and those who can't get a job anywhere else.

Don't be the kind of boss that ends up with that kind of team.

Let me close out this section with a different kind of story. In the world of Australian Rules Football (AFL; the state religion of Melbourne, where I live) Nathan Buckley was a superstar. His career spanned 280 Australian Football League games, 260 of which were with the Collingwood Magpies, where he reigned as captain from 1999 to 2007. In 2003 he was voted best player in the competition by both the umpires (awarding him the coveted Brownlow medal) and by the AFL coaches association. Buckley was named in the all-Australian team seven years running and was captain of the Australian International Rules Team in 1999. Buckley was universally respected as a player and leader, adored as a favourite son at Collingwood.

After his retirement as a player, Buckley joined the coaching staff at the Magpies. In 2011, Collingwood finished second, overrun in the final quarter of the grand final by the fast-finishing Geelong Cats. Buckley took over as senior coach from the legendary Michael Malthouse in 2012. The 'pies finished a creditable fourth that year, winning 68% of their games. The following year, they finished sixth, winning 61% of games. In 2014 Collingwood won half their games and finished eleventh. At the end of 2017 they had won only 41% of their games and had slipped to thirteenth position on the ladder. The Collingwood faithful were losing faith in their favourite son. Amid rumours of player discontent and dysfunction in the coaching group, there was a growing chorus calling for 'Bucks' to be shown the door.

There was no sense of mystery about Buckley's apparent failure as a leader. The antecedents had been there for years. Back in his playing days as captain of Collingwood, a rookie player once quipped, "When I talk to you, I feel like you're thinking about the next thing you're going to say to me, rather than actually listening." Buckley had won football's highest individual award and had topped the ball disposals tally for the entire league for four seasons. He knew football inside and out. He was an undisputed authority on the game, and that was part of the problem.

In his book *Good to Great*,[126] Jim Collins identifies a particular type of leader as an essential ingredient to enduring organisational greatness. The level five leader is both humble and fiercely determined, attributing success to their team members but taking personal responsibility for failure. On the face of it, Buckley's quiet sincerity matched with an iron will seemed to fit the bill. However, Collins contrasts the level five leader with a 'genius with a thousand helpers'. The latter may sometimes achieve quick results with intellect and force of personality but cannot lead an organisation to enduring greatness. Buckley had a reputation for wanting to be across every detail of every detail.

---

[126] Collins, J. *Good to Great: Why Some Companies Make the Leap... and Others Don't* (Random, London 2001).

One staffer remarked, "He'd wanted to know who was folding the towels!" His intense commitment to success was translating into micromanagement, disempowering his assistant coaches and the player leadership group.

Narrowly surviving a probing 2017 end-of-season review, Buckley took some time off, headed for a tropical yoga retreat and immersed himself in Ichiro Kishimi and Fumitake Koga's, *The Courage to be Disliked.*

Buckley returned for the Collingwood 2018 preseason sporting a ginger beard and a markedly changed approach. He began delegating responsibility to his coaching team and gave them space to make decisions. Gone were the questions about minutiae and the intensity of control. He'd recognised the spiral he was in – increasing intensity and control was delivering decreasing performance and poorer results. The new Buckley was more trusting, more empowering, and less intense.

Speaking to a journalist toward the end of the 2018 season, Collingwood defensive coach Justin Longmuir described his experience of working with Buckley: "I've really enjoyed working under him because he's given us, given everyone autonomy to go about their jobs and that was from day one. I've really enjoyed that freedom."[127]

Collingwood finished season 2018 runners-up, losing the grand final to the West Coast Eagles by less than a goal. A far cry from the bottom third of the ladder result a year earlier.

Nathan Buckley took seriously the feedback his system was providing to him. He confronted the brutal facts about his leadership, and had the humility to do the hard work of self-examination and change. As supervisors seeking to make a better world by being a better boss, we would do well to follow his example.

---

[127] Reported to Jake Nial *The Age* September 28, 2018.

Summary

- Formally seeking feedback often results in getting 'nice' responses.
- Generally speaking, if you opt for 360-degree feedback, use a validated instrument.
- If you're seeking very specific feedback, use short answers or interviews.
- Address the feedback you receive and rigorously follow-though .

Discussion

- What kind of feedback instruments have you used or participated in?

Action

- What's one area of your supervisory practice about which you'd like feedback? How could you set about gaining it?

Chapter 22
Supervisor as coach

A quick search on Amazon will reveal that there's no shortage of literature advocating the benefits supervisor/manager/leader as coach. Writers like Daniel Harkavy place primacy on the leader's responsibility for developing others, more than strategy or risk management or generating profit for the organisation.[128] Jim Clifton and Jim Harter go further, dedicating their 2019 work "to those who believe maximising human potential is now the primary purpose of all organisations."[129] Think about that for a moment. Imagine profitability and the return to shareholders being the means by which organisations achieve the goal of developing people, rather than the other way around.

Before we go on, let me insert a caveat. Most people have an innate instinct to learn, to gain skills, to become stronger and wiser (and good luck trying to develop those that don't!). Often development and growth happens while people are busy doing something else. Learning is most effective when the acquisition of knowledge and skill serves a fairly immediate goal. Just-in-Time learning is effective because the information and skills acquired are immediately reinforced by repeated use.

When we put too much focus on individuals and how we might benefit them, and lose sight of the good of the organisation, we put at risk the benefit the organisation generates for all of its stakeholders. Humans are a social species and our success lies in our ability to work collectively for shared benefit. Further, humans tend to mature when they have an appropriate understanding of their contribution to the good of the collective. Humans who begin to think that the collective primarily exists for their individual benefit tend to attract the Freudian label of 'narcissist'. We all roll our eyes at the spoiled child of the helicopter parent. Here endeth the caveat.

---

[128] Harkavy, D. *Becoming a Coaching Leader: The proven Strategy for Building your Own Team of Champions* (Thomas Nelson, Nashville, 2007).
[129] Clifton, J. and Harter, J. *It's the Manager* (Gallup New York 2019).

Coaching is...

There are several lenses through which to view coaching, some specifically from the arena of sport, others from the field of human performance. Sports coaches vary in the way they operate depending on the traditions of their sport. In Australian Rules football, the coach is like a general, directing their troops on the field. They make decisions and give orders. In swimming, the coach is often equal parts technician, a taskmaster and a tactician. At the elite levels of individual sports like tennis and golf, coaches operate as observer-collaborators.

Google the definition of coaching in the business world and you'll get a huge variety of responses, but the common elements are around helping people to improve their own performance, helping people to learn in the context of their challenges, and asking questions that provoke thought. John Whitmore, in his hugely influential 1992 work, *Coaching for Performance*, defined coaching as "unlocking people's potential to maximize their own performance."[130]

The essence of coaching, according to Whitmore, is to raise a worker's *awareness* – gaining a clearer and more complete understanding of the realities they are facing (including their own part in creating them) and facilitating the worker assuming appropriate *responsibility* for taking action in light of their understanding.

Coaching of this kind traces its origins back to psychologist Carl Rogers, who developed the Person-Centred Therapy approach in the early 1950s.[131] Rogers believed that people are inherently motivated toward their own growth, and that the therapist, in providing an empathic environment of unconditional personal regard, could facilitate a person coming to a greater awareness of themselves and taking responsibility for making choices toward their own growth. Rogers believed that the answers to a person's dilemmas lay within themselves, and the therapist's job was not to advise or direct, but to create a context where a person could discover what lay within.

Accordingly, the coach's primary tool is the carefully crafted question. Rather than being the fount of all wisdom, the coach's job is to be a 'thinking

---

[130] Whitmore, J. *Coaching for Performance: The Principles and Practice of Coaching and Leadership* (Nicholas Brealey, London 1992).
[131] Rogers, C. *Client-Centered Therapy.* (Riverside Press. Cambridge Massachusetts 1951).

facilitator'. I like to think about coaching as two brains collaborating to work on the one issue. Primarily the coach curates the process of the conversation while the client or worker wrestles with the content. I recognise this way of thinking has some burrs on it, which we'll get to in a minute. But before that, let's look at a generalised coaching model, as a structured series of questions.

Coaching models

The most basic coaching model is a lot like booking a plane ticket online. The first question is the departure point (Where are you now?). The second is about the destination (Where do you want to go?). Enter these with some indication of preferred dates and the website will throw up a range of options, inviting you to choose one. The third question involves a process of weighing up dates and times with various carriers against cost. The fourth question is answered and the booking is completed when you commit to travel by choosing and paying for your flights (and fending off all the offers for extra baggage, meals, rental car, accommodation, carbon offsets, supporting a global charity and upgrading your booking with your non-existent loyalty program points).

Just about every coaching framework includes or implies these four elements (minus all the offers on extras). Some emphasise particular elements more than others, but the four basic ideas follow the logic of generalised change models:

- Describe your current reality (your departure point)
- Define the result you would like to achieve (what's your destination)
- What are your options for getting from your current reality to achieving the result you want?
- Which option will you commit to action?

GROW

John Whitmore's model follows this pattern almost exactly, except he switches the first two. His GROW model looks like this:

- Goal – What do you want to achieve or attain? This usually refers to the immediate coaching conversation. I'll often ask it this way: "At the end of our time together, what do you want to walk away with?"
- Reality – What are the circumstances, opportunities, constraints, complexities that you need to take into account as you contemplate

339

your goal? What are the contributing factors that have led to your situation?

- Options – What options are open to you to pursue the goal, given your realities? What are the relative advantages, risks and costs of each one?
- Will – What will you do? This includes whatever enablers are required to enact the chosen course of action.

GROW is pretty simple to learn as a construct, although it takes a lifetime to genuinely master. In practice the 'Goal' will often be modified somewhat by examining current 'Reality', and the client will oscillate between the two as their thinking gains clarity.

COACH

Although Keith Webb's work is targeted at leaders of the Christian church,[132] his generalised COACH model can be utilised in just about any context. Webb follows a similar process to Whitmore, with a couple of notable differences. His model looks like this:

- Connect – Establish rapport with the client
- Outcome – Determine what they want to achieve out of the conversation (equivalent to Whitmore's 'Goal')
- Awareness – Examine the circumstance, contributing factors and constraints of your challenge (equivalent to Whitmore's 'Reality')
- Course of Action – What's the course of action to which you will commit coming out of this conversation?
- Highlight – What was the highlight of our conversation: the 'Ah Ha!' moment or the most helpful part of the conversation?

You'll note that Webb intentionalises the human connection aspect with the open and the close, while it's more implied with Whitmore. You'll also note that it's missing an intentional 'Options' section, so the model may not force the client to consider possibilities other than their first big idea.

---

[132] Webb, K. *The Coach Model for Christian Leaders: Powerful Leadership Skills for Solving Problems, Reaching Goals, and Developing Others* (Morgan James, New York, 2012).

Positively framed models

An alternative to the 'flight booking' models are approaches that focus on the positive experiences and results. The idea being to figure out what drives success and look at ways of replicating those drivers more consistently – i.e. What's working for you and how can you get more of that?

Appreciative Inquiry (AI)

Appreciative Inquiry is a consulting approach formulated by management consultant and academic David Cooperrider in the late 1990s.[133] While originally intended as a tool for broad-based consultation, AI adapts readily to coaching and there are dozens of subtle variations in circulation. AI is an asset or positivity-based approach, focusing the attention of the client on what's driving success and what energises them. AI steers the client's attention away from demotivating and anxiety producing problems and barriers.

A simplified AI outline looks something like this:

- Discover – What's working, what's life-giving?
- Dream – What could be? What do you envision?
- Design – What could you do to bring the dream to fruition?
- Deliver/Deploy – What's the plan to put the design into practice?

Some versions open with a preliminary 'Define' – What's the strategic focus for this conversation? Others add at the end, 'Destiny' – How will we evaluate and sustain the change?

Framework for Continuous Renewal

A similar model, but more grounded in the nitty-gritty of organisation life, is the Framework for Continuous Renewal by Oakley and Krug: [134]

- Constantly look for small successes you are achieving.
- Research extensively what you are doing to generate these successes.
- Continually re-clarify (refocus on) in great detail your specific objective(s).

---

[133] Cooperrider, D. and Whitney, D. *Appreciative Inquiry: A Positive Revolution in Change* (Berrett-Koehler, San Francisco 2005).
[134] Oakley, E. and Krug, D. *Enlightened Leadership: Getting to the Heart of Change* (Simon and Schuster, New York 1993).

- Clarify the benefits to all parties (customers, shareholders, the organisation, team, each person) of achieving the objectives.
- Continually search for what you could be doing more, better or differently, to move closer to the objectives.

Oakley and Krug emphasise the centrality of a primary objective, and advocate applying their framework in the pursuit of that objective. With this in view, the Framework for Continuous Renewal, with its focus on the more incremental and immediate, is probably more readily adaptable to the task of supervision.

Blind spots

While positively framed models have the advantage of working with a worker's strengths, initiative and interest, their major blind spot is, well, the blind spot. There are very few jobs that call 100% on a worker's strengths and 0% on anything where the worker is not exactly a standout. This is especially true for younger workers.

Marcus Buckingham and Don Clifton's book, *Now Discover Your Strengths*,[135] understands competency sets using three categories:

- Strengths – the things what you can or have the potential to do with excellence.
- Weaknesses – the things that you don't do with excellence but are an essential companion to the things you can do with excellence.
- Non-strengths – the things you don't do well that you could delegate or just quit.

Let's illustrate. Imagine a brilliant sales rep, who is a spectacularly successful deal closer – put them in front of a client and that client will be begging to buy a product from them in no time. That's their strength, their superpower. Now imagine that same rep is absolutely rubbish at developing promotional materials. What's more, they're chronically disorganised; they miss deadlines, are late for appointments, and don't follow through on customer complaints.

---

[135] Buckingham, M. and Clifton, D. *Now Discover your Strengths: The Revolutionary Program That Shows You How to Develop Your Unique Talents and Strengths – And Those of the People You Manage* (Free Press, New York 2001).

As their boss, you don't want to lose your super-closer, but those areas outside of their strength are beginning to cost you. If you solely concentrated on their strengths, you may coach them into improving their already stellar closing rate by a few percentage points, while you bleed customers because of those deficits. A way forward is to figure out what can be separated from the exercise of that strength, and what can't be.

In this case, you could probably hive off the development of promo material to someone else (a lot of sales reps have no part in developing promo materials). This would make it a non-strength. But personal organisation is prerequisite to being a sales rep. For a sales rep, poor personal organisation is a weakness. They don't need to be an A-grade genius personal productivity guru, just good enough at getting themselves organised that it doesn't undermine their area of special ability.

Coaching your star rep would be around understanding what contributes to their disorganisation and finding the tools, techniques, hacks and helps to get them adequately organised. Then they can get an unimpeded run at what they do best.

Interrogating reality

I've tinkered with the positively framed models and have used the Framework for Continuous Renewal to good effect in a number of settings. However, my 'stock' delivery is essentially Whitmore's GROW model, supercharged by thinking from Susan Scott's book *Fierce Conversations*.[136]

With twenty years of coaching and thousands of coaching appointments behind me, I estimate that about sixty percent of the productive time in a coaching appointment is spent examining the client's reality – trying to get a clear and rich understanding of the challenges, constraints, contributing factors and conflicts. I acknowledge that there are other schools of coaching thought out there that actively discourage spending too much time examining reality in favour of pushing toward action. Jumping quickly to the solution side feels like delivering maximum value to the client, but it risks working at the level of the symptomatic and the easily observable. Resolving problems

---

[136] Scott, S. *Fierce Conversations: Achieving Success at Work and in Life One Conversation at a Time* (Berkley, New York 2002).

generally requires a more sophisticated level of insight than the thinking that generated the problem in the first place.

Further, humans tend to have go-to mental models that provide quick categorization and pattern recognition, allowing for quick, efficient ways of 'getting your head around' situations. Mental models work brilliantly right up until they don't. Frequently a durable solution to a problem requires challenging the mental model that underpinned its creation.

Scott's first principle is to 'master the courage to interrogate reality'. Scott doesn't invite us to politely inquire as to what might be some of the circumstances that could possibly inform our decision-making. She dares us to interrogate reality – to drill into it, to compel our situation to give up the facts unspoken and obscure, the things that we're pretending not to know.

Ground truth

Scott differentiates between the official truth and 'ground truth'. The official truth is the talking points spun by management, like the Lego Movie where "everything is awesome" or the stuff that's supposed to be true but plainly isn't, if only we would come out from behind ourselves and say so.

Ground truth is a military term, describing the actual situation and unfolding realities faced by the active units on the ground. Ground truth is a kind of firsthand intelligence that's almost impossible to gain except by actual presence at the point of engagement. Your primary access to the ground truth your workers are facing, both in terms of challenges and opportunities, is from the workers themselves.

As a boss you already know the official management line – what you need is ground truth from your workers. Workers will tell you ground truth when they trust you, (or when they've just stopped caring about the consequences of their actions). A worker will only trust you with ground truth if they believe you'll take it seriously, non-defensively and won't shoot the messenger. Ground truth is as likely to question your answers as it is to answer your questions. And for that reason, some managers simply don't want to hear it.

As a coach you get to ground truth by courage, persistence, insight and lateral thinking. Scott quotes the adage, "If you're drilling for water, it's better to drill one hundred-foot well than a hundred one -foot wells."[137] It's easy in coaching to shoot for quick answers, casting around a few questions about context and causation before briskly moving on toward options and plans. As a boss it's easy to be so keen to pursue our agenda with our workers that we forget that our workers may have front-line intelligence without which our agenda is doomed.

Broaden the view

In advocating systems thinking rather than simple cause-effect thinking, Peter Senge from MIT's Sloan School of Management points out that today's problems are frequently the result of yesterday's solutions.[138] Too often the 'solution' we shoot for without careful interrogation of reality ends up shifting the symptom somewhere else or forcing the symptom to take a different form. Coaching is about taking the client beyond their current and habitual thinking. As a boss, effectively coaching your workers requires the commitment to develop some decent coaching skills and patience to give your workers the time and the territory to drill down to the less-than-obvious aspects of the realities they face.

To take a broader view, a coaching approach to supervision assumes that there are always opportunities to do things a little differently to the mutual benefit of the worker and the organisation. Regularly asking coaching questions in supervision should lead to a steady stream of improvements to the practices and processes of the organisation, leading to more satisfied workers and improved productivity.

Taking time to listen carefully to our workers, to ask thought-provoking questions and treating their answers with respect is a powerful way to deepen a worker's engagement, which has knock-on effects for motivation, productivity and wellbeing. Further, it leads to better decision-making, based on what's actually going on rather than what we assume is going on. Coaching, rather than simply directing, means you and your workers will be less likely to come up with solutions today that will generate the problems of tomorrow.

------

[137] Scott, S. *Fierce Conversations: Achieving Success at Work and in Life One Conversation at a Time* (Berkley, New York 2002), 39.
[138] Senge, P. *The Fifth Discipline: The Art and Practice of the Learning Organisation* (Currency Doubleday, New York 2006), 57.

Coaching clients with whom I've worked over an extended period report that my questions emerge in their thinking even when I'm not around. Coaching develops habits of thinking deeply, critically and (hopefully) systematically in the mental repertoire of the worker. Coaching helps workers to be habitually circumspect in their assessment of their circumstances, to explore and evaluate options before ploughing ahead with the first idea that occurs to them, and to routinely look at both short- and long-term ramifications of proposed actions. In and of itself, coaching is an effective means of capacity-building.

Autonomy and initiative

There's somewhat of a divide in contemporary leadership thinking – those who think military history and practice is a valuable resource for leadership learning, and those who are repelled by the violence and horror of armed conflict. Whichever side of the divide you might locate yourself, let me say, I agree with you. I don't have a military background and I'm pretty sure I would not be able to coldly end the life of someone else no matter how much it might be my patriotic duty to do so.

Yet, I read military history, simply because military action demonstrates leadership *in extremis* – the stakes are high and time is short. Now we're about to jump into a quick bit of military learning. Even if you find war distasteful, stick with me. I'll keep it PG-rated.

The two most famous Australian servicemen from the First World War are John Monash and Albert Jacka. Monash rose to the rank of general and is regarded by some as the most effective general of any combatant nation involved in the conflict. He is honoured by his name being conferred on Australia's largest university, a prominent local government area and a major arterial road.

If you drive down Fitzroy Street in Melbourne's inner city bayside suburb of St Kilda, before you turn into the Esplanade, you traverse a short, curved stretch of road called Jacka Boulevard. It's named after the one-time mayor of St Kilda, Albert Jacka. Jacka won the first Victoria Cross (the highest award for gallantry) awarded to an Australian in the Great War. He was also awarded a Military Cross and bar for multiple acts of astounding daring and initiative. Over his three years of active service he rose from private to the rank of captain. There's a small plaque commemorating him outside the St Kilda RSL, and a park bearing his name in his hometown of Wedderburn. Hardly the Lincoln Memorial.

Yet the exploits of Jacka, and his Australian comrades, over time led to a significant change in the way military operations are commanded. Although it was his astonishing bravery in the three separate events that won Jacka his decorations, it was Jacka's initiative, flexibility of thought and ability to spontaneously employ novel tactics that provided learning for future generations of soldiers and those that trained them.

The First World War saw the senseless slaughter of millions of young men, commanded from afar to run headlong into a hail of machine-gun fire. Raw bravery and unthinking obedience to command and control did not win battles. Jacka's exploits were not what was expected of a common soldier and too context-specific to be possible to command from a bunker behind the front. They were strategically thoughtful yet tactically impulsive: split-second decisions guided by an overall sense of the broader objectives of his battalion and the wider expeditionary force.

Nowadays military units are granted a great deal of tactical autonomy, guided by broader strategic objectives. It's up to the members of the unit to rapidly assess their environment and the challenges with which they are confronted and respond adaptively. Training soldiers to be reflexively obedient has given way to training to be tactically adaptive. Higher-ranking officers away from the frontline cannot sufficiently appraise ground truth to give tactical instruction with enough speed and detail to be useful. What's required is personnel trained and empowered to evaluate their circumstances in real time, balancing elements of risk, rules of engagement and strategic intent.

The implications for supervision are obvious. Supervision that resembles the command of a nineteenth century Army officer, or the Taylorist 'do as you are instructed and don't think about it', or any supervision that is fundamentally based on Theory X, will at best yield compliance. It forgoes engaging the intellect, the insight and the ground-truth tacit knowledge the worker gathers hour by hour as they work.

Coaching not only invites the worker to put their tacit knowledge and their unique appraisal of ground truth to work for the good of the organisation, it provides a context where they are trained to think about translating the organisation's objectives into tactical responses to immediate challenges. Coach a worker long enough and they'll ask themselves the questions you would ask them if you were present.

Coaching not only delivers better outcomes, it's also a primary means of developing the talent of our workers.

Low control, high accountability

Adopting a coaching approach to supervision can be nerve-wracking, because it requires entrusting the decisions a supervisor might make to those reporting to them. In coaching, your worker will likely come up with adaptations to their challenges that are different to the solutions you might prefer. It takes self-discipline to step back and ask ourselves, "Is the worker's solution flawed, or just different to my way of doing things?" If you can't clearly identify problems with the worker's idea, coaching requires you to let them give it a try. When we override the worker's best thinking with our preferences, we erode the worker's engagement. Play the 'do it my way' card a couple of times and the worker will probably give up offering their thinking and wait for you to tell them what to do.

Coaching requires a supervisory relationship that reduces direct control, trusting the worker to use their judgement and initiative. But that doesn't mean the worker can do as they please. Ensuring the worker's action align with the organisation's purpose and policies becomes a matter of accountability. The emphasis of supervision shifts from following orders to giving account for decisions and results.

Limitations

You'll note earlier in our conversation that the presuppositions that underlie coaching as Whitmore imagines it come from the therapeutic world. Coaching in this form is client-centred (or worker-centred) and ideally occurs outside of the worker's management up-line. Coaching requires a high degree of neutrality or objectivity, allowing the coach to take a dispassionate, non-judgemental posture. Whatever the worker thinks or chooses is up to the worker, and it's not for the coach to criticise or evaluate.

Most of my work as a consultant takes the form of coaching. The people I coach do not work for me, and many of them are not even part of the same organisation as me. I can generally take a reasonably neutral stance with my clients, since my only stake in their game is that their success or failure could reflect well or poorly on my coaching, which has implications for their prospects of referring more clients to me.

Taking coaching into the field of supervision requires another shift, because it brings coaching inside the hierarchy of the organisation. If I'm coaching one of my staff, I have a very large stake in their game – their performance goes beyond being something to which I can lend a hand, to something that is my responsibility. I'm no longer entirely client-centred, since I'm holding the needs and interests of the client (or worker) alongside the interests of the organisation to which I am responsible. I cannot be neutral in this context – I have a significant degree of skin in the game.

A recent article by Herminia Ibarra and Anne Scoular in Harvard Business Review made substantial reference to Whitmore in contrasting coaching with more traditional forms of management: "An effective manager-as-coach asks questions instead of providing answers, supports employees instead of judging them, and facilitates their development instead of dictating what has to be done."[139]

It probably comes as no surprise to you that I'll have a couple of difficulties with their description. It's an example of the unhelpful way of thinking that reduces things to dichotomies. In this case, traditional supervision is portrayed as unenlightened and ineffective and coaching held up as the 'correct' way to manage staff.

Let's go back to first principles. The first responsibility of the supervisor is the prudent deployment of resources to the organisation's benefit and the advancement of its purpose. Certainly, we want people to have a great experience of work, and to develop to their full potential, but that's almost certainly not what's on their PD. Right up front, effective management must define the purpose of the organisation, the purpose of the worker's role and what's expected of the worker in fulfilling that role. To a certain extent you must dictate what is to be done and you can't get there by asking questions.

---

[139] Ibarra, H. and Scoular, A. *The Leader as Coach* (Harvard Business Review November-December 2019), 2.

349

Further, as a supervisor it's your job to exercise a certain degree of judgement upon the worker – by determining and communicating whether they've met expectations or not. If the worker consistently fails to meet expectations, your judgement is required in removing that worker from their role.

Most of the people that I coach translate much of what they experience with me as their coach into the supervision of their staff. I'm often asked, "Can you just use coaching as your supervision framework?" Sometimes I'll return fire with a question like, "What do you think?" But if people genuinely want my opinion I'll say, "About 70% of the time. As a boss you need to define yourself and your expectations, and sometimes you'll need to bang the table."

A coaching posture

Integrating coaching into your supervision doesn't mean you should toss out all the process we discussed in chapters 16-17 and instead use Whitmore's GROW. Coaching as a supervisor is more a matter of the posture you bring to supervision.

I usually open a supervision conversation with a general check in question, like, "How's the role going?" It's not uncommon for a worker to respond by describing a particular difficulty or challenge. Here's an opportunity to apply a coaching approach. I might ask a reality-framed question like, "How long has this been happening?" or I could use a goal-framed question like, "What's the outcome that you want from that situation?" I'll save questions like, "What are you going to do about it?" until after we've explored their realities.

When working through the 'responsibilities' headings in the worker's PD, or touching on their progress with strategy, it's common for challenges to arise where I can employ coaching questions to facilitate the worker devising a solution. If the worker reports success or positive progress, I might adopt a positively framed approach to help them think through how they could learn from their success and apply it more broadly.

Summary

- Coaching is about facilitating thinking to increase awareness and responsibility.
- Models include 'book a ticket' types and 'positively framed' approaches.
- Interrogating reality is where the majority of productive coaching time is spent. This includes:
    - Getting to 'ground truth'
    - Broadening the view to see systems beyond cause-effect logic
- Responding to 'ground truth' requires autonomy and initiative
    - Encourages rapid tactical adaptation
- Coaching as a supervision approach requires a shift in emphasis from control to accountability.
- Coaching has limitations as a supervision method.
    - The supervisor cannot be entirely neutral.
    - Supervision is not solely 'client focused'.

Discussion

- Where could you use coaching as a supervisory technique?
- Which aspect of coaching will you find the most difficult to employ?

Implementation

- Choose a coaching model to research and practice.
- Test-drive it with a trusted friend or colleague.

Chapter 23
Supervision through the lifespan

The question of stewardship becomes a little more complex when we begin to recognise that our lives cross with the lives of our workers at particular junctures in our respective lifespans. Put another way, working for me represents a chapter in the overall life of each of my workers. It might be a formative chapter, where they learn concepts, acquire knowledge and develop skills that will set them up for a productive life. It might be a crisis chapter where they adapt to some confronting realities, it might be a crowning chapter where they get to do their very best work and make the greatest contribution of their lifetime. At the same time, I could well be writing one of those chapters in my own life while I'm supervising others.

Role and expectations through the life cycle

If this all seems like a bridge too far, just stay with me for a while. We'll retreat into the relative safety of theory, which is a little less confronting.

It's so obvious to us that humans go through a series of states in their development that we take for granted. We all carry a rough knowledge of the commonly accepted understandings of what to expect of a baby, a toddler, a preschooler, a child, a pre-adolescent, etc., all the way through to someone who's elderly and frail. There's the acquisition of motor control and language; social skills, a sense of agency and a sense of responsibility; right through to acceptance of loss and mortality. When someone doesn't meet their development timeline as we expect, we might label their behaviour 'immature' or 'maladaptive'. With me so far?

Many pre-industrial or traditional cultures have ideas about life as a series of chapters or phases, sometimes marked by celebrations and rituals. The clearest transition is the one from childhood to adulthood. Some cultures mark this transition by circumcising their boys as they enter adolescence or celebrating the onset of menstruation in their girls. In some cultures, an adolescent goes through an extended ritual after which they are assigned a different place and role in their society.

Partnering and parenthood can mark other transition points, where one is required to adapt to new realities and responsibilities. Some cultures recognise a transition to becoming an elder of the group.

In ancient Hebrew culture, elders held a special position at the city gate, forming a kind of magisterial panel to settle disputes, witness contractual arrangements and even make determinations of criminal culpability and consequences.

Pre-industrial cultures are by nature more cyclical than dynamic, meaning they follow familiar rhythms. There are clear, commonly understood pathways of development through the human life cycle. People know more or less what to expect and what's expected of them.

With the industrial revolution and the rapid urbanisation of Western culture, much of this implied structure was abandoned with the rhythms and familiarity of village life. As people migrated to industrialised cities, they were left to navigate their own way, often as individuals trying to adapt to the changes in society and developmental challenges of life as they grew up, partnered, parented and aged. The well-worn paths were lost and people adapted as they thought best.

Psychology of development

The emergence of psychology as a discipline in the late nineteenth century ignited an interest in human development. But rather than understanding the human lifespan from a functional or societal perspective, the pioneers of psychology were more interested in how the human develops in terms of mental functioning and the formation of identity.

Sigmund Freud has been dubbed 'The Father of Modern Psychology' and much of what emerged through the first half of the twentieth century was in response or reaction to his theories. When we use terms like 'subconscious' or 'anal-retentive', we're drawing on Freudian theory.

Freud proposed that psychological and sexual development were indissolubly linked, mapping out five stages of psychosexual development, punctuated with challenges or 'complexes' (dilemmas and anxieties that are outside of conscious contemplation and typified in the characters of Greek myths such as Oedipus and Electra). Failure to resolve the 'complexes' that emerged at each stage would have broad ranging ramifications into adult life.[140] While psychologists have on the whole moved on from Freud's mythology-based types and sexually attributed ideas of development, we still hear some of the language ('narcissistic personality disorder' is listed in the American Psychiatric Association Diagnostic Statistical Manual of Mental Disorders).

What has persisted from Freud's theory is the idea of developmental tasks that build the internal identity structure for a functioning adult. Failure to complete earlier developmental tasks will, according to the theory, interfere with the completion of subsequent developmental tasks and thus interfere with the emergence of an adult. Numerous theories carry on Freud's idea of staged development where completion of one stage provides a foundation for the next. These include the currently all-pervasive attachment theory popularised by Bowlby and Ainsworth,[141] which built on earlier work by Dollard and Miller,[142] and even earlier work by Harlow and Zimmerman.[143]

Similar to Freud, Jean Piaget developed a four-stage process of cognitive development in children, spanning the years from birth to adolescence.[144] The stages outline the increasing sophistication of children's thought and include ideas about object permanence, symbols representing realities, problem solving and abstract thought. Problems at one stage can lead to difficulty developing the capacities at the following stages. Some have proposed that many adults never reach the stage where they can think in abstractions (don't worry, you've got this far in the book, so you must've done a reasonable job of Piaget's stages).

---

[140] Freud, S. *Three Contributions to the Theory of Sex* (Annotated). Arcadia Ebook; 2016.
[141] Ainsworth, M. D. S. (1973) *The development of infant-mother attachment* In B. Cardwell & H. Ricciuti (Eds.), *Review of child development research* (Vol. 3, pp. 1-94) Chicago: University of Chicago Press.
Bowlby J. **Attachment** in Attachment and Loss: Vol. 1. Loss. (New York: Basic Books 1969)
[142] Dollard, J. & Miller, N. E. (1950). *Personality and psychotherapy*. New York: McGraw-Hill.
[143] Harlow, H. F. & Zimmermann, R. R. (1958) *The development of affective responsiveness in infant monkeys*. Proceedings of the American Philosophical Society, 102,501 -509.
[144] Piaget, J. *Origins of intelligence in the Child* (Routledge & Kegan London: (1936). Piaget, J. and Cook, M. T. *The Origins of Intelligence in Children* (International University Press, New York, 1952).

As Piaget was putting the finishing touches to his theory, German-American developmental psychologist Erik Erikson was building his theory of psychological development of human beings over the lifespan.

Erikson built on Freud's theory, although he emphasised psychosocial development rather than Freud's focus on the psychosexual. Like Freud, Erikson asserted that completion of the developmental challenges at one stage provided a foundation for tackling the next. In Erikson's theory, each stage was marked by adopting a productive or helpful capacity such as trust, autonomy, initiative and industry over the respective opposite, self-defeating tendencies like mistrust, doubt, guilt and inferiority.

Erikson went further than Freud in proposing developmental stages beyond adolescence into adulthood and on through to old age. His theory included eight stages, although much later he added a ninth dealing with very old age. Erikson also took into account cultural variations and their implications for the development of the emerging adult.

The staged developmental theories of Freud and Piaget seemed to assume that the development up to adolescence largely determined the identity and personality of the emerging adult. From there the die was cast – the adult worked with what they had the best they could. Subsequent theories like Bowlby's attachment and the trauma-informed model that has grown out of it follow much of the same line. The therapist's job is to help the adult client to deal with the damage and deficits of their formative years.

Development through adulthood

Erikson's eight-stage framework got us thinking that growth and development could continue, perhaps even must continue, throughout the lifespan. Subsequent to Erikson, a range of stage-based frameworks have sprung up, including Daniel Levinson's work around life's 'seasons'[145] and Bobby Clinton's Leadership Emergence Theory.[146]

Levinson is clearly influenced by Freud and Erikson before him but differs in a couple of important ways. Firstly, his model is concerned with adult

---

[145] Levinson, D. J., Darrow, C. N. and Klein, E. B. *The Seasons of a Man's Life* (Random, New Yok 1978).
[146] Clinton, J. R. *The Making of a Leader* (Navpress, Colorado Springs 1988).

development, and begins in earnest with the period of transition from adolescence to adulthood. Secondly, Levinson differentiated phases as either 'stable' – a time of building structures, consolidating roles and fulfilling goals – or 'transitional', where a person feels the need to question their structures and roles, and adapt to changes. Levinson identifies seven stages and assigns rough timeframes in the life cycle.

To give you an idea of how Levinson's life stages play out, here's the skeleton outline of the stages through a typical working life.

- Age 17-22: Early Adult Transition
- Age 22-40: Early Adulthood
    - 22-28 Entering the Adult World
    - 28-33 Age 30 Transition
    - 33-40 Settling Down
- Age 40-45: Midlife Transition
- Age 45-60: Middle Adulthood
    - 45-50 Entering Middle Adulthood
    - 50-55 Age 50 Transition
    - 55-60 Culmination of Middle Adulthood
- Age 60-65: Late Adulthood Transition
- Age 65-80: Late Adulthood

Along with Levinson, other researchers such as George Vaillant and Robert Kegan have developed alternative theories that map out adult development.[147]

So, let's stop and deal with a couple of questions that you're probably asking. To begin with, "Is this crash course in stages of human development just an elaborate diversion or does it have a purpose?"

Clearly there's not enough information in the headings above for you to make use of them in supervision. I'm hoping to get you thinking about human development, how we grow and change over a lifetime. By introducing you to some of the mapmakers who've tried to make sense of how humans develop,

---

[147] Vaillant, G. E. *Adaptation to Life* (Little, Brown Boston 1977) Kegan, R. *In Over Our Heads: The Mental Demands of Modern Life* (Harvard Press Cambridge MA 1998).

I'm hoping I might pique your curiosity and invite you to consider your development and how you might become more intentional about it.

Then there's your effectiveness as a supervisor. Appreciating the challenges each of your staff are facing, enables you to assist more effectively in their development. Further, sometimes a worker's dissatisfaction or restlessness is driven more by their entry into a transition phase than by their experience of work. If you're mindful of the worker's journey and where they may be in terms of their developmental stages, you can be less reactive and a greater resource to them. I'll give some examples in a minute.

Next question – "Why didn't you summarise each of the theories and set out their various stages? You might have even drawn up a handy comparison table."

I chose against the summaries for a couple of reasons. First, I'm not sure I would do a great job of boiling each framework down in a way that's faithful to the author's intent. I really hate those emails from readers better educated than me that pull me up on something I've misunderstood and quoted out of context. Call it 'small target' strategy.

Second, I'm setting out to give you enough of a glimpse to figure out whether you might be interested in a particular framework, in the hope that you'll let your curiosity take you into researching further. In order to make use of any of these frameworks as a supervisor, you need to do your own work first. You won't make any useful progress in your own development just by reading a sketch summary. If the idea of development over the lifetime strikes a chord with you, I strongly encourage you to choose a framework (and there are plenty of others I haven't mentioned), and begin your own work. If you really want to get the most out of it, work it through with a coach.

For example
Let me give you a quick look at how that's unfolded for me. In doing so, I'll introduce you to some other thinkers. It began for me at age 26. The year was 1993 and Australia was in the midst of that recession 'we had to have'. I had fairly recently thrown in my career as a youth minister (that's a church minister that specialises in working with adolescents) due to my realisation and eventual acceptance of some unwelcome personal realities. Then I went back to uni to finish my undergrad. That's how I wound up in the adhesives

manufacturing plant at Pacific Dunlop (yeah, the image of being beyond my usefulness and sent to the glue factory was not lost on me either). The work was physically hard, dirty, hot in summer and freezing in winter. The hours were long, the pay was just enough to get by. And worst of all, it was mind-numbingly boring. You know how the story pans out, but at the time, I was despairing.

This was not a part of my life plan.

In a chance conversation, a mentor figure listened to my tale of woe and recommended I read Bobby Clinton. I had made an attempt at reading Bobby's work a couple of years before. Bobby is rather technical in his approach and creates a whole lexicon of terms to define his theory of leadership emergence. It's a book that requires you to keep one finger in the glossary as you read.

By this time I was in enough pain to motivate me to persevere, labouring though Bobby's framework of six life stages and list of a dozen or so 'process items' that serve to shape and prepare the leader for greater responsibility and effectiveness. I needed hope and I needed to make sense of being apparently discarded before I even had a chance to make a dent (I admit I was a bit self-absorbed).

Clinton helped me in a few ways right off. According to his research, peak effectiveness in leaders typically occurs in the mid-fifties. That was a relief. I still had time. Also, negative experiences – things like leadership backlash, conflict and tests of my integrity were all part of the development process. I began to wonder if there was some sense to my discomfort.

Clinton's work shares some similarities with Levinson. His stages address some very similar issues and follow somewhat similar age markers. He also observes some similar patterns to Vaillant, especially in the latter stages of life. Clinton shares Levinson's recognition of transition periods (Clinton calls them 'boundaries') and the challenges presented by adaptation and reorientation.

But the real kicker was a process item that Clinton calls 'isolation.' He pointed out chapters in the lives of leaders across history – leaders I had studied, admired and sought to emulate – where they had been sidelined. Some had gotten ill, some had been 'voted off the island' by their organisations, some had been imprisoned by oppressive regimes, some had simply sensed the need to pull back and regroup. As Clinton described the architecture of an isolation, it was as if he was describing my life. Perhaps I wasn't washed-up after all.

From there, I was a Clinton convert. I worked with a coach through the timeline exercise Clinton recommended, using resources developed by his protégé Terry Walling.[148] It was life-changing. Nearly 30 years later, Bobby Clinton's thinking still strongly informs my personal reflection and planning. He's still helping me make sense of what's going on in my life.

It's unlikely to come as a surprise to you that Clinton's work is constantly informing my work as a coach and in supervising my staff. It's not just a novel concept to me, but one of the primary lenses through which I seek to interrogate reality and respond thoughtfully.

Fast-forward 15 years and I found myself in another emotional slump. It wasn't as dramatic as the 'Great Isolation of '93', but it was still unpleasant. (I have a psychologist in the family, who observes that emotional slumps – some large, some small – are a bit of a feature of my emotional landscape.) The most significant contributing factor to my emotional malaise was the growing and inescapable body of evidence that my goals were not being realised, despite my best efforts.

Over the previous ten years I had become increasingly committed to the idea that I could engineer my life – and my life's outcomes – to my specifications through the relentless application of what I determined to be good theory. I assumed that if I read the theory, mastered it conceptually, turned it into a personal strategy and implemented it with discipline and persistence, I would see the predicted outcome. Yet all the indicators were heading in the opposite direction. American social psychologist Leon Festinger would call it a case of 'cognitive dissonance'.[149]

I don't think I'm alone in my embrace and subsequent disillusionment with this approach. I think the whole 'live life according to your personal mission and vision' that's been espoused by writers like Stephen Covey has at times

---

[148] You can access Terry's materials at https://leaderbreakthru.com.
[149] Festinger, L. *A Theory of cognitive dissonance* (Stanford University Press, Stanford, CA: 1957).

been taken too far.[150] That's not to criticise Covey, rather an inkling that I – and I suspect others – may have misused his thinking in the service of the myth of 'you can achieve anything if you try hard enough'.

By chance, the aforementioned psychologist in the family dropped a copy of Dan McAdams book, *The Person*, onto our kitchen table wondering if I might like to read it.[151] I've always got a reading list way longer than I can manage, but for some reason I was drawn to it. Once started, I was hooked.

McAdam's theory of narrative psychology made sense to me – we construct our sense of self out of the story of our life. Which events we choose to make the plot points, and how we interpret them, can make the difference between seeing ourselves and our lives as wonderful or miserable, blessed or cursed – or anywhere in between. He also challenges our assumption that our lives follow some kind of predetermined narrative arc, that all of our trouble will be redeemed and we will find happiness and resolution. There is no evidence that our lives will follow the archetypical fairy story, that we'll struggle, overcome and find our happily ever after.

I can almost hear some of you snorting, 'Nobody believes that!' Well, according to McAdams' research, most of us do, often at the level of an unexamined assumption that perhaps we won't admit to ourselves. As much as I was reluctant to admit it, I was suckered into the myth of what McAdams calls 'the redemptive self'. I believed that through my wit and perseverance and courage I would overcome against the odds, emerging triumphant.

Sure, I hadn't actually stated that anywhere, but it was the summary of my underlying assumptions and it had no basis in fact. Just because other people in other times may have lived lives that followed this arc (or were interpreted as following this arc) gave no reliable basis for believing that mine would. My personal narrative arc was a fairy story. It was not an immutable life pattern.

When I began to challenge the myth, I realised how much of my effort was going into forcing the myth to emerge as reality. I was unhappy because my

---

[150] Covey, Stephen *The Seven Habits of Highly Effective People* (The Business Library, Melbourne. 1997).
[151] McAdams, D. P. *The Person: An Introduction to Personality Psychology* (Wiley, New York, 2006).

lived experience wasn't following the script. And giving up the script felt like giving up hope.

If you take the time to read Levinson, you'll notice my engagement with McAdams looked a lot like the kind of wrestle that goes into the midlife transition he describes, and if you do the maths on my dates (I'll give you a clue – I was in my early forties), it appears I was pretty much on schedule.

Putting theory to work

You might ask, "Which is the most useful of the life-phases theories?" I'm not sure I have a definitive answer. I have benefitted enormously from Bobby Clinton's work, but it really only makes sense if you share Clinton's religious worldview (Dr Clinton served as Professor of Leadership at Fuller Theological Seminary – which holds to Protestant Christian doctrines). If that's not how you see the world, Bobby's probably not your guy.

Levinson is fairly accessible and informed by earlier thinkers like Freud and Erikson, so you may want to begin there, with a couple of caveats. First, Levinson's study sample is small, so tread carefully. Read it for insights to spark reflection, not to lay down immutable laws. Second, his primary research was with men. He published a later study with women, but his primary source is Y-chromosome-centric. If you're over 50, you may want to begin with Vaillant, because the second half of life seems to be his speciality. If you're over 45 and find yourself wondering if you've hit the midlife crisis, and you're ready to do some spiritual work (even if you're not necessarily religious), Richard Rhor's *Falling Upward: A Spirituality for the Two Halves of Life* is worth a shot.[152] I found it super-helpful.

If you haven't already twigged, let me say it explicitly. You'll be a better supervisor and a better resource to your staff if you do some of your own reflection on your life, how you approach it and what kind of presumptions shape your worldview. The life-stages literature is a useful place to begin because it's generally not too pathology-based, it's pretty accessible and will fairly quickly give you some substance with which to work.

---

[152] Rhor, R. *Falling Upward: A Spirituality for the Two Halves of Life* (Jossey-bass, San Francisco, 2011).

Let me give you a few examples of how this plays out.

Using life-phases in supervision

Convergence

I like to run some shared professional development in teams I lead, as well as being committed to providing services that make use of the best theories and techniques available. In one of the teams I have led, each member from time to time was required to design and deliver workshops. Bernice McCarthy's 4MAT learning system transformed my world as a learning facilitator,[153] and I use 4MAT as a design structure for every workshop I create. Because I'm a huge fan of Bernice's work I wanted all of the team to be trained in its use.

The person who stood most to benefit was the most senior member of the team, more than a decade ahead of me in life's journey. At the time that I introduced the idea of learning 4MAT together, this team member probably did more workshop design than the rest of us. When they and I had designed workshops together, I had used the disciplines I learned in my 4MAT training, including the eight-stage learning cycle wheel. My colleague was unimpressed and found my structured and disciplined approach a little mechanical and forced.

In the instructional design space, the rough rule of thumb for workshop design is to allow about three times the delivery time for development. So, a full day workshop should take about three days to create. Without getting too specific, let's just say that my colleague took longer than that. That said, when the time came for delivery – the workshops they built and delivered were always well-received. My colleague came from a corporate consulting background, and their workshops were as good as any you'll see in the corporate world, and better than most.

I knew that using 4MAT made me more efficient. I strongly suspected it could help my colleague. Yet in their own gracious and understated way, my colleague seemed pretty reluctant, and the most basic training would cost between $2000.00 and $3000.00. Here's where the life stages stuff kicks in.

---

[153] https://aboutlearning.com/about-us/4mat-overview/.

At this stage of their career, my colleague has mastered what they're going to master, and they're going to approach their work in the manner that they've crafted over the past half a century in the workforce. A person at this stage of life comes to their job fully formed. It's not that an older worker can't be flexible, it's that by this stage they've taken a long time to develop approaches that work for them. My colleague had established their own groove for workshop design and they were not unhappy with it.

I learned 4MAT at the stage of life where developing skills was paramount (i.e. in my early 30s). I was up for the revolution. My colleague was at a different stage.

Using Clinton's leadership emergence as my frame of reference, I could see that my colleague was clearly in the 'convergence' stage, where all the skills and wisdom they've accrued over their lifetime were being brought to bear for maximum effect. They were probably doing the most effective and the most rewarding work of their life. It's unsurprising that they had no felt need to 'revolutionise' an aspect of their work that was – despite being a little more time consuming than *I* would prefer – delivering excellent results. It was not the time to turn upside down their approach to learning design.

Guided by Clinton, I committed myself to helping my colleague get the very best out of what should be the most satisfying phase of their professional life. The best use of my professional development budget was to provide my colleague with experiences that followed their interests, enriching and energising their work – putting some well-earned 'icing' on their very substantial 'cake'. So, for the most part, my colleague created their own professional development program, and as long as the budget allowed, I signed it off.

That's not how I supervise everyone.

Midlife

Another member of a team I led was clearly unhappy (when one of your team says 'I hate my job' in the middle of a team meeting, it's a fair indicator that things are not going well for them). I'd never had one of my staff say that before. I resisted the urge to remind them that theirs was a great job with good remuneration and lots of flexibility (not to mention a great boss). Something else was up.

In supervision I raised the issue with the unhappy team member and asked them what was behind their outburst. It turned out that the job was not going to script. What had worked in the past was just not working for them now (a classic characteristic of a midlife transition). While I was not unhappy with their work output, the team member was finding the work laborious, and well outside the realm of affairs about which they were most passionate (another midlife transition indicator).

Let me take a quick time-out to clarify something. In the 1960s and 1970s, the 'midlife crisis' was a thing to worry about. It happened to everybody (well, to middle class white men, which in those days was a proxy for everybody). Later research, such as the National Institute on Aging study *Mid-life in the United States*[154], found that only about a fifth of Americans actually experience a crisis of the kind described in the midlife-crisis literature such as Gail Sheehy's *Passages*.[155] Accordingly, I've borrowed Levinson's term 'midlife transition', since change can be experienced as crisis and as process. For some, life seems to progress fairly smoothly and the midlife transition, if there is one, is experienced as uneventful.

Now back to the story. I found myself faced with a choice. My team member was performing adequately and was conducting themselves appropriately, so I had no performance issues to address per se. I could have simply taken a disinterested, "Well, it sucks to be you" approach. I could have suggested that, if this job is such a pain, that they start looking for something else. However, I was concerned that unless my team member could gain some insight into the drivers of their discontent, they could simply jump into another job and find themselves feeling the same way a year or two into it. I knew enough to know that this could be an opportunity for my team member to do a bit of reflection, gain some insight and perhaps gain enough clarity to begin working toward a satisfying and enjoyable role, be it in my team or somewhere else.

While I have coached a number of people through similar challenges to a level of good resolution, I knew that coaching at this kind of depth requires a degree of neutrality that I could not maintain as their boss. My team member needed

---

[154] Mid-life in the United States: A National Longitudinal Study of Health and Wellbeing http://midus.wisc.edu/.
[155] Sheehy, G. *Passages: Predictable Crises of Adult Life* (Dutton New York 1976).

a space where they could say whatever they liked without fear of misunderstanding. They needed someone without stake in the outcome.

I shared my thinking with my team member and offered to divert some professional development budget to them getting some coaching around their vocation. We located a suitable coach and I largely left it with them. Not long after my team member made the transition into a role that virtually had their name written on it.

Early career

I've supervised a number of younger people who've sought my counsel on their career development. As a kid I changed jobs every year, and so I kind of assume that the people in their teens and twenties are only working with me while they're on their way to something else. I tend to get on the front foot and ask them about their hopes and aspirations. If they don't have a post-secondary qualification or a trade certificate, I'll be looking for an opportunity to encourage them toward some formal study. In my observation, the best time to get some foundational studies under your belt is in your twenties, but you probably won't feel the disadvantage of their absence until your late thirties, by which time it's tough to fit in a 24-unit undergrad degree among all the other responsibilities. I'll encourage younger people to get the foundational study out of the way, so that when they're more insight-rich and time-poor in their thirties and forties, they can opt for shorter, more targeted post-grad study that looks great on their resume.

It seems that there's a bit of a narrative doing the rounds that a career has to be carefully curated at every stage and that 'success' (whatever that means) is predicated on making the 'right' choices. Make a 'wrong' choice and you risk wandering into the professional wilderness of the 'bad fit'. Another, complementary narrative is that a young person must discern their 'calling' or sense of 'vocation' at an early age and gain a clear sense of 'giftedness' (translation: what you could be really good at) or forever be doomed to mediocrity and meaninglessness.

Both of these ideas are really important for someone looking to make a career transition in their late forties, where a poor job choice could really do some irrevocable damage to their resume, and where a clear idea of life purpose and unique skill set can assist greatly in making sound career choices. However, in your twenties, you can hardly get it wrong. A clear sense of calling and gifting comes from life experience. Rarely do people have more than a general sense of these in the first half of life.

In my supervision and mentoring conversations with younger people, I reassure them that they have the time and flexibility to try some things. There is so much to learn and so many skills to acquire that just about any context could prove useful, even if it's not exactly pleasant or rewarding. People in their twenties are forgiven for chopping and changing, and they probably don't have an eye-watering mortgage and three kids in high school like they might have a couple of decades later.

As a supervisor of younger people, I'm mindful to help them build foundations that serve them over the long haul, like building skills in communication and influence, and developing habits of self-discipline. The supervision relationship serves as an excellent action reflection context for these to emerge.

It starts with you

In case I haven't sufficiently emphasised it, I'm advocating that you begin by doing your own work on your own life. It's really tempting to grab a theory and immediately apply it to your team members, your boss, your partner, your kids and even your pets (yes, we've had the family discussion about the preferred behavioural styles of our dogs, using the DiSC framework – sad, I know). Life-stage theories, and any other theory with which you might resonate, should be used firstly to help you better understand yourself, and then your staff. It's like the oxygen mask in the aeroplane – fit your own first, then help others. This will provide perspective enabling you to make more thoughtful supervision decisions. It's not about psychoanalysing, diagnosing or fixing people. It is, however about being in a position to offer wise counsel and make decisions in the best interests of your organisation and your worker.

Summary

- Various models map human emergence and development over the lifespan.
- Applying a developmental model can provide perspective and insight in times of crisis and perplexity.

Discussion

- How well can you articulate your sense of vocation? How important is this in your decision-making?
- How do you vary your supervision according to you worker's stage of development?

Action

- Research a development or emergence model and see whether it describes your experience.

Chapter 24
Supervision in strategy and change

Much has been written about organisational change, especially the design and process of change interventions. John's Kotter's *Leading Change* with its eight steps has become sacred writ in the world of change leadership.[156] Strategy carries within it the implication of change, since there's no need to develop a strategy if the organisation's intended course is business as usual.

Much of the strategy and change literature works at the level of ideas and ideals. There are plenty of consultants out there offering to guide organisations through a process of developing a clear vision, a memorable mission statement, a list of organisational values and a set of strategic objectives. While some of the terminology has changed, and the narrative of change has adopted language about constant, disruptive and discontinuous change, the imperative to have ideas like vision, mission and values clearly articulated had been around since the mid-1970s.

While senior leadership teams hunker down for days in off-site workshops to come up with these statements, for the most part the ideas produced never go much beyond a snazzy framed statement in the organisation's office foyer and a strapline on the company letterhead.

Organisations that do put these governing ideas to work generally translate them into a strategy document, which will set out a number of core objectives.[157] More recently, organisations have focused on the importance of embedding values in the organisational culture, and will commonly set out intentional strategies around communicating and reinforcing priorities and behaviours consistent with the stated values of the organisation.

---

[156] Kotter, J. *Leading Change* (Harvard Business Review Press, Boston Massachusetts 1996).

[157] This term comes from Peter Senge's work: Senge, P. *The Fifth Discipline: The Art and Practice of the learning Organisation* (Currency, New York 1990) Jim Collins uses the term 'Core Ideology' to convey the same concept: Collins, J. and Porras, J. *Build to Last: Successful Habits of Visionary Companies BI* (Century, London 1994).

It comes down to supervision

What's lost on most organisations is the critical role supervision plays, both in shaping culture toward the values the organisation espouses, and in bending the organisation's energy and activity toward the objectives set out in the strategy document. Let's take a look at supervision and its role in strategy implementation. In the next chapter we'll take a look at embedding values more specifically.

Strategy

When we explored the process of onboarding a new worker as a kind of template for establishing a supervisory relationship, you'll remember I encouraged supervisors to make reference to the organisation's strategy documents, both to orient the worker toward the current priorities of the organisation, and to ensure any aspects of the strategy that required the direct contribution of the worker were integrated into the worker's work plan.

This of course assumes a couple of things: that the strategy document actually sets out core objectives (I've seen plenty that simply set out the governing ideas and a generalised description of the organisation in the future, apparently hoping it will materialise by osmosis) and that those core objectives have been broken down into concrete, actionable plans. Typical strategy documents set out 3-5 core objectives. In my view, the fewer the better, as it's easier to align effort and allocate resources to one big idea. As more objectives are pursued, attention and effort become diffused and initiatives compete for resources, which leads to competition for control of the organisational narrative.

A relatively straightforward strategy objective like 'grow market share by 20% in three years', would typically be implemented by pushing the product development team to come up with a new line, the marketing department to come up with a new campaign, and tweaking the targets of all the sales reps to push them to increase sales. Dust hands off, job done, check progress every three months. With a bit of luck, the people in products dream up a new line that's a hit, the marketing people manage to find a promotion angle that works, the reps respond to the increased pressure, and the operations side of the organisation has enough latent capacity to deliver. That's hoping a lot of people do what's expected of them and manage to come up with ideas that will be effective. In practice, a large proportion of efforts like this fail because people on the exec level just assume that people will know what to do. They further assume those people have the prerequisite processes and capacity to deliver.

In practice, even such a simple strategy objective will likely require the coordinated involvement of a broad cross-section of the organisation. Nowadays many organisations use project management approaches to initiate their strategic plan, often mapped out using applications like Microsoft Project.

The project management approach breaks the project into discreet phases or sub-projects, then breaks these phases into a series of tasks or milestones. Depending on the size of the organisation and complexity of the objective, these may be further granulated. How far do you need to break things down? Down to the level of actions that can be taken by *individual people* at a *specific time* – i.e. down to the level where it can be itemised on an individual worker's work plan and scheduled into their diary.

Learning from the agile movement

This way of thinking finds its epitome in agile project management techniques like Kanban and Scrum. Kanban dates back to 1940s Japan where an industrial engineer called Taiichi Ohno introduced a visual display system of cards posted on a large board to map the workflow process and monitor work as it progressed through the process. In the early 2000s it was adapted into software development by David Anderson.[158] Scrum breaks a project down into short phases or 'sprints' interspersed by meetings to review and evaluate, often gaining customer feedback that sharpens the project brief.[159] A sprint could be as short as a single day. In general, it's a week or two.

Agile methodologies work in part by breaking complex, multifaceted product development projects into immediately actionable parts and ensuring each team member is absolutely clear on what's expected of them and when they must deliver an outcome. Agile approaches are most commonly found within development teams like software engineering where the whole focus of the

---

[158] Anderson, D. J. *Kanban: Successful Evolutionary Change for Your Technology Business* (Blue Hole Press, Sequim, 2010).
[159] First described by Takeuchi, H. and Nonaka, I. *The New New Product Development Game* (Harvard Business Review January 1986).

team is the project at hand. They may not be universally applicable across all types of change projects, but the disciplines of reducing multifaceted undertakings down to individual responsibilities, making expectations clear and frequently monitoring and reviewing can be applied to just about any effort to implement strategy.

As a supervisor, it's critical to the success of a change initiative that you're absolutely and abundantly clear on the aspects of the initiative that are allocated to the part of the organisation for which you're responsible. If you're not sure or still wondering, it's best to take steps to get clear on what's expected of you before you attempt to delegate various components of the change initiative out to your direct reports. If you can get a written project brief with specifications and timelines for your area, all the better. If that document does not exist, I would suggest you work with your supervisor or the management team to which you belong to generate it.

Once you're clear, it's time to look at how you will break the brief into components actionable by your individual workers. You may choose to undertake this task by yourself or hand the task to your workers as a team. Doing it yourself is quick and unambiguous – but it relies solely on your depth of expertise and forgoes the opportunity to build engagement by getting the workers involved in decision-making.

However you tackle the task, your guiding ideas are clarity and individual responsibility. Representing the overall project or initiative using visual tools like a Gantt chart will assist in achieving clarity and help you figure out the order in which various components should be completed. Ensuring each aspect of the project is assigned to an individual, even if they require the input and collaboration of others, enables you to use the basic discipline of supervision to keep the whole project on track. I have a maxim: *a shared responsibility is a shirked responsibility*. It's almost impossible to hold groups of people accountable.

If you're leading a management team where each member has their own team, it will generally be up to the individual managers to break down their allocated responsibilities and delegate them to their respective workers.

Sure, all of this sounds like a lot of work. That's because it is – which goes some way to explaining why change initiatives and strategic plans so often flounder. Change initiatives that have a broad scope and initiate substantial disruption will generally require a dedicated project manager to hold all the threads. Tacking management of a complex project onto the responsibilities of an already busy manager is a pretty reliable way to ensure the project fails.

Cross-functional and change leadership teams

If we're going to talk about change initiatives, we'll need to talk a little about cross-functional teams, adhocracies and dual operating systems. John Kotter's classic *Leading Change*, calls for the formation of a powerful guiding coalition that will usually operate alongside the structure of the organisation.[160] In his later work *Accelerate*, Kotter advocates using a 'dual operating system' to accomplish change: the regular company structure as described by the organisation chart, which maintains business as usual, and a network-type structure to drive the change initiative.[161] American futurist and businessman Alvin Toffler, best known for his classic *Future Shock*,[162] described such flexible, disposable organisational structures as 'adhocracies'. Various change and process improvement methodologies like Total Quality Management (TQM) advocate forming cross-functional teams made up of people from various departments with a variety of knowledge and skills to tackle a particular improvement project.

What all these approaches share is formation of a working group that sits outside the normal organisational structure. We've spent the last couple of hundred pages talking about clear responsibilities and accountabilities set out in neat and specific documents. How does conventional organisational design thinking square with these non-hierarchical, parallel structures? More pointedly, how does a supervisor manage a worker who is also a participant in a structure where the supervisor has no authority and probably no line of sight?

The resultant ambiguity is a frequent cause of stress for workers involved in change projects. Usually, the change project is energising and exciting, involves interaction with motivated people (often people much more senior than they) and may include some stretch-learning. It feels to the worker like

---

[160] Kotter, J. **Leading Change** (Harvard Business Review Press, Boston 1996).
[161] Kotter, J. **Accelerate** (Harvard Business Review Press, Boston 2014).
[162] Toffler, A. **Future Shock: A Study of Bewilderment in the face of Accelerating Change** (The Bodley Head, London 1970).

they're doing something *really* important. Compare this to the generally less exciting discipline of their business-as-usual role. It's sometimes hard to keep the balance when the change project beckons.

Conversely, as a boss, you've still got work to be done and KPIs to hit, and probably don't particularly appreciate your team workers being absent while they draw up CEDAC charts and chow down on pizza. I've had TQM projects go belly-up simply because the team members' line management made it too hard for them to participate.

Recognising the potential for the adhocracy or the cross-functional team and the conventional hierarchy to either serve or sabotage each other is the beginning of wisdom in the dance of organisational change. Responsible supervision of a worker who's engaged in the change project requires the boss to have a decent line of sight on what's expected of their worker in their participation in the change initiative, and negotiating a fair balance of expectations with their regular, business-as-usual role.

In supervision, it's helpful to make this balance explicit. It may require a conversation with the leader of the change initiative to negotiate some reasonable limits. Getting the expectations clear, even down to the timeslots where the worker is involved in the change initiative, will help prevent the worker being the meat in the sandwich between their regular boss and the leader of the change project.

If you're leading an adhocracy like a cross-functional work team or a change project team, you would do well to be in occasional contact with the regular bosses of your team members. Not only is this a basic courtesy, it also gives you the opportunity to anticipate and negotiate expectation conflicts before the worker becomes a bargaining chip. If there's a clear, common understanding of what's expected of the worker, they won't be forced into choosing a side.

Summary

- Successful change or strategy implementation requires the initiative to be granulated down to the level of individual workers' contributions.
- Supervisors hold workers accountable for completing their respective contributions to the initiative.
- The agile movement exemplifies breaking a strategy down to parts actionable by individuals in short time frames.
- Adhocracies require cooperation between project leaders and line managers so individual workers don't end up being the 'meat in the sandwich'.

Discussion

- What's your experience in implementing change or strategy? How was the initiative broken down into parts to be accomplished by individuals?

Implementation

- If you have responsibility for implementing an aspect of strategy, how can you improve the involvement and engagement of your workers?

Chapter 25
Supervision and culture

How many times have you walked into a foyer, or read an email footer and seen an organisation's values proudly displayed or listed, only to experience close enough to the diametric opposite when you interact with the organisation and its services?

If you've been around the leadership space for a while, you've probably sat through tedious consultations trying to distil a statement of four or five values out of hundreds Post-it notes stuck up on a wall. The result is usually something akin to 'motherhood and apple pie'. The words end up collated into a statement that nobody really cares about.

No wonder most people are a little cynical about values statements.

Organisational values statements have been around for at least 70 years, often embedded in the organisation's proclamations of vision and mission.

Values and culture

Despite the prevailing scepticism, values statements have more recently come into sharper focus as organisations seek to be more intentional about their culture. One of my current clients lists 'grace' as the first of their five values. The major healthcare network in my area lists 'kindness' and 'humility' among theirs.

Simply formulating a values statement to hang in the foyer or include in your email signature block will not do anything appreciable to influence your organisational culture. In fact, it may simply make your workers and customers cynical when they observe behaviour that's inconsistent with the values stated.

If an organisation is going to be intentional about embodying the values it espouses, those with responsibility for supervising people must take primary responsibility for putting some intention behind the aspiration.

As a supervisor, you have a degree of responsibility for the culture of your organisational downline – those workers who report to you, the workers who in turn report to them and so on. Whatever your leadership style, whatever your supervision approach, whether you're relentlessly calculating or irresponsibly *laisse faire*, you will unavoidably shape the culture of your downline. The challenge I'm putting to you is this: do you want that culture to just happen, or do you want to put some thought and intentionality into it?

Presuming we're agreed that you want to be purposeful in the culture you cultivate, the question becomes 'how?'

The psychology of culture

There are all sorts of drivers of organisational culture, from societal forces to the temperament of the organisation's founder. Most of them are not readily visible in themselves and can't be influenced in any direct way. Anthropologists have devised models that trace culture down to epistemological and even ontological underpinnings. These might make for an interesting study, but the realm where culture turns up in an observable and modifiable way is behaviour. The words and deeds of the people who make up the organisation are the products and perpetuators of organisational culture. Every organisation's culture will have subtle and generally unconscious ways of rewarding some behaviours and punishing others. These rewards and punishments are usually so presumed, so habitual and so automatic that nobody notices.

The term behaviourists use is reinforcement. When a certain behaviour results in a desirable outcome, no matter how subtle, that behaviour is thought to be positively reinforced. The inverse is true of behaviours that seem to prompt an undesirable outcome.

If you studied high-school or undergraduate psychology, you'll immediately recognise the previous paragraphs as B. F. Skinner's theory of operant conditioning,[163] which in turn traces its inspiration back to John B. Watson's work at Johns Hopkins University in the second decade of the twentieth century. Granted, the theory is old and tends not to be taught as a therapeutic approach anymore. Further, the idea of intentional punishment raises all sorts of objections, ranging from its failure to promote desired behaviour (only

---

[163] Ferster, C. B. & Skinner, B. F. **Schedules of Reinforcement** (Appleton-Century-Crofts, New York, 1957).

discouraging undesirable behaviour) through to its potential to foster resentment and aggressive responses. Some would claim that behaviourism has been used to justify doing harm. On top of all that, behaviourism has attracted a general disdain because it seems to reduce humans to the status of large, complicated lab rats.

All of those problems notwithstanding, one thing remains uncomfortably unavoidable: the general principles of behaviourism are empirically sound and can be readily observed in any group of social mammals you care to watch. What's worse, it's how you learned the basic social rules and it's the primary means your parents used to shape you into the civilised and sophisticated leader you are today. Not that rats, macaques or frazzled parents tend to read Skinner. It's just how social mammals are wired. What Skinner was observing in his rats was an extreme version of the basic principles of socialisation.

The key concept in creating or shifting culture is the process by which culture is inculcated; people do what they do (in part) because they are socialised or conditioned to do so by the subtle influences of their context. Sure, people have their own values and aspirations, and people's behaviour varies according to context and temperament, but the socialisation forces of a context have the power to curb and even quash these individual variations. The more intense the socialisation pressure, the less variation you'll observe.

This all struck me years ago when I was consulting with a group of leaders in a particular religious group. Now you might assume I'm about to describe a bunch of monks in saffron robes or some brothers in coarse hair habits tied about with a rope. Nope, this was a group that was noted for being contemporary in its style, using rock concert style music, lighting and multimedia (including smoke machines). Yet when the 30 or so leaders showed up for the workshop, they showed up in uniform. They were all men, all dressed in dark business trousers, a light, open-necked business shirt, topped with a black leather jacket. This organisation did not have a stated dress code, and these guys had come from all over the country. Yet here they were, all dressed the same.

It's not that socialisation is bad. When I was a kid, racism and sexism were pretty much ubiquitous. Only the most up-tight and self-righteous member of the joy-police would tut disapprovingly at a joke made at the expense of people other than straight white males. If someone were to act that way nowadays, they would generally experience firsthand how socialisation pressure is brought to bear – eye rolls and groans, disapproving scowls and perhaps direct confrontation. Keep that behaviour up and the only company they'll keep is that of other racist sexists. Mainstream culture has shifted and the conditioning that Skinner observed has played a part.

It's important to note that conditioning works by appealing to some pretty basic human drives and desires. The most basic are food, sex and safety, followed by security, belonging, esteem and significance, as described by Maslow's Hierarchy of Needs.[164] In the example above, the racist sexist is met with overt risks to his sense of belonging and esteem. Supervision that respects workers and is undertaken ethically will generally favour using encouraging reinforcers (i.e. reward or the promise of reward for desired behaviours) and appeal to the drives and needs higher on Maslow's pyramid.

It may seem like manipulation, but the simple fact is that human motivation is emotional, no matter how much we want to enter into a cerebral argument to the contrary. The human intellect serves an important role in regulating motivation and steering it toward the greater good. Jonathan Haidt uses the metaphor of the elephant and the rider to illustrate. The rider represents our conscious reasoning. It can steer and direct, but it's not the source of power. The elephant represents all the rest of our mental processes which are out of our direct conscious awareness.[165] Sometimes the rider can maintain surprising control: humans will endure discomfort and deprivation based on intellectual principle even when their emotions urge them to find relief. But get that elephant sufficiently upset and the rider is powerless.

Haidt further describes how the emotional or intuitive response precedes the rational or intellectual response, and how the intellectual response can be shaped by prior emotional priming.[166] Humans are not rational beings, we're

---

[164] Maslow, A. H. *A Theory of Human Motivation* Psychological Review, *50*(4), 1943 pp370-96.
[165] Haidt, J. *The Happiness Hypothesis: Finding Modern Truth in Ancient Wisdom* (Basic Books, New York, 2006).
[166] Haidt, J. *The Righteous Mind: Why Good people are Divided by Politics and Religion* (Vintage, New York, 2012).

rationalising beings. Conditioning attaches an emotional valence to particular ideas or prompts.

Conditioning at work

For a supervisor who takes seriously their part in shaping organisational culture, the trick is to figure out what you (often unwittingly) reward and punish. The biggest challenge is being able to spot the subtle operation of conditioning in action. An example might serve to illustrate.

Back in my earliest days as an HR manager, I tried my best to provide a great service to my internal customers by doing whatever I could to be helpful. But sometimes my helping ended up being somewhat unhelpful. For instance, a leading hand from the production area might wander into my office reporting a problem with one of their workers. They tell me their tale of woe and I listen with as much empathy as I can muster. I nod sagely. "Leave it with me."

A little while later I stroll out to the production floor, sidle up to the 'problem' worker and have a little heart to heart. Using my best efforts to be charming and diplomatic (no small challenge for me), I seek to win the worker over by eliciting their assistance as a personal favour. Shop floor workers can sometimes be manipulated when people who appear to be more powerful than they appear to take them into their confidence. Like magic the problem is solved. Well, kind of.

My action did nothing to build any kind of self-awareness, skill or knowledge for the leading hand. In effect I just made them dependent on me. Next time they have a problem with a worker, they will predictably show up in my office. Rinse and repeat. I've successfully socialised the leading hand to delegate their responsibilities to me. This could have kept going until every supervisor in the company was queued up outside my door and the entire production floor workforce was engaged in 'doing me a personal favour'.

What's worse, if the leading hand was doing something inappropriate of which I was unaware, I would have been inadvertently colluding with them and building a culture that tolerates behaviour that should be called out.

Fortunately, someone introduced me to the vivid image of seeing every person who walked through my door as if they had a rather troublesome monkey on their back. I could talk to them about the monkey, discuss with them how it got there and how they might take steps to rid themselves of it, but under no circumstances was I to take the monkey from them. "I am not the keeper of monkeys!" I would repeatedly tell myself. From them on I saw myself more as a coach and less of a problem-solver.

Conditioning and emotional process

There's a good chance you're reading this with that uneasy feeling that you kinda get this but aren't sure (I get this feeling all the time when I'm reading). I doubt that anyone ever develops sufficient insight, awareness and observational acuity to clearly and fully see how their choices and the knock-on effects thereof influence the culture of their families, workplaces and community organisations. Yet, if we're going to talk about values, as supervisors we have an implicit obligation to try.

You'll note how much the instinctive human drives were activated in the little anecdote above. The leading hand was feeling anxious and wanted to find quick relief from the unpleasant feelings generated by anxiety. I was made anxious by the leading hand's anxiety and instinctively knew I would feel better if they could feel better. Further, I saw this as an opportunity to be useful, boosting my sense of security by proving my value to the company and accruing some esteem along the way. Then there's me playing with the worker's esteem by offering them status with someone who's perceived to be higher up in the company hierarchy. The emotional process seems subtle until you look at the drivers, then it becomes all too obvious.

Thinking it through

Your most valuable tool in the art of intentionally shaping culture is not a repertoire of hacks and tricks, but the time-consuming and sometimes discomforting discipline of reflection. Reflection for this intent and purpose begins by thinking over your behaviour and asking yourself (with as much honesty as you can rally) questions like:

- *What purpose did my behaviour – words, tone, choices – serve?* Bear in mind that behaviour almost always serves a purpose, especially repeated behaviours. Also bear in mind that most behaviour is driven by our basic needs, no matter how sophisticated the overlying rationale we use to cover it. Figuring out the purpose a behaviour serves requires well developed insight and a willingness to be brutally honest with oneself. It takes practice.

- *Who turned out the winner from my behaviour?* Who had their anxiety relieved, their reputation enhanced, their esteem bolstered, or their workload lightened? What did they do to influence my behaviour? (Figure this out and you just identified the behaviour you're encouraging.)
- *Who turned out the loser from my behaviour?* Who had their anxiety heightened, their reputation tarnished, their esteem eroded, their burden increased? What did they do to influence behaviour? (Figure this out and you just identified the behaviour you're discouraging).

Now ask yourself, with regard to your answers to the three questions above:

- *Did I conduct myself consistently with my own personal values?* This is a question about your integrity.
- *Did I reinforce behaviour that is consistent with the kind of culture we're trying to promote here?* This is a question about your congruence with the organisation's stated intentions.
- *Did I discourage behaviour that runs counter to the kind of culture we're trying to promote here?* This too is a question about congruence, and it also might reveal where you're chickening out on taking a stand.

One of the disciplines I've used to help my reflection is a personal journal. I'll write about four journal entries each month, more if I'm processing a big challenge, less if life is kind of busy but relatively uneventful. You could use the questions above as prompts to journal out critical incidents from your role as a supervisor. You'll be amazed at how much this will sharpen you up and help you supervise in a more thoughtful manner.

Another helpful resource you may wish to employ is a coach. Yes, they're expensive, and yes, they take time, and absolutely yes, they will make you uncomfortable. But a good coach will help you gain insight as to what kind of culture you're creating with greater speed and depth than you'll ever be able to figure out on your own.

Using reflection and a coach are both tools to help you become more thoughtful about your behaviour, your drives and how you influence culture. Undesirable cultural characteristics like favouritism, prejudice, expediency, and deceit may look like carefully crafted tactics, but for the most part they are automatic behaviours, instinctive responses to the challenges and vicissitudes of life in the workplace. Because they're instinctive, they go unexamined and often unchallenged. Shifting to a more honourable and principled culture requires the disciplined and consistent activation of the intellect to moderate and even counter the instincts.

Of course, there are more direct and explicit ways to influence culture, some of which we've touched on in earlier chapters, and we'll get to them in a moment. I've dealt firstly with the more subtle ways that culture is shaped because the mechanisms are so powerful, so pervasive and yet mostly unseen. You can engage in direct means of influencing culture as much as you like, but it will come to nought if you're inadvertently reinforcing the opposite by your instinctive behaviour.

The Germans have a wonderful expression that, roughly translated, goes like this – "What he builds with his hands he knocks down with his butt." Let's look at some direct ways to 'build' culture – just be careful not to knock it over with thoughtless words and decisions.

The standard you walk past

Back in chapter 10 we spent some time considering the idea, 'The standard you walk past is the standard you accept'. I used one example of me flouting the uniform rules at school, and another of a worker who turns up late. While I was not explicit about it at the time, I was indirectly talking about organisational culture.

What if I, having established that I could safely ignore the rules about uniform, started to wonder about the elasticity of other rules, like attendance, or addressing teachers by their correct title, or maybe even 'borrowing' some tools from one of the trade-skills classrooms? What if other students had observed my attire and that of my rule-flouting classmate, and decided that they too could turn up wearing whatever they pleased?

Fortunately for the school and for my moral development, it never occurred to me to test other rules and the rest of my classmates more or less complied with the uniform code. But my trend-setting friend, over the course of the year, became a less and less frequent attendee at classes and I doubt he was challenged about that either. The school did not descend into anarchy, but it had lapsed into a kind of slack, disinterested culture that showed up in a range of other, subtle ways.

Imagine our hypothetical, perpetually late worker had been allowed to continue their tardy ways. It's unlikely they would suddenly get with the program and start being punctual. It's possible that they would gradually begin to turn up later and later. It's also likely that other workers would notice their undisciplined ways and wait for them to be challenged. If no challenge was forthcoming, they're likely to feel a little tempted to see if they too might be able to enjoy a little more sleep before rolling into work each day. Such a contagion of slackness will usually find some kind of limit, but don't be surprised how far things could descend before the limit is reached.

I can't resist a quick illustration. If you've read from the beginning, no doubt you've figured out I'm a churchgoer. Years ago, life circumstances unfolded such that I was looking for a new destination for my churchgoing inclination. A number of my friends were part of a church in the next suburb, and they encouraged me to come check it out one Sunday. The sign out front advised that the Sunday service began at 10:00 AM, so the following weekend, my wife and I showed up a couple of minutes before 10:00.

The doors were unlocked, but the place was deserted, except for one guy busily stoking two roaring open fires that provided heating for the rustic auditorium. We stood perplexed for a couple of minutes wondering what to. I retraced my steps outside and checked the service time on the sign facing the road. Sure enough, the service was advertised to begin at 10:00. We decided to take a seat and wait to see what would happen.

About ten minutes later the musicians began to drift in, casually setting up, plugging-in and tuning-up before beginning a quick run through rehearsal of the music for the day. Around 10:30 congregation members began appearing, some standing about to chat, others ambling toward a seat and settling in. The place was about half-full when someone approached a microphone at the front, extended a welcome to those assembled and the service commenced a little after 10:45.

Chatting with a friend afterward (they had arrived at 10:40), I remarked on the laid-back approach to starting the service. They observed that the time had gradually slipped back because the leaders tended to wait until most people had turned up before starting. So more people started turning up late since there was no point getting there at the posted start time and gradually they'd got to where they were.

I've been to other churches where a countdown is displayed on a huge video screen above the stage. The countdown gets to zero bang-on the advertised starting time, and as 00:00 appears on the screen, the band hits the first chord.

Now, if you're from, or have had exposure to a culture that runs by events rather than by clocks (e.g. most traditional tribal cultures) you'd recognise the cultural presupposition of the first church: the gig starts when the people are there. It's not that one way is right and the other wrong. But as a supervisor, you're responsible for the behaviours you reinforce and the culture that results.

Directly reinforcing values

Some organisations have sought to be more proactive in fostering certain values and have sought to specifically promote and acknowledge behaviour that exemplifies their stated values. There are a number of ways to tackle this, and most rely on the supervisor to maintain the emphasis on particular values and their indicative behaviours.

One way is to ask workers to share stories about them witnessing or experiencing someone acting in a way that exemplifies the organisational values. This can take place in individual supervision or in team meetings. When an anecdote is shared, the importance of the person's action can be reinforced by asking reinforcing questions. Reinforcement is more about basic feelings and drives than it is about cerebral alignment so questions about the subjective experience of the exemplary behaviour will more immediately and powerfully associate the desired behaviour with good feelings.

However, values reinforcement is almost always an appeal to nobler, more thoughtful behaviour in preference to instinctive reactions driven by the less thoughtful parts of the brain. So the reinforcement process will also need to engage the rational parts of the brain – the evaluative and planning functions. This means stimulating thinking about the feelings.

So, are all the parts of your brain hurting yet? Let's paint a hypothetical to illustrate.

Let's imagine a worker at the healthcare network I mentioned earlier, where 'Patient First' and 'Kindness' are listed as their top two values. The worker is a nurse just coming off a gruelling night on the ward. They're tired and they're a bit jetlagged from adjusting their body clock. As the nurse heads out of the main entrance to the hospital, they spy an elderly man in a wheelchair, being pushed by his equally elderly wife, who is struggling against the slope of the wheelchair ramp. The nurse doubles back, assists the couple to navigate the slope and guides them to the admission desk.

This simple act of consideration and kindness was observed by a staffer from an outpatient unit, who was arriving for work just as the nurse reached the struggling couple. In congratulating the nurse on being a customer service superhero, they heard the night shift backstory.

In the daily stand-up meeting of the outpatient unit, the team leader recounts the values of the organisation and asks team members for an example they had seen recently. The staff member shares the story they had just seen unfold on the entrance ramp. The team leader asks, "What do you think was going on for the nurse when she saw the couple struggling on the ramp?" Another team member responds describing the probable conflict between the nurse's instincts – "I'm exhausted, I'll pretend not to see them." – and the more thoughtful, principled response, "Helping those two is more important than me feeling tired."

The team leader nods in agreement and asks, "How do you think the nurse felt after helping the couple?" Various team members respond with comments like "Good", "Still tired" and "Better than if they'd just kept walking." The team leader agrees heartily with the final comment. They might ask, "What do you think that simple action meant to the elderly couple?" And you can probably imagine the responses.

If you examine the process of that simple, 60-second values-reinforcing conversation, you'll see how the team leader invited the team to enter into the nurse's experience. A team member described the 'values vs instincts' tussle in the nurse's mind, and the team leader invited the team to recognise that acting thoughtfully, in accordance with values and principles, ultimately leaves a person feeling better than if they just act on their self-preserving instincts.

I acknowledge the example seems a little bit spoon-fed and a tad cheesy (even though it's based on an actual event), but I'm hoping it illustrates engaging the feeling side while reinforcing thoughtful, principled action through exemplification and acknowledgement. A regular conversation along those lines in every team in every department will do more to embed values in an organisation's staff than an off-site workshop costing thousands and taking all day.

Values and supervision

A further way to embed values with your workers is to ask values-framed coaching questions in individual supervision, and in facilitating team-based decision-making. We looked at coaching as a supervision mechanism back in chapter 22. You'll remember I set out Whitmore's *Goal, Reality, Options, Will* model as a kind of archetype for coaching. Let's look at how each stage of the model can engage values.

When setting the goals for the conversation, you may find opportunity to ask questions like, "What values underpin your goal? What does that goal say about what's important to you?" That might lead to the worker setting out exactly what's important to them. You could draw them out on where their personal values mesh or clash with the values of the organisation. It's not about correcting the worker so much as helping them see where they may be pursuing a direction that doesn't reinforce what's important to the organisation. At some stage you may need to take off the coaching hat and be more directive.

When interrogating reality, there are multiple opportunities to introduce values into the conversation. As the worker describes their situation, their challenges, blockages and the circumstances that have contributed, you can invite them to reflect on the values that lie beneath the behaviours and decisions they describe. You don't necessarily need to use the word 'values'. Questions like, "What does that suggest about that person's priorities?" or "If that's the situation, what does it tell you about what's important to...?" (you, the other person, that work team, etc).

Values-based questions help develop in your worker the habit of thinking in terms of values – not just the explicit values to which the organisation aspires, but the actual, implicit values that are embodied and reinforced in the day-to-day rough and tumble of organisational life. Pretty quickly workers will learn to evaluate whether the implicit values align with those displayed in the fancy frame in the office foyer. The aim is not to make them cynical about the organisation's sincerity in espousing values, but to help workers think through their own contribution to the organisational culture.

As the conversation turns to considering options, it's easy to ask how various options might reinforce or undermine particular values. An obvious question like, "How does that option serve to support the organisation's values?" will get hackneyed pretty quickly so mix it up with questions like, "If you were to implement that option, what kind of behaviour would it reinforce, and what would it discourage?" Another possibility might be, "How will that option support the kind of culture you're trying to create, and what might it undermine?" If the context of the conversation provides the opportunity, especially if the reality exploration shows how a particular organisational value is being eroded, you could ask, "Give me an option that will serve to encourage ..." (insert whatever organisational value applies).

By the time we get to the 'Will' quadrant, the preferred option has probably already been screened for values consistency. Now comes the tricky part of implementation. How we go about pursuing a particular strategy or tactic can speak just as loudly as the action itself. The means of moving forward can either serve or undermine your intentions. For example, if you value being agile, pulling together a large, broadly representative consultative group would pretty much ensure what happens next will be anything but. Perhaps you value being consultative and empowering workers, so you decide to run a series of consultation sessions to brainstorm ideas and workshop some possible actions. But if the timing and process of the session is simply imposed, or happens to disrupt some long-planned high-priority activities of your workers, you risk making things worse. This kind of congruence failure is more common in organisations than you might think.

No one finds this kind of discipline easy, and it will take a great deal of intentionality to develop the habit of bringing values into consideration as you supervise. The weird paradox is this – being intentional about values and the culture they produce is actually a value in itself. To embed that value requires the same degree of intentionality, reinforcement and consistency that it would to build any other value into the culture of an organisation.

Just in case I haven't hammered away on this issue enough already, let me play it one more time with feeling. The values that your words, your behaviour and your decisions convey will be much more readily believed than any statements of aspiration you might make. Unless the way you conduct yourself is congruent with the culture you're trying to create, you'll be knocking down with your butt what you're trying to build with your hands.

Summary

- Values – what's rewarded and prioritised – play a big part in shaping and preserving organisational culture.
- Values are formed and reinforced by conditioning: by what's rewarded and what's punished, even if these are too subtle to notice.
- To intentionally influence culture, we need to examine carefully how our behaviour has a conditioning effect on our workers.
- Values are also shaped by the behaviour we accept or confront.
- We can reinforce values by intentionally associating the desired behaviours with positive emotions.

Discussion

- Think of a prevailing behaviour in your workplace that's counter to your values. How is it reinforced?
- Reflect on a recent interaction with a worker. What behaviours did your behaviour subtly encourage and subtly discourage?

Action

- Identify a value you would like to embed into your team's culture and identify three ways you can reinforce it.

Chapter 26
Supervision and organisational design

Structures like pancakes

The organisational trend in the 1990s was to shoot for super-flat structures. Credit squeezes and a deep recession meant the '90s was the era when the terms 'rightsizing' (a euphemism for wholesale slashing of headcount) came into its own and emphasis was disproportionately toward 'middle management'. Middle managers are a handy target because they tend to have relatively little power (i.e. it's not them making the slash-and-burn decisions) and they're usually not unionised, so any action taken against them will not meet with an organised response.

The result has been the assumed orthodoxy of 'flat structure' doctrine – remove as many layers of hierarchy as you dare. The theory goes that, the fewer layers of bureaucracy between the CEO and the shop floor, the more efficient organisation. This would be fine if maintaining purpose and rolling out strategy was simply a matter of broadcasting information, with everybody immediately and intuitively knowing what to do. The reality is that ideas about purpose and strategy tend to be a little abstract and require translation into concrete behaviour. Strategy implementation involves change, and translating the description of the intended change into actual change itself is a fraught process. It's more about leadership than it is about snappy comms.

If you've read this book from the start, you'll probably be sick of me re-emphasising the idea that supervision is a conversation about clear expectations, and clear feedback about whether the expectations have been met. The chances of everybody immediately and perfectly fulfilling the responsibilities on their Position Description (PD) are remote. Likewise, the chances of a worker implementing an expected change set out in a strategy document on the basis of a single directive is almost nil. People will make all kinds of assumptions, misinterpret directions, put up resistance and go off on tangents. Or they'll just ignore the change directive and see what happens.

If an organisation's leadership has drunk the flat-structure kool-aid, they may have managers and team leaders with up to 25 direct reports – i.e. 25 people to whom their expectations must be clarified, whose performance they need to observe and to whom timely and meaningful feedback must be given. On top of all that, there are 25 locations of potential conflict to manage, 25 opportunities for misconduct or poor performance sufficient to warrant formal corrective action, 25 opportunities for someone to resign and create a recruitment and onboarding challenge – you get the idea. On top of all that, there's that strategy implementation thing we're supposed to be doing...

The deceptive nature of super-flat structures is that they work for a little while. If an organisation guts their middle management tiers or continually spreads their middle management out over more and more reporting relationships as the organisation grows, they will generally not see much downside for perhaps a year or two. The organisation looks more efficient and the proportion of overhead costs to total turnover reduces. The accountants are loving it.

However, over time, the tacit understanding of what's expected becomes foggy. The communications between the decision makers and the decision implementers becomes less clear. Problems that could be simply resolved pile up because managers are stretched too thin. New hires are not properly onboarded and so their performance never quite reaches par, quality standards slip without being challenged. Compliance starts to become an aspiration, and then a running joke. It's usually about this time that consultants like me get called in.

Spans of control

When I enter an organisation as a consultant, one of the first things I do is to ask members of the client organisation to draw the organisation chart. Typically, each member of a team or management group will draw the chart differently. Often there is confusion as to who reports to whom. It's also common to see very broad spans of control. A span of control is simply the number or people reporting directly to an individual. A manager with one direct report has a narrow span of control. A manager with 20 reports has a broad span of control.

Ideal spans of control vary according to a range of factors including seniority of the role, the other non-supervisory responsibilities attached to the role and the nature of the work being supervised. There is a reasonable amount of research available as to the typical functional span of control in different roles and industries, but it's too broad a range to deal with exhaustively here. Instead, let me set out a few principles and some examples.

Basic anthropology suggests that humans can typically manage about a dozen close relationships, and this seems to be replicated in organisational dynamics. It's a stretch for most people to directly supervise more than about 12 people, no matter what the other parameters may be.

The idea of spans of control began in the military. I know we're not fighting a war here, but military endeavour has been around a long time, and the stakes are pretty high. Military structures and broad strategy tend to be fairly consistent across time and cultures, so there's much to learn about effectively organising people to accomplish a goal under high pressure.

In perhaps the first military reference to spans of control, General Sir Ian Hamilton, commander of the British forces in the Dardanelles campaign in World War I, is quoted as stating, "The average human brain finds its effective scope in handling three to six other brains."[167] Later research has coalesced around seven, although some outliers put the number between 20 and 30.

In the Australian Army, it's unusual to find a non-commissioned officer with more than about seven direct reports. A platoon of up to 40 under a sergeant or lieutenant will be structured into a number of crews of about four, each led by a lance corporal. A corporal will oversee two to three crews, and those corporals will report to the sergeant. As you can see, the spans are pretty small. While the terms and titles vary, these numbers are fairly consistent across global militaries.

Further up the chain, the spans don't get any larger. A major will typically command a sub-unit of three platoons assisted by a captain. A lieutenant colonel will command a unit of three to five sub-units.

_____

[167] Quoted by Dale, E. *Management Theory and Practice* (McGraw-Hill New York: 1978), 35.

In the civilian world, organisations tend to work best when they structure in a similar fashion. Given the stakes are a little lower, the numbers can stretch a little but not too much. Let's consider some examples.

A typical CEO will command a senior leadership team of three to four others, typically the leaders of Operations, Finance, IT and People and Culture. Add to that an EA and you have five. Expand that group much beyond five and it begins to get gnarly. What will typically happen is that the person or portfolio to which the CEO least wants to give their attention will find themselves increasingly on the outer – supervision becomes perfunctory, correspondence goes unacknowledged, reports get skimmed, and meetings are postponed or cancelled.

The ratios will usually look pretty similar for any of those executives (i.e. three to five reports). Go much broader than that, and people start drifting off the executive's radar.

When we get to mid-level and first tier supervisors, things become a little more variable, primarily around the degree to which a supervisor has their own set of work outcomes to achieve beyond supervision and the nature of the work being supervised.

A team leader in a call centre will usually be responsible for supervising the team and not a whole lot else. All the team members do essentially the same job, the work is routine and narrow in scope, and basic performance metrics are produced automatically. In that kind of situation, or perhaps an accounts department supervisor overseeing a group of accounts payable and receivable clerks, the supervisor may be able to look after up to fifteen people. Add some extra work for the supervisor (like doing their own recruitment, selection and induction), diversify the work being supervised, make the performance criteria a little harder to measure, and the effective span of control goes down.

Even when everything is uniform, simple and well-defined, we can't escape the fact that people are only human. Put a bunch of them in the same room for long enough and sooner or later they will conflict. They travel a lifespan journey that will include challenges such as partnering, pregnancy, parenting, separation, addiction, bereavement, injury and disease. They can be distressed, distracted and destructive. As a supervisor you might want to write these off as personal challenges that are none of your concern, but they impact the whole person and the knock-on effects will leak into the workplace. When performance and workplace relationships are impacted, they become your concern.

The effective span of control for managers overseeing workers in technically and/or emotionally challenging roles will be smaller. Roles like this include: leading a team of consultant or research engineers (highly technical); leading a team of primary care mental health workers (highly emotional) or leading a unit of ICU nurses (technical and emotional). The workable upper limit of direct reports would be seven at the most, and even that would be a challenge.

By now I am sensing reader objections. You will no doubt be able to cite examples where broader spans of control seem to work just fine. Perhaps you can. I would be keen to look at issues like absenteeism and turnover, along with quality and compliance data. I would also be interested to benchmark the work outputs with analogous teams that have narrower spans of control. Remember, you can get away with a broad span for a little while, and if you're willing to forego optimal performance, a healthy workplace culture and effective implementation of strategy, you can stretch those spans out as wide as you dare. But if you've stayed with me this far, I'm guessing you're not willing to forego them.

The rise of the roboboss

Over the past few years, productivity monitoring software has emerged that may not directly promise to electronically supervise your workers, but offers a performance feedback loop that's intended to give workers real-time information about their performance against a set benchmark, or ranks their performance in comparison to their overall workgroup. The idea is that the supervisor need only pay attention to those who don't meet the stated targets or those who fall one standard deviation below the mean performance level of the group. The rest can pretty much be left to their own devices, just as long as their numbers are acceptable. Large order fulfilment warehouses typically operate by roboboss.

I'm hoping that, given you've read all of the foregoing, you're giving this idea some serious eye rolls right now. Organisations that sell these software packages will give you valid and no doubt truthful data about the almost immediate performance improvement experienced by companies that implement their systems. By the same token, I can almost instantly cut the running costs of your car by telling you to forget about servicing it and only pay attention when a red warning lamp comes on (yellow ones are just a suggestion). In both cases, the immediate cost-benefit will sooner or later be undermined by greater maintenance costs. A bounce in productivity is frequently followed by increased absenteeism and turnover. This in turn increases time spent by first-line managers training people, and the HR team recruiting and engaging in conflict resolution. If the roboboss is applied with sufficient rigour it may even increase workers compensation claims, as any effort toward work intensification is apt to do.

You may remember earlier in the book I introduced you to Frederick Taylor and his theory of scientific management: analyse the job, redesign it for maximum efficiency, and teach the worker to do it exactly according to the new design. Taylor believed it "... is only through enforced standardization of methods, enforced adoption of the best implements and working conditions, and enforced cooperation that this faster work can be assured. And the duty of enforcing the adoption of standards and enforcing this cooperation rests with management alone."[168] Taylor had some uncomplimentary things to say about manual labourers, with pig-iron handlers coming in for some particularly disparaging descriptions. To his mind workers were merely a commodity to be utilised. His is clearly a 'Theory X' philosophy.

For the most part the modern, Western workplace is a far cry from the foundries and factories Taylor studied (with the possible exception of order fulfilment centres and the gig economy). Most of the tasks that Taylor sought to optimise have since been automated or eliminated. What remains for humans are tasks that require flexibility, responsiveness and a degree of judgement, often with a dose of initiative and lateral thinking thrown in.

To my mind supervision by software is essentially neo-Taylorism, reducing the human to a unit of labour. The problem with neo-Taylorism – just like the original Taylorism – is that it engages the science of the task, not the science of the brains of the people completing the task.

Humans, being adaptable creatures, generally figure out how to game the processes in which they participate. They're probably not setting out to cheat, just working out how to deliver what the system demands with minimal effort.

---

[168] Taylor, F. W. *Principles of Scientific Management* (Harper, New York, 1919), 64.

Let me emphasise that this is not about workers being lazy or deceitful, but rather an almost automatic response to challenge. This can throw up some interesting outcomes.

Measure call centre workers on how many calls they get through and they will quickly figure out how to get through each call as quickly as possible. People who are long-winded or have complex service needs will be very quickly shunted off to someone else, who, if they're also being measured on how many calls they can get through, will in turn shunt the customer off to a third person and so on. If you've ever called a bank or a telco with a non-standard or complex problem, you will almost certainly have experienced this.

It's funny that in this exchange, the customer will in all likelihood burn through more employee time as they re-explain their requirements over and over (so the organisation is actually being less efficient) while simultaneously developing an increasing intention to raise a complaint (more work required by the organisation, so more cost) or to quit and go to a rival (while telling at least seven of their friends about their bad experience). All the while, each individual with whom they spoke probably recorded stellar call-clearance metrics. In this example and in hundreds of variations throughout the corporate world, systems designed to make customer service more efficient are inadvertently undermining the interests of organisations. To vary that old German expression I introduced before, what the marketing people build with their hands the customer service team knock down with their... performance metrics.

Engagement versus Roboboss

You'll remember right back in the introduction I introduced you to Gallup's research into engagement, and it's significant, measurable impact on worker performance and employment costs. Work intensification through software may deliver a short-term uptick in productivity, but long-term efficiency and effectiveness comes from human supervision. AI cannot deliver engagement.

Nowadays people are encouraged to interact with government instrumentalities, banks, telcos, insurance companies and utility companies through the internet. If you can't get your dealing done online, you'll contact their call centre and experience two things: firstly, a call direction menu, often several layers deep, to direct your call to the appropriate department.

Secondly, you'll be advised that your call will be recorded for staff training and coaching purposes.

Infuriating multi-level call direction menus and blown out waiting times surely serve to create a certain degree of annoyance and frustration in callers. Yet the demeanour of your average call centre operator remains calm, focused and professional. I'm guessing at least some of that aforementioned training and coaching must actually take place. To the extent it does, it's likely delivered by a supervisor or a person functioning in some kind of supervisory role. Software may help flag the people most in need of coaching and training, but even the most sophisticated online learning module is unlikely to go beyond fairly formulaic responses. Importantly, the call centre operator who's had the caller from hell needs supervision that provides a degree of support and human understanding, not a pre-recorded roleplay or a multi-choice question.

Software may promise to stretch the possible span of control past normal human sociological limits, but without the engagement factors listed above, much of which is supervisor-dependent, the software will likely lead to the same longer-term effects as any other work intensification initiative.

The immediate results of supervision by software may make the labour force appear more efficient on a unit-per-labour-hour basis, but the indirect costs of absenteeism, workers compensation and turnover will erode if not entirely eclipse any benefits. Beyond the mere economics, there are real questions about ethics and potential exploitation. At the end of the day, we need to ask ourselves if we want to participate in a workplace that is happy to treat frontline workers as a commodity.

Strategy and spans of control

Strategy is fundamentally about change, and change is always easier to imagine than it is to implement. When directives for change are made, they almost always hit up against the realities of current practices and resources. It's almost impossible from the rarefied atmosphere of the CEO's office to anticipate all of the practical implications of a change initiative down at the baseline of the organisation (and by baseline, I mean the level where workers, even highly paid ones, don't have anyone reporting to them). You might think that the flatter the organisational structure, the less chance there is for distortion of the change message between the top and the base of the organisation. Let me explain why it's a little more complicated...

The change will require some degree of adaptation. It may mean changes to software or hardware, reorganisation of workflows or re-allocation of responsibilities to distribute the workload. Usually, the individuals involved don't have the authority to initiate these kinds of changes, especially if they involve expenditure.

The supervisory function not only communicates the change required for strategy implementation, but also observes whether the change is made as expected and provides feedback to ensure the response to the change directive is on track. Further, the supervisor can help clear blockages, resolve resource conflicts and provide a conduit for referring issues back up the management line to the level where appropriate expenditure can be authorised, or changes to structure and job classification can be approved.

Here's where the organisational design comes in. In order for the supervisor to play their critical part in implementation, they must firstly be clear on what is expected of everyone in their part of the organisation (i.e. everyone who's in their 'downline').

For implementation to proceed, every aspect of the strategy must be allocated to an appropriate person. Executives are assigned broadly described objectives that might constitute a whole chapter within a strategy document, which are then progressively granulated down through the organisation chart to the level of concrete and specific changes at the operational and administrative baseline – like changes to hiring practices, or changed referral procedures in the customer service centre. In order for those expectations to cascade smoothly down through the hierarchical structure, every line in the organisational chart must represent a functioning supervisory relationship. Find a breakdown in supervision, and the strategy responsibilities of the downline beneath the break are at risk of going unfulfilled.

The design of the organisation is a crucial consideration if supervision is going to play its part in the strategy implementation, especially if you want the implementation to roll out with any kind of appreciable urgency.

Capacity and flexibility

Change is inherent to strategy. Change means doing things differently, and therefore change is to varying degrees disruptive. Allow me to illustrate. In Australia we drive right hand drive cars (steering wheel on the right) and drive on the left side of the road, as they do in the UK, Japan and a handful of other countries. Cars sold here that are made in Japan and Korea have the indicator stalk at your right hand, and the wipers at your left. Cars made in Germany and France have them the other way around.

For a while our family had a mix of European and Asian-built cars. Any time I switched cars I would inevitably turn on the wipers when I intended to use the indicator. The procedural memory that makes routine operations second nature must be suspended, and the more deliberate process of assess-choose-enact must be brought to bear, requiring extra effort and concentration. After a little while I would habituate to the car I was driving, and procedural memory would largely take over. The process then repeated when I drove a different car. Even simple change requires some effort to adapt.

Software manufacturers infuriate us all by changing the functionality and operation of their products, hiding our most used functions in obscure places, or turning a one-click operation into a multi-step rigmarole. It generally takes me a week or two to get my head around a significant software upgrade, and in that time my productivity is reduced.

Now consider how much mental effort is required in your average strategy implementation. It will often involve change to structure so a worker may have a new boss or new team members, new procedures, new software, new vocabulary.

If the strategy calls for adaptive change, there will be a degree of experimentation and provisionality about the change. Time and effort are required to design, trial and evaluate adaptations. All the while, workers are expected to keep turning the wheels of business-as-usual.

The uncertainty of change, the effort of adaptation and the feelings of sheer awkwardness when procedural memory no longer serves, all combine to trigger anxiety. As we saw earlier, anxiety makes our thinking less flexible and less efficient – just when we most need our higher intellectual capacities.

Predictably, the change-induced anxiety will show up as people being avoidant of the perceived source of their anxiety (flight response), or they'll become resistant (fight response) or they'll share their anxious fears and concerns with others (triangling) which can lead to groups 'herding' into camps presenting a 'united front'.

Back in chapters 18 and 20 we spent some time looking at how the anxious brain works. I encouraged you to read Daniel Goleman's work on emotional intelligence, where he talks about the limbic system – the feeling centres of the brain – 'hijacking' the thinking or intellectual centres of the brain when a person perceives threat.[169] Anxiety causes us to literally 'lose' our thinking: sometimes only slightly, sometimes to the point where we can't form a sentence.

An anxious brain focuses narrowly on the perceived source of threat, and will struggle to think more broadly, more laterally and certainly more creatively. Anxiety inhibits our mental flexibility. The frustrating paradox of change in the workplace is that it requires greater flexibility than is demanded by business-as-usual, while at the same time triggering anxiety, which inhibits flexible thought.

The supervisor's role in providing a sense of calm and stability in the face of anxiety-producing change cannot be overstated. Most important is the supervisor being able to stand back a little and observe the anxious process rather than becoming swept up in it. If the supervisor falls into anxious patterns of distance, conflict, and triangling, or if they anxiously under or over-function, they become part of the problem (you'll remember we unpacked these anxious patterns in chapter 18).

Almost as important is the supervisor's ability to stay in calm and thoughtful contact with their workers, and with those leading the strategy implementation. Most helpful is contact that does not overtly seek to fix anything (resisting the impulse to play 'repairman' is a significant challenge), but simply seeks to be fully present. In and of itself, this is one of the most

---

[169] Goleman, D. *Emotional Intelligence: Why it can matter more than IQ* (Bloomsbury London 1996).

helpful actions a supervisor can take. Calm is contagious, and people can think more effectively when they're calm than when they're upset.

In being fully present, the supervisor's first task is to pay attention, seeking to understand rather than offer correction. Next is to shape the conversation toward facts, just as we discussed when thinking about handling a conflictual worker back in chapter 20. Stating things like, "My observation of the situation is...", or "The way I'm thinking about this is..." or even, "My hypothesis at this point..." all focus on observation, thinking and logic, rather than reinforcing feelings. Approaches to questioning like, "I'm interested in your observations about..." or "I'm keen to hear your thoughts on..." or "What's your understanding of...?" all invite the worker to mobilise the intellectual centres of their brains, which helps them to calm down and to get a sense of proportion.

What's this got to do with organisational design? Simply put, people have a limited capacity to maintain thoughtful contact, especially when the people with whom they're interacting are anxious. It's time-consuming and energy-depleting. If a supervisor has 20 direct reports, they will almost certainly lack the emotional juice to be in regular and thoughtful contact with all of them. Supervision is likely to be reduced to transactional, formulaic and perfunctory interactions.

The wider the spans of control, the more difficult it is for the supervisor to play their crucial role in supporting and facilitating a strategy roll-out. While flat structures are supposed to be nimble, they're actually the most apt to be stuck. You'll never see a commando unit with a flat structure, because they need to be instantly responsive and infinitely flexible, which only fairly narrow spans of control can deliver.

The limitations of lean and mean
You'll recall my fairly cynical commentary on the 'productivity dividend' so relied upon by the Australian Federal Government to reduce government departmental overheads, and how it leads to work intensification. The tendency of contemporary organisations to staff to the level of 'barely sufficient' not only means you'll likely wait on hold for hours if you call a government agency, a bank, or a telco – it also means that those very same organisations struggle to implement sustained change.

As we saw in the banal example of indicators and wipers a few paragraphs earlier, doing things differently requires more effort than simply repeating our habitual patterns. We can't work at optimum efficiency and implement change at the same time. Change necessarily brings a drop in efficiency until the new ways are bedded down and habituated. Throw in the anxiety precipitated by change and how it impinges on good thinking, and efficiency is even more compromised. Yet time and again we see organisations slashing headcount while at the same time attempting root and branch transformation and trying to maintain their business operations at the same time. No wonder people hate change.

Depending on where you are in the organisational authority structure, you may or may not have authority to think through the overall workforce capacity implications of a change initiative. However, to the extent that you do, recognising the need for extra capacity in times of change and adaptation will likely augur toward a more successful change initiative.

Hierarchy delivers

Back in chapter five we looked briefly at the concept of hierarchy as a system of delegated authority – a means of organising groups of people, sometimes even millions of people, toward a common goal. Yet say the word 'hierarchy' to most people and you'll be able to observe their visceral reaction, from eye rolls to frowns to heads thrown back in frustration. Try to recall a conversation where 'The Hierarchy' was referred to in positive terms. Can't recall one? Neither can I. You'll probably get similar responses to the word 'bureaucracy', because the two are often conflated.

Pause your reactions for a minute and consider this: the computer, phone or other ICT device you probably use every day was almost certainly made by a large company like Apple, HP or Samsung. The microchips, screen and case materials were probably supplied by other large companies. The raw materials to make those components were mined, refined and transformed by large companies. The same is probably true for the car you drive, or the public transport infrastructure that you use. It takes a large organisation to affordably make complex things at scale.

What do all of these large companies have in common? Hierarchy. They will all have a CEO and other Chief Something Officers all of whom will have heads and managers reporting up to them, and who in turn will have staff reporting up to them.

If you put a group of strangers in a room and assign them a task, the first thing that will happen is that some form of hierarchy will begin to be negotiated. In fact, the quicker a hierarchy can be established and commence operating, the faster the task will be completed.

Hierarchy in one form or another is virtually ubiquitous in any context where humans in groups larger than two are required to cooperate to achieve a goal, even if that cooperative is something as basic as a family, or tribe. Any kind of interdependent functional speciality is impossible without it (even our bodies operate on a hierarchical basis).

Hierarchy has been with us throughout recorded history. The reason nations, militaries and corporations structure on a hierarchical basis is that there is no other working model that will effectively distribute authority and responsibility across a large group toward a collective outcome. Flattening structures may be an attempt to minimise the perceived evils hierarchy, yet at the same time, flatter structures discard the functional benefits of hierarchy that we've been examining in this chapter.

Some may argue that networked structures can deliver innovation and change more effectively than hierarchies, citing successful movements like feminism, environmentalism and religious revivals. Some would go further and observe that these movements lose their effectiveness when they try to corporatise or structure hierarchically, and they would be correct. However, movements are about influence and shaping culture. Movements have shifted public opinion on the status of women, on climate change, on racial equality and dozens of other valid causes – but it takes hierarchically organised institutions to enshrine the changed opinion in law and enforce it as a standard. A movement might create open-source software, but it cannot produce the devices on which it runs.

Functioning hierarchies deliver pretty much everything we buy or use (unless you only ever purchase from farmers' markets). The problem is not hierarchy per se, but the vulnerability of hierarchies to irresponsibility and the abuse of the power that unavoidably aggregates toward the apex. A hierarchy characterised by a responsible and ethical culture has great potential for good.

But that doesn't mean you'll solve all your problems by reducing your spans of control and getting your structure working.

Structural responses to cultural problems

When we decide that the structure is the problem rather than the ethical and responsible operation of the structure, we'll repeatedly try structures and discard them while ignoring the real problem. It's like a bad driver wrecking a succession of cars and blaming the manufacturers.

Jeff Miller helpfully observes that every organisation runs dual operating systems.[170] The rational system of the organisation is the one often documented in core ideals, policies, procedures and of course, an organisation chart. Less well understood is the instinctual system, which can be mapped by allegiances and rivalries, reactions and relationships, emotional triangles etc. You've probably already recognised how this mirrors the intellectual and emotional functions of the human brain.

While the culture of an organisation is a product of both the rational and instinctual systems, the instinctual side is probably more influential. Certainly, when the two systems are in disagreement, it's the instinctual system that will direct the traffic. Too often organisations drag in the consultants and exert a huge amount of energy on organisational change only to find themselves with new statements about vision and values, a new organisational chart with lots of new titles – perhaps even a whole new vocabulary – yet all the while facing the same perennial problems that are largely the product of the unobserved and unaddressed instinctual aspects of their culture.

A high-functioning human is one where the intellectual and emotional processes work more-or-less in alignment for the ongoing success of the individual (and in social species that's indissolubly linked to the success of the group). A high-functioning organisation is one where the rational and emotional systems work in alignment for the ongoing success of the organisation (which is nearly always inextricably linked to the success of the constituent individuals).

---

[170] Miller, J. *The Anxious Organization: Why Smart Companies Do Dumb Things* (Vinculum, Miami 2019).

Before you bring in the consultants to rearrange the structural deck chairs on your organisational Titanic, consider the instinctual factors below the waterline. It could save you a lot of money on consultants (and a lot of people in lifeboats).

Here's a few questions to get you started:

- Does the structure actually impede people in fulfilling their responsibilities, or could there be a relational explanation like unclear expectations or lack of feedback and accountability?
- Does the committee or team need to be restructured, or does it just need to be led competently?
- Does the structure actually prevent effective communication, or is it that people are simply failing to stop and consider who needs to know what and who should be consulted?
- Could you get the outcomes you want with a change in behaviour or some improved systems while retaining the same structure?
- If you're proposing a new structure, can you actually quantify how it will be more efficient and effective than the existing structure?

Often structure is a factor exacerbating more complex problems. For example, we spent some time earlier looking at spans of control (clearly a structural issue). Spans of control that are too wide lead to inadequate supervision. But simply structuring to achieve more functional spans of control will not in itself fix a problem of poor supervision – it simply changes the context to make improvement possible. Ensuring that supervisors have the adequate skills, processes and accountabilities to consistently undertake good supervision is more about process than structure. Creating a culture where excellent supervision is valued goes beyond process and structure to the fundamentals of leadership.

Too often organisations embark on structural change because it's tangible and allows people to escape personal responsibility for shortcomings and problems. Frequently the problem is less about the design of the structure and more about the structure being overridden by instinctual forces. Or it may be that systems of work are inadequate or have broken down. Policies, procedures and reporting lines are of no use if the instinctual forces cause them to be ignored.

A good test is to examine the functioning of the organisation and ask yourself (or your leadership team) whether, if you removed the personalities from the structure and just considered the functions, and if the appropriate policies and procedures were followed, would things function as required? If you can demonstrate how the current structure (not just the personalities that occupy it) is a material contributing factor to a problem and how a restructure will directly and tangibly reduce the problem, then by all means go ahead and restructure.

If you find that the problems lie predominantly with people not executing their required functions, perhaps it's time to look at the relational processes that make up the instinctual system of the organisation. Let's face it, if people aren't following the current design, what makes you think they'll follow a new one? If you're satisfied that the structure really is part of your problem, pull out the whiteboard and begin a redesign. If the systems and processes are not fit for purpose, work on those. If you suspect your problem might be more about the influence of instinctive, anxious forces, you're ready for the next chapter.

Summary

- The quest for flatter structures has become widespread over the past 30 years. Flatter structures require broader spans of control.
- Spans of control impact supervisory capacity. If the span of control is too wide, it will reduce supervisory effectiveness.
- Roboboss software promises to enable wider spans of control, but it's often just an exercise in Taylorist work intensification. There are ethical and risk-management downsides.
- Wide spans of control impede strategy implementation.
- Hierarchy is a necessary aspect of human organisations. The challenge is responsible and ethical operation of hierarchy rather than eliminating it.
- Structural solutions do not solve cultural problems.

Discussion

- Draw out your organisation chart and measure your spans of control. What do you observe?
- Talk over a current challenge in your organisation. As you think about the interaction of the various factors, can you identify where structure, work systems and emotional processes contribute?

Implementation

- If you find yourself in a structure where it appears that the spans of control are not optimal for effective supervision, map out a plan to work with the stakeholders to address the issue.

Chapter 27
Working with the instinctual system

A tale of two systems

Yesterday there was a riot in central Melbourne. After nearly two-years of lockdowns to suppress the COVID-19 virus, a couple of thousand people decided they'd had enough, were not willing to get vaccinated and descended on the city demanding change. About ten percent of the original crowd ended up arrested, a large proportion were identified and will receive large fines and quite a number are nursing bruises after being hit with non-lethal rounds fired by police.

There was never any real possibility of them achieving their goal. The outcome of the 'protest' was entirely predictable. On the same day more than 40,000 people in Melbourne received a vaccine dose. Commentators bemoaned that the rioter's actions defied logic.

Why do people act in ways that defy reason?

In chapter 25 we met Jonathan Haidt, and his metaphor of the rider and the elephant.[171] The rider represents our conscious thinking, while the elephant represents all the rest of our mental processes, most of which we are unaware. Before that in chapter 20 we looked at what happens neurologically when a human becomes angry: the emotional centres of the brain seize the agenda and the intellectual centres become subservient to them.

What happened in the city yesterday? A bunch of riders lost control and the elephants stampeded.

In this chapter we'll explore Jeff Miller's concept of the instinctual or emotional system at play in your organisation.[172] My aim is to help you keep the elephants cooperating with their riders.

---

[171] Haidt, J. T*he Happiness Hypothesis: Finding Modern Truth in Ancient Wisdom* (Basic Books, New York 2006).

[172] Miller, J. *The Anxious Organization: Why Smart Companies Do Dumb Things* (Vinculum, Miami 2019).

The instinctual system is effectively the collective product of all the instincts and emotions of the people that make up the organisation. These in turn are influenced by the instincts and emotions of people connected to the organisation: family members of the staff, suppliers, customers and shareholders.

It's not that the instinctual system is bad. In fact, without our basic instinctual drives, the human race would not be motivated to fulfil the basic necessities of survival and procreation. Motivation is fundamentally emotional. That does not mean the intellect is not involved. The intellect uses information and logic to figure out how we can fulfil our basic needs and drives, and how we can overcome or avoid threats to their fulfilment, whether it's food, shelter, sex, companionship, pleasure, satisfaction or a sense of significance. The intellect steers and directs, but the motivational impetus is emotional.

The instinctual system is therefore an essential ingredient in getting things done in the organisation. Fundamentally, people participate in the organisation to get something out of it, no matter how noble and self-sacrificial they might be. The key to it is keeping the instinctual system aligned with the rational system.

In an individual, when the two systems are aligned, they display thoughtful, goal-directed behaviours for their long-term benefit, working their way up the pyramid of Maslow's hierarchy of needs. When the two systems fall out of alignment, people display reactive, short-term, anxiety-relieving behaviours like addictions, avoidance of responsibility, quarrels, etc. These, in time, generally result in a person tumbling down Maslow's pyramid – sometimes to the point where their very survival may be threatened.

The same goes for the instinctual and rational systems in an organisation. Keep them aligned and the organisation will more likely expend its resources in pursuit of its purpose, while providing a context for its people to pursue theirs. When the two systems fall out of alignment, organisations fall into short-term, symptom-relieving behaviours like chasing silver-bullet solutions, continually changing strategy, hastily firing people, protecting irresponsible managers, industrial disputes, turf wars, managerial turnover – sometimes to the point where the organisation's very survival may be threatened.

First, the bad news...

The instinctual or emotional system of any organisation presents challenges on several levels. Firstly, unlike the rational system, it's never written down, so it's down to individuals to discern it by observation.

Secondly, it tends to shape-shift depending on the emotional forces brought to bear upon it. Two people may have a close, cooperative and collaborative relationship one minute, and the next be engaging in subterfuge against one another. The reason for the sudden shift could be each having separate conversations with a third person. Unless you can observe every single interaction in the organisation, it's impossible to form in your mind a reliable emotional organisational chart. Even if you could, it might be substantially different next week.

Thirdly, as Ed Friedman points out,[173] the outcomes of efforts to influence the instinctual system are often perverse. A leader's efforts to improve morale often produces cynicism, endeavours to build consensus generate sabotage, and trying to keep the peace only spreads the conflict.

Malcolm Gladwell, in his remarkable book *Talking to Strangers* cites a number of studies that demonstrate just how bad humans are at determining what's going on in the hearts and minds of another person.[174] Despite our confidence that we can 'read' people by their demeanour, the best we can do is guess and the evidence suggests we're likely to be way off. At the most basic level, we cannot reliably determine how others feel. The instinctual system is fuelled by emotions, and while our behaviour can influence people's feelings, we have almost no ability to reliably control them.

The clues to the divergence of rational and instinctual systems are easy to spot if you know what to look for. Perhaps the most obvious clue is to observe where the rational system is breaking down. When people aren't following policy and procedure, aren't fulfilling the responsibilities set out in their position description (PD) or aren't putting their efforts toward the purposes

---

[173] Friedman, E. H. *A Failure of Nerve: Leadership in the Age of the Quick Fix* (Seabury, New York, 1999).
[174] Gladwell, M. *Talking to Strangers* (Allen Lane, London, 2019).

of the organisation, there's a good chance emotional processes are working against rather than for the organisation.

It's tempting to try to find a root cause for this divergence. I wish you the best of luck. Causation in the emotional system is always a tangle of interactions, sensitivities and knock-on effects spreading well beyond your field of view and way back beyond any history you can trace.

Other clues are the four basic ways that humans seek to manage their anxiety: conflict, triangling, distancing and either being over-responsible or under-responsible. Trying to control any of these is like trying to compress a balloon full of water. Squeeze it in one place and it will bulge out somewhere else. Push on that bulge and another will appear. With a lot of effort you may be able to keep it all contained but you're not going to make it smaller.

In summary, the bad news about the instinctual system is that you only observe the bit into which you come into contact, your observations will only be reliable in the here and now, and you can't do much to manage it directly.

And then the good news...

The good news is that anyone can exert significant influence on the instinctual system simply by managing themselves. It doesn't need to begin with the CEO or even a senior manager, although the broader a person's influence in the organisation, the greater the effect of their self-management on the instinctual system.

Murray Bowen observed that if one person in an emotional system can lift themselves out of the 'togetherness' that holds everything so stuck, and make even a small step toward being a more responsible self, it will automatically lead to other members of the system taking similar steps.[175]

While you cannot manage the instinctual system, you can take responsibility for managing yourself in the instinctual system. An effort to be a more thoughtful, more principled and less reactive participant will, if sustained, lead to more thoughtful, principled and less reactive behaviours in others. An effort

---

[175] Bowen, M. *Family Therapy in Clinical Practice* (Jason Aronson, New York 1978).

to attend to the rational system and be guided by its requirements will, in time, lead to others also attending to the rational system.

The beginning place for self-management is to step back from the emotional milieu sufficiently to regain our rational thought and gain a little perspective, which leads naturally to a conversation about mindfulness.

Mindfulness

Much has been written over the past two decades about this group of meditative techniques that trace their origins to Buddhism. So much so that mindfulness has become the self-management technique *du jour*. There's an abundance of mindfulness apps to download promising calm, focus and a sense of equilibrium. As with any psychological technique that rises to new prominence, a predictable academic debate has erupted as to the actual efficacy of the technique versus the placebo effect of fad popularity.

Writing in Scientific American, Brett Stetka points out the flaws and failings of many studies purporting to demonstrate the value of mindfulness, and the lack of evidence for mindfulness producing improvements in functioning. However, he goes on to cite valid studies that have found "modest benefits in anxiety, depression and pain."[176] Ruth Baer points to similar findings, especially where mindfulness is embedded into therapeutic approaches like Cognitive Behavioural Therapy and Acceptance and Commitment Therapy.[177] Research by Gaelle Desbordes found that the practice of mindfulness can over time decrease reactivity in the amygdala (the part of the brain that triggers fight-flight responses),[178] while earlier research by Sara Lazar found that the brains of subjects thickened after an eight-week meditation course.[179] Even micro meditations concentrating on deep and slow breathing can sufficiently interrupt our anxious processes to allow us better access to our intellectual functioning.

---

[176] Stetka, B. *Where's the Proof That Mindfulness Meditation Works?* Scientific American October 11, 2017 https://www.scientificamerican.com/article/wheres-the-proof-that-mindfulness-meditation-works1 .
[177] Baer, R. A. *Measuring Mindfulness* Contemporary Buddhism, Vol. 12, No. 1, May 2011.
[178] Cited by Powell, A. *When Science Meets Mindfulness* The Harvard Gazette April 9, 2018.

While not the cure-all it's sometimes held up to be, mindfulness can help us calm down and reduce our feelings of distress. It may even change the way our brain responds to distressing situations. But then what? Being in a calm state is more pleasant than being in a distressed state, but simply detaching and practicing some meditation to calm down could, by itself, simply be a means of avoidance.

However, being calm *and* connected can make a profound difference.

Calmly thoughtful

As we discussed back in chapters 18 and 20, an anxious brain is one experiencing higher levels of activation in the limbic ring, which very quickly gears the body and mind up to deal with an immediate threat. The pulse quickens and blood flow is directed away from the extremities toward the big muscles needed to fight or flee. Adrenaline is released preparing for quick and focused action. The thinking centres of the brain become conscripted to focus and strategise about the immediate threat. The mental and physical resources of the anxious person are increasingly directed toward the perceived source of the anxiety, and the instinctual priority is to do whatever is required to alleviate the sense of crisis. The window of attention narrows and the planning horizon shortens. Sound like anywhere you've worked?

When we're anxiously aroused, thinking about the requirements and constraints of the organisation's rational system are not high on the agenda. Being thoughtful about our responsibilities, the longer-term impacts of our behaviours or the broader implications of a decision are all much less likely when we're anxious. When anxious, we're likely to make snap decisions that cause more problems later on.

Calming down allows us to be a little more circumspect, to remember the contents of our job description and company policies. We can slow down a little and observe things a little more broadly, and then make decisions with an eye on the wider implications.

When calm we're more likely to see when other people's anxieties are being pushed or projected onto us, and we have a chance at thoughtfully and respectfully declining to take it on.

414

We make better decisions when we're calm. Five minutes of mindfulness before a big meeting or a ten-second deep-breathing exercise may just save us hours of damage control later.

Calmly present

Study social animals and you'll soon observe that anxiety is contagious. One anxious wildebeest can trigger a stampede. Put humans under sufficient threat (like a fire in a sporting stadium) and they'll stampede too.

Workers are particularly attuned to the emotional valence of their boss, especially when their livelihood is concerned. An upset boss will fairly quickly lead to an anxious group of workers.

Happily, the inverse is also true. Calm is contagious. A leader who maintains a calm and thoughtful presence has a calming effect on their workers. When the worker's anxiety is low, they too can bring their best thinking to the task – thinking that is broader, longer-term, more creative and more flexible.

We discussed earlier the value of calm, curious, fact-based questions in helping an upset worker regain their thinking. To be in a space to ask helpful questions, we need to be calm enough to bring this approach to mind.

The contagion of calm is transmitted personally. Being a vision of serenity while holed up in your office may be comfortable, but your calm will only be a useful resource if you are actually present and engaged with your workers. In your absence, the anxious worker might imagine all kinds of things, and most likely they'll assume the worst of whatever it is they're worried about. The trick is to be separate enough not to get swamped by the emotional tide, and connected enough to do your job and allow your presence to be a resource to your workers.

Calm individual contact that isn't taking anyone's side is perhaps the most helpful behaviour a boss can bring to an anxious workforce – more helpful than trying to reassure people, more helpful than stepping in to fix things, more helpful than laying down the law (all various forms of over-functioning). When workers are in conflict, provided it's not causing any harm to people, simply being in touch with the combatants and trusting them to figure things out will often be all that's necessary. Sometimes an observation or a thought-provoking question will encourage one of the combatants to pause and think instead of focusing all their attention on the threat posed by their opponent.

Calmly responsible

It's been said that when you're up to your armpits in alligators, it's hard to remember that you're there to drain the swamp. Keeping in mind your own responsibilities, even when others are forgetting theirs, or attempting to recruit you into their conflicts, is an essential means of keeping your head and maintaining your equilibrium. In an acutely anxious system, you may need to remind yourself of your own PD multiple times a day. Your PD tells you where your energy and attention should be going, and anything outside of that is probably not yours to do. Stepping outside of your responsibilities risks feeding the ambiguity, blurring role clarity and contributing to the divergence of the rational and instinctual systems.

Keeping a close eye on your own anxious behaviour is equally important. Watching to see where you're tempted to abandon the rational system can save you a trip to a court or commission, an awkward conversation with HR and the prospect of undermining your own credibility. What's more it will save you from amplifying the anxiety in your workers.

Watching for the four anxious patterns – triangling, distancing, conflict and over- or under-functioning will also give you a clear indication of your part in perpetuating any of the anxiety circulating in the instinctual system. Refusing to be drawn into side taking, refusing to complain to third persons, staying in contact with all the important participants in your part of the organisation, keeping debates to issues rather than personalities, and sticking with you own responsibilities all serve to stop the anxiety flowing around the system like an electric current.

Calmly consistent

Jeff Miller points out that no one has ever met a leader who possesses all of the supposed traits set out as emblematic of great leadership in the various theories of management. Yet "...people can be content enough working for the 'Grinch Who Stole Christmas', so long as he's a *predictable* Grinch."[180] Being predictable is about being sufficiently consistent that your workers know what to expect of you.

---

[180] Miller, J. A. *The Anxious Organization: Why Smart Companies Do Dumb Things* (Vinculum, Miami 2019).

Doing as you say, saying as you do, responding to challenge thoughtfully, and explaining what's going on helps workers to stop worrying about what you might say and do next, allowing them to put more of their attention and energy into their jobs. If they can trust you to reliably do your job, they'll more likely relax and do theirs.

Remember, while we're all emotionally motivated, the rational system is the means by which all our disparate functions coordinate to produce a shared, beneficial outcome. The rational system is the also the system by which we manage risk though policy and procedure. Calm workers are more likely to fulfil their responsibilities, follow procedure and implement strategy. Anxious workers are less likely to, meaning decreased efficiency, increased risk and stifled progress.

Just because the rational system is the stable and predictable one doesn't mean it's set in concrete. You will inevitably find places where it's inconsistent, outdated and even self-defeating. Simply acknowledging these failings and using sensible processes to correct them helps build worker confidence.

Summary

- Organisations of any kind have two operating systems: one rational, one instinctive. The organisation works well when these are aligned.
- Instinct or emotion is the source of motivation.
- The instinctive system is not stable or defined – yet it is observable.
- The instinctive system can be influenced by being a calm presence characterised by being:
    - Thoughtful
    - Present
    - Responsible
    - Consistent

Discussion

- Think of a situation where the rational system of your organisation stopped working properly. Can you observe any of the four anxious patterns at work?

Implementation

- Decide upon a simple calming strategy – a slow deep breath, a micro meditation or similar. Next time your calm demeanour is disrupted, make a point of employing your calming strategy before responding.

Chapter 28
Appraisal and development

A personnel practice with a bad reputation

"I look forward to conducting staff performance appraisals every year!" said no one ever. Performance appraisal is generally seen as a cumbersome burden for supervisors and a motivation-sapping anxiety mill for workers. So why do it?

Let's begin by getting the illegitimate reasons out of the way. Most importantly, appraisal is not your opportunity to deal with long-standing problems – at least not at the symptomatic level. If your worker is underperforming, you should be dealing with it in routine supervision. Leaving tricky conversations until it's time for an annual appraisal is effectively delaying doing your job.

Further, appraisal is not about justifying an annual pay increment. Most economies have some degree of inflation which means the dollar (or euro, pound, yen, peso) value of a worker's remuneration will have less actual purchasing value one year to the next due to inflation. If the worker is making the same labour inputs, it's reasonable to give them a salary increment to hold par. It's somewhat unethical not to.

Some may argue that a pay increment should be balanced by a respective productivity increase. I would argue that your week-to-week supervision should be continually mindful about ways to improve productivity. You'll remember when we looked at the structure of regular supervision meetings back in chapter 16, I encouraged you to include a little stretch as a regular feature of supervision. When we talked about supervision as coaching, I encouraged a collaboration of brains (yours and your workers) to continuously look for ways to improve efficiency and effectiveness. All other things being equal, you and your worker should have been chipping away at productivity improvements all year. Maybe your worker deserves a bigger increase than just the inflation rate!

All that said, the further up the managerial food chain we venture, the more likely it is that performance appraisal and a salary review will be linked –

which makes sense, because the more responsibility a person holds, the more their decisions will impact the overall performance of the organisation. It's not uncommon for a CEO to push for a substantial salary increase if the organisation they lead has performed well, or if they've achieved particularly good outcomes in specific areas.

This isn't a book about executive remuneration, so I'm not going to drill into what's become a complex and emotive topic, other than to state two salient points. Firstly, a salary review should be based on evidence. That evidence includes what the executive is worth on the market. You can find this out by consulting a market or sector salary survey. Further evidence includes sector performance. If the whole sector had a ripping year, it's fair to assume that the organisation's good performance could be due more to environmental factors than executive brilliance. Conversely, if the whole sector tanked, responsibility for the organisation's difficulty may not lie primarily with the executive. Another source of evidence is linking the contribution of the exec's area of responsibility to the overall performance of the organisation.

Secondly, the whole process is far less ambiguous if the basis of salary review is set out clearly beforehand. If at the beginning of the year an exec knows what will be considered in their salary review, they'll have a clear idea of what to expect – it might also serve to focus their attention on particular results. But be careful – focusing on particular results can lead to skewed priorities.

When it comes to profit-sharing arrangements, these are generally based on a balanced scorecard of organisational performance indicators, and are beyond the scope of individual performance appraisal outside of the executive suite.

So back to the original question. Performance appraisal, by its very title, tends to be backward-looking, seeking to make some kind of evaluation or value assessment of a worker's performance. And if that's all it is, I'm all for doing as much of that as possible in routine supervision and consigning appraisals to the employee relations dustbin. So let's reframe it. Let's think about appraisal as performance planning – or perhaps better, relationship optimisation.

Relationship optimisation
You're probably cringing at the title. Yeah, I know, sounds like another vacuous, pop-psychology-derived piece of consultant speak. I'm hearing you. Stay with me for a minute.

If humans were just bits of hardware running bits of software, we could just think about performance as we would any other machine metric. We'd think entirely about employment in terms of the rational system. However, as we discussed earlier, humans are emotional creatures, motivated by drives toward needs.

Just as important, there might be 7,874,965,825 people alive on the planet as I write, but humans are not mass-produced. Each person is an individual with a story, a personality, some hopes and perhaps even some dreams. The rational system is generally designed such that any person with the required competencies can do any given job. Rational systems tend to prioritise standardisation. However, each human will bring uniqueness to a role for which rational systems cannot account.

Optimisation is about finding closer alignment between the rational system which ensures our collective effort is productive, and the needs, strengths and hopes of the individual. It's about both the organisation and the individual extracting optimal benefit out of their relationship, while keeping the cost to both sustainable.

Therefore, appraisal is not an exercise in ensuring an organisation is extracting the requisite pound of flesh, nor is it about justifying a pay increment. Appraisal is an opportunity to move closer toward a worker's realised potential.

Let's take a look at how it might work.

Appraisal as optimisation – the nuts and bolts

Most importantly, appraisal with a view to optimisation is about a series of conversations. You might have a policy and a procedure to frame the process, and you might even use some generic forms to stimulate thought, but all of these are about shaping a conversation.

My kids tell me I'm predictable, so predictably I'm going to begin with the PD. It's the working map for the worker's role as it is, and the contents of the PD provide a good place to begin your conversation.

The next question is about questions. What questions will you bring to the conversation that begins with the PD? My practice is to ask questions in two frames: past up to the present, and future.

Past up to the present

As you read below, you'll note that the conversation is primarily qualitative and tends to lead with the subjective. There's a place for hard data in managing performance, but you should already be dealing with it in routine supervision. Quantitative data has a valid place in performance appraisal, but ideally it's more about bigger questions than metrics. My invitation to my staff is to use appraisal as an opportunity for reflection, to gain some self-understanding. There's a difference between hearing the heart and taking a pulse.

Responsibilities

I'll take the 'responsibilities' headings from the PD and invite some thinking around each of them. I'll usually ask the worker to prepare for the conversation by documenting their responses, while I document mine. In conversation we compare notes. Here's some examples:

- Comment on your performance in fulfilling this responsibility.
- How competent do you feel in fulfilling this responsibility? Is it too easy, a stimulating stretch, a bit beyond you?
- How much satisfaction or enjoyment do you derive from fulfilling this responsibility?
- To what extent does this responsibility play to your strengths?

You may choose to introduce some performance data to bring some objectivity to the conversation, especially if you want to emphasise strengths. If the worker has staff reporting to them, you might use data like turnover and absenteeism in their department versus company average.

Managing the role

This part of the conversation looks at things like managing time, prioritising tasks, and keeping track of the various issues that a worker is required to address in the course of their work. If you've kept track of the worker's execution of their work plans, you should already have a reasonably good idea of how they're managing. I'm interested in the worker's perception of how they're managing. Here are some starter questions...

- Generally speaking, how well does your workload match your capacity? Do you feel like you're under-utilised, carrying a sustainable workload, or struggling to keep up?

- Describe how well you're managing your time and priorities? Do you feel like you're on top of things, playing 'whack a mole', or struggling to keep up?

In reflecting on self-management, it's useful to observe the kind of tasks the worker gravitates toward and which ones they tend to avoid. Avoid the temptation to form assumptions about what that might mean: some people gravitate to the things they like in order to enjoy them, others gravitate to the things that make them anxious in order to alleviate their anxiety. It's most useful just to make the observation and invite the worker to reflect on it.

Engagement with organisation

You may choose to include some questions about the worker's engagement with the wider organisation. The thinking behind the questions in this section is to some extent informed by Gallup's research on employee engagement.[181] Other aspects of the appraisal process address several of the dimensions of engagement as measured by Gallup's Q12 survey.[182] This section deals primarily with issues of belonging. An alternative to discussing these dimensions in appraisal is to simply use the Q12 survey with your team and talk over the results.

This area can touch on some sensitive issues but can also yield some useful data about life at work for your worker. How you phrase the questions and which areas you choose to consider will be a matter for your judgement. Set out below are some sample questions to consider.

- Are there people in the organisation who care about your personal welfare?
- Do you have good friends in this organisation?
- Do you feel like the work you do is important?
- Do you get the help you need from other people in the organisation?
- How motivated are you to help other people in the organisation outside of your immediate team?

---

[181] Clifton, J. and Harter, J. *It's the Manager* (Gallup, New York, 2019).
[182] See https://www.gallup.com/workplace/229424/employee-engagement.aspx.

Gathering other data

There's a lot of discussion about gathering broader data to inform the appraisal process, especially the use of 360-degree feedback. We touched on this back in chapter 21. I've used 360s with senior managers at various times, but I'm not a fan of their routine use for appraisal. Typically, when people receive an appraisal report they head straight for the low scores and begin to worry about or dispute the scores. That's generally not what I want out of an appraisal conversation. The data is coming overwhelmingly from people other than the worker, where I am much more interested in the worker's experiences and perceptions. Sure, there needs to be other perspectives, but using 360s for appraisal runs the risk of appraisal being done to the worker rather than with the worker.

Further, the data coming from 360s may not be all that useful. Let's face it, if 360s are routine in an organisation, you'll be filling out surveys about other people and the others will be doing the same about you. Very quickly a kind of unspoken, subtle contract develops – we'll all tacitly agree to being mildly positive so that no one gets hurt. Often 360 surveys will ask for information that a respondent can't reliably provide, so they'll opt for a neutral score which tends to pull the data toward a middling score.

If you must use 360-degree feedback, I encourage its use less frequently than annually, or at critical junctures in a worker's career. I would recommend using well researched and validated 360-degree feedback instruments like The Leadership Practices Inventory by Kouzes and Posner.[183] Instruments that are based on a large database help the worker know what constitutes an encouraging or worrying score. By itself a score of 3.7 out of five on a question about being a 'good listener' means very little. However, if the average rating across ten thousand managers is 2.5, it's an encouraging score. Not so much if the average across ten thousand managers is 4.1. But even then, what does it actually mean for the worker? That requires a conversation.

Finally, I encourage using a consultant skilled and qualified with your 360-degree instrument of choice. The consultant can help you and your worker make sense of the scores and help you figure out how to make the best use of

---

[183] Kouzes, J. M and Posner, B. Z. *Leadership Practices Inventory (LPI): Leadership Development Planner* (J. Pfeiffer, Hoboken, 2003) .

the data. Otherwise, the survey runs the risk of being done for the sake of it and the results shrugged-off.

Life stage considerations

Taking a worker's life stage into consideration can be helpful for optimising the employment relationship. This takes into consideration issues like parenting responsibilities, health considerations and those stages of life we talked about back in chapter 23.

It's hard to craft generic questions around these, so it's probably easier to give some examples of how this might play out.

- A parent with young kids may want to look at options for finishing work early a few days a week so they can pick their kids up from school.
- A worker in their late twenties, full of drive and aspiration, may want to push hard at their career progression. They may be willing to endure some steep learning curves and some rigorous demands in order to advance.
- A worker facing the midlife transition may be looking to do more of what's truly in their sweet spot and be less interested in positions and titles.
- A worker in their fifties may be more interested in being generative, giving back to the community or mentoring others, rather than taking on the next promotion with more responsibility.

Dreaming

Before you start turning the thinking about the past into a plan for the future, it's worth taking a moment to dream a little. The difference between dreaming and planning is that dreams don't necessarily need to be bounded by the constraints of the moment. I may dream of making most of my living out of writing, but the realities of my current marketability and my financial responsibilities mean I'll front up to work tomorrow and will likely be doing that for years to come. Yet without the dream I would not be writing the words you're reading now. Here are some dream starters...

- Thinking about your strengths and non-strengths, what do imagine as your ideal job?

- If everything went just as you hoped for the next ten years, where would your career path take you?

Development
Needs around life stage and dreaming of possibilities can sometimes dovetail into considerations about further development. Insights from earlier reflections and from that 360 I tried to dissuade you from using can also inform thoughts about development. This will usually take the form of further study and training, or intentionally exposing the worker to experiences that will shape their development.

At this point I encourage you to be thinking possibilities rather than nailing down a plan. It may mean the worker goes away and researches some study options, or you bring someone from your training department into the conversation.

A lot of what passes for professional development is really just routine maintenance for the worker's skill set. If the organisation is about to introduce a new ERP system, or workflow planning application or an enterprise-level technology upgrade, training the workers to use those systems is just part of the implementation program. Sure, it may mean the worker becomes a little more productive and perhaps a little more marketable, but it's just about staying current. Development goes further, enabling a worker to take on broader or more specialised responsibilities.

Study and training could be anything from a short course to embarking on a research degree. Try to keep in mind the worker's developmental needs as well as their life stage and career trajectory. Figuring out what will most set the worker up for their next phase of life will usually take more thought than a web search for a course with a promising sounding title.

Often experiences are conflated with study tours where a group tour around different contexts to learn from the way other organisations operate, or how people in different contexts respond to challenges. These sometimes yield some useful insights, but require careful planning and some very intentional, structured observation and reflection. Setting up a series of meetings post-tour in the shape of a community of practice will further help embed the learning. Etienne Wenger's work on Communities of Practice[184] is worth referring to for further information.

A higher-impact way of developing a worker is to second them to a learning-rich context for an extended period. Learning is much more durable when it's gained in context and the new behaviours are repeated sufficiently to become somewhat automatic. Like the thousands of execs that toured Toyota to learn their methods, most study tours provide opportunity to observe behaviours but don't get to the level of challenging assumptions or forcing people to adapt to a different workplace culture.

A secondment where a worker is embedded into a team that will stretch their thinking, push them to build new skills, engage them in unfamiliar processes and challenge their assumptions, will of course be uncomfortable but may also be life changing. Discomfort is prerequisite to learning.

Leadership pipeline

Many organisations nowadays have an internal leadership development system, sometime referred to as a leadership or talent development pipeline. This concept has to some extent superseded the more established idea of a succession plan. A pipeline is about developing an excess of talent with a suite of generalist leadership competencies. When a vacancy arises, an organisation with a well developed pipeline will be spoilt for choice.

A pipeline conveys the idea of people progressing over time, and that's exactly what a talent pipeline does. A talent pipeline is usually managed by the HR department. If your organisation has an intentional development system, I encourage you to talk over the possibilities with your worker and with the HR people. Even if your organisation does not have a formal talent pipeline, and even if you're supervising volunteers, you can begin to think about opportunities within your area of responsibility to begin developing talent.

Not everybody is up for progressing through the ranks of seniority or developing leadership skills, and there's no point investing organisational resources or your personal energy in workers whose aspirations lie in a

---

[184] Wenger, E., McDermott, R. and Snyder, W. M. *Cultivating Communities of Practice: A Guide to Managing Knowledge* (Harvard Business School, Boston, 2002).

different direction. It's still important to invest in their growth as people, just don't try to push them into leadership.

Even if you're leading a small team of volunteers, you can begin thinking about which of them could in time replace you. Once you've identified potential leaders you can begin to invest in them by providing some basic training in some of the leadership tasks in the organisation and offering them opportunity to take on those tasks, even if it's only once or twice. If they warm to the task, you might delegate it to them on an ongoing basis (note I'm talking about tasks, not roles – that comes a little later).

You may be on the lookout for learning opportunities to share with your leaders-in-development, like seminars or conferences. You may choose to read through a management or leadership book together. If they show interest and promise, you can delegate more tasks to them, and in time ask them to stand in when you're on leave or otherwise unavailable.

You may be leading something a little more substantial than a team of part-time volunteers, and you can take the same approach. You'll remember in the early chapters I introduced you to Mark, for whom I worked at Pacific Dunlop. Using essentially the same process I outlined above, he had more than half of his operations team variously involved in an informal leadership pipeline. I'll give you a closer look at this in the final chapter.

Even if you're a CEO overseeing several strata of management, you could foster that same mindset in every manager at every level, so that leaders are at once being developed by their manager while seeking to develop leaders among their direct reports. You could really turbocharge it by adding some cross-functional coaching and communities of practice.

Competent, committed supervisors with a vision for developing talent can be the prime movers in building a formidable leadership bench in your organisation. Not only will you have leaders who you already know and trust to choose from in order to expand or fill vacancies, you'll also develop the reputation of your organisation as a great place to work – thus attracting more talent and creating a virtuous cycle.

Building a performance plan

So far in the appraisal process we've pulled out a variety of strands: past performance, competency and satisfaction in the current role, using review instruments like 360-degree feedback, hopes and dreams, life stage considerations, and further development. I feel exhausted just writing the list.

Before we try to turn all of that into a super comprehensive performance plan, let's stop for a reality check. We're not going to be able to accommodate everything the worker would like and everything the organisation could hope to gain out of a single annual appraisal. However, in asking the questions and having the conversations we accomplish a couple of things.

Firstly, we build a greater sense of understanding and collaboration with the worker. Even if we can't accommodate everything they hope for, showing interest and effort builds their sense of being valued and raises their engagement.

Secondly, we broaden our thinking to consider possibilities outside the existing PD and organisational structure. We consider what might be in the longer term, so that both the supervisor and the worker can be mindful of opportunities to be sought and taken up, even if they're not explicitly addressed in the performance plan (sometimes development is more serendipity than strategy).

In beginning to craft the performance plan, it's helpful to be clear with the worker that not everything discussed in the appraisal process will find its way into the plan. There are organisational realities and personal constraints that will necessarily limit the possibilities – at least for now.

Running parallel to the reflective and imaginative work you've done with the worker are the requirements of the organisation. The role as described in the current PD fulfils a purpose, and significant change to that role will usually impact related roles in the organisation and may influence broader organisational effectiveness and efficiency. No role is an island. Each role in an organisation will have a degree of interdependence with others – it's the very essence of an organisation.

With that in mind, any changes to a worker's role will need to be guided by understanding the effects on the rational system of the organisation. Keep in mind that your foundational allegiance is to the organisation, otherwise everything becomes vulnerable.

Also influencing the worker's development plan is the forward plan and strategy of the organisation. The individual performance plan should ideally serve the organisation's overall plan and align with the organisational strategy. If everyone's plans are just about the individual's self-actualisation, supervision becomes like herding cats and the direction of the organisation becomes diffuse.

In light of all this, crafting the plan can seem to be more about alchemy than procedure. Set out below are a few questions to help find a meeting point where the worker's development and the organisation's future can serve one another. In the questions below I've drawn on Buckingham and Clifton's thinking around Strengths, Weaknesses and Non-Strengths that we touched on back in chapter 22.[185]

- How could the worker's strengths best serve the organisation? How could they be utilised to maximum effect, especially in light of the organisational strategy?
- How might the worker's strengths be further developed to maximise their impact?
- How do the worker's weaknesses limit their effectiveness? How might this be remedied?
- How can the worker's non-strengths be limited or eliminated from their role?
- What are the worker's life stage needs and how might the role be tailored to accommodate these?
- What skills does the organisation need going forward and is the worker a candidate for developing some of these?
- What kind of training and development experiences can serve to bring these possibilities closer to reality?
- Are there any projects in which the worker could be involved that would benefit both them and the organisation?

---

[185] Buckingham, M. and Clifton, D. *Now Discover Your Strengths: The Revolutionary Program That Shows You How to Develop Your Unique Talents and Strengths – And Those of The People You Manage* (Free Press, New York, 2001).

- What goals, targets metrics and milestones will be used to measure the progress and impact of the changes being considered?

Nailing it down

At the end of the day, appraisal must translate into tangible, concrete outcomes, or the content of the discussion will quickly retreat into the background in the face of the business-as-usual deadlines and demands.

It makes sense to first document changes to the workers PD – these can vary from a few tweaks to a whole new job. You may create a new position, promote the worker into an available vacancy, or so augment their responsibilities that they're effectively in a new role. Conversely, the appraisal conversation may have been an opportunity for some honest reflection that yields an agreement to reduce a worker's responsibilities, or move them into a vacancy that has less responsibility. Moves to a less responsible role can sometimes be a genuine win-win. That said, formal demotion as a consequence of performance management should be entirely separate from performance appraisal. The tone of appraisal must remain collaborative.

Changes to the PD may include changes to reporting relationships – primarily the roles reporting to the role that's subject to appraisal. If the worker's role is being moved into a different reporting line, be careful to ensure the move is about the smooth operation of the rational system, rather than being about enabling 'personality issues' to go unaddressed.

Changes to the PD will also include changes to performance standards – the targets and metrics that are routinely used to measure the worker's performance. This may be as simple as tweaking the numbers, or it may mean changing the actual metrics so that the right outcomes are prioritised.

Other changes to the PD might include days and hours of work, start and finish times or work locations. Working from home can provide flexibility benefits to both the worker and the organisation.

Significant changes to the PD will have remuneration impacts, and you'll need to work these through in terms of award classification (in Australia) or other remuneration standards (such as enterprise agreements and government minimum wages standards, depending on your local jurisdiction). If the role is beyond labour law classification, it would be wise to check a salary survey to ensure you're paying somewhere around the market rate.

Next comes the learning and development plan, which may include some priorities for formal and informal learning, from books and articles to read, seminars and short courses to attend, through to enrolling in an accredited trade or higher education course.

The learning and development plan might also include placements and projects to speed the worker's development. These may take some time to put into place, so be careful to integrate them in future work plans so they don't get lost.

Speaking of which, the final step in an effective appraisal is to ensure changes outlined in the appraisal are reflected in forward work plans. This includes new responsibilities headings in the PD, new measure and metrics and the stepping-stones toward longer-term goals. It's particularly important that some progress toward longer-term goals is made between each supervision session, otherwise the goal is likely to fall out of the field of attention until next year's appraisal.

In the first few supervision sessions after the appraisal is complete, make sure the changes are reflected in the work plan and are informing the worker's priorities and performance. Our tendency to revert to the prior homeostasis has the potential to neutralise all of our good intentions unless we continue to pay attention.

Summary

- While appraisal is viewed negatively by many, when done well it can greatly benefit your workers and your organisation.
- Excellent appraisal is more about optimising the employment relationship than ticking boxes or dealing with problems.
- The nuts and bolts of appraisal include:
    - Reviewing the past up to the present, including fulfilment of responsibilities, managing the role, engaging with the wider organisation and gathering data
    - Considering the worker's life stage with its opportunities and constraints
    - Dreaming a little about what could be
    - Thinking over the worker's development and their place in a leadership pipeline.
- Turning the conversation into a plan will require distillation, and integration with the organisation's strategy.
- Nailing down the forward plan may include:
    - Changes to the PD
    - Changes to organisational structure
    - Updating or creating a training and development plan
    - Integrating all of this into regular work plans.

Discussion

- What's been your experience of appraisal? How is it different from what's been outlined here?
- Which aspect of appraisal do you think has the most potential for benefit?
- Which aspect of appraisal do you find yourself resisting?

Action

- If your organisation does not have an appraisal system, design your own and schedule it into your annual plan. You might want to pilot your system with yourself first.
- If your organisation already has an appraisal process, identify one or two pieces of learning from this chapter that you could integrate.

Chapter 29
Developing people

In this final chapter, I'm hoping to bring it all together: being a boss people want to work for, being a steward of human potential, using good process to effectively supervise and leveraging the potential of supervision for the benefit or your organisation and your workers.

Your worker, while they work for you, is entrusting this era of their career to your care. Decisions you make about that worker's job – their training, the experiences they gain, the teams and committees on which they serve and the projects they undertake – will have lasting, perhaps lifelong impact. Your leadership could set a young kid on a path to CEO. Your decisions could plateau a more mature worker's career and consign them to an inevitable redundancy.

Rather than dive into more instruction, I would like to show you what it looks like. I've given you some snippets of the story of my time with Pacific Dunlop. Let me colour in some details.

Seeing potential

I've already introduced you to Mark, my immediate boss back at Pacific Dunlop in the early 1990s. I'd worked for him at a different company a few years prior. When I finished my on-again, off-again undergrad, I got in touch with him to see if I could find some work in the midst of a sharp economic downturn. He told me that the company was in the process of recruiting a chemical manufacturing process worker, and he gave me the name and contact details of the guy who was running the adhesives manufacturing plant. Mark said he couldn't promise anything. I shot off my rather threadbare resume and hoped. I have no idea whether any strings were pulled, but I got the job.

My first eight months was a daily ten-hour tedium of sweat, dust, and backache, sandwiched between an hour's drive each way in a clapped-out old Ford. Unemployment was running at about ten percent and the pay for this job was okay, so I soldiered on.

Then, out of the blue, Mark called me into his office and advised that I was hitherto appointed to the newly created role of Occupational Health and Safety Officer for the site. The site was home to the group office, comprising about 50 people in finance, accounting, marketing and purchasing. There was a general manufacturing area that employed about 25 process workers, a finished goods warehouse with about four storemen on forklifts, a lab with four white-coated scientists and the adhesives plant. Most of the adhesives were solvent-based. Between raw materials, work in progress and finished goods, there could be anything up to half a million litres of highly flammable liquids stored on site. The adhesives plant had strict controls on ignition sources: no lighters, no electrical devices, no nylon clothing, no steel hammers. Our motto was, "One flash, we're all ash."

All of a sudden, I had system responsibility for the safety of about a hundred people working around a potential bomb. My only qualification for the role was that I was the most accident-prone member of the team (perhaps Mark figured the best way to make the place safer was to get me off the forklift and away from the other machinery).

I was handed a pile of folders, signed up for some training with the risk management consultancy that PacDun had retained and set to the task. I. Had. No. Idea.

What I did have was a weekly 60-minute supervision meeting and Mark's belief that I could learn quickly enough to get up to speed and then keep on top of the ambitious OHS improvement timetable that PacDun was pursuing.

I desperately wanted to reward Mark's faith in me. I read over the files, figured out which required immediate attention and set off trying to get the first of a series of risk-category based surveys underway. I struggled to gain the cooperation of the various area supervisors who were already run off their feet with other things to do. I learned how to earn the right to be heard by finding ways to be a resource to them and flexing my requests to suit their constraints.

There were no spare computers and certainly no budget for me to get one. Back then a basic 386 Windows computer with 8K of RAM and a 250K hard drive was $3000.00 – or fifteen percent of my annual wage. I borrowed an old DOS-based portable (it weighed 12 kilos!) from my father-in-law, learned

WordPerfect 5.1 and began smashing out the policies, procedures and record forms we needed to keep up with the OHS program. In about six months our site was on track and slightly ahead of the deadlines. Our lost-time injury performance was rapidly improving.

Then Mark threw me a project to set up a cross-functional training program site-wide. I researched various multi-skilling initiatives and designed a program. Next came a product costing proposal with various options for calculating overhead recovery (the cents-per-litre model proposed by the accountants would have grossly distorted our product prices, chased off our anchor client and sent us broke). I knew nothing about management accounting, but I learned fast, picking up an array of Lotus 123 skills as I went. These I turned to creating a balanced scorecard system for employee profit-sharing.

Soon after came participation in a Total Quality Management (TQM) project, then leading a TQM team, followed shortly after by running the whole TQM intervention for our site. At the same time I developed and implemented a range of basic HR policies with an emphasis on risk management.

During this time Mark maintained those crucial 60 minutes with me each week. Sometimes there was praise, sometimes there was eye rolling and a bit of scolding. Sometimes there were questions demanding answers I could not give. It was rarely comfortable, but it was inspiring and energising because this guy believed I could do things and achieve things and figure things out. Because he believed I could, I tried, and for the most part, I succeeded.

I performed at a standard I never thought possible and developed skills I had no previous motivation to learn – skills I still use today. I learned principles of leadership and change management that have stood me in good stead for the ensuing thirty years. Two years later I was a Group HR Manager in another business with responsibilities covering twenty sites in four states.

And if it wasn't for Mark's belief and investment in me, there would be no HR career, no transition to consulting and you wouldn't be reading this book. Hence the dedication on the opening page.

Human Resource trustee

My ongoing use of the term 'Human Resources' in preference to the more contemporary 'People and Culture' role is mostly an artefact of my age. When I began in the field 'HR' was the new sophisticated term and the old and stuffy 'personnel' label was still in broad usage. Yet there's a small degree of intentionality behind my retaining the words.

The word 'resource' carries the idea of something to be developed, a raw material, something that's valuable because of its inherent properties and what it could become.

While we look at self-made successes like Steve Jobs and Bill Gates with admiration and envy, they are outliers in almost every sense of the word (as Malcom Gladwell points out in his book of that title).[186] People like Jobs, Gates, and more recently Elon Musk, who make it apparently on their own are a rarity. For every self-made billionaire there are millions of self-made strugglers. Most 'successful' people, whether or not they achieve stratospheric heights, get there in part because of the belief and investment of a series of bosses who provided the opportunity and sponsorship that allowed them to flourish.

The temptation for a supervisor is to see our workers as assets for our own advancement – at worst bosses metaphorically stand on the heads of their workers to make themselves look taller. Most of us think about career progression primarily from our own point of view. I'm inviting you to consider reversing the direction of intended benefit for just a moment – think about offering your own shoulder to help your workers move up and develop.

Just to be transparent, writing and publishing this book is part of a broader plan for my career. I really do hope you'll benefit, but a good deal of the impetus to write and promote the book comes from my hopes for my own progress. I'm not advocating abandoning our own goals, so much as keeping them in perspective.

I'm advocating that we who supervise others see ourselves as trustees – our workers are with us for a season, and during that time we have the opportunity to play a part in the development of their potential. What if we

---

[186] Gladwell, M. *Outliers: Stories of Success* (Allen Lane, London, 2009).

could imagine each worker's season under our care as a kind of stepping-stone – a place where they can gain a foothold as they seek to build their career. This may even mean encouraging workers to think in terms of their longer-term development to avoid becoming plateaued and marginalised.

If you're inspired by American schmaltz (I know I am), watch the 1995 film *Mr Holland's Opus* starring Richard Dreyfus (it's on Netflix at the time of writing). It invites you to wonder if your legacy in the lives of the people who pass through your care is perhaps more important than your own achievement and recognition. It's not that Mr Holland stopped pursuing his own goals, it's just that his impact on dozens of young lives over his career turned out to be his greatest contribution. You'll remember our earlier conversation about servant leadership. This is one way it plays out.

Far from allowing ourselves to be exploited, seeing the development of human potential as an important aspect of the supervisor's responsibility is demonstrated to pay bottom-line dividends to your organisation on a variety of fronts.

Firstly, according to Clifton and Harter, having opportunity to develop and a supervisor who is interested in a worker's development are key aspects of engagement, which correlates to higher productivity, reduced absenteeism, reduced turnover and improved quality.[187]

Secondly, developing workers capabilities through formal training, on the job training, exposure to new responsibilities and involvement in new projects increases the potential contribution of the worker to the organisation, often with no expectation of a formal promotion or a pay-rise (well, not immediately anyhow). On the whole, workers value opportunities to learn and grow.

Thirdly, if you consistently develop talent in your organisation, your organisation will gain the reputation as a great place to work and build a career. People who want to excel will seek out opportunities to work for your organisation. Don't underestimate this factor in volunteer situations, either.

---

[187] Clifton, J. and Harter, J. *It's the Manager* (Gallup, New York, 2019).

I've used development opportunities as a way of attracting high-quality talent and gaining some outstanding volunteer contributions on boards.

Summary

- See people's potential beyond their current job.
- Act as a trustee of the human resources you direct. Perhaps your greatest legacy will lie with the contribution of those you've developed.
- Stewarding human potential pays valuable dividends to your organisation.

Discussion

- Reflect on your career – who are the people who have developed your potential and given you opportunity to flourish?

Action

- Identify an opportunity for development (it may be a project) for each of your workers.

Commission

Now we've come to the end of our journey together. We've covered a lot of territory – why supervision is important, what kind of leader makes an effective supervisor, the theory and practice of supervision and some ways to really leverage your supervision to maximise the benefit to both your organisation and your workers.

If you haven't done so already, I encourage you to engage in your own performance appraisal as a boss, dividing it into the broad section headings of the book. Then set yourself one, or at most two manageable goals under each heading. Set out below are some questions to get you started. The first two are perhaps the hardest and the most important.

- How can I change my priorities so that being an excellent supervisor becomes a matter of increasing performance and focus for me?
- How can I develop my own character and personal disciplines to increasingly be a leader people want to follow?
- What changes can I make to my supervision practices that will deliver tangible benefits to my organisation and my workers?
- How can I further develop my learning about supervision, leadership and human functioning to enhance my effectiveness as a boss?
- How can I leverage my role as a supervisor to enhance the future of the organisation and my workers?

Even if you've readily understood everything I've set out to convey, these are tough questions, especially when we go beyond the conceptual to consistent, concrete action. Yet the reward, in terms of our own sense of purpose and satisfaction, and the potential to enrich the lives of so many others, makes the effort more than worthwhile.

Thanks for taking the journey with me.

I wish you well.

Ken Morgan
Spring 2022